Transnational Trajectories in East Asia

Since the late twentieth century, East Asia has become increasingly interconnected through trade, investment, migration, and popular culture at regional and global levels. At the same time, the region has seen renewed national assertiveness and nationalist impulses. *Transnational Trajectories in East Asia* interrogates these seemingly contradictory developments as they bear on the transformations of the nation and citizenship. Conventionally, studies on East Asia juxtapose these developments, focusing on the much-exercised dichotomy of the national and transnational. In contrast, this book suggests a different orientation. First, it moves beyond the simplistic view that demarcates the transnational as "the West." Second, it does not view the national and transnational as distinct or contradictory spheres of influence and analysis, but rather, focuses on the interactions between the two, with a view on how these interactions work to transform the ideals and practices of the "good nation," "good society," and "good citizen." The book covers a broad empirical terrain – education, science, immigration, multicultural policy, human rights, gender and youth orientations, art and food flows, politics of values and regional identity – which foreground the ways in which the nation is reconfigured, and the relationship between the citizen and (national) collective is redefined, in relation to transnational dynamics and frameworks. Featuring a novel perspective and analysis of transnational processes, *Transnational Trajectories in East Asia* is an insightful account of transformations of the nation and citizenship in the region.

Yasemin Nuhoğlu Soysal is Professor of Sociology at University of Essex, UK.

Asia's Transformations

Edited by Mark Selden, Cornell University, USA

The books in this series explore the political, social, economic and cultural consequences of Asia's transformations in the twentieth and twenty-first centuries. The series emphasises the tumultuous interplay of local, national, regional and global forces as Asia bids to become the hub of the world economy. While focusing on the contemporary, it also looks back to analyze the antecedents of Asia's contested rise.

This series comprises several strands:
Asia's Transformations

Titles include:

1. **Debating Human Rights***
   Critical essays from the United States and Asia
   Edited by Peter Van Ness

2. **Hong Kong's History***
   State and society under colonial rule
   Edited by Tak-Wing Ngo

3. **Japan's Comfort Women***
   Sexual slavery and prostitution during World War II and the US occupation
   Yuki Tanaka

4. **Opium, Empire and the Global Political Economy***
   Carl A. Trocki

5. **Chinese Society***
   Change, conflict and resistance
   Edited by Elizabeth J. Perry and Mark Selden

6. **Mao's Children in the New China***
   Voices from the Red Guard generation
   Yarong Jiang and David Ashley

7. **Remaking the Chinese State***
   Strategies, society and security
   Edited by Chien-min Chao and Bruce J. Dickson

8. **Korean Society***
   Civil society, democracy and the state
   Edited by Charles K. Armstrong

9. **The Making of Modern Korea***
   Adrian Buzo

10. **The Resurgence of East Asia***
    500, 150 and 50 Year perspectives
    Edited by Giovanni Arrighi, Takeshi Hamashita and Mark Selden

11. **Chinese Society, second edition***
    Change, conflict and resistance
    Edited by Elizabeth J. Perry and Mark Selden

12. **Ethnicity in Asia***
    Edited by Colin Mackerras

13. **The Battle for Asia***
    From decolonization to globalization
    Mark T. Berger

14. **State and Society in 21st Century China***
    Edited by Peter Hays Gries and Stanley Rosen

15. **Japan's Quiet Transformation***
    Social change and civil society in the 21st century
    Jeff Kingston

Asia's Great Cities

Each volume aims to capture the heartbeat of the contemporary city from multiple perspectives emblematic of the authors' deep familiarity with the distinctive faces of the city, its history, society, culture, politics and economics, and its evolving position in national, regional and global frameworks. While most volumes emphasise urban developments since the Second World War, some pay close attention to the legacy of the longue durée in shaping the contemporary. Thematic and comparative volumes address such themes as urbanization, economic and financial linkages, architecture and space, wealth and power, gendered relationships, planning and anarchy, and ethnographies in national and regional perspective.

Titles include:

Asia.com is a series which focuses on the ways in which new information and communication technologies are influencing politics, society and culture in Asia. Titles include:

1. **Japanese Cybercultures***
   Edited by Mark McLelland and Nanette Gottlieb

2. **Asia.com***
   Asia encounters the Internet
   Edited by K. C. Ho, Randolph Kluver and Kenneth C. C. Yang

4. **The Internet in Indonesia's New Democracy***
   David T. Hill and Krishna Sen

5. **Chinese Cyberspaces***
   Technological changes and political effects
   Edited by Jens Damm and Simona Thomas

6. **Mobile Media in the Asia-Pacific**
   Gender and the art of being mobile
   Larissa Hjorth

7. **Online@AsiaPacific**
   Mobile, social and locative media in the Asia–Pacific
   Larissa Hjorth and Michael Arnold

Literature and Society
Literature and Society is a series that seeks to demonstrate the ways in which Asian Literature is influenced by the politics, society and culture in which it is produced.

Titles include:

1. **The Body in Postwar Japanese Fiction**
   Douglas N. Slaymaker

2. **Chinese Women Writers and the Feminist Imagination, 1905–48***
   Haiping Yan

3. **Okinawan War Memory**
   Transgenerational trauma and the war fiction of Medoruma Shun
   Kyle Ikeda

Routledge Studies in Asia's Transformations
Routledge Studies in Asia's Transformations is a forum for innovative new research intended for a high-level specialist readership.

Titles include:

1. **The American Occupation of Japan and Okinawa***
   Literature and memory
   Michael Molasky

2. **Koreans in Japan***
   Critical voices from the margin
   Edited by Sonia Ryang

3. **Internationalizing the Pacific**
   The United States, Japan and the Institute of Pacific Relations in war and peace, 1919–1945
   Tomoko Akami

Critical Asian Scholarship

Critical Asian Scholarship is a series intended to showcase the most important individual contributions to scholarship in Asian Studies. Each of the volumes presents a leading Asian scholar addressing themes that are central to his or her most significant and lasting contribution to Asian studies. The series is committed to the rich variety of research and writing on Asia, and is not restricted to any particular discipline, theoretical approach or geographical expertise.

* Available in paperback

Transnational Trajectories in East Asia

Nation, citizenship, and region

Edited by
Yasemin Nuhoğlu Soysal

LONDON AND NEW YORK

First published 2015 by Routledge

2 Park Square, Milton Park, Abingdon, Oxon OX14 4RN
711 Third Avenue, New York, NY 10017, USA

First issued in paperback 2016

Routledge is an imprint of the Taylor & Francis Group, an informa business

British Library Cataloguing in Publication Data
A catalogue record for this book is available from the British Library

Library of Congress Cataloging in Publication Data
    Transnational trajectories in East Asia : nation, citizenship, and region /
edited by Yasemin Nuhoğlu Soysal.
        pages cm. -- (Asia's transformations ; 46)
    Includes bibliographical references and index.
    1. Transnationalization. 2. Nation--East Asia. 3. Citizenship--East Asia.
4. Cosmopolitanism--East Asia. 5. Interregionalism--East Asia.
6. East Asia--Foreign relations. I. Soysal, Yasemin Nuhoğlu.
    DS518.1.T745 2015
    320.54095--dc23
                2014024405

ISBN-13: 978-1-138-81935-1 (hbk)
ISBN-13: 978-1-138-64628-5 (pbk)
ISBN-13: 978-1-315-74459-9 (ebk)

Typeset in Baskerville
by Taylor & Francis Books

Contents

List of illustrations

Figures

Tables

List of contributors

Ly-Yun Chang is Adjunct Research Fellow at the Institute of Sociology, Academia Sinica and Adjunct Professor of Sociology at National Taiwan University. Her current work involves quantitative and qualitative approaches to the organization of health care, health inequalities, happiness, and youth civic development.

Alexis Dudden is Professor of History at the University of Connecticut. During 2013–14 she was a visiting research fellow at Princeton University writing a book about Japan's territorial disputes and the changing meaning of islands in international law.

Adrian Favell is Professor of Sociology at Sciences Po. A specialist on migration, multiculturalism, cities and globalization, he is the author of Before and After Superflat: A Short History of Japanese Contemporary Art 1990–2011 (Blue Kingfisher/DAP 2012).

Koichi Iwabuchi is Professor of Media and Cultural Studies at the Faculty of Arts and Director of the Asia Institute at Monash University. He has worked on issues of media and cultural globalization, cultural connections in East Asia, and multiculturalism, cultural citizenship, and an inclusive reconstruction of the nation in Japanese and East Asian contexts.

Jack Jin Gary Lee is a PhD candidate in Sociology at the University of California-San Diego, where he specializes in political sociology, the sociology of law, as well as global and transnational sociology. He has conducted research on the development of migration policies in industrialized Asia, and his dissertation examines the bureaucratization of British imperial control in Jamaica and the Straits settlements.

David Leheny is the Henry Wendt III '55 Professor of East Asian Studies at Princeton University. A specialist on Japan and international relations, most of his diverse research projects involve Japan's reaction to and adoption of international norms and standards of behavior that have prescriptive and constitutive effects on state action.

Lynne Y. Nakano is Professor of Japanese Studies at the Chinese University of Hong Kong. She is the author of *Community Volunteers in Japan: Everyday Stories of Social Change* (Routledge, 2004).

Yoshiko Nakano is Associate Professor of Japanese Studies at the University of Hong Kong. She is the author of *Where There Are Asians, There Are Rice Cookers: How "National" Went Global via Hong Kong* (Hong Kong University Press, 2009).

Mark Selden is a Senior Research Associate in the East Asia Program at Cornell University and Professor Emeritus of History and Sociology at Binghamton University. A specialist on the modern and contemporary geopolitics, political economy and history of China, Japan, and the Asia Pacific, his work has addressed themes of war and revolution, inequality, development, regional and world social change, and historical memory.

John D. Skrentny is Professor of Sociology and Co-Director of the Center for Comparative Immigration Studies at University of California-San Diego. His research focuses on law, politics, and the comparative analysis of immigration, and his most recent book is *After Civil Rights: Racial Realism in the New American Workplace* (Princeton University Press, 2014).

Yasemin Nuhoğlu Soysal is Professor of Sociology at University of Essex. Her comparative research in the fields of immigration, education, human rights, and regional integration addresses contemporary and historical transformations of the nation and citizenship from a transnational perspective.

Tony Tam is Professor of Sociology at the Chinese University of Hong Kong. His research interests include education, stratification, labor market and health inequality, and economic sociology.

Kiyoteru Tsutsui is Associate Professor of Sociology at the University of Michigan, Ann Arbor. His research on globalization of human rights and corporate social responsibility and their impact on local politics has appeared in the *American Journal of Sociology*, *American Sociological Review*, *Social Forces*, *Social Problems*, and other sociology and political science journals.

Suk-Ying Wong is Professor of Sociology at the Chinese University of Hong Kong. Her comparative-historical research on worldwide social science education, citizenship education, history education and construction of modern nationalism in East Asia appeared in journals such as the *American Sociological Review*, *Sociology of Education*, *Comparative Education Review*, and *Multicultural Education Review*.

Joy Y. Zhang is a Lecturer in Sociology at the University of Kent. She is the author of *The Cosmopolitanization of Science: Stem Cell Governance in China* (Palgrave Macmillan, 2012) and *Green Politics in China* (Pluto Press, 2013).

Preface

The contributors to this volume span new and old liaisons in geographies both sides of the Atlantic and Pacific. Because East Asia was relatively new to me as an empirical field and I was keen about learning from the perspectives and research of my co-authors, I opted not following the famous Peter Katzenstein method of providing a framing introduction from the outset. This turned out to be a great advantage in this case. In the process of producing the volume, back and forth discussions and iterations made the whole journey intellectually rich and rewarding. I am grateful for everyone's patience and diligent work in responding to my endless queries and requests, and most of all for sharing and contributing their outstanding scholarship. I particularly thank David Leheny and Mark Selden for their insightful comments on the structure and intellectual content of the volume. It is a better book, thanks to them.

The beginnings of this book project go back to an international conference I co-organized with Suk Ying Wong at the Chinese University of Hong Kong (CUHK) in 2010. The conference was funded by a joint grant from the Economic and Social Research Council of the UK and the Research Grant Council of Hong Kong. The CUHK not only provided the venue but also additional funds for conference logistics, and the Sociology department lent a highly efficient team of graduate students, whose help was indispensable in realizing those logistics. Simona Szakacs, as always, was most effective contributing research assistance before, during, and after the conference. The Department of Sociology at the CUHK, hosted me several times in the course of this project; it was a great privilege and a great base and opportunity to enhance my knowledge and understanding of East Asia. I am indebted to Suk Ying Wong, my good friend and colleague, and her unsurpassable organizational skills and leadership, for making all of this possible.

At Routledge, Stephanie Rogers, Hannah Mack, Ruth Bradley, and Gill Gairdner walked me through their publication process with great professionalism.

The cover art is by Yuken Teruya – one of the young, internationally mobile Japanese artists included in the contribution by Adrian Favell in this book. I thank Adrian for introducing me to Yuken's work and Yuken for allowing me to use his artwork on the cover. I can not think of a more fitting image that visually speaks to the central themes of the book. The image was also the favorite of Talia, my little niece, who gave the final approval by joyfully and decidedly pointing to it.

Yasemin Nuhoğlu Soysal
London
September 2014

1 Mapping the terrain of transnationalization

Nation, citizenship, and region

Yasemin Nuhoğlu Soysal

In the last two decades, East Asian countries have opened up regionally and globally via deepening investment and trade ties, increasing population mobility, cross-fertilization in popular culture and consumption, and a new political climate of collaboration among Japan, China, and South Korea and between Taiwan and the mainland.[1] The global agendas of human rights and liberalism have penetrated the region and the drive for democratization has intensified. Simultaneously, East Asia exhibits renewed national assertiveness and nationalist impulses, expressed through competition in regional and global markets, geopolitics, as well as new cultural positioning—at times entangled with territorial and colonial legacies. How should we understand such seemingly contradictory developments as they bear on the transformations of the nation and citizenship in East Asia?

Conventionally, studies on East Asia juxtapose these developments, centering on the much-exercised dichotomy of the national (often understood as "unique") and transnational (often understood as "the West"). We have a different orientation in this book project. Rather than treating the national and transnational as contradictory trajectories, we focus on the interactions between the two, with a view to seeing how these interactions work to transform the ideals and practices of the "good nation," "good society," and "good citizen." We inquire into the reworking of the nation and citizenship vis-à-vis the transnational in a variety of institutional, policy, and societal sites. The individual chapters cover a comprehensive empirical range: education, science, immigration and multicultural policy, human rights, gender and youth orientations, contemporary art, "values" politics, and regional politics. These are sites where the boundaries of the nation are contested and the relationship between the citizen and (national) collective is redefined. These are also sites that increasingly engage global norms and forms, and expand networks and markets in the region and beyond. Thus they allow us to address different ways that the national and transnational are intertwined, with intended and unintended, and at times contradictory, consequences.

The volume focuses on aspects of transnationalization that are missing in the accounts of the contemporary East Asian developments. The view of the national and transnational as dichotomous spheres of effect and analysis, which animates much of the social science research in this field, overlooks emerging processes that transform the contemporary nature of the nation and citizen in East Asia. At the same time individual chapters reveal various forms that transnationalization takes and the extent to which the region and the global, as transnational nodes, are constituted at the national level.

Although not unique to East Asia, in the last two decades the processes in which we are interested have intensified in the region. The volume engages the temporal dimension of transnationalization. Unlike the European countries that purposefully pursued transnationalism in the form of region-building in the aftermath of the Second World War, East Asian countries have engaged the transnational at different time points and in the context of different global situations. Japan was a first-comer (through its connection to the hegemonic "West" via the United States) in many of the empirical domains we address in this volume. Thus it provides good comparative leverage for our exploration of the contemporary period in which a common view is that Japan is withdrawing and China is advancing to play a leading role in regional and world affairs. The beginning of the twenty-first century—which is no longer framed by Cold War conflict and in which United States' hegemony is no longer taken for granted—represents overall a more dynamic transnationalization in the region, beyond states' own agendas, and sometimes contradictory to such agendas, impacting different organizational and societal sectors.

Mapping the analytical terrain

In contrast to studies that emphasize discrete national contexts or that simply rehash past conflicts and their contemporary manifestations in the East Asian region, this volume prioritizes transnationalization processes in their regional and global expressions. Our collective effort is not on the theorization of transnationalism as a substantive or normative concern.[2] Rather the individual chapters of this volume offer investigations that help make transnationalization analytically legible in apprehending the seemingly contradictory developments of nation and citizenship in East Asia.

As an analytical node, we suggest the term transnationalization to capture the institutionalization of nation-transcending frameworks, models, and standards, and their constitution of actors' orientations and strategies. It points to the shifting valence of the national as an "organizational logic" and "cultural-cognitive orientation," both as intended and unintended consequence.[3] As such, transnationalization is about transformations of what is historically organized and conceptualized as national, rather than simply reforming at a different level, and may or may not lead to regional or global arrangements (Ramirez 2012, Sassen 2006, 2008). The advance of explicit transborder regimes (e.g. the World Trade Organization and the European Convention on Human Rights) or social formations "spanning borders" (e.g. migrant networks and collective action) is one, but in our view limited, aspect of transnationalization.

Two main analytical threads underline the current volume.

First, the analytical strategy engaged by the authors locates the nation-state and a variety of national actors within their broader transnational environment—in an analytical sense these two levels are inseparable. Here we find affinity with a number of long-established sociological perspectives. Sociological institutionalism, and particularly its world society variety as advocated by John Meyer and his associates, posits that actors are embedded within their wider environments and their actions are only meaningful within the frameworks and interactions provided by such environments (Meyer 2010, Meyer *et al.* 1997, Schofer *et al.* 2012). The research programs of Saskia Sassen (2006, 2008) on globalization and denationalization, and Ulrich Beck (Beck and Sznaider 2006) on cosmopolitanization and methodological nationalism, support a similar analytical imagery that undoes misleading binaries.[4]

Such an analytical move opens up theoretical space for explaining the transformative role of transnational processes not as undermining the nation-state but reconstituting its cognitive, cultural, and organizational premises. It contrasts the simplistic view of "powerful" global institutions weakening nation-state authority by enabling the global corporate economy (e.g. through the IMF) or enhancing global justice (e.g. through the ICC court) (Sassen 2008). In its stead, our analytical strategy leads us to observe the expanded actorhood of the state constituted by transnational frameworks—engaging in region-formation, building a globally agile and able citizenry, and presenting a globally attractive and responsible nation— even when its organization is de- or super-nationalized or integrated with global markets (Leheny, Soysal and Wong, Zhang in this volume).

Second, we note the absence of a centralized global authority in the current world structure. Again in affinity with sociological perspectives, we regard the world as an interdependent state system, in which nation-states, organizations (public and private), and individuals constitute the major actors (Meyer and Jepperson 2000, Sassen 2008). International finance and economic regulators and justice institutions, as commonly posited, are among the driving forces in transnational processes. To this we add a more expansive list of actors—experts, scientists, professionals, social movements—and their expanding resources and linkages into the analytical imagery.

The diversity of actors (with different identities and in different local contexts) and the lack of a centralized global authority do not necessarily mean a chaotic order. One significant aspect of the current world system is the diffusion, however uneven, of discourses, structures, and practices leading to convergence around principles and models of governance (e.g. of good nation, good society, and good citizen). Cognitive and normative expectancy structures, via a broad set of associational and learning processes, constitute the main channels of such diffusion (Jepperson 2002, Strang and Meyer 1993). This view contests much of the literature that pictures the wider world simply as hegemonic powers, or globalized authority structures controlled by them, imposing models and rules on weaker countries (Dobbin, Simmons, and Garrett 2007). Models and rules indeed become hegemonic, often with theoretical and scientific backing, and their diffusion is facilitated by the world structure enabled by hegemonic powers of the time, but the hegemonic powers themselves are not always the proponents of the emerging order. Under US economic expansion and dominance, both economic and political liberalism diffused rapidly in the late twentieth century. Note, however, that while the United States, via global regulators such as the WTO, IMF, and World Bank, clearly pushed market-based policy reforms, much of the liberal human rights norms have diffused despite the United States' notorious resistance during and after the introduction of the UN Covenants on Human Rights (Somers and Roberts 2008).

Moving on from these analytical premises, we specify three different routes through which transnationalization takes place. All three implicate national actors and their engagements that are constituted and enabled by non-nation-specific frameworks, principles, and models. We do not theorize these routes as all-encompassing but offer them as indicative of the empirical observations provided by the individual chapters in this volume.

Transnationalization through externalization of legitimacy: Transnationalization of the nation and citizenship is closely related to broader legitimacy expectations. In an expanded (increasingly connected and institutionally dense) world environment, while states retain their sovereign status, their legitimacy is no longer simply conditioned by a contract with the nation, but also by their adherence to nation-transcending frameworks of appropriate organization and action (Levy and Sznaider 2006, Meyer 2010). The broader environment, via processes of isomorphism, prescribes models of proper nation-stateness and citizenship, which include goals of socioeconomic development and "cosmopolitan" self-definitions and proper forms of participation in global politics, which include regional organization and institutionalization (Leheny, Soysal and Wong, Tsutsui in this volume). States often adopt such models and organizational forms because they risk losing legitimacy in the international system. A range of reform actions and policies follow, not because they are necessarily proved solutions to immediate problems (although they are often thus articulated) but because they signal proper nationhood and competitiveness in the wider world (Soysal and Wong, Zhang in this volume).

Externalized legitimacy also grounds new identity formations at the societal level. The expansion of international movement networks and global campaigns, as well as local activists' cultivation of external allies and projection of their claims onto international institutions, have been noted as instances of transnationalization (della Porta and Tarrow 2005, Sikkink and Keck 1998, Tarrow 2005, Tsutsui and Wotipka 2004). A more radical point is made here: the cognitive and cultural transformation of national (societal) groups in relation to transnational frameworks that consequently facilitates changes in local practices and policies. Tsutsui (in this volume) describes the self-transformation of the Ainu from a small, invisible group to a "proud" indigenous minority by linking to the global indigenous movement and appropriating transnational human rights discourses. These connections brought new meaning, identity, and legitimacy to the Ainu's local struggles. The Ainu became active claim-makers, making significant strides in their struggle for recognition by the Japanese government and abroad. Although discrimination against Ainu in Japan remains an ongoing issue, the greater visibility and formal recognition of the Ainu has all the same contributed to global norm expansion and reproduction.

Transnationalization through "theorized" standards and practices: Nation-states not only operate under externalized legitimacy expectations but are also embedded in a web of expertise. A wide range of experts, consultants, and their associated assemblies (professionals, scientists, businesses, movements), draw standards that enable "non-national organizing logics and operational space" (Sassen 2006, 2008; see also Meyer 2010, Strang and Meyer 1993). Such standards are often theorized as "best practices" and abstracted from national contexts. They are produced not only for markets (e.g. intellectual property rights, accounting principles) but for a variety of fields, in science, education, professions, media and arts, and even social movements. Education and science, domains with explicit theories of collective good, generate universalistic standards that suffuse the international sphere via elaborate organizational carriers (Drori and Meyer 2006, Meyer, Ramirez, and Soysal 1992; Soysal and Wong, Zhang in this volume). This can be contrasted with international migration, a much less institutionalized and much more contested field of policy, resistant to transnational standards (Skrentny and Lee in this volume). In other domains, such as the arts, standards are produced via more informal networks and private schemes that facilitate global consumption (Favell in this volume).

The inconsistencies and discrepancies between transnational standards and local capacities and contexts create much mobilization for change. Nongovernmental and governmental actors both mobilize. Zhang (in this volume) shows how Chinese synthetic biology and stem-cell scientists, as well as grass-roots movements, pressure the Chinese government to introduce national regulations and organizational resources in line with transnational standards in order to increase the capacity of life sciences in China on a par with the most advanced governance structures in this particular field. Transnational standards may also provide the grounds for reimagining of national territories or breaching of others, lending themselves to the creation of a new niche for regional conflicts, as in the workings of the international ocean regime in East Asian seas, described by Dudden (in this volume).

Transnationalization through projected spaces of participation: Immigrant diasporas are often conceptualized as "transnational communities," engaging in practices that thread between places of origin and settlement. This is not the kind of transnationalization we are evoking here, as diasporic communities are more often than not nationally bound (Soysal 2000). We refer to the transnationally shaped imaginaries that inform individual life courses, strategies, expectations, tastes, aesthetics, and value orientations. These imaginaries are enabled by increasingly standardized conceptions of the individual with standardized categorical qualities (Frank and Meyer 2002). They are scripted and transmitted through global businesses and consumption markets (Favell, Y. Nakano), migratory flows (Skrentny and Lee), electronic and other media (Chang and Tam, L. Nakano), professional networks (Zhang), and scientific theories (Chang and Tam, Iwabuchi, Soysal and Wong). Nationally decontextualized, such imaginaries create expectations and avenues for individual mobility and participation, not only for international migrants, but also for those who remain close to home (Sassen 2006).

Transnational reworkings of the nation and citizenship in East Asia

The observations provided in this volume reveal transnational transformations of the nation and citizenship at multiple levels of the social system (policy, organizational structure, social movement activity, individual tastes, attitudes, and values), even as the levels themselves remain loosely coupled. Shifts in the public and policy representations of the nation and citizen are one axis of changes. However even in the absence of explicit policy and organizational reform, we observe changes in individual orientations and private life course practices (see also Frank, Hardinge, and Wosick-Correa 2009).

The national as sanctioned by the transnational

A cursory view of current affairs in East Asia would identify a revitalization of the nation in the region, even as the region gains vitality. By analyzing wide-ranging fields in which the nation is expressed, we offer a much more complex picture: the assertiveness of the nation, as well as its progressively common imaginary, is linked to its transnationalization. This is not to underestimate the potential of nationalist conflicts and their threat to geopolitical stability in the region. However, we suggest in the concluding section that the same transnationalization processes that occasion transformations of the nation and citizenship also underlie some of the tensions in the region.

A significant observation is the emergence of transnationality as an explicit project, pursued by a variety of actors—states, professions, and social movements. Leheny, Soysal and Wong, Zhang (in this volume) show that a ubiquitous aspect of the transnationalization project is nation-states legitimating themselves, internally and to the outside world, as uniquely "attractive." Nation-states systematically insist upon and dramatize their national uniqueness to take part in the transnational, whether in reorganizing their education and science policy (Soysal and Wong, Zhang) or in region-building (Leheny). Yet, as the nation (and its uniqueness) is expressed, at times fiercely, the policy reforms themselves affirm transnationally diffused, common models of social order. Nation and region as "imagined communities" and the individual as citizen acquire increasing commonalities across societies.

The discursive construction of East Asian regionalism reveals not a common cultural or normative identity but one with a common Western "other"—hence the emphasis by East Asian governments and intellectuals on the regional context of difference from the West and its values (Leheny in this volume). However, this emphasis relies on transnationally recognized notions of colonization, modernization, justice, and progress, disabling a meaningfully distinctive and unified regional identity. If anything, the quest of East Asian nation-states to represent the most appealing values and contributions to the region (including transnational awareness and constructiveness) creates further political tensions and rifts (Rozman 2012).

National distinctiveness also appears in much of education and science policy discursive spaces. Chinese school history programs are riddled with statements about the great contribution of Chinese civilization to greater humanity. In Japan, the returning conservative government of Shinzō Abe in 2012, along with proposals to revise the constitution to reflect Japan's uniqueness, restated its aspiration of teaching more of "the 2000-year history of Japan's wonderful traditions and culture" as the basis for a caring and persevering citizenry (*Japan Times Online* 2012).[5] Neither country on the other hand has so far proposed a citizenship education model or pedagogy that can be recognized as uniquely Chinese or Japanese. Instead they reach for models with high indicators of "success" and legitimacy in transnational educational circles—models that emphasize individual capital and autonomy and notions of progress and justice (Soysal and Wong in this volume).

Chinese scientists, who themselves are energized by the transnational standardization of science and their extensive global networks, pressure the government to implement a rigorous national science policy (Zhang in this volume). While they appear to advance a China-specific "big-question" approach to science, at the same time they appropriate a universalistic progress discourse and advocate universally applicable organizational schemes that locate them firmly within transnational scientist identities. In the same vein, only by transnationalizing their networks and appropriating transnational standards could the civil society initiative Sunshine Stem Cell Bank gain visibility and incentivize the Chinese government to rationalize its own cell bank operation. The transnational figures prominently in the restructuring of national scientific governance structures.

However, transnationalization is not always a deliberate project of political actors; at times it is an unintended consequence of policies. Skrentny and Lee (in this volume) hint at how women-centered marriage-immigrant family networks might enhance transnationalization even when, and partly because, East Asian migration policy frameworks remain nationalistic and the policy intends national closure. The insecurities of migrants' citizenship status in East Asian societies and weak societal mechanisms for their incorporation encourage family strategies and intimacies beyond nationally bound imageries.

Similarly, in the absence of national reforms and policy, the possibility emerges for everyday multicultural interactions and various forms of local participation to transform the nature of Japanese society toward one that is more open and cosmopolitan (Iwabuchi in this volume). Such multicultural coexistence, however, has the danger of leaving the nation "intact," Iwabuchi points out observantly, unless there is a willingness to question homogenous conceptions of the nation more broadly, by local and non-local actors alike. The Ainu's self-transformation into an active transnational movement and their recognition by the Japanese government as indigenous people in 2008 is a step in this direction (Tsutsui in this volume).

The rising individual and citizen

A dominant view is that East Asian cultures place the well-being of groups above that of the individual and individuals are subordinate to the group or collective.

The empirical observations provided in this volume diverge from such a view, pointing to values, tastes, life-course, and citizenship orientations in which the individual increasingly figures.

In education and science policy, the two policy spheres that are most susceptible to transnational isomorphism (Drori *et al.* 2003), new individual attributes and solidarities are projected. Japanese, Chinese, and Taiwanese school citizenship curricula increasingly assume standardized citizen qualities and bonds transcending gender, national, and geographical boundaries in line with global educational trends (Soysal and Wong, Chang and Tam in this volume). East Asian education systems have uniformly reformed since the 1990s to stress individual agency and capabilities, individual self-development, and reflective and critical thinking.[6] In school curricula, emphasis is put on democracy and the expectation of participation in public life, even when there is not a systemic possibility for democratic participation. Consequently, such expectations can be loosely coupled with individuals' participatory practices.

Discrepancy between projected citizenship qualities and participatory practices notwithstanding, among the youth, and particularly women, we note presentations of self and personhood with new moralities and aspirations for the future that reflect greater attention to transnational frameworks. Life-course ideals and orientations are increasingly expressed through self and individual positioning, replacing the previously dominant collectivist terms (family, the party, community, workplace). Chang and Tam's survey of civic engagements (in this volume) evidences the dominance of individualistic pursuit and orientation among Taiwanese youth—particularly those birth cohorts which came into adolescence when expressive idioms of self were legitimated and fostered through a variety of diffuse institutional and media sites, from consumption and entertainment to pedagogical and human rights ideologies. Taiwanese youth, and East Asian youth more generally, have been highly exposed to such transnational influences since the late 1980s.

Y. Nakano (in this volume) shows how in the context of international mobility of capital and businesses, middle-class aspirations for distinctiveness (and the quest for a separate identity from mainland Chinese) create possibilities for transnationalization of taste in Hong Kong. Japanese national food products, which originally served as "comfort food" for Japanese expats in the city, have in time transformed into expressions of transnationally indexed sophisticated taste and choice, particularly for young Hong Kongers.

Individual choice and pursuits are also strongly expressed in young professional women's narratives regarding life and mate choices. Marriage and work are personal projects they construct for themselves. As L. Nakano (in this volume) shows, the narrated individual biographies of women in big Asian cities, although constructed as unique selves in relation to specific family and societal constraints, reveal similarities. Despite lagging public attitudes, East Asian urban women display a sharp demographic shift since the 1990s to later marriage or indefinite singlehood—confirming to a broader trend often noted as "Western." In their life decisions, independence, self-realization, personal achievement, and satisfaction emerge as leading motivations. Maybe more striking than their insistence on choice in intimacy (the changing conditions of the marriage market in East Asia inadvertently strengthen women's position in choosing mates) are the "romantic ideals" and the "language of love" that penetrate their narratives as an expression of their individuality (Swidler 2001). Even as they rely on locally rooted traditional arrangements and networks as a resource to meet prospective mates, young women pay attention to individual characteristics such as respect and caring and the communication and emotional skills of their future spouses. They convey their marriage and labor market trade-offs not simply as financial considerations but as means for realizing self-worth, fulfilling dreams, and exploring the world beyond the immediate, again highlighting their individuality. Lest one think that these developments are confined to the highly educated and urbanized, in his extensive ethnographic work in rural China, Yan (2009) reports rising expectations and expressions of freedom, choice, and individuality in marriage relations and self-positioning of women in public and private spheres. Equally telling is the development of juridical individuality through the extensive rights activism of workers, property-owners, and farmers both in urban and rural areas (Kwan Lee 2008).

It is of course possible to interpret such ascendancy of the individual (in relation to traditional social groups and the state) as integral to the general modernization process driven by rapid industrialization and accelerated by the developmental strategies of the East Asian states since the 1980s. The analyses we offer however challenge the view that local conditions of modernization, via either market expansion or the party-state, stand alone in catalyzing the changes we convey.[7] We note the individualization of life-course strategies and choices even when the structural transformation of the local is missing, and when policy and public commitments are contrary to such strategies and choices. East Asian women express themselves as independent and self-determined "agents," and thus worthy good daughters and good citizens, distant though such qualities seem to be from local political and social expectations (L. Nakano in this volume). The moral dilemmas, choices, and strategies we encounter in their narratives and actions strike a transnational chord. Many young Japanese and Chinese women of today imagine life courses and possibilities common to female persons not only in East Asia but everywhere.

Limits of transnationalization

As postulated by sociological institutionalism, a connected world polity and the transnational frameworks it enables expand and diffuse in times of economic growth (Meyer 2010). The empirical trajectory of an ascending liberal world polity following the Second World War, under the hegemony of the United States but much supported by a tremendous network and infrastructure of international (inter- and nongovernmental) organizations, has been studied extensively (Boli and Thomas 1999, Meyer *et al.* 1997). Mark Selden (2009, 2010, in this volume) conveys historically how the East Asian region itself was facilitated by the expansion of economy and market, first under the Sinocentric tributary trade system (the sixteenth through to the eighteenth century), and then in the second part of the twentieth century, with the US–China opening of the 1970s. The first regional order was dissolved by the forces of colonialism, nationalism, endemic wars, and revolutions that lasted between 1840 and 1970. The second one is being trans-formed by China's dramatic ascent and the United States' waning power. In relation to such historical background, Selden reflects on the possibility of region formation in East Asia that does not rest on the hegemony of a single power. In the context of the region's economic dynamism and deepening ties (trade and investment, technological partnerships, labor migration, cross-border tourism, urban networks, and popular culture exchange) one would expect such a possibility to avail itself. However as Selden astutely points out, it is not possible to isolate East Asian regionalism from the broader global dynamics and particularly the Asia-Pacific conjuncture (see also Katzenstein and Shiraishi 2006). That is, East Asian regionalism ultimately needs to accommodate the United States, still the most influential geopolitical actor even in a period of China's rise.

The economic downturn and crisis climate of the first decade of the twenty-first century certainly hampered the global dynamics that facilitated nation-transcending configurations in the second half of the twentieth century. Indeed, developments in East Asia give pause to visions of expansive transnationalization. From 2010 on, the region has been embroiled in a series of clashes over territorial sovereignty, materialized in the form of island and seabed disputes (Dudden in this volume).[8] The disputes have evoked strong nationalist emotions and popular protests, shaping popular elections and politics in the region. They have generated major losses for businesses in the region; the strong regional profile of popular culture and tourism has been similarly affected (*New York Times* 2012). Japan's quest for constitutional reform to allow the deployment of its military—a move supported by the US–Pacific pivot—and China's military build-up contribute to regional tension and worries. On the other hand, the region's export-oriented stagnating or slowing economies mean that East Asian countries need each other more than ever. While the island disputes unfold, East Asian governments delicately thread through hawkish and diplomatic strategies.

As significant as the current geo-political conjuncture is in shaping the future of the region, we maintain that the observations this volume presents on East Asian transnationalized trajectories point toward a more complicated picture. We highlight two reflections against which we suggest current East Asian developments should be understood. First, the chapters in this volume reveal the temporal aspect of transnationalization; East Asian countries' engagement with transnational frames and agendas vary in time, exposing different transnational imaginaries. Second, much of the conflict in the region follows from the transnationalization processes themselves, within which national geographies and histories are reinterpreted. We take up these points in turn.

The periodization in our chapters reveals different transnational contexts in the postwar period, into which East Asian countries enter (see particularly Selden in this volume). Under the tutelage of the United States and within the context of the Cold War, Japanese involvement with the transnational followed a relatively straightforward course—not simply through the building of a competitive industrialized economy from the 1960s on, quickly allowing it to assume a position as the world's second largest and most advanced economy, but also by taking advantage of the protection afforded by the Western security regime and appropriating the agenda of internationalization as a language of "peace" (Katzenstein 2005). In the 1970s and 1980s, Japan became a globally visible producer of popular and high culture, its "innovative" variations on global culture allowing transnational consumption and access (Favell in this volume, Iwabuchi 2002).

Unlike Japan, which internationalized in tandem with the West at a time when it did not face any formidable competition in the region or beyond, China has advanced into the world in a climate of fierce competition, a time when the region is going through vast and deep transformations. While Chinese opening to the outside world since 1970 has been rapid, it has not been linear. China had already engaged with internationalization previously via socialist ideals while subject to US-led blockade and isolation from 1950 forward. But since the 1980s, and integral to its "modernization" agenda, China has displayed a more enthusiastic and broadly conceived transnationalization project than one led by or centered on the West. For South Korea and Taiwan, an export-based economic strategy initially forced their state-sponsored internationalization as early as the 1960s. However, as the authoritarian regimes in both countries gradually relinquished their place to democracies in the late 1980s, many aspects of society beyond a high-performing economy have opened up. We note, however, that even under authoritarian regimes, these countries were not totally cut off from broadly diffused cultural ideas and models of society and citizenship (Chang and Tam in this volume). All East Asian countries are also facing demographic pressures that challenge their long-standing homogenous nation-building strategies (Skrentny and Lee in this volume). For Taiwan, cross-Strait tensions with the Mainland have played an added role in its efforts to shape a multicultural self-identity and consciousness distinct from an encompassing Chinese nationality and embracing the transnational, while integrating its economy deeply with China all the while (Hsiao 2012). In the 2000s, East Asian states anticipate a transnationalized world and future in which they try to reinforce their presence through their soft- and not-so-soft foreign policy strategies and science and education policies (Dudden, Leheny, Soysal and Wong, Zhang in this volume).

Among the societal sectors, we find that the transnational is encountered axiomatically. While political commentaries highlight "introvert" Japan's return and "self-isolation" and the risk of such a return to regional and global peace, Favell's (in this volume) account reveals a young generation of artists who are transnationally aware and able. For this generation the national and transnational no longer constitute a dichotomy. They are at ease with their identity and apply universalistic concepts and trends (e.g. environmental sustainability and social therapy) using local Japanese styles and materials in their art. They are not cut off from the rest of the world (far from a return to an isolated Japan) and their mobility seems to be both within Japan and abroad. This is different from the earlier post-bubble generation of artists, such as Murakami and Nara, who were promoted by globally savvy art dealers and who everyone recognizes as global faces of "cool Japan." As much as they sought out and found their place in global art capitals, these artists are still ambivalently located within the radar of the national and global.

A further comparison with "olden day" Japanese internationalists—the cultural and political elites who explicitly positioned themselves in relation to Western modernity in the early twentieth century and who came into adulthood in the aftermath of World War Two when the country was "catching up" to the West—is also instructive. The kind of internationalism that was held up by the establishment elite did not necessarily imagine a world of commonalities. On the contrary it was the "differences" that motivated internationalism in the quest to become like the West. Young contemporary Japanese artists, while being cognizant of their origins, traverse lives in global art hubs—New York, Berlin, London, but also rural Japan—with universalistic theoretical and social sensibilities.[9]

In their search for better societies and citizens, East Asian scholars also impart strong transnational sensibilities (Chang and Tam, Iwabuchi in this volume). Their objections to excessive nationalisms and excessive individualisms are framed within transnationally informed concepts and theories. The views expressed are certainly critical of "hegemonic impositions" and question both Western and East Asian practices; the alternatives articulated are however remarkably bound within a set of standardized theories about individuals and groups. A set of standardized individual and societal traits—being democratic, egalitarian, participatory, diversity-respecting, and conscientious—emerge as desirable virtues for good citizenship and good society in academic debates and nationally set surveys.

The second reflection we wish to offer is that transnationalization often involves a realignment of the states with the broader frameworks while reiterating and reinterpreting national positions. The ensuing conflicts are not necessarily straightforward. Consider the island disputes in East Asia as an instance of transnationalization. As they unfold in the 2000s, island disputes involve two internationally institutionalized frames: the UN-affirmed ocean regime (which allows Japan's claims for redefinition of national geography)[10] and the UN-affirmed human rights regime whose institutional foundations are tightly linked to condemnation of nationalist crimes and atrocities of the past with a view to the "correct" future (which exposes Japan's legitimacy deficit, not only internationally but also nationally, with regard to the "history issues").

Aside from its provisions defining ocean boundaries, the ocean regime (the UN Convention on the Law of the Sea as its base) establishes obligations for protecting the marine environment and ensuring freedom of scientific research on the high seas. In respect of the "common heritage of mankind" principle, it also stipulates for controlling mineral resource exploitation in deep seabed areas beyond national jurisdiction. The regime relies heavily on technical definitions, "geometrically objective" methods, and input from scientists, in cooperation with other stakeholders such as policymakers and government officials, in delineating the contents and limits of the continental shelf. The assumption is that cooperation between these stakeholders will reveal boundaries "naturally." As Dudden (in this volume) argues, however, such delineations and the determination of legal ownership of the isles (around which the continental shelf is located) are far from "natural" and are riddled with "claims of history," even though the Law itself does not include a statement to this effect.[11] It is exactly the expectations on the part of its neighbors and Japan's failure to fully conform to the global trend of "national introspection" and own up to its past "human rights violations" that make its new island geography contested (Barkan 2000, Berger 2012, Levy and Sznaider 2006).[12]

In this book project, while favoring the concept of transnationalization, we did not necessarily move from a theoretical and analytical position that would designate transnationalization and the diffusion of transnational frameworks as a unilinear or inescapable process. Neither do we suggest transnationalization as an all-consuming process in explicating the changes that the nation and citizenship are undergoing in East Asia at the beginning of the twenty-first century. We consider this a matter of empirical inquiry. On the other hand we strongly believe that such inquiry should be conducted without being trapped in a Huntingtonian world.[13] While analyzing the nation and citizenship and their changing contours requires contextual knowledge, their content cannot be deduced from the civilizational heritage or regional and national identities but only through their interactions with the broader world and the institutional and cultural frameworks that this world espouses. The empirical analysis we provide in this volume, though its coverage is wide, is far from complete. We believe, however, it is an important step in the direction of a more robust understanding of East Asian developments and their transnationalized context.

Notes

1 Despite overtures toward a thaw since 2000, the tension between two Koreas, one of the lingering legacies of the Cold War, remains to be eased.
2 We consequently find the vast literature on transnationalism of limited use (for reviews of this literature within migration studies, see Faist 2010, Vertovec 1999, Waldinger and Fitzgerald 2004).
3 On "organizational logic" see Sassen (2006) and (Meyer and Bromley 2013); on "cultural-cognitive orientation" see Meyer *et al.* (1997).
4 See Soysal 2010 for a review of Beck's cosmopolitanism in comparison to Meyer's World Polity institutionalism and Sassen's denationalization. In conceptualizing transnational contention and transnational dynamics of social activism, della Porta and Tarrow (2005) and Tarrow (2005) also iterate the local and international as overlapping analytical spheres.
5 Since from its inception, Japan's Liberal Democratic Party (LDP) has repeatedly called for revision of the constitution, which was imposed by the occupying US. Over the decades, these calls did not go beyond the discussion stage; however, under Abe's leadership the LDP has stepped up its zeal. LDP's draft for revisions, which was published in April 2012, proposes that Japan's long history and unique culture and traditions should constitute the basis of the constitution, rather than the universalistic principles, including human rights, that the current constitution espouses (Repeta 2013).
6 Given its quest to become an independent and democratic nation, Taiwan's reforms go far to distance school education intentionally from the collectively oriented, authoritarian moral hierarchy rooted in traditional Chinese culture (Hsiao 2012).
7 In China, the move toward individual self-autonomy (from the family and community) and self-development and agency (for both sexes) can be traced back to the socialist

period, earlier than other East Asian countries. Although as Yan (2009: 280) remarks, after the revolution, while "individuals were liberated from kinship and community power by the party-state" they were "re-embedded in the […] 'socialist big family'." Thus, the asserted individuality of Chinese youth at the beginning of the twenty-first century is both a continuation of and a break with this past.

8 Although receiving most publicity, the scope of disputes is not limited to Japan and China. Japan has also had skirmishes with Taiwan, Russia, and South Korea; and China with Vietnam and the Philippines.

9 As Favell (in this volume) points out, surprisingly these young artists are largely ignored in art circles and also political debates, which invariably focus on an Japanese youth "alienated" from both the West and the rest of the Asia, with a "regressive Japanese 'island' mentality."

10 Following the 1996 ratification of the UN Convention on the Law of the Sea (UNCLOS), Japan made expansive maritime claims in the Japan/East Sea, impacting on Takeshima/Dokdo islets. Since 2008, Japan and China filed claims and counterclaims with UNCLOS involving territorial seas around Senkaku/Diayou islands. It is worth noting that since 2009, several ASEAN states (including Vietnam and the Philippines) have also made claims to maritime zones in conformity with UNCLOS, with territorial implications in the South China Sea.

11 Such ambiguities are typical of international laws as they have conflicted "authorship." The protagonists of laws are often experts who introduce non-national and scientific definitions, but the subsequent formulations and interpretations are subject to negotiations among different views and interests.

12 In the case of Europe, condemnation in the post-Second World War era did not only involve the genocide of the Nazis and their collaborators but also the crimes of colonialism, which created an externalized (beyond the region) sphere of shared guilt. In East Asia, Japan as the sole colonizer within the region (and the colonizer of its neighbors) is easily singled out for its "international legitimacy deficit." Since 1992, the UN Human Rights Commission and committees issued several prompts to the Japanese government to offer an official apology to the Korean "comfort women" victims. It is the "memories" of these "human rights failures" and the "continual recourse to international opinion" that ground Japan's legitimacy deficit (Levy and Sznaider 2006: 61). The revisionist perspective (proposals to revise the 1993 Kono statement that apologized for the military's involvement in wartime sex slavery and the 1995 Murayama Statement on Japan's aggressive wars, as well as the textbook-screening policy) that animated the 2012 electoral politics of Shinzō Abe invited further international, as well as national, reaction. In late 2012, another monument that commemorates the suffering of Korean women forced by Japan into sexual slavery during World War II was launched in California. In 2013, events were held across Canada (attended by citizens of various origins, including Japanese, Chinese, Korean, and European) to remember the 75th anniversary of the Nanjing massacre.

13 Samuel Huntington's essay, "The Clash of Civilizations?", which renders civilizations as "primordial" and "unique" entities with insurmountable differences among them, set off extensive debate about culture and identity in world politics.

References

Barkan, E. 2000. *The Guilt of Nations: Restitution and Negotiating Historical Injustices*. Baltimore, MD: The Johns Hopkins University Press.

Beck, U. and N. Sznaider. 2006. Unpacking Cosmopolitanism for the Social Sciences: A Research Agenda. *The British Journal of Sociology* 57(1): 1–24.

Berger, T. U. 2012. *War, Guilt, and World Politics after World War II*. Cambridge: Cambridge University Press.

Boli, J. and G. Thomas. 1999. *Constructing World Culture: International Nongovernmental Organizations since 1875*. Stanford, CA: Stanford University Press.

Chang, K. S. and B. Turner, eds. 2011. *Developmental Politics, National Unity, and Globalization*. Abingdon: Routledge.

della Porta, D. and S. Tarrow, eds. 2005. *Transnational Protest and Global Activism*. Oxford: Rowman and Littlefield.

Dobbin, F., B. Simmons, and G. Garrett. 2007. The Global Diffusion of Public Policies: Social Construction, Coercion, Competition, or Learning. *Annual Review of Sociology* 33: 449–72.

Drori, G. S. and J. W. Meyer. 2006. Scientization: Making a World Safe for Organizing. In *Transnational Governance: Institutional Dynamics of Regulation*, M.-L. Djelic and K. Sahlin-Andersson, eds. Cambridge: Cambridge University Press.

Drori, G. S., J. W. Meyer, F. O. Ramirez, and E. Schofer, 2003. *Science in the Modern World Polity*. Stanford, CA: Stanford University Press.

Faist, T. 2010. Diaspora and Transnationalism: What Kind of Dance Partners? In *Diaspora and Transnationalism: Concepts, Theories, and Methods*, R. Bauböck and T. Faist, eds. Amsterdam: Amsterdam University Press.

Frank, D. J. and J. W. Meyer. 2002. The Profusion of Individual Roles and Identities in the Postwar Period. *Sociological Theory* 20(1): 86–105.

Frank, D. J., T. Hardinge, and K. Wosick-Correa. 2009. The Global Dimensions of Rape-Law Reform: A Cross-National Study of Policy Outcomes. *American Sociological Review* 74(2): 272–90.

Hsiao, I. 2012. *Taiwan as an "Uncertain Imagined Community" in Transformation: Changing the History Curriculum in the post-Martial Law Era (from 1990s to 2008)*. PhD dissertation, Department of Sociology, University of Essex.

Iwabuchi, K. 2002. *Recentering Globalization: Popular Culture and Japanese Transnationalism*. Durham, NC: Duke University Press.

Japan Times Online. 2012. Rightwing Minister Seeks to Radically Revamp Education System. December 30. www.japantimes.co.jp/news/2012/12/30/national/rightwing-minister-seeks-to-radically-revamp-education-system/#.USkm-4Ubg7A (accessed June 2014).

Jepperson, R. L. 2002. The Development and Application of Sociological Neoinstitutionalism. In *New Directions in Contemporary Sociological Theory*, J. Berger and M. Zelditch, Jr., eds. Oxford: Rowman and Littlefield.

Katzenstein, P. 2005. *A World of Regions: Asia and Europe in the American Imperium*. Ithaca, NY: Cornell University Press.

Katzenstein, P. and T. Shiraishi, eds. 2006. *Beyond Japan: The Dynamics of East Asian Regionalism*. Ithaca, NY: Cornell University Press.

Kwan Lee, C. 2008. Rights Activism in China. *Contexts* 7(3): 14–19.

Levy, D. and N. Sznaider. 2006. Sovereignty Transformed: A Sociology of Human Rights. *The British Journal of Sociology* 57(4): 657–76.

Meyer, J. W. 2010. World Society, Institutional Theories, and the Actor. *Annual Review of Sociology* 36: 1–20.

Meyer, J. W., J. Boli, G. Thomas, and F. O. Ramirez. 1997. World Society and the Nation-State. *American Journal of Sociology* 103(1): 144–81.

Meyer, J. W. and P. Bromley. 2013. The Worldwide Expansion of "Organization." *Sociological Theory* 31(4): 366–89.

Meyer, J. W. and R. L. Jepperson. 2000. The "Actors" of Modern Society: The Cultural Construction of Social Agency. *Sociological Theory* 18(1): 100–120.

Meyer, J. W., F. O. Ramirez, and Y. Nuhoğlu Soysal, 1992. World Expansion of Mass Education, 1870–1980. *Sociology of Education* 65(2): 128–49.

New York Times. 2012. China's Territorial Disputes. December 13. http://topics.nytimes. com/top/news/international/countriesandterritories/china/territorial-disputes/index.html (accessed June 2014).

Ramirez, F. O. 2012. The World Society Perspective: Concepts, Assumptions, and Strategies. *Comparative Education* 48(4): 423–39.

Repeta, L. 2013. Japan's Democracy at Risk – The LDP's Ten Most Dangerous Proposals for Constitutional Change. *The Asia-Pacific Journal* 11(28/3), July 15. Available at: www. japanfocus.org/-Lawrence-Repeta/3969 (accessed June 2014).

Rozman, G. 2012. *East Asian National Identities: Common Roots and Chinese Exceptionalism*. Stanford, CA: Stanford University Press.

Sassen, S. 2006. *Territory, Authority, Rights: From Medieval to Global Assemblages*. Princeton, NJ: Princeton University Press.

——2008. Neither Global nor National: Novel Assemblages of Territory, Authority, and Rights. *Ethics and Global Politics* 1(1–2): 61–79.

Schofer, E., A. Hironaka, D. J. Frank, and W. Longhofer. 2012. Sociological Institutionalism and World Society. In *The Wiley-Blackwell Companion to Political Sociology*, K. Nash, A. Scott, and E. Amenta, eds. Oxford: Wiley-Blackwell.

Selden, M. 2009. East Asian Regionalism and its Enemies in Three Epochs: Political Economy and Geopolitics, 16th to 21st Centuries. *The Asia-Pacific Journal* 9(4/9), February 25. Available at: www.japanfocus.org/-Mark-Selden/3061 (accessed June 2014).

——2010. Nation, Region and the Global in East Asia: Conflict and Cooperation. *The Asia-Pacific Journal* 41(1/10), October 11. Available at: www.japanfocus.org/-Mark-Selden/3422 (accessed June 2014).

Sikkink, K. and M. Keck. 1998. *Activists Beyond Borders: Advocacy Networks in International Politics*. Ithaca, NY: Cornell University Press.

Somers, M. R. and C. N. J. Roberts. 2008. Toward a New Sociology of Rights: A Genealogy of "Buried Bodies" of Citizenship and Human Rights. *Annual Review of Law and Social Science* 4: 385–425.

Soysal, Nuhoğlu Y. 2000. Citizenship and Identity: Living in Diasporas in Postwar Europe? *Ethnic and Racial Studies* 23(1): 1–15.

——2010. Unpacking Cosmopolitanism. An Insider-Outsider's Reading. *The British Journal of Sociology* 61(Suppl.1): 405–11.

Strang, D. and J. W. Meyer. 1993. Institutional Conditions for Diffusion. *Theory and Society* 22(4): 487–511.

Swidler, A. 2001. *The Talk of Love: How Culture Matters*. Chicago, IL: Chicago University Press.

Tarrow, S. 2005. *The New Transnational Activism*. Cambridge: Cambridge University Press.

Tsutsui, K. and C. M. Wotipka. 2004. Global Civil Society and the International Human Rights Movement: Citizen Participation in Human Rights International Nongovernmental Organizations. *Social Forces* 8(2): 587–620.

Vertovec, S. 1999. Conceiving and Researching Transnationalism. *Ethnic and Racial Studies* 22(2): 447–62.

Waldinger, R. and D. Fitzgerald, 2004. Transnationalism in Question. *American Journal of Sociology* 109(5): 1177–95.

Yan, Yunxiang. 2009. *The Individualization of Chinese Society*. Oxford: Berg.

Institutionalized projects

2 Citizenship as a national and transnational enterprise

How education shapes regional and global relevance

Yasemin Nuhoğlu Soysal and Suk-Ying Wong

Despite their different trajectories and institutional set-up, East Asian education systems increasingly locate individual nations within broader global contexts. This orientation creates its own paradoxes. At the same time that citizenship becomes more and more a transnational enterprise, replacing earlier forms that favored national collectivity as the moral source for rights and conduct, "distinct" national cultures and values gain commanding positions as legitimate and effective entry points to world politics. In this chapter we track changes in the way that nation and citizenship are conceptualized and presented in school curricular material, focusing on China and Japan from 1945 until now as our case studies. We give particular attention to the periodization of change, engagement with broader (regional and global) dynamics, and converging and diverging patterns across case countries. We show that over time both countries assume a globalized society and the active role of individuals and nations in making this society. The region, East Asia, is a sub-plot to this globalization narrative. We also note that in the case of China this image of citizenship incorporates a more energized, forthcoming national framework depicting a shift from "communist" to a "normalized" portrait of the nation and citizen, whereas Japan straddled a national and international outlook earlier on. In both cases, the accent on the uniqueness of the nation and its distinct values is accompanied by increasingly abstract notions of active and autonomous citizenry. We suggest that these changes are brought on by a variety of (not necessarily coordinated and often conflicting) factors, including the changing position and competitiveness of the country in the region and the world, shifts in educational and pedagogical doctrines, and the dominant transnational frameworks and models of how societies should work.

Education as a national and transnational good

Historically, national citizenship and education have been tightly connected (Schissler and Soysal 2005). Curricula and textbooks are canonical knowledge forms that reflect institutionalized understandings of how society works and how it should work and projections about the proper membership of individuals in national polity. As an institution, education imparts both individual and collective goals. As such, educational agendas are bound with the political priorities of the time, but they are also subject to extensive academic approaches and pedagogical theories. Thus, despite contestations, and despite significant organizational differences across national contexts, we find common assumptions and models in the education policy field, more so than in other policy fields.

Ideas and discourses regarding educational priorities and content are highly institutionalized at the transnational level through a network of specialized organizations (Benavot and Braslavsky 2007). The international organizations in the field of education (UN, UNESCO, IBE, OECD) have authority and expertise and are often tightly connected to governmental bodies. Educational models, goals, and "best practices" are produced and conveyed effectively. These models are increasingly presented as global collective goods (e.g. education for all and lifelong learning) and strongly supported by scientific evidence. At the same time, education, like science, is regarded as providing a competitive edge for nation-states. A whole range of standardized indicators is produced to confirm the relationship between educational progress and national competitiveness. Thus, there is much attention to the successful models and ideas practiced by others and codified and legitimated transnationally.

Certain aspects of education are highly politicized. Textbooks, as the central instructional media, have been the subject of intense historical memory politics, public controversy, and media attention in East Asia (Hein and Selden 2000, Müller 2011; see also Dudden, Selden in this volume). Although highly visible, such controversies are not representative of the whole range of educational reforms and agendas that inform transformations of the nation and citizenship.

In this chapter we take a broader view to reflect on generalized educational agendas and the curricula organization of these agendas for compulsory school teaching. We consider such a focus justified given that in the postwar period youth have been exponentially incorporated into the nine-year compulsory-education trend across the world and in East Asia. Furthermore, given the centralized nature of East Asian educational systems, curricula production and content are highly revealing with regard to the teaching in schools of what constitutes proper citizenship and nationhood. In our discussion, we purposefully leave out institutional reforms (organization and administration of compulsory schooling), not because they are less relevant to the questions addressed in this volume, but because they have been already addressed in detail by others (Tsang 2000, Willis and Rappleye 2011). Our focus is instead on educational goals and curricular contents as they relate to the conceptualizations of the nation and citizen. History and citizenship education in schools, as well as the general educational reforms in East Asia, has been the subject of recent scholarship, but much of this literature remains within the boundaries of the education discipline and rarely engages broader questions of the transformations of the nation and citizenship (see for example Grossman, Lee, and Kennedy 2008, Lee *et al.* 2004). We employ a longitudinal perspective (starting from 1945) to capture long-term shifts and trends in regional and global contexts.[1]

Curricular reforms and periodization of change

In the postwar period, both Japanese and Chinese educational systems went through significant reforms and periods of opening up and hunkering down with an explicit focus on the nation. In each period we find that both countries had significant engagements with the "outside" world and the predominant educational models, either rejecting or endorsing them.

Educational reforms are often seen as responses to changes in political and economic circumstances, but such functionalist explanations are wanting. During the sixty years or so with which our analysis is concerned, Japan and China have had different political and economic trajectories and different positions vis-à-vis the region and the world. Our review shows that Japanese and Chinese educational priorities and curricular goals diverged up until the mid-1980s. Since then, however, their educational reforms decidedly converge in terms of the priorities and goals they set.

Japan's economy-sponsored transformations: coming to terms with a stagnated nation

Postwar remodeling, 1947–69

The first educational reforms in the aftermath of the Second World War were imposed by the United States, as the occupying force, with the intention of transforming Japan from a military dictatorship into a democratic society. The reforms followed American educational ideals infused with progressive pedagogy rooted in Dewey on active, participatory students in school and society and rejecting elitism and authoritarianism. Educational priorities were reoriented to put the "liberation of the individual" before the purpose of the state, schooling to produce individuals who would actively participate in their communities and in democracy, empowered against authoritarian control by the state.

The first article of the Fundamental Law of Education passed in 1947 reflects this orientation:

> Education shall aim at the full development of personality, striving for the rearing of people, sound in mind and body, who shall love truth and justice, esteem individual value, respect labor, have a deep sense of responsibility, and be imbued with an independent spirit, as builders of a peaceful state and society.
>
> (Article 1, p. 1)[2]

The law laid the foundations for the democratic and egalitarian ideology of schooling in Japan. The differentiated multi-track system was replaced by a nine-year compulsory single track. The law also effectively undermined the moralistic nature of education as the official national philosophy since the Meiji period (Shibata 2003). Japanese history and geography curricula were discontinued along with moral training, since excessive focus on the nation and national history was seen as an impediment to world peace and democracy. A new social studies curriculum was introduced similar to the one in the United States. Overall the curricula emphasized greater individuality, freedom of inquiry, self-development, and learning by experience.

However, the following decade saw a reaction to the "Americanization" of education. In particular, the bias toward social and economic history and the lack of moral teaching were problematized. In 1958 the first "Japanese" curriculum after the war was introduced. Moral education was re-introduced as a separate class hour but with a new orientation that did not conflict with the general direction of democratization in education:

> Moral education aims to develop a Japanese who will never lose the consistent spirit of respect for his fellow man, who will realize this spirit in home, school and other actual life in the society of which he is a member, who strives for the creation of a culture rich in individuality and for the development of a democratic nation and society, and who is able to make a voluntary contribution to the peaceful international society.
>
> (Ministry of Education, "Outline for Implementing Moral Education,"
> 1958, quoted in Beauchamp 1994: 11)

Moral education nevertheless remained on the public agenda for years to come as a point of tension.

Consolidation and success of the "Japanese" model, 1969–84

The general consensus in favor of a continued democratic system and the new context of the Cold War meant that Japan retained the essence of the American-initiated liberal-democratic educational framework after the Occupation era. However, by the 1960s, Japan was experiencing high economic growth and development and, more self-confident, introduced a series of curricular reforms. One of the most significant ways that Japanese education moved away from "Americanization" was the rejection of the "progressive education model" and return to disciplinary teaching in 1969. Formulated as back-to-basics and a systematic acquisition of academic discipline-based subject content, this move came to define what was considered the "Japanese model." Associated with postwar Japanese economic recovery and development, the model was assumed to be effective in educating competent workforce and responsible citizens and began to attract international attention as a successful example.[3]

While a significant motivation was to strengthen science and technological training with a view toward national development goals, the new curricular structure also allowed the teaching of history, geography, and civics as separate subjects, with stronger emphasis on the Japanese nation and national consciousness and values. Where science education provided an understanding of nature as the basis of natural sciences, history education provided knowledge of the nation as the basis of social studies. Teaching of the "distinct character" of Japanese history, culture, and traditions received further reinforcement in this new course structure. This was a period of nation re-building and consolidation for a successful Japan in the world scene.

The dilemma of "catching up," 1984–2008

In the 1980s and early 1990s, Japan's education system seemed to offer a compelling model to the rest of the developed world. From the 1970s through the 1990s and even as late as 2000, Japan consistently ranked among the top three countries on major international tests of student performance in math and science (e.g. the International Association for the Evaluation of Educational Achievement [IEA], and the OECD Program for International Student Assessment [PISA]). This reinforced international attention on the "Japanese model."

Despite indications of success and high achievement in international tests, and despite a stable economy and prosperity from the mid-1980s on, Japan embarked on a route of educational reforms. Unlike the major reform debates in other countries, such as United States in the 1980s (low ranking of American students in international tests and low SAT scores) and Germany in the 2000s (poor performance in PISA studies), there was no "achievement crisis" in Japan when the reform proposals were first introduced (Tsuneyoshi 2004).

These reform efforts were set in motion during the administration of Prime Minister Yasuhiro Nakasone, who recast the idea of the "completion of the national goal of catching up with the West" through educational arena (Rappleye and Kariya 2011: 69). It would be through the education that Japan would articulate its "unique" path to the challenges of the post-catch-up period.

The Ad-Hoc Council of Education, appointed by Nakasone himself, issued four reports between 1984 and 1987. Although elaborated the shortcomings of "catching-up type of modernization," particularly for Japanese youth, and the need for re-appropriating Japan's own unique traditions and culture, the educational agenda set by the reports mirrored the ongoing educational debates in other industrialized countries. The reports focused on four main ideas: greater individuality and flexibility, internationalization, information technology, and lifelong learning. Measures suggested slimmed-down curricula (in terms of both time and content), more elective and interdisciplinary subjects to allow pupils to study things that would fit in their personal interests and aspirations, exploratory, self-motivated, and creative learning. The reports also emphasized the importance of a deeper understanding of the tradition and culture of Japan and developing student awareness of themselves as Japanese citizens. These ideas pretty much constituted the gist of reforms to follow in the next two decades and also paralleled prevailing transnational frameworks. The quest and claim for uniqueness, however, has remained in the political discourse.

Throughout the 1990s, reform ideas regarding student-centered and flexible education (*yutori kyōiku*) were supported by different groups but for different reasons. Politicians, business leaders, and educational critics all questioned the effectiveness and efficiency of education to meet the challenges of intensified international

competition and globalized society. While the educationalist experts and professionals (intellectuals, teachers, trade unions, and human rights organizations) focused
on the need for educational practices that nurture autonomy, liberation, and
self-realization, business circles focused on the failings of schools to produce
human resources for a competitive international market. This was accompanied
by political interests that played up to the panic about the state of youth and their
morals (Cave 2001, Takayama 2011). To be sure, there was much public controversy about the overall direction of educational reforms. Concerns were raised
about the inequalities and stratification that deregulation and privatization would
exacerbate (Kariya 2010) and the cut to instructional hours which did not
leave enough time for "basics." But the thrust of the reforms regarding student
autonomy and participation and relaxation of school education found widespread
support.

The 1998 curriculum stated the purpose of school education to be fostering a
"zest for living" (*ikiru chikara*) (Central Council for Education 1997). This terminology, albeit foreign to the Western ear, is emblematic—drawing upon current
educational psychology and pedagogical approaches that stress individuality,
creativity, and learning via practice and enjoyment. The introduction of "integrated study" was one of the strategies toward these ends. Left to the devices of
individual schools, integrated study lessons (more than two hours a week) have no
prescribed textbooks or examinations. Instead, individual schools develop lessons
and activities to encourage independent and creative thinking, reasoning, and
investigation through interdisciplinary topics including international understanding, information technology, environmental education, and education on
welfare, taking into account children's interests and the particular characteristics
of the school and community (the goal being to make learning more stimulating
and personally relevant for students).

In 2006 the Fundamental Law of Education was revised for the first time in
sixty years, under the government of Shinzō Abe, replacing the education law of
1947 that was introduced during the US occupation to undo the authoritarian
educational doctrines of the imperial era. The nationalist undertones and the
state's expanded dominance in Abe's education agenda received extensive criticism (Lebowitz and McNeill 2007). The preamble of the 2006 law declares "the
promotion of an education which transmits tradition and aims at the creation of a
new culture," and "honoring the public spirit"—rather an amorphous statement.
The principle of lifelong learning ("to improve oneself at every opportunity and at
every setting to lead a fulfilling life") is added as a separate article (Ministry of
Education, Japan 2006, Article 3). The new curriculum guidelines, released in 2008,
mandate increased classroom hours, adjusting the previous emphasis on "relaxed
education," with the goal of ensuring students get a solid grounding in "basic
knowledge"—in line with the turning tide of individual capabilities and human
capital development in educational reforms worldwide. The objectives of education
listed in the new law and as reflected in the new curricula reveal the dilemmas
Japan encounters today. On one hand the objectives insist on "respecting Japanese
traditions and culture." On the other, converging on global trends, the law and

curricula envisage "an education-based nation" and an autonomous, creative, able, and actively contributing citizenry which values democracy, (gender) equality, and respect for the environment, peace, and other cultures (Ministry of Education, Japan 2008a, Chapter 1, Article 2).

China's state-sponsored transformations: the quest to be a world player

Socialist construction, 1949–78

After the establishment of the People's Republic of China (PRC) in 1949, the state took full control of education in the country. In the early years, a pronounced Soviet model was adopted in which the inculcation of communist ideology and politics were prominent goals in education. The education system was looked upon as a mechanism for fostering love of communist ideals and the construction of socialist men. The learning basics gave much emphasis to language studies, science, and technology—the core components of nation-building. The appropriation of the "nation" was not necessarily confined to a politically or culturally bounded entity, however: it belonged to the masses—of the country and the world—who would share the fruits of this grand socialist experiment. The first proper Constitution of the People's Republic of China (1954) defined the country's grand developmental project for the good of the humanity as a whole (Chen 1981: 104–9).

It was not until 1957 that a Chinese educational model began to emerge, one that was characterized by a rejection of any imperialistic or capitalistic (Western) elements and their replacement by a radically progressive socialist model, namely, Marxism-Leninism and Mao Zedong Thought. During this period of socialist construction, China experienced a series of national experiments in which a mobilization on all fronts for the final realization of utopian communism was the primary goal. The scale of these experiments organized through political movements and campaigns is unparalleled in history. Not surprisingly, education as an ideological source became instrumental. In the period between 1958 and 1965, various measures were taken to accelerate communist-building through education. In 1958, political and ideological education was made compulsory at all levels of schooling. To strike a balance between the "red" and the "expert," manual labor was incorporated into the formal curriculum. It was a period that set forth the momentum for a full-fledged socialist construction program while leaving no ambiguity for a turn-back.

During the Great Cultural Revolution, the education system was characterized by a low degree of formalization and standardization (Hawkins 1983, Li 2006, Liu 1993, Su 1991). From 1966 on, all educational institutions were idle for almost ten years. The Ministry of Education and schools were closed. Politics was in command, along with the cultivation of citizens who could meet the requirements of class struggle and the socialist state. There was an overt rejection of intellectualism, disciplines and academics. Accordingly, citizenship was not at all a favorable concept as it overlooked class differences. Individuals' place was strictly located in collectives in which many had to be "re-educated."

China's purposive move to socialist construction during this period is characterized by strong state control over ideological inculcation and training through education. While nation-building called for individual self-sacrifice and altruism as its legitimate base in the early years of the PRC, such "nation" referencing soon succumbed to massive ideological mobilization and political movements. The general goals of education in 1952 gave a vivid description of a visionary socialist citizenry to be nurtured, involving an amalgamation of nationalism, patriotism, and socialist ideals presented as a Chinese model of education for national development. The 1952 official statement for planning of secondary education is illustrative. While educating youth with Marxism-Leninism and Mao Zedong Thought as the central and common knowledge frames, students were also expected to exhibit loyalty to the motherland, serve people, love labor, and develop public morals as well as a brave character (He 1998).

It is possible to consider this period of socialist nation-building, including the gradual departure from the Soviet model, as an initial move on the part of China to path its long-term goal of welding autonomy and self-determination in the international community. Undoubtedly, the Chinese Communist Party's determination to "struggle against imperialist and hegemonic forces" was the major ideological drive, but such an undertaking was also rationalized by appealing to world progress and justice, the universalistic notions with much currency in the international community. The 1975 constitution, promulgated in the midst of the upheaval of the Cultural Revolution, described socialist nation-building as a striving for equality and respect among nations, peace, and progress in the world—a theme to be picked up again by the following two constitutions (1978 and 1982) in reformed post-Mao China.

Post-1978 reform and opening-up

The post-Mao era in China was marked by the grand transition from a centrally planned economy towards a market-oriented socialist economy. Already by the late 1970s the anti-capitalist and pro-socialist educational content had been toned down. By the end of the 1990s, China had seen through a series of major structural changes in education: the redirection of education policy by Deng in 1978, the 1985 Decision of the Chinese Communist Party (CCP), Central Committee on the Reform of the Education System and the Compulsory Education Law, the 1993 Outline of Educational Reform and Development, as well as the 1999 Action Plan for Educational Development (Tsang 2000). Economy, rather than culture or politics, was the driving force in reforms, with the goal of fast economic modernization and prosperity in order to enhance the status of the nation in the world. This is also the juncture when the state enthusiastically began seeking inspiration from "successful" models irrespective of their capitalist or socialist origins while at the same time reviving the local Confucian tradition. Debates on the direction of reforms drew heavily on the Chinese civilizational and cultural base to fend off Western value orientations such as extreme individualism and hedonism (Lee 2001). However, a substantial part of the reforms focused on methods of learning and imagining the ideal citizen—this is where Chinese education got closer to the dominant transnational models.

It is worth noting China's intensive engagement in this period with the wider educational and cultural circles through various international exchanges. These exchanges included scholarly visits, academic conferences, and joint research programs in the development of education. Various national organizations for coordinating and managing these exchanges also emerged. For instance, the Chinese National Commission for UNESCO was established in 1979 and Beijing Normal University became the host for the first research center for educational technology as a UNESCO project. The China Education Association for International Exchange was set up in 1981. All these early initiatives were crucial in reshaping Chinese education anew in its quest to re-integrate in the world (Liu 1993, Wang 2001, Zhu and Hu 2009).

The first national curriculum after a ten-year hiatus from formal schooling was implemented in 1978. While training virtuous socialist citizens was still the primary objective, new pedagogical approaches were filtering into educational agendas. Self-learning, analyzing and solving problems, and student interest and creativity in learning activities are all mentioned in the 1978 instructional regulations for junior high schools (Ministry of Education, PRC 1978). The major shifts in education however took place after the introduction of nine-year compulsory education in 1986. Occasional debates still cast doubts on the compatability between capitalist liberalization and an effective socialist citizenry, but the 1988 curricula for compulsory schools set the overall direction of changes to come. Political education was "diluted" into three separate areas of instruction: "Civics," "Social History," and "Construction of Chinese Socialism" (Zhong and Lee 2008). The official document issued by the ministry further reinforced the shift to the learning interest of students by promoting a "motivational approach to develop self-esteem, self-reliance (independence), and self-strengthening in students" (Curriculum and Teaching Materials Research Institute 1992: 69–74).

This is a significant epoch for China's reformulation of its self-positioning both nationally and internationally. Education once again became a vehicle for transformation, constituting the backbone of modernization. The route to modernization was twofold: on the one hand, an accentuated morality (enterprising on the convenience of traditional Confucian values such as care for others, care for collectives, integrity, diligence, and optimism), on the other an accentuated individuality (drawing on widely available ideas in the transnational educational discourses such as ability to observe, self-reflection, creativity, and analytical and scientific thinking). The tension between the morally sanctioned individual and her rights was acknowledged, while "individual growth" was understood as an integrating force through everyday practice. At the same time, nation was portrayed as a mobilizing narrative, both inwardly and outwardly, to legitimize the developmental trajectory of a China that fully engaged in a search for a unique model of Chinese socialism.

A New Millennium: The determined "way forward"

China entered the twenty-first century with great determination to deepen the reforms and consolidate its status as an integral and active world player. A more nurtured and appreciated national self was required for this outward positioning; the "affective, value-based" nature of education became even more manifest and replaced the previous obsession with a technological and scientific orientation (Müller 2011). The broadened conception of the individual as a builder and successor instead of mere worker also signified this shift, as reflected in the curricular programs for teaching training (Gu and Tan 2005, Ho 2014). The education reforms in 2001 called for an overhaul of the objectives, content, curricular materials, and pedagogical philosophy. The new curriculum revealed two foci: nurturing the nation and nurturing the individual. On one hand the reforms aim to cultivate patriotism and immersion in traditional culture, along with socialist values. On the other, fostering the individual well-being and psychological health of students and their creativity and independence are given primary importance. The reforms pointed to several "deficiencies" in the former compulsory curriculum: an over-emphasis on transmission of facts and disciplinary knowledge, over-crowded content, and mechanical learning. To correct these problems, the new guidelines specified that teaching should closely relate to students' lives, interests, and experience, and encourage initiative-taking, participation, and activity-related learning (Ministry of Education, PRC 2003, Section 3): much that was reminiscent of the Japanese "zest for living" principle. Knowledge and skills for lifelong learning is also mentioned to further the new educational goals. As part of follow-up, two new integrated subjects were introduced: "integrated science" (physics, chemistry, and biology together) and "history and society" (history and geography together).

China's determination to have a world role is also reflected in its continuing engagement with the international education community. At both global and regional level, China has strengthened its participation and commitment, taking part in initiatives such as the E-9, a platform for exchanging educational experiences among the nine most highly populated countries in order to realize the globally established goals of Education for All (UNESCO 2001). It has also begun to offer help to other developing countries in the form of international exchange programs and scholarships (e.g. "The Great Wall Fellowship Program") as well as research and training opportunities, assuming a more active global role from the 1990s (Wu and Wu 2001). Maybe more telling is China's decision to participate in international tests such as the Program for International Student Assessment (PISA) for the first time in 2009. The 15-year-olds from Shangai scored top scores in both 2009 and 2012, and although the Chinese officials did not allow the scores from rural areas to be published, the insider view was that they also indicated "remarkable performance" (Coughlan 2012). Nevertheless, as in Japan, the PISA participation fuelled discussion on the need to reform the teaching and learning of students in China in order to better cope with international competition. It also generated momentum for re-directing and accelerating the process of educational reform to attend to individual needs and diversity so as to foster all-round development of students (Lu and Zhu 2011: 17–19).

The Outline of the National Medium- and Long-term Program for Education Reform and Development (2010–20), issued in 2010 (Ministry of Education, PRC 2010), explicitly links the betterment of the nation and the world with the betterment of the individual, as foreseen by transnational educational models, while also highlighting the importance of the distinctive Chinese culture in realizing such a goal. The educational model adopted starts from the "self" (personal growth) and follows the child's ever-expanded communities—school, the country, and the world. Simultaneously, the model insists on the legacy—and appreciation—of the "excellent" culture and traditions the Chinese nation represents. The belief in Chinese culture and its role in making a visionary future is clear. What this role entails is not. Thus, despite following a drastically different postwar trajectory, China finds itself on the same page and in the same dilemma as Japan at the beginning of the twenty-first century.

Different paths, converging reforms

Two observations emerge from our review of educational reforms in Japan and China. Given their core status in national development and national self-projections, educational reforms often stir controversy, quickly becoming an arena for fleshing out different political orientations, as is the case in Japan. Even in state-controlled scenarios, such as in China, educational reforms generate significant public interest. Furthermore, educational reforms are often set in the context and urgency of a "crisis of national society" (Japan) or "rapid economic and social transformations" (China). However, the trajectory of changes is long-term and incremental. The latest reforms in Japan were set against a background of deteriorating skills, vitality, and morality in the post-bubble economy and society. And China's "rise" in global positioning contextualized much of its reforms in the first decade of the twenty-first century. Yet, many elements of these reforms were introduced in the previous periods. In Japan, from the late 1970s on, a set of measures was in place to support "relaxed education," including trimming the content of core curricula (1977, 1989, 1998), with the goal of allowing students to feel more engaged in the classroom and to enjoy learning. Internationalism has also been on the agenda since the 1970s. In China, similar ideas made an appearance in curricular statements from 1978 on. Indeed, before the latest wave of changes in 1998 and in 2008 in Japan and 1999 and 2010 in China, the content of subjects and textbooks already reflected the new orientation toward child-centered teaching and internationalism (Bromley, Meyer, and Ramirez 2011, Meyer, Bromley, and Ramirez 2010, Soysal and Wong 2007, Tsuneyoshi 2004). As such, these changes correspond more to evolving educational ideologies than immediate solutions for societal crises and needs.

Equally revealing is the lack of reference to "indigenous models" in both Japanese and Chinese reforms (see also Goodman 2003, Kariya and Rappleye 2010). The trails of the current Japanese and Chinese educational reforms go back to the mid-1980s, even though Japan and China started from different dispositions. Just as Japan announced the end of its catching-up, China started its opening-up to the outside world. While these dispositions generated extensive political talk regarding the uniqueness and traditions of each nation, the language and scope of education policy reforms in the last two decades largely followed the transnationally avail-able models.[4] The reforms and the preceding and subsequent debates remarkably included all the buzzwords of recent worldwide educational reforms: individual autonomy, personal development and well-being, creativity and the knowledge society, participation in and skills for a globalized world. As such, they revealed a standardized knowledge and discourse among education professionals, as well as a policy sector which is sensitized to transnational frameworks. Governments, policy-makers, administrators, academics, and educators pay attention to transna-tionally affirmed models. Thus, despite the controversies they stimulate, national educational reforms increasingly converge around priorities and instruments. Postwar curricular reforms in China and Japan attest to this.

Reworkings of the nation and citizen in history and civics curricula

We now turn to the goals and teaching content stated in the curricula as they portray the nation and citizen. Official curricular bulletins often state educational aims that reflect normative expectations of what each schooled individual should become, as well as her relationship to the broader collective (be it the nation, region, or world). We compare the history and civics curricula from 2000s[5] (a period of manifest transnational engagements) with the ones in 1969 from Japan and 1988 (history) and 1993 (civics) for China (periods of national consolidation in both countries).

Reinvigorating the national via transnational

The teaching of the "nation" has commonly commanded a central place in history instructions in both China and Japan. The Japanese history curriculum is forthright in stating "national consciousness" as a main concern and "patriotism" is consistently a pronounced goal in the Chinese curriculum. However, there is a shift in tone and in the elaboration of teaching themes over time in both countries.

While the 1969 history curriculum in Japan makes an explicit reference to "our" culture and land as a basis of individual pride and rights (Table 2.1a, point 2), in 2008 the idea evolves into an abstract "love for one's own country" in the context of world history and the appreciation of "historical figures who con-tributed to national, social, and cultural development" (Table 2.1a, points 5 and 6). Social and nation-building are dominant goals in the 1969 civics curriculum in Japan, with the emphasis on science and technology, and industry and economics (Table 2.1b, points 2 and 3). Corresponding to a period of high growth in Japan, this nuance is not surprising and it underscores the country's optimism, confidence, and commitment to continuing development. In 2008, democracy and demo-cratic politics take the driver's seat; the references to economic development are

Table 2.1a Curricular goals of history teaching in Japan

1969	2008
Subject label: Social Studies (*Shakai*)	Subject label: Social Studies (*Shakai*)
1. Developing a broad perspective in relation to politics, economy and society. 2. Understanding our country and our land as well as history in order to develop a sense of individual pride and rights that forms the foundation of democratic life. 3. Understanding our country's role in the world and raising the consciousness of being a member of the nation; mastering knowledge of the international world and upholding the spirit of international cooperation so as to contribute to world peace and human prosperity. 4. Learning well fast-changing Japan and the world's economy, society, and culture through exercising objectivity when making judgments based on data evidence.	5. Heightening concern for history; learning national history by placing world history as the background to cultivate national consciousness and love for one's own country. 6. Understanding and respecting those historical figures who have contributed to nation-building and the social and cultural development of the country. 7. Understanding international relations, cultural exchange and cultural relations between our country and other countries; developing concern for other ethnic cultures and ways of life; cultivating the spirit of international cooperation. 8. Developing an interest in studying specific case studies from a historical approach; acquiring an unbiased attitude towards the use of data from different angles.

Sources: Ministry of Education 1969, Ministry of Education 2008b.

dropped (Table 2.1b, point 7). Democracy rather than economic development is designated as the virtue of the nation.

In the case of China, although the country has opened up over time through a set of reforms, the teaching themes of patriotism and nationalism have remained on the agenda, albeit with altered orientation. The 1988 curriculum specifies the adoption of dialectical materialism and historical materialism as the ideological base to inculcate patriotism and internationalism (Table 2.2a, point 2). Such specification is virtually absent in the 2011 curriculum. Instead, patriotism is treated as an affective component that should be cultivated through acknowledgement and appreciation of the "great Chinese culture and history," along with "great achievements of human civilization." Such appreciation is expected to enrich the individual with the capacity to formulate "ideals and life goals that aim at making contribution to the human race and peace" (Table 2.2a, points 5 and 6). As in Japan, democracy appears as an important principle for both the nation and citizen (Table 2.2a, point 6), replacing the "inevitability" of socialism and communism in the earlier Thinking and Politics curriculum (Table 2.2b, point 2).

These curricular goals are reflected to a large extent in the content specified, although the detailed topics and their presentation reveal long-term trends, a persistent one being the articulation of the nation with the broader world, as a way to revalorize the nation. According to both the 1969 and 2008 curricula,

Table 2.1b Curricular goals of civics teaching in Japan

1969	2008
Subject label: Social Studies (*Shakai*)	Subject label: Social Studies (*Shakai*)
1. Understanding the significance of respect for individual dignity and human rights, especially freedom/rights and responsibility/duties; cultivating the concept of democracy and citizenship as well as the awareness of sovereign rights of a national citizen.	6. Understanding the significance of respect for individual dignity and human rights, especially freedom/rights and responsibility/duties; cultivating the concept of democracy and citizenship as well as awareness of sovereign rights of a national citizen.
2. Understanding the close relationships between family, geographical communities, the state and other social groups in society; nurturing an attitude of giving through profound understanding of an individual's role in contributing to national development based on the fact that individual wellbeing is closely related to social and national development.	7. Appropriating the meaning of democratic politics, its effect on daily lives and the economic activities of citizens; understanding various problems in society and developing an attitude of making own judgment.
3. Developing a wider perspective and ability to improve a less than satisfactory social environment in which problems emerge due to rapid developments in science and technology, industry, and the economy.	8. Acknowledging the importance of respect for both sovereignty rights and advancement of international cooperation among countries, along with love of one's own country, which are crucial for world peace and human welfare.
4. Acknowledging the importance of respect for both sovereignty rights and advancement of international cooperation among countries, along with the love of one's own country, which are crucial for world peace and human welfare.	9. Forming interest in modern social phenomena; acquiring skills in collecting and selecting proper data materials in order to understand and evaluate these phenomena without bias.
5. Forming interest in modern socialphenomena; acquiring skills in collecting and selecting proper data materials in order to understand and evaluate these phenomena without bias.	

Sources: Ministry of Education 1969, Ministry of Education 2008b.

learning history in Japan involves a distinct reference to the importance of understanding international relations and other cultures so that the spirit of international cooperation and peace is cultivated. This is not surprising. Unlike European developments, where economic and political unification provided the script for building futures in the region, Japan's postwar outlook was heavily dominated by its security alliance with the United States. This orientation still dominates the way that history is narrated to some extent. While Japan's current and historical relationship with other East Asian countries is neglected, a strong internationalism makes its way in. Japan turns to the world as a reference point, to bridge its "difficult past" (in the region) with an "acceptable present."

Table 2.2a Curricular goals of history teaching in China

1988	2011
Subject label: History (*Lishi*)	Subject label: History (*Lishi*)

1. To help students attain a basic knowledge of history; to be familiarized with events, facts, and historical figures in Chinese and world history; to be exposed to important historical concepts.
2. To transmit knowledge of dialectical materialism and historical materialism with special emphasis given to social development order; to instill patriotism and internationalism; to understand the basic development trajectory during the primary stage of socialism; to expose students to the concept of revolutionary transition; to develop good morals, historical consciousness and responsibility for contributing to socialist modernization construction while striving for peace and development.
3. To develop the ability to analyze historical facts and make keen observations based on the concept of historical materialism.

4. To help students master a basic knowledge of history including important historical figures, events, phenomena, concepts and historical development trajectory; to be familiarized with a chronological approach, to develop independent thinking; to understand the developmental order of history; to learn to collect valid historical facts and information from different sources as basis of supporting evidence for analyzing and solving historical controversies; to learn to discuss historical events and figures in both written and verbal communication.
5. To understand the development of diverse cultures in human society and learn to appreciate the great achievements of human civilization; to develop an independent view in analyzing history and exercise learning skills through collecting, generalizing, comparing, and summarizing data materials and historical facts when developing argument.
6. To understand the country's conditions and develop love for the great Chinese culture and history; to develop pride in the long history of the interdependence of all nationalities in China; to learn the significant contribution of the Chinese Communist Party to nation-building and reforming China; to devote oneself to the motherland's socialist construction; to form ideals and life goals that aim at making a contribution to the human race and peace; to develop good character and healthy aesthetic sentiments; to advocate the development of science and scientific attitudes, to pay attention to practical issues and foster creativity; to understand the changes of political systems from autocracy to democracy, from rule of man to rule of law, and their inevitability, to strengthen consciousness of democracy and law; to understand the diversity of social development, to understand and respect the culture of different countries, different regions and different nations in the world; to develop international consciousness, to face the world in the future.

Sources: Ministry of Education, PRC 1998; Ministry of Education, PRC 2011a.

Within this type of international project, the treatment of the two world wars has always been a point of continuing tension between Japan and her Asian neighbors. The topic does not take up much space in the Japanese curriculum. Instead, there is substantive exposure to the sufferings of war and the "evil" that ensues. The emphasis is on the avoidance of war and the pursuit of international cooperation and democracy, "common challenges for all people in the world"

Table 2.2b. Curricular goals of civics teaching in China

1993	2011
Subject label: Thinking and Politics (*SixiangZhengzhi*)	Subject label: Thinking and Moral Education (*SixiangPinde*)
1. To provide the fundamental basis for becoming socialist citizens with ideals, morals, culture, and discipline and understanding the socialist moral standard; to build up the concept of collectivity; to nurture good virtues in students, including loyalty to the motherland and people, concern for community and abiding by the law; to nurture a love of labor and hardwork; to instill respect for parents and others; to maintain social morals, honesty and integrity, and the ability to distinguish between right and wrong. 2. To educate about social development; to promote understanding of the objective pattern of human social development and that socialism and communism are inevitable trends in human history. 3. To develop understanding of our country's situation and the construction of socialism with Chinese characteristics, especially under the leadership of CCP; to understand the nature and mission of socialist nation-building. 4. To emphasize an education in socialist democracy and legal concepts; to instill the importance of law; to build up the concept of upholding the authority of constitutions; to develop the exercise of citizenship through abiding by the law and accepting sanctions if breaking the law; to develop the exercise of human rights properly and correctly; to develop citizens' social responsibility.	5. To instill the core values of socialism as the guiding framework; to integrate students' daily life with social practice; to develop good moral standards and psychological quality, and the habits of abiding by the law; to be polite; to enhance patriotism and collectivism; to develop common ideals of socialism with Chinese characteristics; to develop correct outlooks and worldviews as well as high values. 6. To instill the foundations of humanity: to emphasize national spirit and outstanding cultivation; to be attentive to students' needs and life experience during puberty; to emphasize students' learning and development, to enrich their emotions and feeling, to develop positive and enthusiastic life attitudes, to encourage the spirit of teamwork and individual creativity; to enhance moral integrity; to adopt pedagogical approaches that are congruent with students' everyday life and experience. 7. To instill the foundation of practicality: to integrate daily life with social practice; to enhance knowledge in technology and life experience; to develop good morality through spontaneous participation in different kinds of activities. 8. To integrate moral values and elements of psychological health within which an independent self should be fostered; to develop the ability to appreciate nature, protect the environment, and understand the law; to learn about the current development of the world and its future trends.

Sources: Ministry of Education, PRC 1993; Ministry of Education, PRC 2011.

(Ministry of Education, Japan 1969: 19). Both 1969 and 2008 curricula highlight the importance of peace and how Japan has persistently incorporated the peace principle and practice into its national restructuring and development program. The picture drawn is of a modern Japan that actively participates in the world arena, with references to current world events and the organizations through which Japan plays an important role in world society.

The picture is even stronger in civics teaching in Japan. The 1969 civics curriculum reveals efforts to move the nation to the center as a cooperative international player. National sovereignty is mentioned in connection with almost all international institutions (e.g. the United Nations, UNESCO), and in relation to international law (Ministry of Education, Japan 1969: 25). But strong emphasis is put on how Japan has pushed forward for international peace and understanding after World War II as both national and international common goals for eternal peace. In the 2008 curriculum, both the globalized world and Japan's place in it are much more taken for granted. Students are sensitized to identifying problems faced by a "common all" despite their diverse origins. Environmental degradation, depletion of natural resources, and poverty are mentioned as the main problems that the world as a whole should solve. Sustainable development of "global society" is set as a goal towards which Japan has to work with other countries (Ministry of Education, Japan 2008b: 33, 35).

It is worth noting that the coverage in the curricula of the world at the expense of the region is partly to do with a pedagogical shift which is itself a global trend. Over time, Japan's history teaching moved away from chronological content to a more conceptual arrangement of time, with greater emphasis on modern history (taking as a vantage point social and cultural history rather than militaristic and dynastic)—a common trend across countries (Wong 2003). Paradoxically, this shift meant that much of the early historical regional context was also omitted. Egypt, Mesopotamia, and India, which were mentioned as part of the coverage of ancient civilizations and their contribution to human progress, are not mentioned in 2008. China and Korea receive fewer mentions and have less visibility than in the 1969 curriculum. The 1969 curriculum makes several references to China, particularly in the context of "change and progress in Ancient Japan": diplomatic contacts with China, trade exchange between Japan and China, and the import of Buddhism. In the 2008 curriculum, the development of Buddhism and the language system in Japan are conveyed as a national project, the incorporation of "international civilizational elements" as Japan's own without specifying the origin, marking a distinct departure from a regional focus and reorienting it toward the international. Buddhism and Kana language system are referenced as part of a wider international cultural environment; their origins in China and Korea are not mentioned.

The 2008 curriculum covers the modern period under two separate headings: Modern Japan and the World, and Current Japan and the World. The first section allows for praise of Japan's long-term modernization—from Meiji restoration to democratic reforms and fast economic development in the postwar era—contextualized with reference to developments in the Western world (no difference here from the 1969 curriculum). In the second, scientific, technological, cultural, and social developments and progress receive even more significant mentions, and within these areas the United States and the global world become even more visible. Surprisingly, even as late as 2008, the curriculum does not mention transcultural exchanges within East Asia, which increasingly dominate popular culture.

Japan's "peaceful internationalism" finds its match in China's civilizational perspective. Unlike Japan, even after the latest reforms in 2000s, the Chinese history curriculum remains highly chronological, with the emphasis on civilizational achievements. Almost equal emphasis is allocated to ancient, medieval, and modern history. Instruction begins with the civilizational root of the Chinese people and culture [e.g. "the Yellow River, where the Chinese culture was first nurtured" (Ministry of Education, PRC 1988: 516)], followed by China's distinguished achievements and subsequent contributions to world human civilization [e.g. "the four big inventions: the compass, gunpowder, paper-making, printing" (Ministry of Education, PRC 1988: 514–15)]. For a country like China whose history accounts embody both a "glorious" past and a whole century's assault by foreign powers in modern times, such an arrangement of history provides a convenient base for nation-building and national mobilization under the CCP leadership. While the celebrated civilizational dimension provides the national pride that must be secured and sustained, the setback of the recent past bolsters the determinedness and the revitalization of a forward-looking China.

In the 2001 curriculum, modern Chinese history makes special references in order to glorify achievements in science and technology in the development project of capitalist exchange. The United States, the former USSR, and Japan are cited as examples of technological and economic success (Ministry of Education, PRC 2001, Section 3: vi). While China is positioned to represent a theory of civilization, the United States is seen as embodying a theory of progress in the modern world, both nevertheless contributing to the "advancement of humankind." Reference to such a club of world achievers was not part of the curriculum in 1988.

In contrast to Japan's avoidance of confronting conflicts, the Chinese association with Japan rests upon a sentiment of ambivalence in the history narratives. Japan as an invading power and the subsequent suffering of and injury to the Chinese people are mentioned, as well as the Japanese postwar economic miracle (Ministry of Education, PRC 2001, Section 8). Indeed, the commitment to modernization on the part of China "makes the other modernizers in the region visible" (Sun 2011: 10). Participation in the ASEAN is also mentioned in this context. Although East Asia does not receive treatment as a region, the European Union is highlighted as a prominent regional organization along with its role in the revival of European economy. In the same context, international organizations of various sorts, their role, and their work are also mentioned.

The geographical coverage of the world history teaching is expansive. In the earlier curriculum, world history was organized chronologically with references made to the internationalist communist worldview or socialist internationalism—an understandable emphasis when revolutionary movements commanded much attention around the world in the 1960s. World history teaching in the 2000s portrays a much closer and more connected world, not only politically but also economically and culturally through trade, science, art, and popular culture. China enthusiastically projects itself onto this globalized world as an active contributor.

The "ideal" citizen as a national and transnational enterprise

The common view on Asian citizenship education is that it centers on the development of self and social relations, with focus more on "morality" than politics, more on self-cultivation (good personal attributes and character) and public spirit than exercising rights and democracy. For example, moral education classes are required in junior high schools in Japan (Otsu 2008) and China has also incorporated the teaching of youth and adolescent psychology as well as morals into the junior secondary level of education since the early 2000s. Our review of Japanese and Chinese curricular content reveals an increasing emphasis on the autonomous and able individual as a sovereign actor in social life, located within civil society and the broader world, and much less within corporate groups such as family or the collective nation.

While individual dignity, human rights, and democracy, along with national consciousness and moral behavior, have been the underlying principles of citizenship education stated in every Japanese civics curriculum in the postwar era, the 2008 curriculum stresses more than before individual autonomy, participation, and democratic processes (Table 2.1b, points 6 and 7). The shift mirrors changes in other education systems, which move away from docile citizens to competent and active individuals.

The 1969 Japanese curricular content includes extensive information on local and national administrative structures and procedures and economic, financial, and political systems within which the individual is fused in the building and maintenance of major institutions. Specifically, the individual's relationship with family, occupation, and work are highlighted as a way of exercising rights and responsibilities. The 2008 curriculum departs from a different pedagogical viewpoint, which inevitably reflects the way that topics are dealt with. A much more issue- and problem-based approach is adopted, with coverage of the aging society, the information society, globalization, efficiency versus justice and fairness, individual dignity, and gender equality. While the 1969 curriculum stated the role and contribution of individuals in direct relation to social and national development enterprise (Table 2.1b, point 2), this is no longer the case in 2008. In its place there is a broad expectation of individuals' active involvement in small or large society. An empowered but amorphous body of citizens is assumed, as reflected in the titles of the sections: "Us and Modern Society," "Us and Economy," "Us and Politics," "Us and International Society." The focus has shifted from common knowledge of Japanese society and its functioning to individual ability and responsibility "to construct a society" (Ministry of Education, Japan 2008, Civics section: 34–6).

In China, the typical model of socialist citizenship that values collectivism and self-sacrifice gradually transforms to one that emphasizes the nurturing of the right virtues in order to relate sensibly to the wider web of social relations. These intrinsic qualities are integral to citizenship-building in contemporary Chinese society as specified in the 2003 civics curriculum, an area of instruction formerly called Thinking and Politics, now renamed Thinking and Moral education.

Patriotism (putting the interests of the country over the interest of individuals) and love for the "great" Chinese culture (including socialist culture) have been constant themes in the Chinese civics curriculum. However, the 2003 and 2011 curricula organize the "self" as an independent unit—"self" not simply submerged in people, motherland, or socialist ideals. Self-awareness, self-reflection, self-strengthening—all have become means of interacting with others, no longer confined by customary settings (i.e. school, family, party). This "self" on the other hand is also expected to have the "correct" virtues and morality to take part in and contribute to different fields (Table 2.2b, points 5 and 8; Ministry of Education, PRC 2003: 3). As in Japan, public spiritedness is a running theme in the curriculum, covering a wide range of topics from own self, family, nature and environment, science, creativity, motherland, peace, and a cosmopolitan point of view. The new curricular content also specifies citizenship rights and responsibilities much more clearly than before (e.g. individual privacy, dignity, private property, right to education, life and health, consumer rights, rule of law) (Ministry of Education, PRC 2003, Thinking and Moral Education section: 63–78). Understanding and respecting social justice and equality and abiding by the laws and regulations constitute some of the core responsibilities. It is clear however that rights are to be exercised concomitant with virtuous personal attributes and character. China still perceives the development of noble morals and character as a prerequisite for effective citizenship.

The fostering of civic-mindedness goes beyond the national domain in both countries. The evolutionary development of human rights with Western origins is a topic in the Japanese history curriculum, covering the origins of human rights in the English, French, and American revolutions, their arrival in Japan during the Meiji period, and their establishment as universalistic standards in 1947. The 1969 civics curriculum has a separate section on human rights, directly linked to the constitution and the rule of law. In the 2008 civics curriculum, human rights gain a more taken-for-granted nature, assumed to be global and naturally unfolding in every society. The assumed "naturality" of human rights means that they are removed from the national or regional political context. Thus the new civics curriculum does not entail as much explicit discussion of human rights and national structures as before (see also Meyer, Bromley, and Ramirez 2010).

Tolerance and co-operation among peoples beyond national borders are also a continuous topic in the Japanese civics curriculum. Cooperation with and care for others have always been a significant principle of Japanese civics teaching as a way of creating sense of belonging (Parmenter 2006). The same logic extends beyond the immediate confines. Global awareness of and respect for different national cultures becomes an individual responsibility, creating an empathetic community with "others" beyond borders. The teaching of "diversity" as such implicates rightful and virtuous individual citizens, as well responsible nation-state societies, in the "betterment" of the world (Soysal and Wong 2007).

Although the curriculum reveals a distinct commitment to social harmony and solidarity among different cultures, this commitment in the main is externalized. The 2008 curriculum specifically mentions gender equality as the basis for human dignity. However, there is no mention of different cultural or ethnic groups inside Japan. The Korean minority and various migrant origins are missing altogether. And while the global indigenous movement is celebrated, specific references to the Ainu (Japan's own indigenous minority) are also missing.

Compared to the earlier curricula, the 2003 history and society curriculum in China offers a distinct endorsement of many ideas associated with ideal citizenship as promoted in transnational spheres: awareness of individual rights; enhancing women's position in society; protection of children, elderly, and ethnic minorities; protection of the environment and promotion of sustainable development; understanding and appreciating Chinese and other peoples' struggles for human rights; and appreciation of and respect for different cultures and traditions (Ministry of Education, PRC 2003, History and Society section: 35–6). Although on this last point the curriculum clearly moves to emphasize the unity of the nation and the interdependence of ethnic minorities that make up the nation, there are limitations of such claimed cosmopolitanism in China. The effort to foster citizenship values has been one that focuses on the consolidation of the rule of law and order.

Concluding remarks

With regard to understanding the role of the transnational:

a) In the educational sphere, a recent and formidable literature understands and studies globalization in terms of a "neoliberal turn" (Dale and Robertson 2002, Kariya 2010, Kariya and Rappleye 2010, Mitchell 2003). The educational reform projects of the 1990s and later are linked to "neoliberal" transformations that took place simultaneously in North America, Europe, and Asia. The institutional structure of the Japanese education system has changed significantly, along with changes in socio-economic and political arrangements that had sustained Japan's postwar stability since the 1960s. China's ten-year program for institutional reform and development, issued in 2010, imitates some of the neo-liberal agendas in education (decentralization, privatization, and outcomes-based academic standards and testing).

However, our review of the periodization of reforms in East Asia shows that the educational doctrines that are now closely associated with neoliberal economic ideologies took root in national education systems without neoliberal economic imperatives. The focus on individual autonomy, well-being, creativity, participation, realization of one's abilities and self, lifelong learning—these ideas have had a career in the international educational scene for a long time (promoted by the likes of UNESCO, the United Nations, the Council of Europe).

What makes the recent neoliberal reforms "successful" is that they are cast as models promising collective good and they embrace progressive/liberal educational ideals (with individual dignity, autonomy, and well-being at their center) that are already legitimated transnationally, with the backing of professional expertise and intergovernmental organizations, as collective goods

(see Schofer *et al.* 2012; Simmons, Dobbin, and Garrett 2006). In the expectations and projections surrounding the nation and citizen, "political liberalism"
(participatory individual with universal rights, responsibilities, and actorhood)
and "economic liberalism" (requirements of regional and global markets, international mobility, the hegemonic rise of human capital ideas in facing global
competitiveness) are increasingly entangled, leading national education systems
toward outward orientations.

b) Education, as a modern institution and an individual and collective good,
has long been susceptible to transnational flows. Both Japan and China
had extensive encounters with "outside" educational models long before the time
period upon which we focus our analysis. In both cases these encounters
generated intense discussion and disputes as to whether the borrowing of
"foreign" educational systems (be they Western or Marxist) would be appropriate, given the countries' long-standing traditions in learning and training.
The "outside" models no longer seem to generate tension; the nation and its
traditions are expressed through education, but they do not constitute alternative
educational models.

With regard to substantive changes in history and civics teaching:

c) Despite convergent educational models, claims are made for cultural uniqueness as the basis of the nation's appeal and participation in the broader
world. This constitutes a contrast to the European educational context; in the
case of Europe, ideals (human rights, democracy, gender equality) owned as
"national" are often universally projected (Soysal, Bertilotti, and Mannitz
2005).

d) Increasingly moralized and empowered individual citizens are the designated
sovereign actors in civil society and social life (as opposed to the collective nation
or corporate group), not necessarily confined by national boundaries. This
orientation is prevalent in both countries but appropriated differently—virtues
(China) vs. public spiritedness (Japan).

e) History teaching particularizes the nation (more so in China than in
Japan); in civics education we find an increasingly expanded individual in an
increasingly standardized mode of society. The comparison with earlier curricular periods reveals a shift in aim from knowledge of the nation (its history,
values, geography, etc.) to the ability to construct and be part of a functioning
society.

f) Territorial spheres of civics and history education have expanded, with a
noticeable emphasis on the active individual and citizen, not only within but
also beyond the nation, particularly from the mid-1990s. However, unlike
Europe, "beyond the nation" does not necessarily entail a regional project.
The reference to region is not a positive one as in European education (Soysal
2002) but rather a context of conflicts, despite the extensive integration that
has already taken place through trade, consumption, and circulation of arts
and popular culture.

Notes

1 Empirically, we report findings from a research project in which we investigated the changing concepts of "Good Citizen" and "Good Society," focusing on comparisons between Europe and East Asia with a view on regional and global dynamics (funded by the Economic and Social Research Council in Britain and the Research Grant Council of Hong Kong). The project analyzed school curricula, as well as textbooks and the policy debates around them, from 1945 until now (including the case countries of England, Germany, and France in Europe; and China, Japan, South Korea, and Taiwan in East Asia). The data were sampled from history and civics school subjects intended for the 12–14 age group, which is generically called "lower secondary" and is part of compulsory education, before the differentiation of curricular subjects takes place, thus better reflecting the mass aspect of schooling.
2 The law replaced the 1890 Imperial Rescript on Education, which was seen as the legal and moral force behind the militaristic and ultranationalist emphasis in education (Beauchamp 1994: 5). Although modeled after the Prussian military and education system, the "ills" of the Japanese system were attributed to its Confucian and traditional cultural elements. Thus the US Occupation Force efforts to remake the system went much deeper than their interventions in Germany (Willis and Rappleye 2011).
3 The 1970s' US education reform movement "back to basics" and the 1980s' "excellence movement" referred to the successful Japanese model.
4 UNESCO, EURYDCE, IBE, OECD all keep track of educational reforms across countries and time, and consultative reports and white papers on reforms today invariably include a review of educational reforms worldwide. See for example Ministry of Education, Japan (2001).
5 For Japan, the latest available curricula are from 2008. In China, the 2011 curricula formalized the 2001 (history) and 2003 (civics), both of which were introduced initially as experimental versions.

References

Beauchamp, E. R. 1994. Introduction: Japanese Education since 1945. In *Japanese Education Since 1945: A Documentary Study*, E. R. Beauchamp and J. M. Vardaman, Jr., eds. Armonk, NY: M. E. Sharpe.

Benavot, A. and C. Braslavsky, eds. 2007. *School Knowledge in Comparative and Historical Perspective: Changing Curricula in Primary and Secondary Education*. New York: Springer.

Bromley, P., J. W. Meyer, and F. O. Ramirez. 2011. Student Centrism in Social Science Textbooks: 1970–2005. *Social Forces* 90(2): 1–24.

Cave, P. 2001. Educational Reform in Japan in the 1990s: "Individuality" and Other Uncertainties. *Comparative Education* 37(2): 173–91.

Central Council for Education, Japan. 1997. *The Model for Japanese Education in the Perspective of the 21st Century* (2nd report). Available at: http://warp.ndl.go.jp/info:ndljp/pid/286794/www.mext.go.jp/english/news/1997/06/970601.htm (accessed June 2014).

Chen, T. H. E. 1981. *Chinese Education since 1949: Academic and Revolutionary Models*. New York: Pergamon Press.

Coughlan, S. 2012. China: The world's most clever country? *BBC Online*, 9 May. Available at: www.bbc.co.uk/news/business-17585201 (accessed July 2013).

Curriculum and Teaching Materials Research Institute. 1992. *Ershi Shiji Zhongguo Zhong Xiao Xue Kecheng Biaozhun Jiaoxue Dagang Huibian: Sixiang Zhengzhi Juan* [Collection of Standard Curriculum Guidelines for Primary and Secondary Schools in the Twentieth Century: Thinking and Politics]. Beijing: Renmín Jiaoyy Chuban She [People's Education Press].

Dale, R. and S. L. Robertson. 2002. The Varying Effects of Regional Organizations as Subjects of Globalization of Education. *Comparative Education Review* (Special Issue on Globalization and Regionalization) 46(1): 37–66.

Goodman, R. 2003. The Why, What and How of Educational Reform in Japan. In *Can the Japanese Change Their Education System?* R. Goodman and D. Phillips, eds. Oxford: Symposium Books.

Grossman, D. L., W. O. Lee, and K. J. Kennedy, eds. 2008. *Citizenship Curriculum in Asia and the Pacific*. New York: Springer.

Gu, M. and C. Tan. 2005. *2004 China Education Development Annual Report: Teacher and Teacher Education in Innovation*. Beijing: Beijing Shi Fan Da Xue Chu Ban She [Beijing Normal University Press].

Hawkins, J. N. 1983. *Education and Social Change in the People's Republic of China*. New York: Praeger.

He, D., ed. 1998. *Zhonghua Renmin Gong He Guo Zhong Yao Jiao Yu Wen Xian: 1949–1997* [Important Educational Documentary Sources of the People's Republic of China: 1949–97]. Haikou Shi: Hainan Chuban She [Hainan Publishing].

Hein, L. and M. Selden, eds. 2000. *Censoring History: Citizenship and Memory in Japan, Germany, and the United States*. Armonk, NY: M. E. Sharpe.

Ho, C. 2014. *Teacher Education as an Institution in China: A Discursive Study, 1949 – Present*. PhD thesis, Department of Sociology, the Chinese University of Hong Kong.

Kariya, T. 2010. *Education Reforms and Social Class in Japan*. Abingdon: Routledge.

Kariya, T. and J. Rappleye. 2010. The Twisted, Unintended Impacts of Globalization on Japanese Education. *Research in Sociology of Education* 17: 17–63.

Lebowitz, A. and D. McNeill. 2007. Hammering Down the Educational Nail: Abe Revises the Fundamental law of Education. *The Asia-Pacific Journal: Japan Focus*, July 9. Available at: www.japanfocus.org/site/make_pdf/2468 (accessed June 2014).

Lee, W.O. 2001. Moral Education Policy in China: The Struggle between Liberal and Traditional Approaches. In *Education and Political Transition: Themes and Experiences in East Asia* (second edition), M. Bray and W. O. Lee, eds. Hong Kong: Comparative Education Research Centre, University of Hong Kong.

Lee, W. O., D. L. Grossman, K. J. Kennedy, and G. P. Fairbrother, eds. 2004. *Citizenship Education in Asia and the Pacific: Concepts and Issues*. New York: Springer.

Li, Q. 2006. *"Dayuejin" Shiqi "Jiaoyu Geming" Yanjiu* [Education Reform During the Great Leap Forward Movement]. Beijing: Zhong Gong Zhong Yang Dang Xiao Chu Ban She [China Central Party School Press].

Liu, Y. 1993. *Zhong Guo Jiao Yu Da Shi Dian, 1949–1990* [Book of Major Educational Events in China, 1949–90]. Hangzhou: Zhejiang Jiao Yu Chu Ban She [Zheijang Education Press].

Lu, J. and X. Zhu. 2011. *Ru He Kan Dai Shanghai 2009 Nian PISA Ce Ping Jie Guo* [How to Appropriate and Evaluate the Testing Results of the Shanghai 2009 PISA]. Shanghai Academy of Educational Sciences. Available at: www.cnsaes.org/homepage/Upfile/2011224/201102457291077.pdf (accessed June 2014).

Meyer, J. W., P. Bromley, and F. O. Ramirez. 2010. Human Rights in Social Science Textbooks: Cross-National Analysis, 1970–2008. *Sociology of Education* 83(2): 111–34.

Ministry of Education, Japan. 1969. Chugako Gaushyu Shotou Youryou [Social Studies Guidelines for Middle School]. Available at: www.nier.go.jp/guideline/s44j/index.htm (accessed June 2014).

Ministry of Education, Culture, Sports, Science and Technology, Japan. 2001. Educational Reform as a Global Trend. *Educational Reform for the 21st Century* (Chapter 8, Section 1). Available at: www.mext.go.jp/b_menu/hakusho/html/hpac200101/hpac200101_2_061.html (accessed June 2014).

——2006. *Basic Act on Education (provisional translation)*. Available at: www.mext.go.jp/eng lish/lawandplan/1303462.htm (accessed June 2014).

——2008a. *Basic Plan for the Promotion of Education (provisional translation)*. Available at: www. mext.go.jp/english/lawandplan/1303463.htm (accessed June 2014).

——2008b. Chugako Gaushyu Shotou Youryou [Social Studies Guidelines for Middle School]. Available at: www.mext.go.jp/a_menu/shotou/new-cs/youryou/chu/index.htm (accessed June 2014).

Ministry of Education, PRC. 1978. *Ershi Shiji Zhongguo Zhong Xiao Xue Kecheng Biaozhun Jiaoxue Dagang Huibian: Ke Cheng (Jiao Xue) Juan* [Collection of Curriculum Standards and Teaching Guidelines of Primary and Secondary Schools in the Twentieth Century: Curriculum and Pedagogy]. Beijing: Renmín Jiaoyy Chuban She [People's Education Press].

——1988. *Jiunianzhi Yiwu Jiaoyu Quanrizhi Chuji Zhongxue Lishi Jiaoxue Dagang 1988* [Curriculum Outline of History for Nine-year Fulltime Compulsory Education: Junior Middle Schools, 1988]. In *Ershi Shiji Zhongguo Zhong Xiao Xue Kecheng Biaozhun: Lishi Juan* [Standard Curriculum Guidelines for Primary and Secondary Schools in the Twentieth Century: History]. Beijing: Renmín Jiaoyy Chuban She [People's Education Press].

——1993. *Jiunian Yiwu Jiaoyu Quanrizhi Chuji Zhongxue Sixiang Zhengzhi Jiaoxue Dagang— Shiyong 1993* [Curriculum Outline of Thinking and Politics for Nine-year Full-time Compulsory Education: Junior Middle Schools, 1993]. In *Ershi Shiji Zhongguo Zzhong Xiao Xue Kecheng Biaozhun: Sixiang Zhengzhi Juan* [Standard Curriculum Guidelines of Thinking and Politics for Primary and Secondary Schools in the Twentieth Century]. Beijing: Renmín Jiaoyy Chuban She [People's Education Press].

——2001. *Quanrizhi Yiwu Jiaoyu Lishi Kecheng Biaozhun Neirong Biaozhun—Shiyangao* [Curriculum Outline of History for Nine-year Full-time Compulsory Education: Junior Middle Schools (Experimental Version)]. Beijing: Beijing Shi Fan Da Xue Chu Ban She [Beijing Normal University Press].

——2003. *Quanrizhi Yiwu Jiaoyu Sixiang Pideke Kecheng Biaozhun—Shiyangao* [Curriculum Outline of Thinking and Politics for Nine-year Full-time Compulsory Education: Junior Middle Schools (Experimental Version)]. Beijing: Renmín Jiaoyy Chuban She [People's Education Press].

——2010. *Guo Jia Zhong Zhang Qi Jiao Yu Gai Ge He Fa Zha Gui Hua Gan Yao, 2010–20* [Outline of the National Medium- and Long-Term Program for Education Reform and Development, 2010–20]. Available at: www.moe.gov.cn/publicfiles/business/htmlfiles/ moc/A01_zcwj/201008/xxgk_93785.html (accessed June 2014).

——2011a. *Yiwu Jiaoyu Lishi Kecheng Biaozhun 2011Nianben* [Curriculum Outline of History for Compulsory Education, 2011]. Beijing: Beijing Shi Fan Da Xue Chu Ban She [Beijing Normal University Press].

——2011b. *Yiwu Jiaoyu Sixiang Pideke Kecheng Biaozhun 2011Nianben* [Curriculum Outline of Thinking and Moral Education for Compulsory Education, 2011]. Beijing: Beijing Shi Fan Da Xue Chu Ban She [Beijing Normal University Press].

Mitchell, K. 2003. Educating the National Citizen in Neoliberal Times: From the Multicultural Self to the Strategic Cosmopolitan. *Transactions of the Institute of British Geographers* 28: 387–403.

Müller, G. 2011. Teaching "The Others' History" in Chinese Schools: The State, Cultural Asymmetries, and Shifting Images of Europe (1900 to Today). In *Designing History in East Asian Textbooks Identity Politics and Transnational Aspirations*, G. Müller, ed. Abingdon: Routledge.

Otsu, K. 2008. Citizenship Education Curriculum in Japan. In *Citizenship Curriculum in Asia and the Pacific*, D. L. Grossman *et al.* eds. New York: Springer.

Parmenter, L. 2006. Asian(?) Citizenship and Identity in Japanese Education. *Citizenship Teaching and Learning* 2(2): 8–20.

Rappleye, J. and T. Kariya. 2011. Reimagining Self/Other: "Catch-up" Across Japan's Three Great Education Reforms. In *Reimagining Japanese Education: Borders, Transfers, Circulations, and the Comparative*, D. B. Willis and J. Rappleye, eds. Oxford: Symposium Books.

Schissler, H. and Y. Nuhoğlu Soysal, eds. 2005. *The Nation, Europe, and the World: Curricula and Textbooks in Transition*. New York: Berghahn Books.

Schofer, E., A. D. Hironaka, J. Frank, and W. Longhofer. 2012. Sociological Institutionalism and World Society. In *The Wiley-Blackwell Companion to Political Sociology*, E. Amenta, K. Nash, and A. Scott, eds. Oxford: Wiley-Blackwell.

Shibata, M. 2003. Destruction and Reconstruction: A Comparative Analysis of the Education Reform in Japan and Germany under the US Military Occupation after World War Two. In *Can the Japanese Change Their Education System?* R. Goodman and D. Phillips, eds. Oxford: Symposium Books.

Simmons, B. A., F. Dobbin, and G. Garrett. 2006. The International Diffusion of Liberalism. *International Organization* 60(4): 781–810.

Soysal, Nuhoğlu Y. 2002. Locating Europe. *European Societies* 4(3): 265–84.

Soysal, Nuhoğlu Y., T. Bertilotti, and S. Mannitz, 2005. Projections of Identity in French and German History and Civics Textbooks. In *The Nation, Europe, and the World: Textbooks and Curricula in Transition*, H. Schissler and Y. Nuhoğlu Soysal, eds. New York: Berghan Books.

Soysal, Nuhoğlu Y. and S. Y. Wong. 2007. Educating Future Citizens in Europe and Asia. In *School Knowledge in Comparative and Historical Perspective: Changing Curricula in Primary and Secondary Education*, A. Benavot and C. Braslavsky, eds. New York: Springer.

Su, Z. 1991. An Organizational Analysis of Central Educational Administration in China. In *Chinese Education: Problems, Policies, and Prospects*, I. Epstein, ed. New York: Garland Publishing.

Sun, G. 2011. The Predicament of Compiling Textbooks on the History of East Asia. In *Designing History in East Asian Textbooks Identity Politics and Transnational Aspirations*, G. Müller, ed. Abingdon: Routledge.

Takayama, K. 2011. Reconceptualizing the Politics of Japanese Education, Reimagining Comparative Studies of Japanese Education. In *Reimagining Japanese Education: Borders, Transfers, Circulations, and the Comparative*, D. B. Willis and J. Rappleye, eds. Oxford: Symposium Books.

Tsang, M. 2000. Education and National Development in China since 1949: Oscillating Policies and Enduring Dilemmas. In *China Review 2000*, M. C. Lau and J. Shen, eds. Hong Kong: The Chinese University of Hong Kong Press.

Tsuneyoshi, R. 2004. The New Japanese Educational Reforms and the Achievement "Crisis" Debate. *Educational Policy* 18(2): 364–94.

UNESCO. 2001. *Report of the 4th E-9 Ministerial Review Meeting in Beijing*. Paris: UNESCO.

Wang, Z. 2001. *Zhongguo Shi Fan Jiao Yu Gai Ge Yu Fa Zhan Yan Jiu* [Research in Reforms and Development in China's Teacher Education]. Guilin Shi: Guangxi Shi Fan da Xue Chu Ban She [Guangxi Normal University Press].

Willis, D. B. and J. Rappleye. 2011. Reimagining Japanese Education in the Global Conversation: Borders, Transfers, Circulations, and the Comparative. In *Reimagining Japanese Education: Borders, Transfers, Circulations, and the Comparative*, D. B. Willis and J. Rappleye, eds. Oxford: Symposium Books.

Wong, S. Y. 2003. The Globalization of World History Instructions: A Comparative Study of Three Chinese Societies. In *Jujutsu no Sutairu to Rekishi Kyouiku Kyoujuhou to Kyoukasho no*

Kokusaihikaku [Styles of Narrative in History Education: International Comparisons of Pedagogy and Textbooks], M. Watanebe, ed. Tokyo: Sangensha Academic Press.

Wu, S. and F. Wu. 2001. *WTO Yu Zhongguo Jiao Yu Fa Zhan* [WTO and the Development of Education in China]. Beijing: Beijing Keji Daxue Chu Ban She [University of Science and Technology Beijing Press].

Zhong, M. and W. O. Lee. 2008. Citizenship Curriculum in China: A Shifting Discourse toward Chinese Democracy, Law Education, and Psychological Health. In *Citizenship Curriculum in Asia and the Pacific*, D. L. Grossman *et al.* eds. New York: Springer.

Zhu, X. and Y. Hu. 2009. *Zhongguo Jiao Yu Gai Ge San Shi Nian: Jiao Shi Jiao Yu Juan* [China's Thirty Years' Reform in Education: Teacher Education]. Beijing: Beijing Shi Fan Da Xue Chu Ban She [Beijing Normal University Press].

3 Synthesizing the "national" and the "cosmos"

The case of life sciences in China

Joy Y. Zhang

The life sciences are often seen as "a 'Sputnik opportunity' for Asian states seeking to 'catch up with' and potentially surpass 'the West'" (Ong 2010: 5). As such, surging R&D investment and the rise of biotechnology in East Asia are often interpreted as being part of a nation-building process (Chopra 2008, Mizuno 2009, Wang 2002). This nationalistic gaze may be especially dominant when decoding China's burgeoning bioindustry. While many recognize that, due to the increasing ratio of scientific personnel trained abroad, China's domestic research is "becoming more and more cosmopolitan" (Qiu 2007), "top-down interference" from government institutions are still seen as an overriding influence (Cao and Suttmeier 2001: 972). For example, government institutions are seen as the main sources of funding (Cheng et al. 2006), the designers of scientific infrastructures (Zhong and Yang 2007), and the decision-makers in choosing which industrial standards to follow (Mu and Wu 2005). In short, China's scientific development is coined as "neo-techno-nationalism"—that is, "a deep-seated-nationalism, albeit one accommodated to the realities of techno-globalism" with government agencies as the principal driver (Suttmeier, Yao, and Tan 2006: 31).

My investigation of Chinese stem cells and synthetic biology, however, suggests the need for an alternative view in comprehending how the interplay of the national and global shapes the organization of science on the ground and who the architects of the research system are. Originally, stem cells were promoted by top-down government directives and state funding. But during my fieldwork between 2006 and 2010 there emerged a multiplicity of social actors (individuals, professional networks, civil groups) influencing the governance of stem cell research. Not only was there a diversification of research funding and a developing constellation of localized research policies, but certain areas which were traditionally under national monopoly (such as stem cell banks) had been challenged by globally connected civil initiatives. Meanwhile, the emergence of synthetic biology in China since 2007 has shown a reverse pathway. In contrast to stem cell research, its early progress was closely aligned with transnational scientific initiatives and largely supported by foreign funding. However, this origin did not lead to an abandonment of a national agenda. In a joint proposal made by leading Chinese synthetic biologists to the Ministry of Science and Technology at the end of 2009, a "Big Question" approach was put forward, which in effect inaugurated a centralized national agenda to bring synergy among domestic experts.

Stem cell research and synthetic biology offer complementary insights on the nature of scientific governance in China. Contradictory as their development trajectories seem, both the displacement and reinstatement of government dominance challenge a simple techno-nationalism explanation. In fact, as I demonstrate in this chapter, they highlight an emerging cosmopolitan mindset in China's life sciences. I call it cosmopolitan because, for stakeholders I interviewed, the development of biotechnology was not achieved through a zero-sum wrestling between the national and global, but rather through a social synthesis of aligning national R&D resources and actors with the transnational scientific community. A further argument of this chapter is that instead of the domination of a top-down command from government authorities, there seemed to be a bottom-up instrumentalization of the nation-state, an effect of the increasing cosmopolitanization of scientific governance. That is to say, the utility of government agencies to scientific development is no longer taken for granted, but is constantly assessed, contested, constructed, and, in some cases, altered.[1]

To further these arguments, I organize my discussion around two case studies, drawing on data from two separate research projects I conducted between 2006 and 2010. The case study on stem cell research was funded by the Wellcome Trust. In total I interviewed 48 key Chinese stakeholders (scientists, ethicists, and regulators) in six cities (Beijing, Tianjin, Shanghai, Guangzhou, Hangzhou, and Changsha). The case study on synthetic biology was funded by the UK's Royal Society Science Policy Center. As part of a larger study on the international governance of synthetic biology, I visited four leading research teams in three cities (Beijing, Tianjin, and Hefei) and interviewed ten researchers.

Case Study One: the displacement of government dominance in stem cell research

It was not until after the birth of Dolly the sheep in 1997 that stem cell became a buzzword in biomedical research. As with many developing countries, the Chinese government sees stem cell research as an opportunity in joining the "top squad" of the global scientific force. Apart from its permissive governance stance, the Chinese government has also been a major sponsor in this area from the start. The number of stem cell-related projects funded by the National Natural Science Foundation of China (NSFC) has increased from nine projects in 1999 to 166 in 2007. The amount of investment also rose steadily, reaching CN¥44.09 million (US$7.05 million) in 2011. Attention from the National Basic Research Program (the 973 Program) and the National High Technology Research and Development Program (the 863 Program) administered by the Ministry of Science and Technology (MOST) have also upgraded stem cell research's profile.[2] Key stem cell research centers were set up from 2000, all supported by government funding and hosted by state research institutions.[3]

Many scientists I interviewed highlighted government channeling of scientific resources and its consequential control over research as a particularity in the early stage of stem cell development in China. They described the funding procedures not so much as a scientific decision but rather an administrative one, or a form of government "task commissioning." Similar to China's hierarchical authoritarian administration in other scientific fields (Cao and Suttmeier 2001), such task commissioning was to ensure that a national development strategy for stem cells was entrusted into the "safe hands" of few elite senior scientists. This semi-commission relationship made stem cell scientists directly accountable to government agendas and subsequently enforced compliance with ministerial soft rules as a condition of receiving financial backing (Barr and Zhang 2010). This may help to explain why, to foreign observers, China's loosely termed guidelines on stem cell research seemed alarmingly deficient (Giles 2006: 9), yet in the eyes of Chinese researchers they were considered adequate, since "nearly all scientific research in China relies on government funding" (Cheng *et al.* 2006: 992).

An overview of China's administrative system of stem cell research is summarized in Figure 3.1 below. Administrative powers radiate from one centralized office, the State Council's State Steering Committee of S&T and Education (Guowuyuan Keji Jiaoyu Lingdao Xiaozu) and are disseminated through a parallel division of executive branches. In terms of stem cell research, the Ministry of Health (MOH) and MOST were the main regulators, while MOST, NSFC, and the Chinese Academy of Sciences (CAS) were the main funders. In short, at the beginning of stem cell development in China, all regulatory decisions and scientific resources could be traced back to a handful of national ministry-level organizations.

As the Chinese stem cell community expands and starts to establish regular transnational scientific exchange and collaborations, the exposure to criticism,

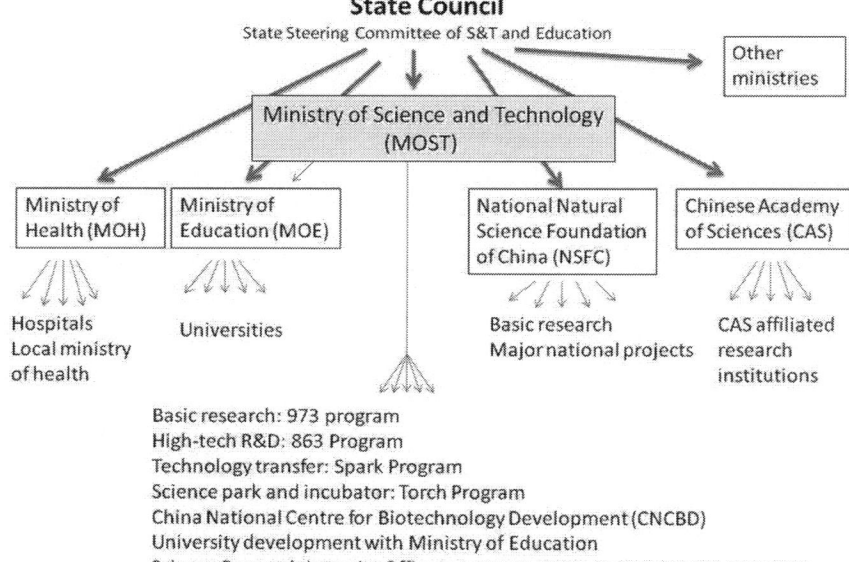

Figure 3.1 China's administrative system of stem cell research

alternative practices, and resources challenges China's national control from at least two perspectives. First, there is a "dilution" of government dominance, in which the national agenda and centralized government directives are increasingly required to incorporate, work with, and respond to an emerging multiplicity of funding sources, regulatory authorities, and governing visions within and without national borders (Sleeboom-Faulkner 2010, Zhang 2010a). Second, there is a "disruption" of government dominance, in which the role of the nation-state and its governing approach is directly questioned, contested, and transformed. This point is best illustrated by the development of two bone marrow donor programs, commonly referred to as "blood stem cell bank" in China: China Marrow Donor Program (hereafter the "China Stem Cell Bank") founded in 1992 and Sunshine Marrow Donor Program ("Sunshine Stem Cell Bank") founded in 2002.

The significance of blood stem cell banks, apart from their scientific implications, is that they are key to advancing stem cell transplants to cure leukaemia. To put their basic operations in a nutshell, these banks recruit and register volunteers for potential donation. They then collect blood samples and record relevant data specification, provide hospitals with database search service, make donation confirmation when an ideal match is found, and set up necessary medical coordination when donation is agreed. A large database, efficient communication among stakeholders, and reliable working standards are all positively related to higher success rates in such treatments (Han and Wang 2004).

In the absence of private funding, for a long time it was thought that such enterprises could only be managed by the state. Sure enough, for almost a decade, the China Stem Cell Bank was the only stem cell bank in China. According to its Beijing branch director, almost 90 percent of the stem cell bank's expenditure came directly from the government. Its daily operation also depends on sister government or semi-government agencies, such as the Beijing Red Cross, key transplant hospitals, and the local Communist Youth League committees.

However as the national bank is comfortably positioned in the web of government institutions, it showed little interests in promoting public understanding of the risk and benefits of blood stem cell transplant. For its Beijing branch, a better managed division of the national bank, most donor recruitments relied on volunteers sent by universities or work units to meet the annual semi-political mandates issued by the local Communist Youth League and Offices of Conduct (*Jingshen Wenming Ban*). Although many submitted their blood sample, few would eventually agree to be registered as potential donors. During the period between 1992 and 2001, the China Stem Cell Bank had a registry of only 20,000 records, a database that was only one-tenth the size of the stem cell bank in Taiwan. The national database was too small to provide service for the four million newly diagnosed patients each year. In fact, by the year 2009, seventeen years after its founding, the national bank was able to serve only 1100 patients, a small fraction of those in need of stem cell transplants. Many mainland patients relied on help from the Taiwan Tzu Chi Stem Cell Centre (Lu 2009).

In 2001, Liu Zhengchen, a Peking University student was diagnosed of leukaemia and needed a blood stem cell transplant. As with many leukaemia patients, the national bank failed to find Liu a match at the time. Fortunately for Liu, his condition allowed him to switch to medication as alternative treatment. Liu survived but was deeply disappointed by the national bank. In the following year, he and his fellow students initiated the Sunshine 100 Project at Peking University, with the aim of promoting public awareness and recruiting 100 volunteers for their own blood stem cell bank. With much help from student associations of Peking University and a bit of luck (the project had a limited number of registered donors and little private funding), it was able to pair the first transplant match in January 2003. Two years after its foundation, Liu's stem cell bank already upgraded its aim to Sunshine 10000 (Xiao 2004).

It was around this time that the national bank first contemplated a merger with the Sunshine Bank. At the time, such a proposal was considered a "friendly gesture" and "favor" by the national bank, as my interviews revealed. It would create a win-win situation, whereby the Sunshine Bank would not only receive political endorsement but also automatically benefit from national scale institutional support, while the national bank would benefit from the positive societal image created by this burgeoning student initiative. But this offer was turned down by Liu. The Beijing branch director's initial reaction was: "What do they think they can achieve? They've got no government endorsement or backing. They are just a student association."

However, it turned out that Sunshine Bank's potential was underestimated by the national bank. Not only did their registry expand, but they also set up a donors club, offered free data searches, and hosted public concerts, university lectures, and other fund-raising activities. What is worth highlighting is that, unlike the national stem cell bank's reliance on governmental support, Liu and his colleagues closely worked with global organizations such as the US Marrow Donor Program, Bone Marrow Donors Worldwide, and Gift for Life. According to Liu, the aim was both to seek technical assistance and to incorporate managerial experiences and public engagement strategies. In the years that followed, several attempts to negotiate a merger were made by the national bank, but all were turned down by the Sunshine Bank. Liu explained his stubbornness as follows:

> My initial motivation in setting up a blood stem cell bank was because I was denied treatment since the national bank cannot find me a donor. And I thought it would help other patients if we can set up an alternative source for people to look for transplant matches. ... I can set up an individual organization and let them [the national stem cell bank] see how things could have been done differently and influence them. But of course, this is not to say that the national bank is all bad; we also learned a lot from them.

An official correspondence from the Sunshine Bank to the China Stem Cell Bank in 2008 made two points clear: a) the Sunshine Bank welcomed any form of collaboration with the national bank and opened its database to the national bank so as to facilitate donor searches; and b) the Sunshine Bank reaffirmed its position on remaining an independent organization (Sunshine Stem Cell Bank 2008). In fact, after years of application and appeal, in April 2009 the Sunshine Bank was granted full legal status as independent civil organization by Beijing's Civil Affair Bureau. By that time the grassroots student association was more than a stem cell bank: it had become a comprehensive leukaemia-focused health institution, known as the New Sunshine Charity Foundation.

It then became clear that a merger might never take place. However, during the years of skepticism and rivalry, the China Stem Cell Bank also greatly improved its work efficiency, its database increasing almost fourfold. As I observed during my site visits to the Beijing branch in 2007 and 2009, the national bank also became active in assimilating transnational experiences and standards, supporting patient group events and hosting regular public engagement activities. Thus to some extent there *was* a win-win situation in the field of blood stem cell banks. It was just a different sort of win-win from what the national bank had originally envisaged.

To summarize, at the onset, stem cell research in China was organized through a hierarchical nation-state apparatus. Ministerial institutions functioned as the main gateway for commissioning scientific resources and national agendas to selected scientists. With increasing transnational communication and exchange, it is not too far-fetched to expect the nation-state dominance to be "diluted" by new possibilities and alternatives, but its "disruption" and "transformation" is maybe more revealing for the processes I am trying to convey in this chapter.

The Sunshine initiative was first and foremost founded on the questioning of the national bank's capability to promote leukaemia treatments and protect patients' welfare. More specifically, Liu and his colleagues challenged the existing structures and administration of the stem cell bank, such as its reliance on government financial allocation and its semi-political recruitment mandates. The aim of terminating the government monopoly in stem cell banking was clear, for the Sunshine Bank turned down several advantageous offers by the national bank. Their persistence in maintaining organizational independence was, in the eyes of Liu, an effective way in demonstrating "how things could have been done differently" and in "influenc[ing]" changes in the national bank. It is worth noting that Liu's challenging of state dominance did not necessarily aim at replacing the national bank with a globally resourced model. Indeed, Liu and his colleagues opened their database to the national bank and were ready to engage in all forms of collaboration. Through decades of contention, the Sunshine Project was more interested in stimulating than destroying the national bank's capacity building. It may be a stretch to argue that the once government-led operation was steered by grassroots initiatives. However, it is safe to say that the national bank's social and scientific functions were greatly improved due to the bottom-up efforts of Liu and his colleagues.

The Sunshine Bank's disposition towards national and global resources echoes a cosmopolitan outlook. In the absence of government backing, involvement in global networks and the assimilation of transnational experiences and standards were key to sustaining a healthy development of the Bank. Its success lies largely in its vernacular translation of these broader experiences into local commitments (e.g. donors club, free data searches) and customized public engagement (e.g. lectures and charity events). At the same time, while well networked globally, Liu did not shun from admitting that the Sunshine Bank also "learned a lot" from the national bank and was keen on drawing support from local authorities (e.g. Beijing's Civil Affairs Bureau). Liu and his colleagues had little interest in demarcating the local, national, and global. Rather, they indiscriminately perceived these categorical terms as representing a myriad of social spheres that intersect on the issue of leukaemia treatment. In this way, the development of the Sunshine Bank displayed a pragmatic approach—not framed by a conceptual dichotomy (or trichotomy) but navigated through exploring and synthesizing a world of options.

Case Study Two: the demands for a national agenda in synthetic biology

In contrast to stem cells, synthetic biology's initial development in China was not driven by national developmental directives but mainly benefited from transnational initiatives. China's first synthetic biology-related project, launched in October 2006, was part of the "Programmable Bacteria Catalyzing Research" (PROBACTYS) project, funded under the EU's Sixth Framework Program (Yang 2010). China's first synthetic biology centre, the Edinburgh University-Tianjing University Joint Research Centre for Systems Biology and Synthetic Biology, was also the fruit of cross-border collaborative efforts (Zhang 2008). In addition, China's involvement in synthetic biology was largely promoted by the participation of students in the International Genetically Engineered Machine competition (iGEM)—an international undergraduate contest initiated by the Massachusetts Institute of Technology in the USA. Before the iGEM training workshop hosted by Tianjin University in spring 2007, there were no research records and only two literature reviews on synthetic biology in Chinese scientific databases (Zhao and Wang 2007). According to Chunting Zhang of Tianjin University, a leading figure in promoting synthetic biology in China, it was during these workshops that Chinese research institutions joined their efforts for the first time. From the onset, the organization of these workshops engaged the transnational scientific community. World-leading synthetic biologists, such as Drew Endy and Christina Smolke, were invited. Later the same year, another training camp for iGEM tutors was organized in Tianjin and included delegates from Australia and Japan (Zhang 2008). During the 2010 competition, eleven teams from nine universities in six provinces/municipalities participated.

Training for iGEM has grown beyond winning student awards and has become a key component in Chinese researchers' exchanges with the transnational community (Ding 2010). The scientists I interviewed recounted how their initial involvement in synthetic biology overlapped with their participation in tutoring iGEM teams. One associate professor at Tianjin University, who wrote China's first undergraduate textbook on synthetic biology, half-jokingly said, "I mainly learned [synthetic biology] through tutoring new iGEM teams every year."

Increasing involvement with these initiatives not only helped to popularize synthetic biology in China but also influenced how Chinese scientists situate themselves in transnational scientific community. The iGEM competition involves using standard biological parts (BioBricks) and subsequently submitting new BioBricks to an open registry based in the United States (biobricks.org) for future sharing. During my fieldwork I asked one team whether there has been any plan in setting up a national bank for hosting all designs from Chinese iGEM teams to benefit domestic teams. Both the tutor and team members thought this proposal a bit "strange." The team captain responded:

> But why? There is no need. With BioBricks Foundation, we can get any parts we want quite easily. Plus, it directly connects us with all the data produced by iGEM teams around the world, let alone in China. A national bank would just be a small-scale duplicate.

The response was pragmatic, and as in the case of cell stem research, it did not honor national and transnational dichotomy. The main point, as far as Chinese teams were concerned, was to employ standard biological parts in their laboratory designs. As long as they have access to a good pool of resources, they were indifferent to whether it carried an "international" or "national" label, or whether it was based in the United States or in China.

Their sense of integrally belonging to the fabric of transnational scientific society is also exhibited in Chinese synthetic biology community's proactive approach in engaging with international debates. Chinese scientists are keen to increase their visibility in the formulation of international regulatory norms. Through the application of engineering principles to the design, control, and construction of living systems, synthetic biology seeks to integrate a number of research disciplines and industrial sectors, such as computational science, engineering, information technology, material science, biology, and nanotechnology. One major challenge for synthetic biology is "the synthetic integration of existing disciplines" and setting interdisciplinary regulatory standards (NEST 2005: 10). The CAS and the Chinese Academy of Engineering are currently engaged with their peer institutions in the United Kingdom and the United States to "design more robust frameworks for oversight, intellectual property, and international cooperation" on synthetic biology (The Royal Society 2009: 11).

Yet in discussing the roadmap for further advancement of synthetic biology, these globally well-networked individuals turned to the nation-state for support. Towards the end of 2009, the Chinese Academy of Science hosted a series of conferences on synthetic biology. One of the main outcomes was the founding of a "China Synthetic Biology Coordination Group," an informal association of around thirty conference delegates from various research institutions. This group formulated a "Regulatory Suggestion" to the MOST, which stated the necessity and implications of support for synthetic biology-related research. More specifically, the coordination group appealed to the MOST to play a key role in integrating national expertise through a "Big Question" approach.

To some extent, this grassroots proposition implies a stronger nation-state presence and government leadership than in the case of early stem cell development. According to my interviewees, the proposed approach aims to organize dispersed national R&D resources into one grand project that is essential for the technical development of this field, preferably along some industry-related theme that would appeal economically to the Chinese public. Structurally, this means the foundational (industry-related) research question is to be branched out into various streams of supporting research and more specific short-term research topics. Within such a framework, a variety of Chinese universities and research institutions can be recruited and coordinated at different levels towards solving the Big Question. At the time of my fieldwork in 2010, MOST had already taken up the role of coordinating a nation-wide consultation. Some interviewees described the excitement it generated amongst the Chinese scientific community as comparable to establishing "a new 'moon-landing' project."

In 2011, synthetic biology was listed as one of the core essential technologies (*hexin guanjian jishu*) in the government's Twelfth Five-Year Plan for Biological Technology (MOST 2011: 12). The first national basic research program on synthetic biology, SynCell, was launched as an "orientational program on major scientific problems" (*zhongda kexue wenti daoxiang xiangmu*). Drawing on expertise from ten research institutes in six cities in China, this project aimed to "promote the formation and development of a new strategic industry of bio-manufacturing" (see the project's official website, *www.syncell.org*). Similarly, the first national synthetic technology project launched in 2013 comprised an equivalent structure and ambition (Zhou 2013).

It might be tempting to equate these "moon-landing projects" as yet another national stride towards modernity. However, it is noteworthy how the organization of these projects actually echoed the "Big Question" approach envisaged by Chinese scientists. Reducing what is happening in China's synthetic biology research to techno-nationalism and focusing on the nation-state as the key unit of analysis, as is commonly done in the literature (Edgerton 2007), would miss the actual dynamic and significance of this scientific development.

First, to date, the principal drivers of synthetic biology in China have been not state authorities but individual scientists from different parts of China. It is useful to recall that even before synthetic biology appeared on MOST's agenda, these grassroots scientists had collaboratively set up an elaborate network of training programs and an informal coordination group. Not only was state involvement a result of grassroots requests but the role of such involvement was, to some extent, prescribed in the Regulatory Suggestion submitted. As one academician, who regularly contributes to MOST consultations, explained:

> It [the Big Question approach] was initially conversations among us scientists over the past couple of years. We saw this as an alternative way to keep up with international development and possibly lead to some scientific breakthrough. But we are happy to see that the ministry is excited and wants to support such an idea as well.

It is, of course, still too early to tell how MOST will fulfill its expected coordinating role and how power relations may evolve after the state institution enters the picture. But what is already apparent is that the state involvement in science should not be taken for granted. It was urged and shaped by a series of bottom-up endeavors: assessment of the value and strength of national and transnational resources (such as BioBricks, professional networks, cross-border funding, and national administration), reflection on existing operational arrangements, and actions on the basis of these considerations. In the case of synthetic biology, it was cross-sector organization that needed to be enhanced, and scientists demanded such performance from state ministries.

Second, the primary concern of the Big Question project was clearly embedded in scientists' respective professional interests, rather than their nationalistic vision. According to one professor in Beijing, who was a key initiator of the Big Question approach, the proposition of a nation-wide synergy was not so much about "national pride" or the goal of developing a "Chinese" synthetic biology; it was about research practicality. She explained:

> Synthetic biology is at the convergence of many disciplines, computing modeling, nanotechnology, bioengineering, genomic research etc. Individual researchers like me can only operate on part of the production chain. But I would like to see where my findings would fit in a bigger picture as well. It just makes sense for a country the size of China to set up some collective and coordinated framework so as to seek scientific breakthrough.

Similar to the case of stem cell research, the development of synthetic biology in China has a cosmopolitan feel to it. In the eyes of Chinese scientists, national and international resources are but one accessible global pool. From its emergence to its ongoing development, transnational initiatives such as international student competition and cross-border funding opportunities all played a vital role. Yet factors such as geographical proximity, language, collegial familiarities, and shared interests in economic development also attracted Chinese scientists to the national strategy as a sustainable mid- to long-term coordination amongst various research groups across scientific disciplines and industrial sectors. Neither the national nor the global frame of analysis would allow us to perceive the relations of dominations at work in full. Rather it requires a combination of the two.

Synthesis of the "national" and the "cosmos"

While techno-nationalism has often been ascribed as a main driver in the rise of the life sciences in China, the findings conveyed in this chapter necessitate revisiting at least two questions: a) how the national and the global constitute their influence in research on the ground, and b) who are, in practice, refining scientific governance structures.

As demonstrated with my case studies, the development of stem cell research and synthetic biology in China are advancements not only in the scientific construction of artefacts but also in the social synthesis of national and transnational research strengths and possibilities. In the case of stem cell research, the synthesis can be seen from a decrease in national government dominance and an increase in assimilation of transnational experience and standards. In the case of synthetic biology, the opposite holds true. A transnationally located research community appeals for a national research agenda and centralized coordination among domestic scientific groups.

I argue that the interplay between the national and transnational elements in China's life sciences suggests an emerging cosmopolitan mindset. The reasons are as follows. To begin with, in both case studies, the framing of stakeholders' rationales was not primarily based on national borders or on national causes, but on exploiting a world of potentials. For Liu, his stem cell bank was not so much targeted at eliminating national inputs or competing with national institutions as leaving the door open for introducing models "to conduct things better," independent of the origin of such models. Similarly, for synthetic biology, the Big Question approach did not so much originate from national pride as from a grassroots call by scientists to "make a difference" among their international peers. Moreover, the steering capacity for such practical thinking was, to a large extent, empowered by access to transnational scientific frameworks and resources. It would have been extremely difficult, if not impossible, for a leukaemia patient to launch a competitive stem cell bank in the absence of technical support from global agencies. Chinese synthetic biology scientists would probably not have gained leverage or have been persuasive with the Ministry of Science and Technology had they not already networked with the transnational scientific community.

Second, both cases were initiated and advanced by what Ulrich Beck (2002: 17) terms "globalization from within" or a contextual reflexivity towards global alternatives. In neither stem cell research nor synthetic biology were there blanket installations of global or national conventions. Rather they were constituted out of continuous processes spread over the span of several years. During this time, stakeholders (such as the Sunshine Bank, the national stem cell bank, iGEM tutors, and scientific academies) compared domestic and global contexts, weighed the merits of various options, questioned the existing organization of research, and instrumentalized a selection of glocal social capitals they had access to. Furthermore, orchestrating national and global influences was also far from straightforward. In the case of the stem cell bank, it took years of failed communication until the value of a civil bank was appreciated. In the case of synthetic biology, how the Big Question project balances different domestic interests remains a challenge. This contextual reflexivity and dialogical process in mediating local particularities and competing global alternatives were seen by many social theorists as essential characteristics of contemporary cosmopolitan outlook (Appiah 2006, Beck 2006, Harvey 2009).

Subsequently, this emerging mindset among stakeholders begs for a re-examination on the suitability of a traditional techno-nationalism lens in studying Chinese scientific developments. In both cases of stem cells and synthetic biology, bottom-up initiatives were most visible. The Sunshine Stem Cell Bank was initiated by a leukaemia patient, started with limited private funding, and operated, for the larger share of the last decade, as a student association. The new "moon-landing" grand scheme of synthetic biology also originated from grassroots communications amongst Chinese scientists and was jointly proposed through an informal ad hoc scientific group. This finding is in line with empirical studies of cosmopolitanism in the field of migrations (Cabrera 2010), financial integration (Brassett 2010), innovation (Tyfield and Urry 2009), and scientific governance (Zhang 2010b), which all illuminate the capacity of a multiplicity of social actors, especially at grassroots level, in mediating immediate social particularities and global alternatives. Correspondingly, there has been an increasingly shared recognition, at least amongst social scientists, that the nation-state is no longer the prime unit of scientific development, but should be regarded as one among many important governance and analytical units (Beck and Grande 2010).

However, I want to push this point further and argue that the empowerment of bottom-up actors through transnational frameworks and networking does not simply add another dimension to local development dynamics. Rather, it may necessitate a more radical change in our understandings of how relations of power and dominance are shaped. Through a techno-nationalism lens, scientific governance has always been premised on how formal state authorities (such as ministries) could best define the relevance of grassroots social actors (Callon, Lascoumes and Barthe 2009, Stirling 2008). However, I argue, we should at least be aware of the possibility (or in the two cases of China's life sciences, the reality) of a fundamental overturning of how this dynamic is formulated. That is, in the context of transnationalization of scientific governance, it may be the relevance and utility of a nation-state that is subjected to a bottom-up evaluation, criticism, questioning, and (re)conceptualization in the development of scientific governance.

Of course, this is not to say that the nation-state is irrelevant or insignificant. In both the cases of scientific development I investigated, the Chinese government remained vital. In a negative sense, the irresponsiveness and inefficiency of the government hampered the development of science, such as in the case of stem cells. In a positive sense, government input and national coordination were still essential in securing mid- to long-term research advancement and promoting regional scientific competitiveness. But then again it is essential to be reminded that the Chinese iGEM victories, Chinese joint synthetic biology projects and ethical discussions all took place before the state got involved. In the case of stem cells, despite the complex, lengthy establishment of the national stem cell bank, a patient's discontent eventually led to a disruption of government dominance in this field.

More importantly, contrary to an implicit techno-nationalism assumption that the nation-state is essential for scientific progress, in both case studies the nation-state presence was decoupled from national scientific competence. For example, a nationally owned biobrick registry was considered redundant in improving national competitiveness at iGEM. Despite China's early foundation of a national stem cell bank, it was not until the establishment of a civil bank a decade later that the national database started to show rapid expansion. Thus, in addition to moving away from a nationalistic gaze to attend a multiplicity of social actors, it may also be important to consider a possible reformulation or even an overturning of social dynamics among these actors.

Concluding words

How nation-states instrumentalize science and scientific communities in driving its development agenda has long been a central question in feeling the pulse of scientific advancement in Asian countries (Ong and Chen 2010, Schneider 2003). However, the development trajectory of stem cell research and synthetic biology in China questions the appropriateness of a conventional nation-state-focused line of inquiry.

For both the development of stem cell research and synthetic biology, the significance and relevance of government institutions were not taken for granted by Chinese stakeholders. Rather, the relevance of government input was, to various degrees, challenged, reflected upon and reshaped through grassroots practicalities in reference to transnational standards and practices. In the case of stem cells, despite generous state funding and permissive regulations, Chinese stakeholders discerned that following national directives alone was not enough in ensuring scientific excellence or efficiency. Transnational frameworks and resources were utilized as an extension or corrective to existing national ones. In the case of synthetic biology, the state originally played little role. It was the scientists with connections to the transnational scientific community that steered China's ministerial involvements into this field.

Such bottom-up synthesis of the national and global denotes the cosmopolitization of scientific governance, with at least twofold implications. First, even in cases where the structure of the national innovative system remains the same, the actual governing dynamics at work may be in constant flux. In the case of China, it is well acknowledged that its science and technology administrative framework "has not implemented any major changes for more than twenty years" (Zhong and Yang 2007: 324). The two case studies this chapter examined took place in an overlapping period of time. However, the relations between grassroots actors and state institutions were quite different, and they have changed within respective scientific context over time. For example, the relation between the Sunshine Bank and the national bank evolved from antagonistic to mutual respect with a view to good scientific conduct. At least at the time of my fieldwork, there was a sense of collegiality rather than a chain of command between synthetic biologists and the MOST, with the goal of further scientific advancement.

Second, and related to the first, the empowerment of a multiplicity of social actors may expand the sources and incentives for regulatory change. To be sure, the national agenda is still important in advancing science. Yet in both stem cell research and synthetic biology, progress in the organization of sciences was not guided by the concern of the national economy or national competitiveness but generated by a diversity of influences, such as alternative patient care, professional codes of conduct, funding opportunities and industrial concerns, all of which were articulated with transnational standards and frameworks.

Correspondingly, for us social scientists, there may also be a need for reframing our analytical frameworks. This means not only an expansion of our analytical gaze to accommodate diverse actors, but also a sensitivity to the fluidity of power dynamics within and without national borders. Instead of confining our sociological analysis to a national/global dichotomy, it may be more fruitful to empirically examine how dominance is formulated and steered on the ground.

Notes

1 My usage of the term cosmopolitan and focus on such processes follows that of Beck (2002, 2006).
2 According to its official website (www.973.gov.cn), the 973 Program initiated two major national projects on stem cell research as early as 2001. Among the 82 major projects it launched in 2006, seven are stem cell-focused. In 2006, the State Council issued the National Mid-term and Long-term Science and Technology Development Plan (2006–20), in which stem cell research was identified as one of the frontier development subjects. In the same year, the 863 Program launched a new major project on Stem Cell and Tissue Engineering (MOST 2006).
3 For northern China, the Peking University Stem Cell Research Center was founded in 2000, in collaboration with the Embryology Department in Peking University Health Science Center. For central China, the National Human Stem Cell Engineering Research Center in Hunan province was established in 2001 on the basis of the Human Reproductive Engineering Laboratory. The biggest stem cell research center in southern China, the Center for Stem Cell Biology and Tissue Engineering, was founded in 2002 at Sun Yat-sen University.

References

Appiah, K.A. 2006. *Cosmopolitanism: Ethics in a World of Strangers.* London: Penguin Books.

Barr, M. and J. Y. Zhang. 2010. China: Bioethics Education, Biosecurity, and the Rise of its Science. In *Ethics, Education, and the Life Sciences*, B. Rappert, ed. Canberra: Australian National University Press.

Beck, U. 2002. The Cosmopolitan Society and Its Enemies. *Theory Culture & Society* 19(1–2): 17–44

——2006. *The Cosmopolitan Vision.* Cambridge: Polity Press.

Beck, U. and E. Grande. 2010. Varieties of Second Modernity: the Cosmopolitan Turn in Social and Political Theory and Research. *The British Journal of Sociology* 61(3): 409–43.

Brassett, J. 2010. *Cosmopolitanism and Global Financial Reform.* Abingdon: Routledge.

Callon, M., P. Lascoumes, and Y. Barthe. 2009. *Acting in an Uncertain World: An Essay on Technical Democracy.* Cambridge, MA: MIT Press.

Cabrera, L. 2010. *The Practice of Global Citizenship.* Cambridge: Cambridge University Press.

Cao, C. and R. P. Suttmeier. 2001. China's New Scientific Elite: Distinguished Young Scientists, the Research Environment and Hopes for Chinese Science. *The China Quarterly* 168: 960–84.

Cheng, L., R-Z. Qiu, H. Deng, Y. A. Zhang, Y. Jin, and L. Li. 2006. Ethics: China Already Has Clear Stem-cell Guidelines. *Nature* 440: 992.

Chopra, R. 2008. *Technology and Nationalism in India: Cultural Negotiations from Colonialism to Cyberspace.* Amherst, NY: Cambria Press.

Ding, B. 2010. Sannian Fengyu Lu, iGEM ZhaiJin: Caijia Guoji Jinyin Gongcheng Jiqi Jingsai de Xinlulicheng [Three Years of Struggle for the Gold Medal: Experience at the iGEM Contest]. *University of Science and Technology of China News.* Available at: www.chinaumu. org/content/2010–01/12/content_3033016.htm (accessed June 2014).

Edgerton, D. 2007. The Contradictions of Techno-Nationalism and Techno-Globalism: A Historical Perspective. *New Global Studies* 1(1): 1–32.

Giles, J. 2006. Rules Tighten for Stem-cell Studies. *Nature* 440: 9.

Han, Z. and Y. Wang. 2004. HLA Kangyuan yu Zaoxue Ganxibao Yizhi Jinzhan ji Gusuiku Jianli Yiyi Chutan [Progress on HLA-antibody and the Hematopoietic Stem Cell Transplant Research and Initial Discussion on the Founding of Bone Marrow Registry]. *Zhonghua Yixue Yanjiu Zazhi* [Chinese Medical Research Journal] 4(1): 42–3.

Harvey, D. 2009. *Cosmopolitanism and the Geographies of Freedom*. New York: Columbia University Press.

Lu, D.P. 2009. Blood and Marrow Transplantation in Mainland China. *Hong Kong Medical Journal* 15(3): 9–12.

MOST (Ministry of Science and Technology), China. 2006. 863 Jihua "Ganxibao he Zuzhigongcheng" Zhongda Xiangmu Lixiang Gongzuo Shunli Wancheng [Successful Completion of 863 Program's Launching of the Major Project, "Stem Cell and Tissue Engineering"]. Beijing: MOST. Available at: www.most.gov.cn/ztzl/863cj/863cjswny/200612/t20061229_39304.htm (accessed June 2014).

——2011. "Shier-wu" Shengwu Jishu Fazhan Guihua [Twelfth Five-Year Plan for Biological Technology]. Beijing: MOST. Available at: www.most.gov.cn/fggw/zfwj/zfwj2011/201111/t20111128_91115.htm (accessed June 2014).

Mizuno, H. 2009. *Science for the Empire: Scientific Nationalism in Modern Japan*. Stanford, CA: Stanford University Press.

Mu, R. and Z. Wu. 2005. The Role of Standards in National Technology Policy in China. Institute of Policy and Management, Chinese Academy of Sciences. Available at: www.strategicstandards.com/files/China.pdf (accessed June 2014).

NEST. 2005. *Synthetic Biology: Applying Engineering to Biology*. Report of the NEST (New and Energing Science and Technology) High-Level Expert Group. Luxembourg: Office for Official Publications of the European Communities. Available at: www.bsse.ethz.ch/bpl/publications/nestreport.pdf (accessed June 2014).

Ong, A. 2010. Introduction: An Analytics of Biotechnology and Ethics at Multiple Scales. In *Asian Biotech: Ethics and Communities of Fate*, A. Ong and N. N. Chen, eds. Durham, NC: Duke University Press.

Ong, A. and N. N. Chen, eds. 2010. *Asian Biotech: Ethics and Communities of Fate*. Durham, NC: Duke University Press.

Qiu, R. 2007. After the Future of Science in China: Techno-nationalism or Cosmopolitan Innovation? Paper presented at The Atlas of Ideas: Mapping the New Geography of Science, Demos, London, January 17–18.

Schneider, L. 2003. *Biology and Revolution in Twentieth-Century China*. Oxford: Rowman & Littlefield Publishers Inc.

Sleeboom-Faulkner, M. E. 2010. National Risk Signatures and Human Embryonic Stem Cell Research in Mainland China. *Health, Risk & Society* 12(5): 491–511.

Stirling, A. 2008. "Opening up" and "Closing Down": Power, Participation, and Pluralism in the Social Appraisal of Technology. *Science, Technology & Human Values* 33(2): 262–94.

Sunshine Stem Cell Bank. 2008. Zhi Zhonghua Guosuiku he Hongshizihui Han: Yangguang Jihua Huibao [Correspondence with China Hematopoietic Stem Cell Bank and the Red Cross: Reports on Sun Shine Project]. Internal publication, August 31.

Suttmeier, R. P., X. Yao and A. Z. Tan. 2006. Standards of Power? Technology, Institutions, and Politics in the Development of China's National Standards Strategy. NBR Special Report. Seattle, WA: The National Bureau of Asian Research.

The Royal Society. 2009. *Science Policy Centre: 2010 and Beyond.* London: The Royal Society. Available at: https://royalsociety.org/~/media/Royal_Society_Content/policy/Science-Policy-Centre-Prospectus.pdf (accessed June 2014).

Tyfield, D. and J. Urry. 2009. Cosmopolitan China? *British Journal of Sociology* 60(4): 793–812.

Wang, Z. 2002. Saving China through Science: The Science Society in China, Scientific Nationalism, and Civil Society in Republican China. *Osiris* 17: 291–322.

Xiao, F. 2004. "Yangguang Yiwan Jihua" Qidong, Gongyi Gucuiku Zhengji Wanming Juanxianzhe [Launching the "Sunshine 10,000 Project": Public Donor Recruitment on Public Bone Marrow Banks]. *Xinhua News Press*, November 2. Available at: http://news.xinhuanet.com/newscenter/2004-11/02/content_2166627.htm (accessed June 2014).

Yang, H. 2010. Synthetic Biology and the Future of Man. The International Symposium on Opportunities and Challenges in the Emerging Field of Synthetic Biology, Washington DC, July 9–10. Available at: http://sites.nationalacademies.org/PGA/stl/PGA_051983 (accessed June 2014).

Zhang, C. 2008. Hecheng Shengwuxue Yanjiu Jinzhan [The Development of Synthetic Biology]. *China Science Foundation* 2: 65–69.

Zhang, J. Y. 2010a. The Cosmopolitanization of Science: Experience from China's Stem Cell Scientists. *Soziale Welt* 61(3–4): 255–74.

——2010b. Is the Cosmopolitanization of Science Emerging in China? *Études Internationales* 41(4): 571–95.

Zhao, X. and Q. Wang. 2007. Hecheng Shengwuxue: Xueke Jichu, Yanjiu Jinzhan yu Qianjing Zhanwang [Synthetic Biology: Foundation, Development, and Prospect]. *Qianyan Kexue* [Frontier Science] 3: 56–66.

Zhong, X. and X. Yang. 2007. Science and Technology Policy Reform and its Impact on China's National Innovation System. *Technology in Society* 29(3): 317–25.

Zhou, X. 2013. "Shierwu" 863 Jihua Hecheng Shengwu Jishu Zhongda Xiangmu Qidonghui Juban [The Kick-off Meeting for the "Twelfth Five Year Plan" 863 Program's Major Project on Synthetic Biology Technology]. *Tianjin University News*, April 22. Available at: www.tju.edu.cn/newscenter/teaching/201304/t20130422_172365.htm (accessed June 2014).

4   From resistance to attractiveness

The politics of values and regionalism in East Asia

David Leheny

In a speech in Tokyo in 2002, Prime Minister Mahathir Mohamad of Malaysia discussed the twentieth anniversary of his "Look East Policy." Partly a criticism of British diplomatic policies toward the region, the Look East Policy was premised on the idea that the best solutions for the region's problems—particularly those involving economic development—could be found not by learning from the West but rather by rediscovering the successes of Asia itself. He made the point dramatically, and in a manner that turned Japan's modern history into a veritable case study of resistance to Western imperialism:

> The people of East-Asia had been Looking East long before Malaysia adopted the Look East Policy. When Japan started modernizing during the Meiji Restoration, East Asians who were then faced with aggressive European and American free traders to open their countries for trade, looked at Japan's handling of this problem.
>
> The assumption by China that its culture was superior and the foreigners were barbarians could not be sustained in the face of Western successes in forcing open the country. Elsewhere in the East the Europeans simply occupied the countries in order to gain access to their products. By the middle of the nineteenth century only Thailand and Japan remained free. China had many ports converted as European trading stations.
>
> Japan was able to ward off European and American hegemony by adopting the administrative systems and the commercialization of the economy. Large numbers of Japanese were sent to Europe in order to acquire industrial technology. Very quickly Japan became as much as industrial and commercial power as the Europeans. Any idea that the Europeans had of colonizing or dominating Japan was shattered when in 1905 a modern Japanese Navy defeated the Russians decisively. From then on, Japan was looked up to by East Asians.
>
> Attempts were made by East Asians to emulate Japan's modernization. Siam, now Thailand being independent followed in Japan's footsteps. Looking East is therefore not a new thing. The people of East Asia had been Looking East at Japan even when they looked up to the West. Japan's success in modernizing gave them hope. They believed they could become as good as Japan.

The success of the Japanese Army in the early days of the Pacific war finally broke the spell cast by the Europeans regarding their invincibility. East Asians were able to see that their European overlords could be defeated. Their yearning for independence gained strength.

True, Japan was eventually defeated by superior Western arms, including the atom bomb. But the post-war years saw yet another demonstration of Japan's capability. From almost total destruction, Japan rose to become the second most powerful economy in the world.

(Mahathir 2002)

Considering Mahathir's words in context requires recognizing not only his awareness that neoliberal economic reforms by the Japanese government had pushed Japan away, not toward, an idealized East Asian development model in the late 1990s and early 2000s but also his efforts to buttress a line of attack on Anglo–American capitalism that he had pushed for two decades. In what would be his last full year as prime minister of Malaysia, Mahathir was moreover clearly deploying well-worn sentiments about Japan's economic success while steering clear of any debate about Japan's wartime behavior, which would likely have appeared in at least a few sentences during visits by many other Asian heads of state.

The speech is instructive for Mahathir's choices in constructing an East Asia not only largely as a postcolonial territory but also as a territory whose colonizer was the West rather than the subsequent Japanese empire. By referring to China, perhaps in an effort to flatter his Japanese hosts, Mahathir also offered the possibility that there were different ways for the East to differ from the West: at the level of civilization or culture, or in terms of development and progress. These differences need not be dichotomous; recent East Asian politics is littered with projects designed to explain and promote the region's high-speed economic growth partly through reference to culture or to values that emanate in a loose way from Asian civilization, whether understood as Confucian, Buddhist, or something else. But their existence underscores the way in which the definition of East Asia—or what makes East Asia East Asian—can involve not just intellectual parlor games but real struggles over power and politics and the construction of intellectual and ideological frames that support them.

This chapter aims to denaturalize the idea of East Asia as a region. On the one hand, its very existence is often premised on its putative opposite. To quote the historian Victor Koschmann (1997), "Without the West, there is no East." Particularly in the 1990s, the region's putatively unifying "Asian values" were usually described as resistance to the supposed "universal" values emanating from North American and Western Europe. But on the other hand, East Asia is also shaped by various soft-power projects designed to emphasize the attractiveness and uniqueness of national cultures, which are then projected as regional in nature. In making this case, the chapter builds from the "world polity" perspective, especially the global processes of isomorphism that dictate legitimate forms of participation in global politics, including through regional organization and institutionalization (Meyer *et al.* 1997). It departs, however, from recent accounts of regional institutions from within the world polity literature, suggesting instead that the framework may be able to provide important clues to not only the existence of regions but also the distinctiveness of their content. It suggests that we should consider how the construction of regions may be specific and deliberate challenges to the supposed universality of rules and norms embedded in international organizations, even as these challenges are best understood as the contested and unstable outcomes of an increasingly universal demand that states offer something uniquely attractive and appealing to the outside world (see also Soysal and Wong in this volume). My point is not that the world polity perspective, including its focus on the transnational legitimation of specific organizational forms and substantive practices, is unable to deal with regions. Instead, I argue that the political tensions involved in the definition of regions may result from the same cultural processes that militate toward their formation in the first place.

The respectability of regions

As a topic of analysis, regionalism differs from globalization and nationalism. Even a harried undergraduate would be unlikely to write with much excitement about globalization, so clichéd is the notion of a world coming together through the movement of people, capital, and information. Nationalism is a better bet for a research topic, but almost always viewed with some normative skepticism; it is the clinging to an atavistic identity that threatens cosmopolitan values and seems hopelessly provincial in a world hurtling toward togetherness. Regionalism, on the other hand, is simultaneously uncontroversial—who doubts that there are regions and that they matter in some way?—and inherently constraining in a way that seemingly lends itself to rigor that might be denied the more capaciously global. Unlike the globe, a region differentiates, conferring expertise and authority on some (whether natives or foreign specialists) to discuss it while allowing them to bound and limit their analyses in ways that globalization theorists cannot.

But to write of East Asian regionalism is to engage in politics, the issue of "who gets what, when, and how" (Lasswell 1990). Defining the boundaries of the region as well as the ties and flows that bind it together involves distributional claims about who and what are inside and who and what are outside, and therefore about what the region itself is. Lacking the global cohesiveness produced by astronomy and gravity, as well as the emotional commitment of an "imagined community" (Benedict Anderson's famous formulation of the nation), East Asia might well be understood as a straightforwardly intellectual conceit. No one calls himself or herself "East Asian," and yet the concept of East Asian regionalism has been so widely proffered as to be nearly accepted as true, with pundits and researchers primarily interested in who defines East Asian regionalism correctly rather than in what we are doing politically and culturally when we define it. Depending on how one depicts East Asia—what it is and what it means—one might come to legitimately different claims about how it ought to be run and, by extension, who should lead it. The same cannot be said as easily of thumbnail sketches of globalization or analyses of nationalism.

Analyzing East Asian regionalism as an aspect, perhaps even a symptom, of the development of a world polity requires both a critical take on regionalism itself and a sense that globalization is about more than the obliteration of boundaries—rather, it involves global processes of isomorphism. These confer legitimacy to regional groupings but primary authority to the highly institutionalized nation-states that comprise them. Even as regions, like states themselves, are expected to share certain cultural or civilizational values, the efforts to define those values bear the imprint of states, themselves always engaged in efforts to define themselves as unique. The global polity virtually demands the construction of regional cultural frames—e.g. what makes Asia Asia—even as clear and sustainable consensus on them is elusive. In a certain sense, as Mahathir's strange history of Japan's international relations suggests, Asia lies not in a distinctive and clear set of values but rather in practices that can be rationalized as resistance and defined against a West. This malleable Asia, however, is increasingly constituted by the expression of values that are articulated first as national and then legitimated by their presumptive attractiveness around the region.

Regions in the world polity

The "world polity" literature emanates from Stanford's Department of Sociology, particularly from the work of John Meyer and his colleagues. The research undertaken in this vein—often heavily quantitative, with a primary focus on the spread of institutional forms across the globe—has generally found that "many features of the contemporary nation-state derive from worldwide models constructed and propagated through global cultural and associational processes" (Meyer *et al.* 1997: 144–5). Endowed with such components as ministries of education, legislatures, and environmental agencies, states largely resemble one another even as their components are turned to different purposes and uses in local political contexts. As a state, for example, South Korea resembles Brazil in most ways as much as it does China or Vietnam.

But it is never grouped that way. Few would note a connection or similarity between Korea and Brazil—whether in the popularity of beef or the role of labor unions—and identify it as something meaningful, but such depictions are routine between Korea and its neighbors. Contemporary trade and investment links and the legacies of Confucianism are frequently invoked in describing Korea's relations, but decades of military authoritarianism and import-substituting industrialization as well as the popularity of Roman Catholicism are rendered irrelevant, as are other similarities that might be understood to be mere coincidences. The framing of Korea as Asian means something more than geography; it both allows the post facto explanation of its attributes as Asian and guides observers to notice certain kinds of similarities rather than others.

Regionalism thus poses certain kinds of challenges to a global polity framework. One way is the possibility that global polity theorists might well be able to account for the existence of regions but be less sensitive to or interested in their specific content, the things that make Asia Asian or Europe European. Some writers in the field have attempted to account for regionalism, though normally in somewhat stylized ways. In discussing the remarkable postwar increase in regional organizations, many of them mimicking the functions of global institutions, John Boli and George Thomas argue:

> Given the establishment of a firm world-polity foundation via extensive universalistic organizing into the 1930s, the increased corporation of peripheral areas into the world polity, and the practical advantages of shared language, culture, and history as tools for mobilization with respect to the larger world, regional bodies became a favored organizing form. A seemingly simple and straightforward process, its result is a world polity of considerably more complex structure.
>
> (Boli and Thomas 1999: 31)

A more recent effort to embed regions in the world polity framework takes it as axiomatic that regions—not just states—can be the sources and loci of institutional isomorphism; just as all states are expected to have legislatures and health ministries, so too are they now expected, like the member states of the European Union, to belong to and constitute regional organizations whose widely remarked existence may mask dys- or non-functionality (Jupille and Jolliff 2011). Jupille and Jolliff are primarily concerned with the region-building efforts of the European Union, an organization that simultaneously confers legitimacy on others by encouraging their institutionalization while also benefiting from the global spread of regions as primary forms of geopolitical organization.

This framing of regionalism as, in a sense, localized globalism connects some important developments neatly to the world polity framework, but risks robbing regions of their meaning—at least in terms of what people mean when they define, often quite assertively, what constitutes East Asia, or Latin America, or Africa. After all, to describe regions as reflecting the "practical advantages of shared language, culture, and history" not only presupposes a very great deal about areas as diverse as Latin America, Africa, and Asia, but also misses the fraught nature of regional definitions and delineations.

After all, the emergence of a region may reflect transnational flows more recent than the ancient or civilizational ties that judgments of "shared language and culture" might suggest. In an important statement about the development of East Asia as a region, Pempel (2005) distinguishes meaningfully between different sets of actors and their effects in region-building. Private actors may be uninterested in the creation of a region per se, but the net consequence of their combined investment, production, and trade strategies may help to establish certain bottom-up tendencies toward integration that Pempel describes as "regionalization." State actors, on the other hand, may push for the creation of political institutions, a top-down process that Pempel describes as "regionalism." In arguing that East Asia displays denser patterns of regionalization than regionalism, Pempel distinguishes the area from Europe, and calls attention especially to the frustration frequently voiced regarding the region's seeming inability to build institutions as comprehensive and binding as the European Union: "Using the European or other regional experiences to critique East Asia for lagging 'behind' in its level of regional integration is an impractical, if understandable, mistake" (Pempel 2005: 5).

It may not be "A World of Regions," as Peter Katzenstein says in his famous account, but it is impossible to imagine a world without them: perhaps a world of atomized nation-states all vying for position on a global chessboard, or one in which legitimacy is conferred solely by global institutions? In his capacious definition of regions, Katzenstein refers to their material and ideational bases as well as to the practices that draw them together: regions "have both material and symbolic dimensions, and we can trace them in patterns of behavioral interdependence and political practice" (Katzenstein 2005: 2). Katzenstein calls attention in particular to the complex roots of Asia and to the ways in which people battle over its definition:

> In Asia, these interconnections are hierarchical, crystallize around different urban nodes, and are based on different historical foundations—a Sinocentric tribute system in northeast Asia, a precolonial maritime system in Southeast Asia. As a concept, 'Asia' lacks an obvious focal point or common tradition. And for some countries, especially the United States and Japan, Asia-Pacific and the Pacific Rim are concepts that denote an Asia that is inclusive. These new concepts are examples of an institutionalized language, what Bruce Cumings calls 'rimspeak.' As a term, rimspeak may be annoying as a matter of plain English, but it undoubtedly matters politically. Such language captures and reflects political, economic, and cultural processes in East Asia that are creating new relations between places and peoples.
>
> (Katzenstein 2005: 10)

That is, regions are not simply there, and they are not naturally produced; they can develop and become more region-y. The symbolic and ideological dimensions accompany and are reshaped around material forms of integration, like the business networks involved in regionalization and the political practices that help to define regionalism. And these help to militate against the kind of easy teleology that Pempel (2005) astutely criticizes: Europe's present is not necessarily Asia's (or Latin America's, or Africa's) future. The global polity literature has long recognized that political efforts by states vis-à-vis international organizations stem in part from concerns about legitimacy. In considering regions, however, we might go a bit further and suggest that the legitimacy of regional organizations stems not only from their service as entry points into international relations but also as political and symbolic challenge to a "universal" (or Western) order. East Asian regionalism—or the political efforts to build institutions that draw together specifically countries along the western side of the Pacific Ocean—has frequently been justified by its most stalwart adherents not primarily with reference to efficiency or to geography nature but rather to resistance. As in Mahathir's speech about what Japan has long represented to those countries willing to "look East," Asia is defined largely by what the West is not.

How the West was spurned

These West vs. East dichotomies are of excellent vintage, and they have spawned not just books but entire literatures—on Orientalism, on subaltern studies—that critically engage and even upend them. But they live on as politically weighty phenomena, informing popular tracts like Samuel Huntington's *The Clash of Civilizations* and often fact their most obvious challenges in equally problematic accounts that emphasize universal teleologies, like Francis Fukuyama's *The End of History*. And perhaps it is little surprise that the notion of an Asia unified largely by its non-Westernness became most powerful and compelling at a time when the West (at least the United States and its closest allies) seemed to have triumphed over its chief Cold War foe but arrogantly ignored the shift in economic power toward the Pacific Rim. After all, Fukuyama's enthusiasm about the collapse of communism, like fascism before it, followed by just a few years the hand-wringing about the rise of Japan as an economic competitor to the United States, even as there had been no real resolution to the question of what kind of challenge Japan posed.

When the World Bank published its weird, deeply conflicted report *The East Asian Miracle* in 1994, it fed into a growing debate about the possibility that the Asian region had established an alternative growth model that was premised at least in part on distinctive cultural values that might be shared within the region. Viewed today, the report is remarkable in part for how closely it hews to the market-oriented logics that have long animated World Bank programs and recommendations. At the time, however, it was noted for how far it seemed to stray from neoliberal orthodoxy, supporting a positive state role in development that goes beyond the merely regulatory and moves toward active planning (Seddon 2005, Wade 1996). In this view, the success of an "Asian development model" provided an alternative avenue for generating economic growth that would not rest so clearly on the pure and unadulterated wisdom of the market.[1]

At least in terms of its formulation as such, the "model" itself was, of course, clearly linked not only to Japan's own economic growth, itself famously described as a "miracle" by, among others, the distinguished political economist Chalmers Johnson (1982) but also to its stewardship of other countries in the region. In this view, Japan could be understood as not only a source of capital for other neighbors embedded in Japan's production network (see especially Hatch and Yamamura 1996) but also the wellspring of institutional innovations that played key roles in high-speed growth in neighbors (and former colonies) like South Korea and Taiwan (see Woo-Cummings 1999). One particularly visible advocate of an East Asian development model, Malaysia's longtime prime minister Mahathir Mohamad, established the "Look East" policy that was designed in part to valorize Japan's contributions to the region while distancing it from the West.

East Asia's economic growth was arguably the most important global phenomenon of the latter half of the twentieth century and the opening years of the twenty-first, likely vying for that distinction with the expansion of women's rights, decolonization, the end of the Cold War, nuclear proliferation, and global warming. Perhaps a billion people were lifted out of poverty, transnational production chains were increasingly shaped around the Pacific, and the dominance of manufacturers in Japan (and later South Korea) hollowed out previously competitive sectors in the advanced industrial West. And while scholars have debated extensively the roots of economic success (for a brief survey, see Pei 1998), there were high stakes involved for leaders trying both to claim credit for the region's successes and rejecting the ostensibly global spread of democratic and liberal norms that might shift the political landscape.

Chief among these was, of course, the "Asian values" debate of the early 1990s. Mahathir, along with Singapore's authoritarian leader Lee Kuan Yew, became key proponents of the view that the region's values—drawing from a diverse array of sources but clearly involving modern interpretations of Confucianism—had undergirded its economic growth. Drawn in part from early twentieth-century "pan-Asianism," these values were also those previously derided by Western modernization theorists as the ones that had prevented the East from developing as quickly and successfully as the West (de Bary 2000; see also Aydin 2007).

In a widely quoted interview, Lee himself disputed the notion of an "Asian model" and highlighted differences between northeast and southeast Asia, but emphasized broad differences between the East and West, rooted in the relationship between the individual and his larger community:

> I don't think there is an Asian model as such. But Asian societies are unlike Western ones. The fundamental difference between Western concepts of society and government and East Asian concepts—when I say East Asians, I mean Korea, Japan, China, Vietnam, as distinct from Southeast Asia, which is a mix between the Sinic and the Indian, though Indian culture also emphasizes similar values—is that Eastern societies believe that the individual exists in the context of his family. He is not pristine and separate.
>
> (Zakaria 1994)

Lee went further, however, in detailing how Asians are distinctive. They are culturally predisposed toward a belief in hard work, education, and responsibility, which are responsible for their economic success. Not sharing these cultural values, even those other developing countries seeking to learn from the Asian economic experience would be unable to do so successfully:

> Getting the fundamentals right would help, but these societies will not succeed in the same way as East Asia did because certain driving forces will be absent. If you have a culture that doesn't place much value in learning and scholarship and hard work and thrift and deferment of present enjoyment for future gain, the going will be much slower.
>
> (Zakaria 1994)

In other words, culture matters, and it matters a great deal. To Lee, and to a number of the myriad authors who began to pen articles and books on the subject, East Asia's economic success had to be understood as emanating from different sources than those idealized in the Western literatures of economics. These sources could be viewed as largely institutional—wise state administrators cleverly guiding the economy toward outcomes better than those a self-regulating market might produce on its own—but would likely have to be supported by wide cultural beliefs. These beliefs could sustain trust and faith in political authority to make the right decisions regarding allocation while channeling personal effort and initiative into productive and family-oriented endeavor rather than toward individual avarice, selfishness, and distributional conflict. And these values could be connected somehow to the region, to a cultural background (Confucian, Buddhist, communitarian) unifying the region and distinguishing it from others, particularly the individualistic West.

In the broadest logic, the comfort that East Asians ostensibly felt, by dint of broadly shared religious and social values, with protective authoritarian governments would allow wise and responsible leaders to care for their people effectively. Unlike the divisive consequences of democracy, in which selfish parties could deploy discourses of rights and individualism against the state, Asia's authoritarian governments had constructed an alternative and culturally relevant form of social and political cooperation that had led to better outcomes for all. "What use," one young Southeast Asian bureaucrat training in Japan in the early 1990s asked me, "are individual rights if you haven't got enough to eat?" The logic of benevolent state leadership and the resistance to democratization is hardly unique to East Asia. The nickname of Brazil's longtime leader Getulio Vargas, *Pai do Povo* (father of the people) could hardly be more clearly paternalistic, and Vargas was as eager as Mahathir to represent himself as a distinctively modern thinker eager to break away from the ravages of predatory capitalism by the advanced industrial West.

The rise of Asian individuals?

Lee's and Mahathir's depictions of "Asian values," in particular, were frequently derided by critics (Western and otherwise) as shabby defenses of authoritarian rule. The most widely read response was from Nobel laureate Amartya Sen, the Indian-born economist who claimed democracy to be a "universal value" necessary for all (Sen 1999). To be sure, whatever the popularity of their challenges to the apparent arrogance of Western governments demanding political and economic reforms in the region, Lee and Mahathir were confronting political shifts that went far deeper than speeches by American and European leaders and diplomats eager to castigate the practices of non-democratic governments. As scholars from the global polity literature have noted, discourses of human rights, usually based on ontological claims about the primacy of the individual (as opposed to the society or the community), have long been prevalent in international relations and have become ever tighter.

That is, the processes that shape state expectations and practices are not necessarily the outcome of obvious power politics or even the direct legacies of colonialism. They are often produced through the interaction of states (one needs a foreign ministry, for example, to talk formally with neighbors), the practices of supranational organizations (without a ministry of education, a state cannot coordinate expectations set by UNESCO), and the efforts of transnational non-governmental organizations. Indeed, there has been increasingly universal membership across the globe in international human rights organizations and conventions, largely because of the organization of citizen action through institutionalized and scripted formats for the sanctification of certain rights (Tsutsui and Wotipka 2004; see also Tsutsui in this volume).

The work of Kiyoteru Tsutsui, Christine Min Wotipka, Emilie Hafner-Burton, and their colleagues has continued to show the pervasiveness of organization and institutions oriented around the concept of human rights (e.g. Hafner-Burton and Tsutsui 2007, Tsutui and Wotipka 2004). This does not mean, of course, that human rights are uniformly observed and respected; many governments that have signed human rights agreements have flagrantly violated their content. But it does suggest an organizational basis for the collapse of alternative claims about agency, participation, and responsibility. In this sense, the world polity comprises not only institutional forms but also rationalized practices that are premised on a common understanding of individual action. There is still plenty of contestation of what rights are or how to judge the relative moral weight one places on certain choices, but the world is one of citizens:

> Everyone is an individual endowed with certain rights and subject to certain obligations; everyone is capable of voluntaristic action seeking rational solutions to social problems; everyone has the right and obligation to participate in the grand human project; everyone is, therefore, a citizen of the world polity. It infuses each individual with the authority to pursue particularistic interests, preferably in organizations, while also authorizing individuals to promote collective goods defined in largely standardized ways.
>
> (Boli and Thomas 1999: 39–40)

And this is true of East Asia itself. Even in the comments of Mahathir and Lee, with all their criticism of Western democracy and their emphasis on different cultural values, there is little clear articulation of what specific form of political organization— non-democratic, premised on something other than individuals—might be legitimate. Lee himself struggles with the question. He knows what ought to be criticized but cannot move far enough away from an assumption of individual choice and agency to create a full alternative:

> The system of government in China will change. It will change in Korea, Taiwan, Vietnam. It is changing in Singapore. But it will not end up like the American or British or French or German systems. What are we all seeking? A form of government that will be comfortable, because it meets our needs, is not oppressive, and maximizes our opportunities. And whether you have one-man, one-vote or some-men, one vote or other men, two votes, those are forms which should be worked out. I'm not intellectually convinced that one-man,

one-vote is the best. We practice it because that's what the British bequeathed us and we haven't really found a need to challenge that. But I'm convinced, personally, that we would have a better system if we gave every man over the age of 40 who has a family two votes because he's likely to be more careful, voting also for his children. He is more likely to vote in a serious way than a capricious young man under 30. But we haven't found it necessary yet. If it became necessary we should do it.

(Zakaria 1994)

If we consider East Asian regionalism to have a cultural component, the debates that might define it have thus had to coalesce around a dwindling number of core ideas. It cannot be all about economic success, because the 1997 financial crisis and its aftermath created challenges that—while easily blamed on nefarious outside forces—still challenged a singular narrative of regional growth. It cannot be all about community, as the individual has become a universally legitimate signifier that makes alternative political claims difficult to frame convincingly. Instead, we see a central and continuing critique of a moralistic/judgmental West against which Asia might be defined, and we also see the lionization of that Asia as a region comparable to other areas where the West's lessons are unhelpful. Kishore Mahbubani, the most internationally recognizable proponent of the idea of a regional political culture (as well as dean of the Lee Kuan Yew School of Public Policy at the National University of Singapore), said in 2008:

Well, the Asian values debate, unfortunately is the most mistitled, that mostly badly mistitled debate in the world, because the Asian values debate came about at the end of the Cold War, because there was an Asian reaction to western triumphalism. I mean I was there. I went to Europe. I went to America and that was I mean, the western intellectuals where just plain cocky. Their attitude towards the rest of the world was "hey! the cold war is ended. The west has won. Now you the rest of the world, you have only one road of history. You all have to become cultural clones of the west" and that's what the Asians rejected. They said, "No, we will not become cultural or political clones of the west" and it was that reaction that was named the Asian values debate. It's not that the Asians disagree about the values of democracy, or the values of human rights, or we disagreed about the way the west said it should be implemented and history, by the way, has vindicated what the Asians said, because the societies that tried to go overnight, like Yugoslavia, it was a disaster.

(Mahbubani 2008)

This conception, needless to say, leaves a great deal of space and flexibility: Asians believe in the values of democracy, of human rights, just not in cultural cloning. And yet the construction of this space, this Asia, has repeatedly involved not just the negative case of the West but also the articulation of the cultural values that supposedly binds it together. Over the past few years, the structure and mechanisms of cloning have become increasingly apparent. They lie in the articulation of national values and their connection to a sympathetic region; they also suggest further deepening of a global polity.

The soft power of national values

While Asian champions of Japanese success, like Mahathir with his "Look East" policy, received significant and enthusiastic press in Japan, it was actually an American writer who in some ways spurred some of the language regarding Japan's overseas impact. Based on research in Tokyo in spring 2001, the journalist Douglas McGray wrote a widely cited (particularly in Japan) article entitled "Japan's Gross National Cool" in the public intellectual magazine *Foreign Policy*. Using the Harvard political scientist Joseph Nye's (2005) concept of "soft power" (the ability to attract and persuade rather than to coerce), McGray posited that Tokyo—with its vibrant arts scene, the success of its pop music groups overseas, and the seemingly endless popularity of anime—would likely be able to spread its "message" in the way that it had not previously (McGray 2002).

But what was that message? In his pathbreaking study of Japanese popular culture overseas, Koichi Iwabuchi provocatively argued that Japan's pop culture overseas had succeeded in part by being "odorless," earning a recognizability for its Japaneseness because it was so malleable within local contexts, so hybridized in its influences, and so lacking in explicit references to Japan itself (Iwabuchi 2002). Without some kind of explicit message, without some kind of expression of what Japan represents, how could the Japanese government hope to harness any of the good will that might be engendered by the popularity of Japanese products overseas?

In some ways, this putative limit fit well with Nye's original views on soft power. In his 1990 book *Bound to Lead*, in which he argued that American soft power resources were considerable sources of strength in the post-Cold War world, Nye suggested that the United States would not be replaced by then-rising powers like Japan and (West) Germany, in part because of the ubiquity of American media channels to the rest of the world and in part because of the attractiveness of American values. Compared to the universal values of openness, democracy, tolerance, and freedom that the United States could represent, Japan's basic insularity would make it an unlikely beneficiary of soft power. Crucially, Nye's image arose not only out of faith in the attractiveness of American values but also from genuine concerns about America's potentially declining place in a multipolar world (see Nye 1990).

It would not be much of a stretch to point out that Nye's "soft power" is almost the flip side of the "Asian values" debate, reflecting not the abrasive demands of an America eager to remake the world in its image, but rather the inherent magnetism of American values. To be sure, Nye discusses a material basis for American soft power—particularly American dominance over the channels of communication—but he repeatedly returns to the idea that there is something inherently appealing and attractive about the United States, and that core elements of Americanness are central to its global weight. One might ask whether this is an argument that could or would have been produced in an era of American confidence, and, if not, whether soft power was in part a compensation meant to console American readers worried about the decline in American power.

Viewed from that perspective, it is not terribly surprising that Japanese debates about soft power would arise and spread in an equally nervous environment. The Japanese economic miracle had, by 2002, long since been replaced by years of uncertainty and even decline, and Japanese policymakers could see a resurgent United States, a self-confidently expanding Europe, and a rising China, all replacing the juggernaut that Japan had seemingly represented only a decade earlier. To be sure, a number of policymakers and theorists had already explored the possibility of enhanced soft power before McGray's piece, but the general conclusion was that this would be unlikely (see especially Takenaka 2001). But the phrase "gross national cool" echoed like a gunshot in Japanese public administration, and a number of policy white papers and approaches over the succeeding years emphasized that the spread of Japan's popular culture overseas, as indicated by McGray and proved by the victory of Miyazaki Hayao's *Spirited Away* as Best Animated Film at the 2003 Academy Awards, would lead to soft power. This position was as popular to progressives who viewed soft power as a replacement for military power as to conservatives who argued that a better understood, better appreciated Japan, would face less opposition overseas to the well-meaning development of military force, both for Japanese defense and for participation in international peace-keeping forces. And while the source for this post-2001 appraisal might have been American, the target of Japan's soft power was almost invariably Asia (Leheny 2006).

What made Japanese popular culture attractive? There are as many answers as there are commentators, but they frequently coalesce around their non-Westernness. In a quasi-official account, Japan's former ambassador to UNESCO, Seiichi Kondo, implicitly uses the United States as a foil for Japan:

> One of the reasons why Japanese anime appeals to young people around the world today may be that the end of the Cold War has liberated human beings from ideological confrontation, creating an environment where they can freely pursue diverse cultures. Many people in the world now prefer contemporary expressions in art and culture instead of the missionary preaching of ideals. This is a situation apparently favorable to Japan, which is not good at projecting ideals. ... The most important factor on the receiving side probably has to do with the psychology of contemporary human beings. While enjoying the freedom and material prosperity that are the fruits of modern rationalism, people feel perplexed at the growing divide between rich and poor, cutthroat market competition, environmental destruction, and identity crises, as well as the social unrest and terrorism that have arisen partly because of their inability to resolve these issues. For those who have some doubts about modern life but cannot articulate them, the messages from Japanese anime emphasizing human complexity and the importance of coexistence with nature may appear to offer some hints for problem-solving

options superior to reliance on the simple dichotomy of rewarding good and punishing evil.

(Kondo 2008: 199)

And so Japan's soft power might emanate from its representing something different from and better than the Manichean, neoliberal world of the United States. But much of this discussion went on without much reflection on whether the United States—understood by most Japanese authors as the key holder of soft power—had actually benefited from its putative soft power resources, or how one could actually measure or test the extent of American success. On the one hand, with the long-term visibility of American popular culture in Japan, not to mention the often-criticized fidelity of the Japanese government to American foreign policy goals in the postwar era, one might easily have viewed the extent and utility of American soft power resources to be beyond any dispute. On the other hand, long-term resentment in Japan (particularly among the far right and the far left, but continually visible even in the political mainstream) might have led to the conclusion that omnipresent American icons could produce only so much good will. Similarly, with the United States providing both the most important foreign market for Japanese goods as well as a substantial military force aimed in part at defending Japan, one might have also asked whether Japanese acquiescence to the demands of its alliance partner was really the result of persuasion rather than coercion. There is, therefore, no clear and obvious reason, in looking at Japan over the past thirty years, to assume the viability of American soft power; and yet it was usually presumed to be the model to which a newly "cool" Japan might aspire.

Indeed, this flexibility, even to the point of non-falsifiability, of soft power is likely one of the features that has encouraged its deployment in not only Japan but also its neighbors in the region. After all, if there is no easy way to argue that country does not have the ability to persuade, or if its coercive capacity can be masked (even to its wielders) as persuasive, there is little to be lost in suggesting (usually) low-cost strategies to promote overseas one's own culture or values, whatever that might mean, with the hope that they might find some traction or provide a boost to one's foreign policy. And in this vein, it would be easy to read the visibility of cultural icons as providing some sort of power to the state with which they are associated. As South Korean became more internationally visible in the 2000s, for example, Japanese writers began to consider the possibility that Korea itself was developing significant soft power resources. With the immense popularity of the television drama Winter Sonata, as well as the arena-filling skills of Korean pop stars throughout East Asia, Korea could be seen as harnessing the good will of foreign audiences, just as those audience members might be ridiculed by their compatriots as dupes of a spreading Koreanness (Hayashi and Lee 2007).

Seen from home, however, the popularity of Korean television, music, and movies overseas might just as easily be described as an appropriate reflection of the Korean people, of Korea itself. One Korean sinologist who has written extensively on Korean popular culture overseas argues:

I have always been one to insist that the true origin of the Korean Wave is the cultural vivacity of Korean society and the fervent belief in social progress and democracy pervasive to Korean people. … This popular refusal to condone any and all obstacles to justice and progress, I am deeply convinced, is the chief source of Korea's cultural vibrancy. The phenomenon of the Korean Wave certainly owes its breadth and impact to the wholesale economic and industrial restructuring undergone by both Korea and Asia as a whole in the recent decade. … What has really enabled the transnational adoption and consumption of Korean cultural products is the so-called phenomenon of pop-Asianism, a tendency among the people of the region to prefer Asia's own home-grown pop culture. Hence, through pop culture a sense of self was awakened in Asia, and Asians were brought closer to each other. It is hardly an exaggeration to say that what the Korean Wave has done for the Asian region is to create a true cultural common ground for it, giving it something that could be called a regional identity.

(Paek 2009)

In many of the claims about Korean and Japanese soft power, Asia thus becomes a mirror against which values that might be judged as largely consistent with global norms—humanism and warmth, or justice and progress—can be defined and assessed *in national terms*. And like a mirror, it has no real content except its capacity to reflect the actor gazing into it. Asia is the warm and human region that especially reflects Japan's emphasis on holistic complexity, or it is the wellspring of a desire for just and democratic development. For all its humanism and justice, however, the language of soft power in these accounts is irreducibly and obviously competitive. Countries have soft power vis-à-vis one another, and their soft power is premised on their competitively arrayed attractiveness of their national values.

This competitive aspect of soft power is most apparent in the myriad discussions of China's soft power. It has been the source of tremendous debate in recent years, with some (usually foreign) authors writing with great alarm about the government's efforts to promote its values overseas (see Kurlantzick 2007), others assessing with somewhat more skepticism China's ability to create a favorable image in global media markets (Huang and Ding 2006, Manzenreiter 2010). Still others have hinted that China should improve its soft power prospects by altering its policies or adopting practices among more, to put it as delicately as possible, well-liked states (Ding 2008).

In a careful discussion of China's soft power, two authors simultaneously call attention to active efforts to craft an image of China while also emphasizing something essential about its cultural links to the Asian region:

The rise of China is, however, once again making it possible to pursue Asian values based on Chinese civilization, at least in Confucian East Asian countries. These values include the importance of family as the focal point of social structure formation; concerns over virtues and ethics; the primacy of the group over the individual; emphasis on unity or harmony and order; and hard work, frugality, and the importance of education. … China's Asian values are based on the rapid expansion of the Chinese economy following the model of previous arguments over Asian values that championed the East Asian economic miracle. Furthermore, China's civilization and historical legacies add weight to Chinese advocacy of Asian values.

(Cho and Jeong 2008: 470)

Since Japanese leaders began to grapple with Chinese claims about soft power in the mid-2000s, they have been forced to confront the possibility that nearly anything Asian that Japan might represent for the region could be matched, even trumped, by China: Confucian China has unimpeachable Asian credentials. And so conservatives like Shinzō Abe (2006) and Tarō Asō (2007) began to speak of Japan's special ability to represent a local take on universal values and to encourage the region to move toward a democratization that China could not support, while progressives like Hatoyama Yukio (2009) have emphasized Japan's ability to act as a bridge between East and West. Asia is always open to interpretation, but always amenable to the expression of locally defined values, whether of economic growth, Confucianism, harmony, democracy, progress, or the like, provided that the source of these values can be defined unproblematically as part of the region.

Paradoxes of regional politics

The Asian values debates of the 1990s may have grown out of local resistance to foreign pressure to democratize and open markets, but it has morphed into an opportunity to express the natural, even essential affinity between one's own national values and those of the larger environment. In doing so, it has mapped onto exactly what helped to encourage the Asian values discourses in the first place: the expression of soft power, of the inherent attractiveness of one's own culture and the amenability of the outside world to persuasion. Where Nye might have seen the world as America's oyster, however, East Asian claims about soft power derive their legitimacy from the essential boundedness of the region: it is what the West is not. My point is not that there is hypocrisy in statecraft; I suspect I could find much easier examples than this one, and far closer to home. It is instead to suggest that the construction of a region may reflect larger issues in the global polity—there must be an "East Asia" to go alongside "Europe"—and that the content of that region is increasingly defined by the near mandate of a country to have soft power. Perhaps states do not want to be loved, but no one seems to trust in the existence of power that is not coated in a layer of attractiveness and persuasion.

And so in considering the existence of regions and their relationship to the global polity, we would do well to understand how East Asia itself is the product of both a series of challenges to the West, or to ostensibly Western-led globalization, and the struggles among its members to define what makes the region East Asian. Asian regionalism is, among many other things, a point of entry for states in the area to engage other regions as well as global institutions. But it is also a site for intense contestation, and I have argued above that this contestation itself reflects cultural processes that seem entirely consistent with the main tenets of the global polity literature. For all that East Asia might represent as resistance to the West or to the ostensibly universal values encoded in international institutions, it seems almost poignant that this resistance is an almost inescapable aspect of legitimate state practice: each state must be unique, and its uniqueness must make uniquely important contributions to its region. But the boundaries of this uniqueness have become ever tighter, noticeable in the similarities between appealing national values and recognized global ones, and therefore in the inability to frame the content of regional identity as anything stable or meaningfully distinctive.

Note

1 For a brief and representative discussion, see development specialist Kenichi Ohno's comments in RIETI (2002).

References

Abe, S. 2006. *Utsukushii Kuni E* [Toward a Beautiful Country]. Tokyo: Bungeishunju.

Asō, T. 2007. *Totetsumonai Nihon* [Tremendous Japan]. Tokyo: Shinchosha.

Aydin, C. 2007. *The Politics of Anti-Westernism in Asia: Visions of World Order in Pan-Islamic and Pan-Asian Thought*. New York: Columbia University Press.

Cho, Y. N. and J. H. Jeong. 2008. China's Soft Power: Discussions, Resources, and Prospects. *Asian Survey* 48(3): 453–72.

Boli, J. and G. M. Thomas. 1999. INGOs and the Organization of World Culture. In *Constructing World Culture: International Nongovernmental Organizations Since 1875*, J. Boli and G. M. Thomas, eds. Stanford, CA: Stanford University Press.

de Bary, W. T. 2000. *Asian Values and Human Rights: A Confucian Communitarian Perspective*. Cambridge, MA: Harvard University Press.

Ding, S. 2008. *The Dragon's Hidden Wings: How China Rises with its Soft Power*. Lanham, MD: Lexington.

Hafner-Burton, E. M. and K. Tsutsui. 2007. Justice Lost! The Failure of International Human Rights Law To Matter Where Needed Most. *Journal of Peace Research* 44(4): 407–25.

Hatch, W. and K. Yamamura.1996. *Asia in Japan's Embrace: Building a Regional Production Alliance*. Cambridge: Cambridge University Press.

Hatoyama Y. 2009. Address at the Sixty-Fourth Session of the General Assembly of the United Nations. Available at: www.kantei.go.jp/foreign/hatoyama/statement/200909/ehat_0924c_e.html (accessed May 2014).

Hayashi, K. and E-J. Lee. 2007. The Potential of Fandom and the Limits of Soft Power: Media Representations on the Popularity of a Korean Melodrama in Japan. *Social Science Japan Journal* 10(2): 197–216.

Huang, Y. and S. Ding. 2006. Dragon's Underbelly: An Analysis of China's Soft Power. *East Asia* 23(4): 22–44.

Iwabuchi, K. 2002. *Recentering Globalization: Popular Culture and Japanese Transnationalism*. Durham, NC: Duke University Press.

Johnson, C. 1982. *Miti and the Japanese Miracle: The Growth of Industrial Policy: 1925–1975*. Stanford, CA: Stanford University Press.

Jupillle, J. and B. Jolliff. 2011. Regionalism in the World Polity. Paper presented at the European Union Studies Association Annual Meeting, Boston, MA. Available at: euce. org/eusa/2011/papers/11g_jupille.pdf (accessed January 2012).

Katzenstein, P. J. 2005. *A World of Regions: Asia and Europe in the American Imperium*. Ithaca, NY: Cornell University Press.

Kondo, S. 2008. Wielding Soft Power: The Key Stages of Transmission and Reception. In *Soft Power Superpowers: Cultural and National Assets of Japan and the United States*, Y. Watanabe and D. L. McConnell, eds. New York: M. E. Sharpe.

Koschmann, J.V. 1997. Asianism's Ambivalent Legacy. In *Network Power: Japan in Asia*, P.J. Katzenstein and T. Shiraishi, eds. Ithaca, NY: Cornell University Press.

Kurlantzick, J. 2007. *Charm Offensive: How China's Soft Power Is Transforming the World*. New Haven, CT: Yale University Press.

Lasswell, H. D. 1990 [1936]. *Politics: Who Gets What, When and How*. New York: Peter Smith.

Leheny, D. 2006. A Narrow Place to Cross Swords: Soft Power and the Politics of Japanese Popular Culture in Asia. In *Beyond Japan: The Dynamics of East Asian Regionalism*, P. J. Katzenstein and T. Shiraishi, eds. Ithaca, NY: Cornell University Press.

Mahathir, M. 2002. Look East Policy: The Challenges for Japan in a Globalized World. Keynote speech during official visit to Japan, December 12. Available at: www.mofa.go. jp/region/asia-paci/malaysia/pmv0212/speech.html (accessed May 2014).

Mahbubani, K. 2008. What Are Asian Values? Bigthink.org interview. Available at: http://bigthink.com/ideas/2052 (accessed May 2014).

Manzenreiter, W. 2010. The Beijing Games in the Western Imagination of China: The Weak Power of Soft Power. *Journal of Sport and Social Issues* 34(1): 29–48.

McGray, D. 2002. Japan's Gross National Cool. *Foreign Policy* (May/June): 44–54. Available at: www.foreignpolicy.com/articles/2002/05/01/japans_gross_national_cool (accessed May 2014).

Meyer, J. W., J. Boli, G. M. Thomas, and F. O. Ramirez. 1997. World Society and the Nation-State. *American Journal of Sociology* 103(1): 144–81.

Nye, J. S. 1990. *Bound to Lead: The Changing Nature Of American Power*. New York: Basic Books.

——2005. Soft Power Matters in Asia. *The Japan Times*, December 5. Available at: http://belfercenter.ksg.harvard.edu/publication/1486/soft_power_matters_in_asia.html (accessed March 2008).

Paek, W. 2009. Beyond the Wave: In a Post Korean-Wave Era. *Column & Issue* 1080, May 21. Korean Studies Promotion Service. Available at: http://ksps.aks.ac.kr/default_eng/board_issue.php?md=V&idx=1080 (accessed January 2012).

Pei, M. 1998. Constructing the Political Foundations of an Economic Miracle. In *Behind East Asian Growth: The Political and Social Foundations of Prosperity*, H.S. Rowen, ed. London: Routledge.

Pempel, T. J. 2005. Introduction: Emerging Webs of Regional Connectedness. In *Remapping East Asia: The Construction of a Region*, T. J. Pempel, ed. Ithaca, NY: Cornell University Press.

RIETI (Research Institute for Economy, Trade, and Industry). 2002. Growth Driven by Trade, Investment and Economic Cooperation – The East Asian Experience in Economic Development and Cooperation. RIETI conference in Johannesburg, South Africa, September 1. Available at: www.rieti.go.jp/en/events/02090101/report_1.html (accessed December 2011).

Seddon, D. 2005. Japanese and British Overseas Aid Compared. In *Japan's Foreign Aid: Old Continuities and New Directions*, D. M. Arase, ed. Abingdon: Routledge.

Sen, A. 1999. *Development as Freedom*. Oxford: Oxford University Press.

Takenaka, H. 2001. Nihon Keizai Saisei no Kagi [The Key to Japan's Economic Revitalization]. In *"Sofuto Pawa" Nihon Fukken e no Michi: Posuto IT Kakumei* ["Soft Power," the Road to Japan's Reinstatement: Post IT Revolution], H. Takenaka, ed. Tokyo: Fujita Institute of Future Management.

Tsutsui, K. and C. M. Wotipka. 2004. Global Civil Society and the International Human Rights Movement: Citizen Participation in Human Rights International Nongovernmental Organizations. *Social Forces* 83(2): 587–620.

Wade, R. 1996. Japan, the World Bank, and the Art of Paradigm Maintenance: The East Asian Miracle in Political Perspective. *New Left Review* 217 (May-June): 3–36.

Woo-Cummings, M. 1999. Introduction: Chalmers Johnson and the Politics of Nationalism and Development. In *The Developmental State*, M. Woo-Cummings, ed. Ithaca, NY: Cornell University Press.

Zakaria, F. 1994. A Conversation with Lee Kuan-Yew. *Foreign Affairs* (March/April). Available at: www.foreignaffairs.com/articles/49691/fareed-zakaria/a-conversation-with-lee-kuan-yew (accessed May 2014).

Mobilities

5 Creative East-West cosmopolitanism?

The changing role of international mobility for young Japanese contemporary artists

Adrian Favell

As with other facets of social change, innovation and creativity explored in this volume—such as science and technology, education, cuisine, youth orientations, gender identities—the rise of distinctive new contemporary art from East Asia offers possibilities for exploring the interaction of the local, the national, the regional and the global, in a particular field of cultural production and from new world perspectives. My chapter offers another angle on the "transnational trajectories" in East Asia by considering the cross-border dynamics of Japanese modern and contemporary art—and particularly the international mobility of artists—as part of an Asian-led cultural globalization.

It is widely accepted that the economic rise of Asia in recent decades has in effect produced an alternative Asian modernity (or modernities) that is capable of challenging American and European global hegemony, not only economically or politically, but also in terms of cultural production. In this, clearly, Japan was a leader (see, for example, Clammer 1997). Having absorbed the Western lessons of modernization in its emergence as a modern nation state in the early part of the twentieth century, and then as a global economic power from the 1960s onwards, in the 1970s and 1980s it began to produce innovative and distinctive variations on modern global culture that swept through both regional and global markets (Iwabuchi 2002, Moeran 2000). Japan became a globally visible producer of new culture, not only in terms of the wildly popular culture of *anime* (animated cartoons), *manga* (comics), tv and film, toys, electronic games, and brand characters—Godzilla, Pokemon, Hello Kitty, and all that (Allison 2006, Kelts 2006)—but also the "high culture" branches of, for example, contemporary design, catwalk fashion, and architecture (Japan Foundation 2008, Kawamura 2004, Koolhaas and Obrist 2011). Japan in effect patented a model of Asian modernity that, in the 1990s and 2000s, has become a path for others: pop culture from Hong Kong, K-Pop from Korea, Singapore or Taipei as creative cities and, above all, the rise of China.

The production, consumption, and appreciation of contemporary art from Asia is another key index of this so-called "world class" modernity. In the 1990s and 2000s, indeed, it might be argued that contemporary art became *the* quintessential global high culture, a form of culture itself very characteristic of the era's global capitalism. The globalization of contemporary art produced an apparently borderless global art world that stretched from the auction halls of New York and London, via the high art temples of MOMA, Tate and Pompidou, to the new museums of Istanbul and Dubai, and the biennials and art fairs of East Asia. In parallel with the deregulated markets and finance knocking down national borders, the free-spirited *avant garde* intellectual discourse of artists and art curators complimented perfectly the free-moving money of venture capitalists who bought the works or built the museums (Stallabrass 2004). Amidst a vast inflationary boom, contemporary art became the calling card for newly rich oligarchs in emerging economies everywhere, as well as the signature form of city branding for "global cities" the world over. It might even be argued—as captured beautifully in the ethnography of this world by Sarah Thornton (2008)—that contemporary art became a truly sublime form of the global, approaching a new religion for the secular, atheist, "post-modern" elites that followed and believed in it.

Part of this story was an Asian art boom as the world discovered new Asian art and artists, a boom unquestionably centered on Chinese artists but which progressively involved many other sources of origin (Chiu and Genocchio 2010, Ciotti 2012, Philipsen 2008, Vine 2011). The presence of Asian artists on the global market and the curatorial and museum prestige which has been invested in their works, alongside the physical location of many huge global events (such as art fairs and auctions in Hong Kong, or biennials in Shanghai and Singapore), might be seen simply as affirming the rise of a truly de-centered, de-colonized contemporary world or global art sensibility; something that might be identified with the "cosmopolitan imagination" identified by recent critical social theory (Delanty 2009, Papastergiadis 2012). Western art history as a discipline has been very slow to question its own ethnocentric assumptions, but in the wake of this world art boom, there has been a veritable deluge of reflection in these terms on globalization in art theory (Harris 2011).

This reflection was, of course, the back end of the post-colonial critique which swept across the humanities since the 1960s. Yet the self-styled "cosmopolitan" global art of the 1990s and 2000s was at the same so patently anchored in the economic liberalism of rampant global capitalism of that era (see also Kofman 2005). As the sublime, utopian form of these material global forces, contemporary art could—to echo the famous works of Hardt and Negri (2001, 2005)—in effect unify both "empire" and "multitude" in the critical discourses of the free-moving global curators who very self-consciously selected, promoted and put (extraordinary) value on the art from new, non-Western sources. The most fashionable Asian artists might slam global capitalism or evoke universal environmental ideals, but those selected for stardom on the global art market or museum circuit often looked very similar as they were presented for global consumption. Superstar new Asian artists such as the Chinese Ai Weiwei or the Indian Subodh Gupta were always positioned as liberal, cosmopolitan heroes, critiquing the forces of modernization sweeping their countries as well as their restrictive political regimes, yet producing very nationally specific icons and images of their home countries that could be easily packaged into simple sociological lessons about exotic (and sometimes still dangerous) locations to curious Western viewers and buyers. The cosmopolitanism of the new global art, and its selective presentation, may thus easily be questioned as a sophisticated new form of orientalism that was not challenging the global order anywhere near as radically as supposed. Behind the apparently free-flowing global circuit, for all the new Asian talent it could also be seen that the personnel powering this world—the institutional "art power" of top curators, dealers, collectors and art writers—were still as solidly as ever anchored in the usual Western hub locations (Quémin 2006).

The story with global contemporary art in East Asia, though, is complicated by the positioning of Japan in this picture. Japanese artists were among the first to be presented as part of the "discovery" of world art in the late 1980s, a moment usually linked with the famous *Magiciens de la Terre* show, curated by Jean-Hubert Martin at the Pompidou, Paris in 1989 (McLean 2011). Yet although a vibrant commercial and conceptual contemporary art scene has continued to develop in Japan during the next two decades, Japanese contemporary artists have been surprisingly marginal to the Asian art boom in global art. This is a long and complex story, but it is largely because the Western global curators have been unable to get in to Japan and shape the contemporary art scene as they have in China. With one or two notable exceptions, then, Japanese artists have been neglected in global art history narratives of the 1990s and 2000s. The perfect evidence is the canonical handbook of modern Western art history, *Art Since 1900*, edited by the five ruling modern art historians of the East Coast Ivy League: Hal Foster, Rosalind Krauss, Yve-Alain Bois, Benjamin H. D. Buchloh, and David Joselit (Foster *et al.* 2011). Only one Japanese contemporary artist since the 1960s is discussed. That artist is, of course, Takashi Murakami: Japan's version of Ai Weiwei or Subodh Gupta, Japan's only true global superstar artist since 1990, who is central to my story below.

The dominant Western narrative is, to say the least, not a representative history from a Japanese point of view (Favell 2012).[1] And despite all the talk about global art and cosmopolitan sensibilities, the "national" point of view is still very relevant here because it does not align with the global view. This in fact is also a peculiarly distinct feature of Japanese contemporary art in comparison to other Asian countries, whose art has been assimilated more easily into global art theories and narratives. At the same time, Japan's relative neglect is also symptomatic of the Japanese art world's long history of self-understanding and positioning in relation to Western modernity (Clark 1998). The story of Japanese modern and contemporary art in relation to transnational flows and mobilities indeed reveals an ambivalent globalization. It suggests that, in this field of cultural production at least, Japan has preserved a certain independence, less obviously dominated or colonized by global forces. And that by analyzing the international mobility of Japanese artists it is possible to chart the changing forms of both cosmopolitanism and nationhood in the ways their experiences have been expressed through artistic forms.

The chapter proceeds as follows. In the first section, I take the story back to the historical pre-World War Two origins of modernist Japanese art, tracing the role of self-positioning in relation to Western modernity and the dynamics of international mobility and return in international Japanese artists' careers. This introduces the notion of the *gaisen kōen* (the "triumphant return performance")—that is, the acclaim at home after perceived success on a tour abroad—which has hitherto always been thought necessary to cement a Japanese artist's international (i.e. "world class") reputation. Along the way, the story introduces a number of the most famous figures in Japanese modern and contemporary art from different periods in relation to our broader themes. These distinct generations can be thought of as cohorts who have varying interactions with their global and national contexts, thus revealing how forms of cosmopolitanism and nationhood have changed over time. It also lays a groundwork to understand the problematic evolution of the Japanese modern art tradition and art world institutions and assess the effects of their domination and resistance up to and through into the global art era from the late 1980s onwards.

In the second main section, I shift to the younger "post-Bubble" or "zero zero generation" who came of age amidst the economic decline, social malaise and shattering disasters of Japan in the mid- to late 1990s. Their evaluation as emergent artists is not as yet settled—neither in Japan nor internationally. Japan in the 1990s and after experienced economic hardship and global contraction while the rest of the world, in particular the rest of Asia, was going through a development boom. I suggest that this disjuncture with world trends has caused important changes in the dynamics of influence and recognition on the part of these younger Japanese artists in a global context. While they have been largely ignored by the mainstream global art world, the need for the *gaisen kōen* in their work is arguably being transcended.

The argument is that the qualitative change of Japan from being a rising Asian power and alternate modernity to one pioneering forms of post-Bubble, post-growth society, has largely confounded dominant Western understandings of this new Asian culture. These understandings assume a modernizing developmental paradigm and create their narratives of artistic importance accordingly: essentially in terms of global market value and "political" art theoretical interest—and hence as a "challenge" to the West. But what works for China and India does not work for Japan. Rather, the new post-Bubble generation offers a different way of pinpointing how East Asian society and culture may interact with regional and global forces or embody the national and transnational in a post-growth future. It is a rather different narrative to the one told about contemporary Chinese or Indian artists, as well as one comparatively free of the typical dominated passive-aggressive position of Japanese artists from previous generations. I illustrate my interpretation with a number of artists born in the mid-1970s who have all drawn diversely on *both* national themes and material sources *and* global contemporary theoretical sensibilities. While acutely aware of their origins and trajectories, they all have wide experience of travel and life in different Western global hubs. They are therefore fashioning convincingly cosmopolitan and Japanese contemporary art—not least because the "global" or "cosmopolitan" influence of cities where they have lived and work, such as New York, London and Berlin, are all quite different.

Gaisen kōen ("triumphant return performance"): the international as the source of legitimacy in Japanese modern and contemporary art

How were Japanese artists from different generations during the twentieth century received and understood on the international stage? I examine this history in relation to three distinct cohorts, who emerged to prominence in Japan, via international mobility in the 1920s/1930s, 1960s, and 1990s respectively.

After the opening of Japan to the modern world with the Meiji Restoration of 1868, the traditional arts in Japan—as with all areas of technology, consumption, and public life—were all progressively joined by imports from the West, which the nation took upon itself to reproduce and master as part of the modernization process (see especially Sato 2011, also various essays in Rimer 2012). At the same time, the imported arts took on institutional structures similar to those that so tightly organized the traditional forms: for example, "schools" (*iemoto*) led by a single master (*sensei*) who would train follower to reproduce particular styles and techniques. These structures and distinctions continue to have an impact on art in Japan, which in turn impinges upon the automatic adoption of Western or global forms. Even contemporary art training, in art school departments that embrace global styles and references, as well as careers within a recognizably modern art system of commercial galleries and museums, still reflect elements of the old institutional structure that go back to pre-modern times.

After Meiji, art in Japan was essentially divided between *nihon-ga* (Japanese art), rooted in certain styles, forms, and materials that required specific training, and *yō-ga* (Western art), which consisted of the appropriation of Western materials and forms, particular oil painting and forms of Western representation. As art forms, of course, neither was fixed. Even traditional arts in Japan, such as *ikebana* (flower and plant arranging), have in time evolved in their highest forms to take increasingly modern, even post-modern forms; contemporary *ikebana* can look like a kind of abstract installation art. But the old distinctions still matter, and this has always permeated the classification and recognition of artists who adopt Western (and later global) forms of artistic expression. When recognizably modernist art emerged in Japan in the late nineteenth and early twentieth century, it inevitably put these *yō-ga* artists, inspired by twentieth-century European or American techniques and ideas, in a difficult position (on these issues, see Lucken 2001, Winther-Tamaki 2012). From both sides they could easily be seen as nothing more than local derivations of Western trends—for example, in impressionism or surrealism. At the same time, they could not, by definition, be part of the wave of "japonisme" that was simultaneously sweeping the Western artworld as it awoke to the traditional arts of the newly opened Japan. This was the discovery of Edo-(pre-Meiji) era arts such as screen painting, *ukiyo-e* (wood block prints of the "floating world") and materials from *nihon-ga* (such as gold leaf or traditional ink line drawing) that had such a massive impact on the art of many leading names of European modernism, such as van Gogh and Klimt. *Yō-ga* artists, in contrast, would usually be seen as naive versions of Western styles in, say, portraiture or sculpture; at best, they might, with a certain stylistic or material element, catch a Western collector's or curator's eye as an slightly exotic variant on the Western norm.

The hierarchization at work here, in terms of the global art historical evaluation, was locked in a dominant colonialist logic. And yet, at the same time there was a resistant art system within Japan that defined itself in opposition to Western (and even other Asian) influences, defying its unitary categorizations. For those artists, part of the opening up/modernization, international mobility was an obligation, with distant Western capitals the Meccas towards which the artists must face. As for every artist in the world, in the high modernist period of the 1920s and 1930s the global art world centered on Paris. It too attracted its Japanese heroes, as small exotic bit-part players in the wider creative trends of the city. Two, in particular can be mentioned: "Leonard" (Tsuguharu) Foujita (1886–1968), a painter and celebrated member of the Picasso circle in Montparnasse from 1914 to 1931; and Tara Okamoto (1911–96), a surrealist painter and sculptor, influenced by Bréton and, again, Picasso, who studied extensively in Paris during the 1930s (Birnbaum 2006, Gomez 2000).

Today, Foujita and Okamoto are probably the two biggest popular names in Japanese modernism. Their styles which found marginal success in Europe were eventually accepted back home on the back of their reflected foreign glory—what is often referred to as the paradigmatic *gaisen kōen*, when the artist who is often long-time despised or not properly recognized in their country of origin finally gains massive acclaim via their perceived success abroad. There is both a clear general mechanism at work and subtle variations in these two archetypal stories from the 1920s and 1930s, as in others from later periods.

Foujita is now certainly celebrated by Japan as a modernist classic. After also working in Latin America, he returned a hero to Japan in 1933. His formidable talents were called on to mythologize rural life, with paintings of his native Akita, and then during the war he was pressed into service as a famous "war artist." Nowadays he is regularly shown in Japan, collected in museums, and his most famous works from the 1920s can still be seen in France. He left Japan after the war and resettled back in his adopted European home. Okamoto, meanwhile, went in and out of favor over the years, often seen by his peers in Japan as a "foreign" artist aping Western modernist styles. Eventually, though, his notoriety won him acclaim. His famous *Tower of the Sun* symbolized Japan's great display of futurist modernism at the Osaka Expo of 1970, and after spending his later life popularizing Japanese national myths, he is now cherished as a populist icon. His massive atomic bomb mural, for example, adorns part of Shibuya train station, following its discovery and return from Mexico. Yet to achieve this he had to step outside of the mainstream art system, creating his own media identity, with a museum and art prize in his own name—an anti-institutional strategy that has strongly influenced Japan's star artist of the 1990s, Takashi Murakami.

By the 1960s, New York had supplanted Paris. And the heroes of the 1960s *gaisen kōen* were heroines: the *avant-garde* women artists, Yoko Ono and Yayoi Kusama (Munroe 2000, Yamamura 2009). Closely connected with Fluxus and John Cage, Ono's humanistic performance art was a significant part of the

New York *avant-garde* of the period, although her reputation took a heavy knock from her notorious association with John Lennon after she moved to London. But she has slowly transcended this, and by 2009 Venice Biennale she was being officially celebrated as one of the greats of the twentieth century and a true pioneer. Ono is also ubiquitous in Japan, the one household name (along with Genpei Akasagawa) from the *avant-garde* of the 1960s (see Marotti 2013). Kusama, meanwhile, was even more radical. A young troubled prodigy, she finally escaped to New York in the late 1950s. Her early work, which was initially close to Jackson Pollock, evolved into experimentation with relentless repetition, *mise en abyme* mirrors, and sexually charged installations that closely paralleled the leading American pop art of the period, such as Andy Warhol and Claes Oldenburg. By the mid-1960s she was organizing "orgies" and "happenings," a significant figure in the New York counter-cultural scene, as well as feted across Europe in major art museums. Here, it has been argued, Kusama's reputation underwent a sinister gender- and ethnic-based marginalization (Yoshimoto 2005). Her own originality and groundbreaking conceptual vision, which tended towards almost absurd extremes, was ultimately upturned in its importance: as an easy-to-dismiss Japanese "copy" of or derivation from American male pop artists, who subsequently took much of the credit for ideas she in fact pioneered. Kusama went home broken to Japan in the 1970s, reviled as a crazy old lady in her home country. Only the interest of international curators such as David Elliott and Alexandra Munroe later in the 1980s and 1990s and the key support of a highly internationalized Japanese curator, Akira Tatehata, helped put her back on the global map. By the 2000s she was apparently thriving in her seventh active decade as an artist, living as a permanent mental patient, and now managing a vast portfolio of easy-to-recognize, brandable work that would appear in global cities everywhere—a late career canonization paralleled only by the French artist Louise Bourgeois—although in Japan there has always been a little more hesitancy in embracing her radical libertarian vision of the 1960s.

Again, the *gaisen kōen* was at work in these women's careers, although it played a complicated role. Ono is effectively a New York artist; "Japanese" is a convenient adjective, but not particularly significant, except in the somewhat "zen"-like atmosphere of many of her works. Back home it is the classic *gaisen kōen*, endowed with a weighty worldwide respect, although sometimes undermined by her more trivial fame as someone famous's widow. Kusama, whose touch for exploring leading edge global currents in her work was no less secure, made it and lost it in New York. It took a later global reconstruction of her reputation to secure her recognition at home and abroad. It is important to note that other vitally important *avant-garde* movements in Japan in the 1950s and 1960s, such as *Gutai*, *Mono-Ha*, and *Anti-Art*, established themselves and have claims independent of the global trends they nevertheless related to; where they have been discussed as part of a bigger global narrative, the discussion has often been distorting and is generally patronizing, again relegating them to a derivative relationship with supposed Western pioneers (Tiampo 2011a, Tiampo 2011b, Tomii 2011). It has taken significant art historical reconstruction for the appropriate recognition to start to be given by the global mainstream (Merewether and Hiro 2007, Munroe 1994, Tomii 2009, Yoshitake 2012).

In the post-1990 era, Japanese contemporary art has continued to have a difficult time being understood in its correct context (Favell 2011). This concern is a pre-occupation of traditional specialist art historians. When the dominant selections of global curators or global markets can be seen as too narrow, distorted and non-representative, there is clearly a need to represent artists correctly in terms of their career trajectories and meaning in relation to their origins in the Japanese art world. Although it was initially a part of the late 1980s discovery of world art as part of a vision of global contemporary art, Japanese contemporary art lost ground massively in subsequent years to the appreciation, consumption, and under-standing of other Asian art. Korea, then China, then India, and a growing list of other smaller Asian countries, all became more exciting targets for global curatorial and art market discourse, somehow easier to process than Japan through the stylized, development and rising-power obsessed political and sociological context-setting frames that were produced to select and make sense of the art—for example, famous international and touring shows such as *Alors, la Chine?* (Pompidou 2003), *China Power Station* (Serpentine 2006), *China Onward* (Louisiana 2007), *The Revolution Continues: New Art from China* (Saatchi 2008), *Indian Highway* (Serpentine 2008), *The Empire Strikes Back: New Art from India* (Saatchi 2010), and *Paris-Delhi-Bombay* (Pompidou 2011). The one exception to the failure of Japanese contemporary art to provide a resonant story about itself for global art consumption has been the spectacular international success of pop artist, Takashi Murakami: an entrepreneur, impresario, art theorist, and curator as much as he is an artist. Alongside him, out of the 1990s, the only other two names to make it onto the global art radar were the similarly "pop," easy to brand and consume charms of Yoshitomo Nara and Mariko Mori.

Takashi Murakami's relation to the *gaisen kōen* mechanism is self-conscious and explicit. A young prodigy at the heart of an explosive and brilliant pop art scene in Tokyo in the early 1990s, he worked out his full global strategy while on a one-year residency in New York 1994/5. In it, he seized upon the manifold delights of Japanese urban sub-cultures such as the sci-fi and sexual obsessions of "loser" *otaku* (male nerds), the Japanese commercial talent for producing endless *kawaii* (cute), infantilized brands and characters, and the rising fascination in the West for *anime* and *manga*. He then, very deliberately, packaged these "low" cultural forms in elite gallery and catalogue spaces as a world-beating formula for the highbrow Western art market. By the end of 1995, his peers and rivals back home were pronouncing the death of *otaku* and Tokyo's pop art scene as a result of the shock of the disasters earlier that year: a massive earthquake in Kobe followed by a stunning terrorist poison gas attack on the Tokyo metro. They were moving on to new and darker artistic concerns, just as Murakami was beginning to gain his first victories in the West using his colorful pop culture themes. By 2001, he was able to coordinate a smash hit show in Los Angeles, selecting a mix of popular and unknown young Japanese artists under his name and framed by his theory, "Superflat," to the applause of an almost entirely ignorant Western audience, totally seduced by the cartoon-like representation of this weird and wonderful Asian paradise (Murakami 2001). The trick was reproduced on an even bigger scale in New York in 2005 (Murakami 2005a). It was a Japanese contemporary art very deliberately lost in translation, with Murakami playing a knowing double-faced game: a laughing pop impresario for his (gullible) Western audiences, while triumphantly announcing his success as a bitterly instrumental, resentful nationalist for his (smart) Japanese audiences back home. In a self-help autobiography (Murakami 2005b)—a bestseller in Japan, and addressed to the young amateur artists whom he calls upon to be his followers—he bragged immodestly while coolly analyzing how he had made a million dollars out of his work. The overall package was both a clever Japanese variation of global commercial superstars, Jeff Koons and Damien Hirst, and a sincere homage to his heroes Warhol and Okamoto.

Murakami's astounding rise underlines those aspects of the *gaisen kōen* that are genuinely convertible back home in a universal sense: massive sales in New York auction houses, and his impressive citation index rating in worldwide art press and academic scholarship. He is constantly in the news, all the major international collectors have a piece of him, his prices outstrip all other Japanese artists (although total sales are closely followed by Yoshitomo Nara), and he always gets a page or two in global art reviews, or a solid paragraph in any narrative of modern and contemporary art (see, for example, Foster *et al.* 2011: 734–7). Much of his art world reputation rests less on the content of his art than the methods by which it has pursued a Warholian pop art right to its logical ends (Lubow 2005, Schimmel 2009). Murakami's production is a seamless corporate factory-like operation, and in dabbling with *anime* production or designing brands for American pop stars or global fashion companies, he works indifferently across the line between high art and low consumer culture (Gingeras 2010). That part of his work, beyond the art world, hitched itself during the 2000s to the somewhat desperate policies of the Japanese government to find an alternative to its declining manufacturing and financial might in its creative and content industries: Murakami was always was one of their key "global performers" (Favell 2010). And so he duly became a face of "Cool Japan." In doing so he also engendered a sort of *neo-japoniste* phenomenon in world art consumption, in which any and every representation of contemporary Japan became a "fun" cartoon: a futurist paradise of high tech urban landscapes, cute kids and wild sub-cultures, and endlessly adorable characters (all with a satisfyingly dark hint of weirdness underneath). Effectively, the complexity and often unpalatable realities of contemporary Japan were, to paraphrase Koichi Iwabuchi (2002), turned into a simple, "odorless" code: signifying "Japan" but easy to sell as *mukokuseki* (nationless) product. In Murakami's case, though, behind the happy smileys and pop art flowers lay the double-faced, rather angry irony of an unrepentant nationalist artist.

As a footnote to Murakami's success, the parallel global art triumphs of Mariko Mori and Yoshitomo Nara in the late 1990s confirmed and extended Murakami's stunning success. Mariko Mori knew even earlier success in New York, then Venice, in the mid-1990s (Borggreen 2008, Holland 2009). She was one of several Japanese "neo-pop" artists that entrepreneurial gallerist Jeffrey Deitch tried to take to fame as a token Japanese in New York. In her sensational series of robot and sex-plaything "Japanese girl" photos, set in a touristic fantasy of Tokyo, Mori just happened to be the most photogenic and easy to sell of these artists. "Made in Japan" was Deitch's slogan; it was not entirely accidental either that she was a close relative of one of the richest and most powerful families in Japan, the Mori Building Corporation, whose Roppongi Hills development and art museum dominates the skyline of south west Tokyo. Nara meanwhile quietly built a cult name as a people's artist in Japan, with a solid global career anchoring his untouchable fame back home. For him, the *gaisen kōen* drew on the mythology of the international *freeter* (free arbeiter) artist: the young creator-on-the-road, soaking up international experiences, living like a student well into his forties, pursuing his dreams and obsessions in countless art works and books before going home to Japan to cult fame (Tezuka 2010). Nara's naive image and simple lifestyle have engendered a fanatical fan base, who help him produce his shows and buy his endless spin-off commercial products (Ivy 2010). Nara's life and work, meanwhile, is a paradigm that literally thousands of young Japanese artists and creative types have followed in cities around the world. They are the legions of young fashionable Japanese who can be seen today in any hip and happening neighbourhood of Los Angeles, New York, London, or Berlin.

Murakami's story, in particular, articulates a view that is still unquestionably accepted as a truism by all in Japan: to make it globally you have to go abroad. Yet there is a double irony with Murakami's success in this respect. First, he was never really an American artist. Although he made all his connections during his time in New York and Los Angeles and keeps offshore bases in both places, Murakami essentially lives and works in Tokyo—developing an alternative corporate organization, media presence, gallery, and cult-like school that he presents as a revolutionary alternative to the moribund mainstream Japanese art system. Second, and frustratingly for Murakami, in his case the *gaisen kōen* is not really working well in all respects. Everyone in Japan is impressed by his global achievements, but the Japanese art world—with its stubborn spirit of distinction and categorizations still partially independent of the "foreign" global criteria that Murakami has learned to manipulate so well—is quite resistant to many of the criteria that might be presented as "proof" of his importance. In terms of Japanese critical evaluation, museum visibility and popularity, influence on new young artists, or site/location-specific impact, Murakami's international reputation as the most important Japanese contemporary artist is quite heavily contested in Japan.

After "Cool Japan": new forms of mobility in the next generation

Takashi Murakami's problems with the *gaisen kōen* perhaps indicate another shift in the context of cultural production in Japan, as the country has slipped out of the front rank of nations seen to be driving the alternative Asian modernity challenging the dominant West. A younger generation of artists, born in the 1970s and coming of age amidst the disasters and decline of the 1990s, is arguably pioneering a new kind of Japanese art. The work of this generation illustrates both Japan's changing relationship with the world and a different kind of cosmopolitan aspiration to the quite instrumental use of international experience and the *gaisen kōen* that marked Murakami, Nara, and Mori's career trajectories. It becomes apparent with the younger artists that, unlike with previous generations, there is no longer a dichotomy between the local/national and the global/transnational. These levels are no longer clearly distinguishable, and perhaps no longer need to be distinguished as such.

Murakami, Nara, and Mori were part of the generation born between the late 1950s and mid-1960s whose pop art work strongly reflected the emerging Japanese and consumer culture of the 1970s and 1980s. While in popular culture these pop art forms have continued to proliferate and sub-divide into numerous sub-cultures, their influence on Japanese contemporary art has waned. Western art shows and surveys that have continued to focus on the significance for art of *manga* and *anime*, *otaku*, and *kawaii* are significantly out of touch. Only in the first decade of the twenty-first century have discussions emphasizing the new trends after Murakami begun to emerge (Baldissera and Knelman 2008, Cavaliero 2011, Favell 2008, Ha Thuc 2012). The global art world ignored it, but there was indeed a significant generational change in the creative environment as a result of the end of Japan's economic boom years in the early 1990s, and especially after the shattering disasters of 1995.

In global terms, the only narrative of the shift that is known outside of Japan is Midori Matsui's *Micropop* (2007), a series of shows and books written by the one internationally published curatorial/theoretical name to have risen globally with Murakami and Nara (the other well-known name, Noi Sawaragi, publishes much less in English). *Micropop* collects together a series of younger artists who came of age during the "lost decade" of the 1990s and who use adolescent, low-tech, and/or ephemeral styles as painters, installation and video artists. Matsui's argument is that their art reflects an introverted "politics" that uses the everyday resources of the private bedroom or alienated observation of daily life to resist, from a "minor" position, the hegemonic domination of (Western) global capitalism.

Aside from freighting a very partial selection of this generation's art with a lot of rather overstated theory—mostly influenced in the usual one-way colonial style by French master thinkers, in this case Deleuze and Guattari—Matsui does offer a substantial sociological analysis of the difficult new world into which this generation had to make its way as mature artists. They lived in (or fled from) a Japan whose corporate stability was shattered, with an economy embracing flexibilization and marginalization of the young, a depressed recognition of American dominance and China's rise, and an increasing tendency to escape into private, self-isolating fantasy and obsessions. Yet they were also a generation with a full and relaxed knowledge of global culture from internet connections and international travel, especially the cheap "HIS" travel agent packages, which had enabled them to explore quite routinely both Asian countries and the West when they were young. Murakami was admired for his business entrepreneurship and Nara for his globetrotting lifestyle (Mariko Mori, for other reasons, has faded in importance since her heyday in the late 1990s). But Matsui, who has remained loyal to the two male artists who she made her career writing about, tends to overstate their stylistic influence by selecting a lot of artists who were clearly followers of these "godfathers": especially the young girl artists groomed as part of Murakami's company Kaikai Kiki. Her own *otaku* generation tastes predominate, but the ephemeral, everyday style of some of the artists—with its emphasis on irony and quixotic observation—does capture one important dimension of the artists of the "lost generation," often referred to as the unlucky *zero nen kai* (the zero zero generation) as it came of age around the year 2000.

Although she was symptomatically missing from *Micropop*, the most successful and representative artist of the zero zero generation is in fact the young women video artist Tabaimo. A discussion of her work is essential to understanding the shift in Japanese contemporary art as it has moved further into the post-Bubble, post-disaster condition and away from other global trends (see also Rawlings 2010). Born in 1975, Tabaimo was famous and feted in Japan almost before she left school: the new, experimental Kyoto University of Art and Design, which is headed by the famous philosopher Akira Asada.

Her breakthrough work was her sensational graduation piece: the prize-winning *Japanese Kitchen* (1999). It is an adolescent work but one which has the essence of all her best set pieces. *Japanese Kitchen* is, like most of her work, a large-scale color video installation, in which a short five to ten-minute video animation plays in a specially constructed theatrical environment. In this case, she built a small wooden house, with the Japonist paraphernalia of *tatami* mats and a temple-like atmosphere. Profanely, though, visitors to the house are advised by a sign outside that you do *not* need to take off your shoes (Japanese people can almost never bring themselves to obey this sacrilegious suggestion). Inside, it is a claustrophobic space, with an animation playing out on three screens. In the centre we watch an overweight mother making a *nabe* (stew) in a cluttered kitchen amidst the sweat of high summer; on side screens, we see an anonymous city environment, with ugly high-rises and wires cutting across the blank sky of an archetypal Japanese urban sprawl. Bugs crawl across the screen, humidity rises on the wall, a politician screams on the television screen; then we see inside the fridge where a depressed-looking salary man is sitting at a desk awaiting his fate along with the other vegetables. The mother reaches in for him, and cuts off his head on the chopping board. Outside, a couple of schoolgirls pass by, laughing, followed by a battered Toyota car; then, mysteriously, past the high-rise windows, bodies start falling from the sky, one by one.

Western audiences, in a cognitively limited way, tend to see Tabaimo's work as a piece of cute manga-like *anime*, referencing clichés of Japan. It is true that a certain traditionalism lies under the imagery and techniques she uses: *ukiyo-e* colors and line drawing techniques predominate in her style. But Tabaimo resents this association with pop culture. Her world is not at all the "Cool Japan" Western tourists love to imagine and which Murakami celebrated, but a distinctly "uncool" place: one in which people live in unglamorous and densely packed urban sprawl threatened by earthquakes and chronic social dysfunctions, and where on average nearly thirty people a day commit suicide. This is a Japan that has been of little interest to an outside world fixated on Asian dynamics and rising Asian power.

In other internationally successful work—all single room videos—Tabaimo used other archetypal Japanese settings to tell an unfamiliar story about quite grim and sometimes gothic everyday life. She goes inside a public bath full of frustrated middle-aged and elderly men, with a latent air of violence everywhere (*Japanese Bathhouse*, 2001); a packed commuter suburban train full of isolated travellers unable to communicate (*Japanese Commuter Train*, 2001); a woman's latrine, in which young women are apparently giving themselves abortions (*public conVENience*, 2006); a doll's house, in which neurotic, scratching hands destroy the furniture before mysteriously waters come and flood everything away (*house*, 2008). For Tabaimo, no *gaisen kōen* was necessary; international recognition simply came knocking soon after her discovery in Japan. She was feted with solo shows at both Hara Museum Tokyo and Fondation Cartier in Paris before she was 30. There was no need for a self-conscious international strategy. Here was someone from the zero zero generation who was able to make an art that reflected the harsh reality of this era while finding a form of presentation that was perfectly attuned to the trends in global installation art.

Tabaimo is exceptional in that by her mid-thirties she has attained a level of unambiguous national and international success that means her representative significance cannot be doubted. As the problems with Midori Matsui's selection attest, it is perhaps (still) too early to make a choice of other representative artists of her age group. Nevertheless, certain features of this generation, common to Tabaimo, can be pointed to. These include features not highlighted in Matsui's emphasis on introverted, naive, and adolescent styling. Other aspects less clear in her presentation include the still striking technical ability of many young Japanese artists (a virtue of an art education that still values technique over conceptual teaching); their often "cool" and quite "neutral" commentary on politics and society; the influence of the white screen and non-spatial networks of computer technology; their strong interest in low-cost, craft-intensive, sustainable practices; and the sophistication with which traditional Japanese influences or local references intermesh with a knowing awareness of global trends, such that it is difficult to distinguish these various levels of context.

As Tabaimo has also emphasized in her work—one show (*Danmen*, 2009) focused on what she called the *danmen no sedai* (the cross-sectional generation), of which she is part—the generational features of the 1970s-born cohort are significant. Here I introduce three further artists, among the most interesting of this generation, who each in turn embody aspects of cosmopolitanism and nationhood particular to younger artists from Japan. Each relates to three of the key international destinations that still routinely form part of the career development of young Japanese artists.[2]

New York: Yuken Teruya

New York remains the global art capital, still attracting a major slice of young international artists hoping for a world-scale breakthrough. The Japanese presence in New York is pronounced, and strong networks and organizations link the artists who have made their home there. With Yoko Ono a kind of patron saint in the city, a well-received show in 2007, *Making a Home,* celebrated the particular kind of "global Japan" reflected in the Japanese artist residents in the city (Shiner and Tomii 2007).

One of the most successful of the younger generation, both in the US and at home in Japan, is Yuken Teruya, who is best known for making extraordinary environmental and political commentaries out of tiny and intricate installations made of cut-up cardboard boxes and paper bags.

Born in Okinawa (1973), Teruya always felt himself an outsider while studying in Tokyo; this sense of identity was then only sharpened by the subsequent move to live and work in New York. Distinctively Japanese in his sense of craft detail, as well as in his humour and in the only obliquely articulated conceptual ideas— Japanese artists are rarely comfortable articulating clear big "theoretical" ideas of the kind loved by global art discourse—Teruya says he finally felt comfortable as himself in the "global" New York environment. Yet New York is both global— the world in a city—and a very particular American environment, provincial and specific in its own way. Teruya has absorbed the New York environment clearly in the way he has been influenced by the typically American obsession with articulating one's identity and one's own migrant trajectory as a form of politics and selfhood in society. For example, there are his installation pieces (2008) in which a series of videos installed in improvized cardboard box "cinemas" tell the story of tiny paper ships, each marked with flags of Brooklyn's resident immigrant

Figure 5.1a Yuken Teruya, born 1973

Figure 5.1b Installation view of *Notice – Forest (Madison Avenue)*, 2011, 25 x 15 x 9 cm
Photograph by Jeffrey Prehn, by permission of the artist.

populations, as they follow their way towards the sea in the flowing waters of the borough's gutter system. Teruya positions himself as another immigrant among others in the city—a cosmopolitan artist identifying with the poorer classes around him.

So far, so transnational. Characteristically global environmental concerns also might be read into his extraordinary *Notice-Forest* (2005) series that gave him his first important breakthroughs as an artist. In each work he turns a luxury branded paper bag (such as Hermés, Vuitton, etc.—although one is made out of a McDonalds bag) into an improvised art space: peering in we can see a tiny, minutely cut and composed tree made out of cuts in the paper bag then placed inside. These works offer a quiet statement about consumer waste and environmentalism, as well as illustrating a sustainable art economy of creating your own miniature white cube out of everyday recycled waste. There is of course an allusion at work here to traditional Japanese paper art techniques such as *origami*: Western viewers often want to read it this way, although Teruya himself does not present it as such. On the other hand, a specific local origin does surface in the way his work draws on traditional Okinawan techniques—stencils and fabrics, as well as the recycling of familiar global commercial branded packaging (that is, Okinawan delicacies such as Kellogg's cornflakes or local fashion such as Adidas). In more recent works, he also mixed in American icons—using traditional, almost kitsch, Okinawan stencils to portray typical American heroes, such as native American leader Geronimo, and a reworked version of the *Newsweek* cover of Barack Obama. In other works, these same almost kitsch touristy stylings are

mixed with alarming military images and references to General MacArthur's
speeches and statements of the 1940s, that remind all that Okinawa (now part of
sovereign Japan since the 1970s) is still America's biggest floating aircraft carrier
in the Pacific. Teruya processes the familiarly American cosmopolitanism of New
York: the American "capital" as the paradigmatic global experience. The mix is
distinctly cosmopolitan, "American," and local, all at once.

London: Satoru Aoyama

Artists that have chosen to live and work in other global cities can be seen to
embody different forms of cosmopolitanism refracting their Japanese national
origins, each city inflected by local variations in the global. London, in many
ways, offers a quite different context to New York.

For example, there are the elaborate tableaux made from a sewing machine by
Satoru Aoyama (born 1973), who spent several years of his formative education
in London, at Goldsmith's, during the heady years following the breakthrough of
the YBAs (Young British Artists, i.e. Damien Hirst, Tracey Emin, Sarah Lucas,

Figure 5.2a Satoru Aoyama, born 1973

Figure 5.2b Glitter Pieces #1, 2008. Embroidery with metallic and black thread on polyester
By permission of the artist and Mizuma Gallery, Tokyo.

and so on). Aoyama is another younger Japanese artist who rejects the mass
production of pop art in favor of painfully honed craft skills and laborious han-
diwork: in other words, the polar opposite of Murakami's factory production
lines. At Goldsmiths he soaked up some of the atmosphere of arch conceptualism
that marked the height of the YBAs, but he actually trained on the unfashionable,
almost women's only, BA course in textiles. There, he adopted a peculiar meth-
odology from a despised women's "craft": reproducing painterly images using an
archaic Singer sewing machine.

At one level his work echoes the themes of Gerhard Richter and David Hockney
involving painting as reproduction and the use of technology in art; in their
case, the impact of photography on artistic representation. Like them Aoyama
deliberately "copies" given photographic or painted images, only with a sewing
machine. On the one hand, then, Aoyama's method is an anachronistic art form
long swept over by the march of technological progress. Maybe this is the point of
contemporary art, Aoyama is saying, rather than pop art's attempt to keep up
with and process the latest in design or fashion technology, which is Murakami's
hopeless quest. Aoyama thus explores and re-values art forms and techniques that
have been rendered obsolete in the usual linear, developmental reading. Yet,
from another angle (the sewn "paintings" are in fact hard to detect as works of
needlework), Aoyama is practicing a form of "digital" production, with each stitch
approximating the pixel of a computerised image that transforms analogue
brushwork into digital code. Explicitly evoking the spirit of nineteenth-century
labor organization and the ideas of William Morris, Aoyama thus makes contemporary reproductions that question the hierarchy of modern media images.
Aoyama's craft-based style echoes the intricacy and intensity of much Japanese

design work and fits within a contempoary trend in Japan to re-evaluate craft arts (*Ko-jutsu*) as distinctively "Japanese" arts. Yet Aoyama rejects any notion that he is a Japanese artist, positioning his work firmly in a theoretical line at ease amidst the conceptualism of high global art theory.

Berlin: Kei Takemura

Despite the claims of New York and London, or Paris and Los Angeles (which might be similarly contrasted), it is Berlin in the first decade of the twenty-first century that has become the most fashionable *avant-garde* global art capital. As other global cities went through real estate and finance booms that priced artists out of the residential and studio spaces they need to live and work, Berlin became the prime destination for this younger generation of footloose international *freeter* who sought opportunities outside of Japan during the depressing late 1990s and 2000s. Germany has also proven unusually generous in its provision of grants and welfare benefits (including child support) for Japanese artists, as well as in its laxity over their residence status.

In this respect, it is illuminating to consider the work of Kei Takemura (born 1975). Takemura is another artist of this generation who left Japan in search of global experience and opportunity. For her, it was the typical Berlin

Figure 5.3 Kei Takemura, born 1975. Working on *A.N.'s Living Room in Tokyo: Premonition of an Earthquake*, 2005. Italian synthetic cloth, Japanese silk thread, transparency, permanent pen. 380 × 1120 cm
By permission of the artist.

artist's aspiration for an authentic, cosmopolitan expression: something which can draw on the international resources of a world city and the conceptual language of global art centered there but is untainted by the exigencies of the art market and commercial space as New York inevitably is and London has become.

Takemura also uses needlework, linking different ends of the historical silk road from Asia to Europe, with fine Japanese silk threads and Italian synthetic fabrics applied to huge tapestry-like works that evoke memories of travel, people, and a life lived between Japan and Europe. As with most of her peers in this generation, she found little inspiration in the pop culture and consumer ideologies that drove the interests of Murakami's generation. Influenced by the local performance scene in Berlin, Takemura also acts out her memories, living out words or songs of the characters she remembers as part of her installations. The emphasis on the work is always on the small and the sustainable. In another line of work, evocative of Yoko Ono's famous "mend pieces," she "sews together" broken objects, renovating them while preserving the meaning of the break, "veiling" the damage, she says, rather than restoring it. Takemura's work is uncanny, yet distinctly humanistic in attempts to find transcendent forms of communication, which as with Aoyama and Teruya draw in form, though not content, on Japanese craft traditions. At the same time the translucent, ghostlike objects floating on her tapestries, as with Aoyama's tableaux and Teruya's stencils, also evoke contemporary digital or media images. Yet working from Germany, Japan is still ever-present: such as in the powerful and disturbing *A.N.'s Living Room in Tokyo, Premonition of an Earthquake* (2005), a work Takemura says she made well before the disaster of March 2011, because she just could not get Japan out of her mind.

These artists of the zero zero generation made their careers in a hostile environment. Those that did not give up to go abroad, struggled long term to make viable careers in a depressed Japan, only to face continual set backs as the nascent contemporary domestic art market failed to ignite. Meanwhile, the Japanese art world has watched all the global attention pass straight over, to China and the rest of Asia—with the exception of Murakami and Nara's easy-to-consume pop art, which almost entirely monopolized the perception and understanding of Japanese contemporary art from the 1990s. Yet there is a return to Japan among many of these young artists, both physically (as they come home during the approach to middle age), but also stylistically. Not to dig into the nationalist myths and war-obsessed fixations of the past, but rather to produce an art that respond to the condition of a post-Bubble, post-disaster society, which has learned a new, non-linear attitude to low or no-growth development. There is undeniably an influence at work of emergent global environmental concerns, as well as a critique of global capitalism that has become clearly worldwide since 2008. Yet the emphasis on renovation, sustainability, and aesthetic reflection among these young Japanese artists sits in stark contrast to the rampant technology and consumer-driven development sweeping the rest of Asia: the concerns of Asian modernity more reflected in many contemporary young Chinese and Indian artists, who are also more visible and successful internationally. In contrast, the younger generation's art in Japan is well suited to the new post-crash age now emerging, even before the latest disasters of 2011—events that should have surely interred any further notions of promoting Japan globally as "Cool Japan."

Conclusion: going "home" and the new *Sakoku*

Tabaimo was honored in the 2011 Venice Biennale, chosen that year for the Japanese pavilion. The enigmatic video installation she produced was announced as a work that evoked the notion widely discussed in Japan of "Galapogosization," exploring the country's identity as island state. This is the idea that the islands of Japan had become something akin to the Pacific islands explored by Charles Darwin, disconnected from evolutions elsewhere in the world, producing weird and wonderful flora and fauna more advanced than anywhere else, yet doomed to extinction in the face of dominant global currents. It is a gloomy idea, recognizing Japan's objective decline internationally, while proudly upholding some of the national products that the country produced in spite of American, European, and (other) Asian norms. A classic example was Japan's 3G phone technology which led the world for years while being incompatible with global norms. It finally succumbed to crushing American business interests with the introduction of the iPhone; within a year the influence of Apple's products had virtually wiped out the "native" technology.

A part of the reaction to the disappointments and incursions of the global in Japan has been the re-emergence of an introversion often mentioned in terms of the new *sakoku*: the foreign policy of the pre-Meiji era based on wilful closure and self-isolation from the world. Sometimes, it is said, ordinary Japanese people still dream of a time before the black ships of 1853 (the American gun boats of Commander Perry which forced Japan to open to trade) and a return to a pristine national culture untouched and untroubled by (foreign) global influences. Con- temporary artists position themselves differently: their self-consciously border-crossing trajectories often embody the complex relationship between local, national, regional, and global contexts. Yet, as I have argued, in terms of the creative impulses of artists and art world professionals from Japan, the contrast across generations is stark. Murakami's generation and those older were, above all, in awe of and fascinated by the power of foreign Western culture. Following a colonial pattern, they sought out the global art capitals, such as Paris and New York, and tried to assimilate and re-import their cultural forms and aesthetic trends, while still sometimes expressing nationalist resentment and despair at the cultural power and domination that this relationship expressed. By the zero zero generation, young Japanese artists seemed to have come to a more relaxed rela- tion to the rest of the world: with international travel and ease of internet con- nections, they absorbed the world while confidently developing their own original forms, enmeshing Japanese traditions and global conceptual trends. Moving in a world in which these binaries have broken down, the mechanism of the *gaisen kōen* has become less relevant. The talk now amongst older generations is that even younger people in their teens and twenties, disillusioned with the global and alienated from both the West and Asia, are going back more forcefully to a regressive Japanese "island" mentality: self-sufficient with Japanese popular culture, escapist via the internet, and ambitionless in terms of a global world apparently no longer interested in Japan—except as an object of pity or as a fantasy cartoon (Favell 2014).

This kind of reaction is not unfamiliar in other parts of the world that have experienced the incursions of a globalizing economy and culture in a difficult, sometimes destructive way. Whatever new generational shift may be underway, the cosmopolitanism of the zero zero generation in Japan remains a complex, original, and hopeful response. Having transcended the problematic colonialist paradigm of the *gaisen kōen* and the reductive stereotypes of "Cool Japan," they also offer an art signally at odds with the development and power-obsessed narratives of a rising Asian modernity but very much in tune with the emergent post-2008 global concerns of a world economic and environmental crisis. Largely ignored by the blinkered readings of the global art world, it is to be hoped that their vision of Japan in the world will find better appreciation in the future.

Notes

1 Here and throughout, I draw upon my own narrative and analysis in Favell (2012). My work is based on a five-year-long ethnography of the Japanese art world, particularly as seen from the Tokyo contemporary art scene.
2 Material in the following sections is largely based on interviews and repeated meetings with the three artists: Satoru Aoyama (Tokyo, July 2007), Kei Takemura (Yokohama, June 2008), and Yuken Teruya (New York, March 2012).

References

Allison, A. 2006. *Millenial Monsters: Japanese Toys and the Global Imagination*. Berkeley: University of California Press.

Baldissera, L. and S. Knelman. 2008. *Great New Wave: Contemporary Art From Japan* (exhibition catalogue). Art Gallery of Hamilton, Victoria, Canada.

Birnbaum, P. 2006. *Glory in a Line: A Life of Foujita*. London: Faber and Faber.

Borggreen, G. 2008. Japan in Scandinavia: Cultural Clichés in the Receptions of Works by Mori Mariko. *HZ*, No. 4.

Cavaliero, S. 2011. *Nouvelle Garde: de l'art Contemporain Japonais* [New Vanguard: Contemporary Japanese Art]. Paris: Lézard Noir.

Chiu, M. and B. Genocchio. 2010. *Contemporary Asian Art*. London: Thames and Hudson.

Ciotti, M. 2012. Post-colonial Renaissance: "Indianness," Contemporary Art and the Market in the Age of Neoliberal Capital. *Third World Quarterly* 33(4): 637–55.

Clammer, J. 1997. *Contemporary Urban Japan: A Sociology of Consumption*. Oxford: Blackwell.

Clark, J. 1998. *Modern Asian Art*. Honolulu: University of Hawaii Press.

Delanty, G. 2009. *The Cosmopolitan Imagination: The Renewal of Critical Social Theory*. Cambridge: Cambridge University Press.

Favell, A. 2008. After the Gold Rush: Japan's New Post-bubble Art and Why it Matters. In *The Echo: An Exhibition of Young Japanese Artists* (exhibition catalogue). ZAIM, Yokohama, Japan.

———2010. Tokyo to LA story: How Southern California Became the Gateway for a Japanese Global Pop Art Phenomenon. *Kontur: Tidsskrift for Kulturstudier* 20: 54–68. Available at: http://kontur.au.dk/fileadmin/www.kontur.au.dk/Kontur_20/Microsoft_Word–VAM-FAVELL_MOD.pdf (accessed May 2014).

———2011. Bye Bye Little Boy. *Art in America*, April 1. Available at: www.artinamerica magazine.com/features/bye-bye-kitty/ (accessed May 2014).

———2012. *Before and After Superflat: A Short History of Japanese Contemporary Art 1990–2011*. Hong Kong: Timezone 8.

———2014. Visions of Tokyo in Japanese Contemporary Art. *Impressions: Journal of the Japanese Art Society of America* 35: 68–83.

Foster, H., R. Krauss, Y-A. Bois, B. H. D. Buchloh and D. Joselit. 2011. *Art Since 1900: Modernism, Antimodernism, Postmodernism* (second edition) (Vol. 1–2). London: Thames & Hudson.

Gingeras, A. M. 2010. Lost in Translation: The Politics of Identity in the Work of Takashi Murakami. In *Pop Life: Art in a Material World*, J. Bankowsky, A. Gingeras, and C. Wood, eds. London: Tate Museum.

Gomez, E. 2000. Breathing Life, Posthumously, into Japan's Art Scene. *New York Times*, August 20.

Hardt, M. and A. Negri. 2001. *Empire*. Cambridge, MA: Harvard University Press.

———2005. *Multitude*. New York: Penguin.

Harris, J., ed. 2011. *Globalization and Contemporary Art*. Malden, MA: Wiley-Blackwell.

Ha Thuc, C. 2012. *Nouvel Art Contemporain Japonais* [New Contemporary Japanese Art]. Paris: Scala.

Holland, A. 2009. Mariko Mori and the Art of Global Connectedness. *Intersections* (November) 23.

Ivy, M. 2010. The Art of Cute Little Things: Nara Yoshitomo's Parapolitics. *Mechademia* 5: 3–29.

Iwabuchi, K. 2002. *Recentering Globalization: Popular Culture and Japanese Transnationalism*. Durham, NC: Duke University Press.

Japan Foundation, 2008. *WA: The Spirit of Harmony and Japanese Design Today*. Tokyo: Japan Foundation.

Kawamura, Y. 2004. *The Japanese Revolution in Paris Fashion*. Oxford: Berg.

Kelts, R. 2006. *Japanamerica: How Japanese Pop Culture Has Invaded the US*. New York: Palgrave.

Kofman, E. 2005. Figures of the Cosmopolitan: Privileged Nationals and National Outsider. *Innovation, The European Journal of Social Sciences* 18(1): 83–97.

Koolhaas, R. and H-U Obrist. 2011. *Project Japan: Metabolism Talks*. Köln: Taschen.

Lubow, A. 2005. The Murakami Method. *New York Times*, April 3.

Lucken, M. 2001. *L'art du Japon au Vingtième Siècle* [Japanese Art in the Twentieth Century]. Paris: Hermann.

Marotti, W. 2013. *Money, Trains, and Guillotines: Art and Revolution in 1960s Japan*. Durham, NC: Duke University Press.

McLean, I. 2011. Aboriginal Cosmopolitans: A Pre-history of Western Desert Painting. In *Globalization and Contemporary Art*, J. Harris, ed. Malden, MA: Wiley-Blackwell.

Merewether, C. and R. Hiro, eds. 2007. *Art, Anti-Art, Non-Art: Experimentations in the Public Sphere in Postwar Japan 1950–1970*. Los Angeles, CA: Getty Research Institute.

Midori, M. 2007. *The Age of Micropop: The New Generation of Japanese Artists*. Tokyo: Parco.

Moeran, B. 2000. Commodities, Culture and Japan's Corollanization of Asia. In *Japanese Influences and Presences in Asia*, M. Söderberg and I. Reader, eds. London: Curzon Press.

Munroe, A. 1994. *Japanese Art After 1945: Scream Against The Sky*. New York: Abrams.

——2000. *YES Yoko Ono*. New York: Abrams.

Murakami, T. 2001. *Superflat*. Los Angeles, CA: The Museum of Contemporary Art.

——ed. 2005a. *Little Boy: The Art of Japan's Exploding Sub Cultures*. New Haven, CT: Yale University Press.

——2005b. *Geijutsu Kigyo Ron* [The Art Entrepreneurship Theory]. Tokyo: Gentosha.

Papastergiadis, N. 2012. *Cosmopolitanism and Culture*. Cambridge: Polity.

Philipsen, L. 2008. *The Globalization of Contemporary Art*. PhD dissertation, University of Aarhus, Denmark.

Quémin, A. 2006. Globalization and Mixing in the Visual Arts: An Empirical Survey of "High Culture" and Globalization. *International Sociology* 21(4): 522–50.

Rawlings, A. 2010. All that Creeps Below the Surface: Tabaimo. *Art Asia Pacific* 71 (Nov/Dec).

Rimer, J. T., ed. 2012. *Since Meiji: Perspectives on the Japanese Visual Arts*. Honolulu: University of Hawaii Press.

Sato, D. 2011. *Modern Japanese Art and the Meiji State: The Politics of Beauty*. Los Angeles, CA: Getty Research Institute.

Schimmel, P., ed. 2009. © *Murakami*. Los Angeles, CA: The Museum of Contemporary Art.

Shiner, E. C. and R. Tomii, eds. 2007. *Making a Home: Japanese Contemporary Artists in New York*. New York: Japan Society.

Stallabrass, J. 2004. *Art Incorporated: The Story of Contemporary Art*. Oxford: Oxford University Press.

Tezuka, M. 2010. Music on My Mind: The Art and Phenomenon of Yoshitomo Nara. In *Yoshitomo Nara: Nobody's Fool*, M. Chiu and M. Tezuka, eds. New York: Asia Society.

Thornton, S. 2008. *Seven Days in the Art World*. London: Granta.

Tiampo, M. 2011a. *Gutai: Decentering Modernism*. Chicago, IL: University of Chicago Press.

——2011b. Cultural Mercantilism: Modernism's Means of Production: The Gutai Group as Case Study. In *Globalization and Contemporary Art*, J. Harris, ed. Malden, MA: Wiley-Blackwell.

Tomii, R. 2009. "International Contemporaneity" in the 1960s: Discoursing on Art in Japan and Beyond. *Japan Review* 21: 123–47.

——2011. The Discourse of (L)imitation: A Case Study with Hole-digging in 1960s Japan. In *Globalization and Contemporary Art*, J. Harris, ed. Malden, MA: Wiley-Blackwell.

Vine, R. 2011. *New China, New Art*. New York: Prestel.

Winther-Tamaki, B. 2012. *Maximum Embodiment: Yoga, the Western Painting of Japan 1912–1955*. Honolulu: University of Hawaii Press.

Yamamura, M. 2009. Re-viewing Kusama, 1950–75: The Biography of Things. In *Yayoi Kusama: Mirrored Years* (exhibition catalogue). Rotterdam.

Yoshimoto, M. 2005. *Into Performance: Japanese Women Artists in New York*. New Brunswick, NJ: Rutgers University Press.

Yoshitake, M. 2012. *Requiem for the Sun: The Art of Mono-Ha*. Los Angeles, CA: Blum Edition.

6 Eating one's way to sophistication

Japanese food, transnational flows, and social mobility in Hong Kong[1]

Yoshiko Nakano

Hong Kong rightly prides itself on being a Chinese food paradise, a consequence of the free port's dual status as a Chinese migration hub and one of Asia's greatest financial centers. Following the establishment of the communist government in China in 1949, chefs from Guangdong (Canton), Chaozhou (Chiu Chow), Shanghai, Beijing (Peking), and Sichuan increasingly crossed the border to enter the territory, and found employment in the kitchens of restaurants that were often financed or frequented by business tycoons. This combination of money and mobility raised Chinese regional cuisines to a level that has, over the years, consistently attracted and delighted visitors from around the world. Today, however, this food paradise is no longer uniquely Chinese. Its definition has expanded to include a variety of international cuisines, most particularly Japanese.

This chapter traces a six-decade-long transnational odyssey—one that saw Japanese food evolve from providing a sense of home to Japanese expatriates in Hong Kong to representing a symbol of sophistication for local residents. According to *OpenRice.com*, the territory's most popular dining guide that relies on user-generated reviews, in 2014, "Japanese" was the fourth largest category with 2,093 restaurants and takeaways; it followed local "Hong Kong-style" (8,401), eclectic "Western" (2,892), and adjacent "Guangdong" (2,374). The "Japanese" eateries accounted for more than 5 percent of all entries on the site, and outnumbered other popular "national" cuisines such as "Italian" (765), "American" (696), and "Thai" (523).[2] In 2011, the Japan External Trade Organization, an independent government agency, surveyed 400 Hong Kongers on their consumption of Japanese food. The poll confirmed that a meal at a Japanese eatery is a part of everyday life for the territory's residents: 99 percent of respondents aged between 20 and 59 had eaten at least once at a Japanese restaurant. Furthermore, nearly one third of respondents (33 percent) stated that they visited Japanese eateries on a weekly basis. This pattern was even more prominent among the more affluent respondents who gave their monthly income as HK$60,000 (US$7,692) or above: 43 percent of them said that they ate at a Japanese restaurant more than once a week (JETRO 2012: 16–7).

Separately, an estimate in 2011 by the Hong Kong Eating Establishment Employees General Union put the number of Japanese restaurants in the territory at approximately 600, employing 7,000 people in a city of seven million (*South*

China Morning Post 2011). In other words, there is one Japanese restaurant for every 12,000 Hong Kong residents. This figure of 600 includes dozens of high-end restaurants that serve the fresh catch flown in daily from not only Tokyo's Tsukiji, the world's largest fish market, but also other markets across the country. It includes an even greater number of highly localized dining establishments which Japanese expatriates eschew as *nisshiki* (Japanese-style) imitations and which Japan's Ministry of Agriculture, Forestry, and Fisheries dismisses as restaurants that provide a "cuisine that is removed from traditional Japanese cooking" (MAFF 2007). However, the sheer volume of these "bastardizations" only goes to prove that Japanese dining establishments in Hong Kong have gone far beyond simply providing a taste of home to the territory's more than 23,000 Japanese expatriates (Consulate General of Japan, Hong Kong 2013).

In fact, Hong Kong imports more Japanese food items than any other country or region in the world. In 2007, it surpassed the United States, with a population forty times greater than that of the territory, and became the biggest international market for Japanese produce. In 2013, 23 percent of Japan's agricultural and marine products—worth ¥124.9 billion (US$1.15 billion)—was exported to the territory (see Figure 6.1).

Young Hong Kongers not only eat Japanese food for their main meals but also snack on it between meals. Local retailer Okashi Land specializes in neatly packaged Japanese snacks and carries an overwhelming variety of cookies, crackers, chips, candies, and chewing gum from major manufacturers such as Meiji, Glico, Lotte, Kabaya, and Calbee. The chain operates 51 outlets throughout Hong Kong, in shopping malls, subway and ferry stations, and at the airport (Okashi Land n.d.). Alongside such specialty stores as Okashi Land, Japanese snacks dominate the shelves at countless convenience stores across town. They are 20 to 50 percent more expensive than in Japan, once the cost of transportation and handling has been added, and usually more expensive than Chinese and

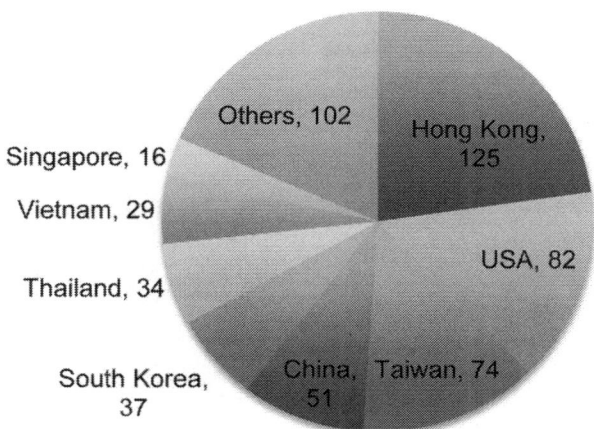

Figure 6.1 Japan's agricultural and marine product exports in 2013 (in billion yen)
Source: Ministry of Agriculture, Forestry, and Fisheries of Japan (MAFF) 2014.

Taiwanese varieties. Despite this they have a strong following among young Hong Kongers who find them tasty, are drawn to their sleek packaging, and trust Japanese food safety standards (JETRO 2002: 22–3).[3]

Furthermore, there are countless Japanese-style supermarket and convenience stores operating in the territory, acting as advertisements for both Japanese food and its lifestyle. The Japanese general merchandise store giant AEON alone operates 58 stores in Hong Kong, including 34 outlets of its "100-yen shop" spin-offs that offer a wide range of Japanese-style household goods and dry food items at bargain prices (AEON Stores n.d.). AEON is also home to outlets of the Yamazaki Baking Company. Yamazaki, which offers freshly baked bread made with wheat flour and other ingredients imported directly from Japan, opened its first overseas venture in Hong Kong in 1981(JETRO 2002: 10) and now counts 47 outlets throughout the territory. Most of the Yamazaki shops are located in suburbs away from the areas where Japanese expatriates normally reside and cater to the local middle class (Yamazaki n.d.).

Among Hong Kong's high-end supermarkets, the trendsetter is city'super. The retail chain's chairman is a Japanese fashion entrepreneur who introduced Italian luxury brand Prada to Hong Kong in 1986, and later to Korea, Singapore, and Hawaii. City'super currently operates four "Mega Lifestyle Specialty Stores" in the territory, each carrying gourmet products sourced from around the world, with an emphasis on Japanese tastes and display. For example, by my last count, the chain carries 77 different types of Japanese curry sauce alongside the 58 choices of olive oil it offers. Its storefronts feature fresh Japanese fruit, such as peaches, grapes, and strawberries, all of which are prized gift items in Hong Kong. Gourmet *amaou* (sweet king) strawberries from Fukuoka, Kyushu, are in the same league as Godiva and Leonidas chocolates. A box of a dozen *amaou* retails for as much as HK$158 (US$20).

How did Japanese food evolve from being a niche cuisine for Japanese executives in Hong Kong to a symbol of sophistication for local high school students? The first axis of this story relates to the expansion of Japanese business in Hong Kong and Southeast Asia from the mid-1950s onwards. As "Made in Japan" products began to find their way into regional markets, Japanese food was brought into the territory to satisfy the demands of homesick senior Japanese executives and their family members.

The signing of the 1984 Joint Declaration, which set out the terms of the British colony's return to China in 1997, provoked an unprecedented discussion of issues of identity and social mobility among the city's inhabitants. Japanese staples, such as sushi and sashimi, made accessible by the opening of Japanese super-markets in the suburbs, became emblematic of the cultivated lifestyle that set Hong Kong's middle class apart from their cousins across the border in Mainland China. Thus, the second axis of this story relates to how the consumption of Japanese food helped foster the development of a distinct Hong Kong identity among the territory's predominantly Chinese population.

The third axis concerns the emergence, from the 1990s, of a younger set of local consumers of Japanese food, at a time when it was gaining the status of a worldwide indicator of cosmopolitan sophistication. As Hong Kong's economy continued to grow, Hong Kong teenagers began to expand their culinary horizons, from typical local noodles and American fast food to Japanese *ramen* noodles and *gyōza* dumplings. In effect, both *ramen* and *gyōza* have their roots in China: they represent a refined Japanese take on two basic Chinese dishes. These Japanese adaptations have been embraced by young Hong Kongers since they add a touch of luxury to what might be an otherwise mundane dining experience. Through the examination of these three axes, this chapter frames the relationship between a people's foodways and transnational mobility as an interactive process; and discusses how the consumption of food from one Asian country has become an index of social mobility and identity in another.

A taste of home for the Japanese *salaryman*

Hong Kong has been Japan's gateway to Asian markets for nearly six decades. The free port was, and remains, an Asian transportation hub, facilitating the formal—and informal—flow and exchange of products, people, and ideas. The former British colonial city was not only the place where East met West, but also where "Made in Japan" products met Chinese distributors and consumers at a time when protectionist trade policies were the norm in many other parts of the world. Countless Japanese products made their overseas debut in Hong Kong, which served, in effect, as a test market (Nakano 2009: 85–109). In the mid-1950s, under the US government's grand initiative to contain the spread of communism in Asia, the Japanese government encouraged major Japanese corporations to expand their businesses into Southeast Asia (Shiraishi 2000: 127–43). Hong Kong assumed a strategic role in this process, and senior Japanese executives from industries such as banking, trading, shipping, insurance, and textile began to arrive in the territory on their multi-year assignments, along with their cravings for familiar food.

In February 1955, Japan's newly established national flag carrier, Japan Airlines, started service to Hong Kong, its second international destination after San Francisco. It provided a means of transportation for the businessmen who paved the way for the globalization of Japanese products and services. Six months after the carrier's inaugural flight to the territory, the Hongkong Japanese Club was established with 16 corporate and 90 individual members (HKJC 2006: 95). It began to offer a modest Japanese dining service to its membership, and soon became the place where Japanese salarymen and their family members headed for their comfort food.

The non-fiction book *Sanwa Bank Hong Kong Branch* gives an account of the first day in the territory of a newly arrived bank employee, Shohei Saiga, and his family in 1964. The 31-year-old salaryman transferred to Hong Kong following a two-year assignment in London to set up the local branch of Sanwa Bank, which would eventually merge with the UFJ Bank in 2002 and the Bank of Tokyo-Mitsubishi UFJ in 2005. Upon arrival on a Japan Airlines flight, the Saiga family unpacked at a budget hotel in Causeway Bay on Hong Kong Island and headed to the nearby Japanese Club for their first dinner in the colony. The family ordered sukiyaki hot pot with beef and vegetables, a dish that was often reserved for special occasions:

> As Saiga tasted the delicately sliced beef, he became nostalgic, "I haven't had such finely sliced meat for a while; it was all cut in chunks in London."
>
> (Tateishi 1997: 24)

While for many Japanese expatriates, the Hongkong Japanese Club was considered the sole purveyor of authentic Japanese food in the territory, it was not the only choice available. By 1960, "Made in Japan" products had gradually built a solid reputation for themselves in Hong Kong and Southeast Asia, with the introduction of affordable sewing machines, cameras, and transistor radios. In addition to those stationed in Hong Kong, Japanese business executives flew in and out of the territory on their way to develop new markets. As a result, upscale restaurants with *tatami* rooms and kimono-clad waitresses were established by Japanese entrepreneurs and frequented by Japanese executives. Most popular among them was the Imperial Hotel's Tokyo Restaurant, which opened its doors in December 1960.[4] The hotel stood on a prime location in Tsim Sha Tsui, Kowloon, where the majority of Japanese executives stayed. A leaflet of the Restaurant from the time promotes its services as follows:

> The one and only real Japanese restaurant in Hong Kong with charming Japanese waitresses and Japanese cooks. Genuine Kobe Beef Sukiyaki, Sushi, and Sushi Counter.

To mark its opening, Tokyo Restaurant ran advertisements in both English- and Chinese-language newspapers featuring six *geisha* girls (see Figure 6.2). The menu listed Kobe beef sukiyaki and tempura, two dishes that had proven popular among international visitors to Japan, as well as with men serving in the Allied Occupation Forces.

The restaurant became such a landmark that it repeatedly figured in Japanese popular culture, including the blockbuster comedy series *Shachō*, which starred Hisaya Morishige as a company president. Tokyo Restaurant, under the fictionalized name of Tokyo-tei, features in a 1962 episode that revolves around a market development trip to Hong Kong by Morishige's character. A running joke has all Japanese executives heading to Tokyo-tei for their meals. When Hong Kongers spot a Japanese businessman looking lost in Tsim Sha Tsui, they automatically direct him to the restaurant. Tokyo Restaurant thrived throughout the 1960s, benefitting from the plans of Japanese corporations for international expansion in Southeast Asia, which had them send their homesick executives to the territory, along with a large entertainment budget. The meals at Tokyo Restaurant were considered extravagant and most junior salarymen could not afford to eat there (HKJC 2006: 157).

Figure 6.2 Tokyo restaurant advertisement, 1960
Source: *Overseas Chinese Daily*, December 15, 1960.

Similarly, Daimaru department store in Causeway Bay was the preserve of the privileged. In November 1960, Daimaru, which owned and operated stores in Osaka, Kyoto, Kobe, and Tokyo, became the first of 14 Japanese retailers to open a department store in the territory after World War II. However, this was not Daimaru's first overseas branch. The company had operated ten stores and numerous procurement offices throughout Asia during World War II, starting with its Shanghai branch in 1937, and followed by ten stores in Suzhou, Tianjin, Canton (Guangzhou), Fengtien (Shenyang), Hsingking (Changchun), Hsuchou (Xuzhou), Tsingtao (Qingdao), Rangoon (Yangon), Penang, and Singapore (Daimaru 1967: 435–80). Thus, Daimaru had both the aspiration and the know-how to expand its business to continental Asia despite lingering anti-Japanese sentiment.

Another factor prompting Daimaru to look overseas for growth involved the domestic restrictions it faced at home. In 1956, Japan's Ministry of International Trade and Industry imposed regulations which made it difficult for existing Japanese department stores to open new branches within the country. As a result, they began to focus on opportunities abroad: in 1958, Takashimaya opened a branch in New York; in 1959, Tokyu followed suit in Honolulu, and Hankyu in Los Angeles. For Daimaru, it was Hong Kong. A retail space of approximately 90,000 sq ft (8,361 m^2) became available in Causeway Bay, and the company made the decision to invest in a joint venture with a Chinese entrepreneur. Together they opened a modern department store that adhered to a fixed price policy. The Daimaru executives saw their investment in the Hong Kong branch as supporting the development of the Southeast Asian economy. At the same time, the store was to be a means of gathering market intelligence from around the world (Daimaru 1967: 522–3, 541–2).

Daimaru Hong Kong contributed to the transnational odyssey of Japanese food in two ways: it opened a restaurant that served Japanese haute cuisine as well as Japanized forms of European dishes; and it established the first modern supermarket selling Japanese food products in the territory. On the second floor, the store had two dining facilities: a restaurant and a coffee shop operated by Shin-Osaka Hotel, which was one of Osaka's most prestigious hotels (HKJC 2006: 95).[5] The company's advertisements in local papers featured menu items such as sukiyaki, tempura, and Kobe beef, but not sushi or sashimi. A Daimaru Hong Kong employee who was in charge of importing Japanese food products from 1960 to 1966, Frankie Wu, explains the choice of featured items as follows:

> It's not that these (sukiyaki, tempura, and Kobe beef) dishes were well known (to Hong Kong residents), but if we were to promote Japanese food, we had to stick to cooked varieties, because they would not eat raw fish.
>
> (Interview, Hong Kong, November 22, 2012)

In fact, Japanese food was not at all popular in Hong Kong in the 1960s. Chinese residents who had traveled to Japan used to warn their friends saying, "There is nothing to eat in Japan." But at the same time, a sukiyaki meal at Daimaru Hong Kong prepared with Japanese-imported ingredients and cooked at the table by a Japanese waitress was considered a luxury. One serving came to HK$80 (US$10.3); by contrast, the monthly salary for a clerk on the Daimaru sales floor was HK$210 (US$27).

Along with sukiyaki and tempura, Daimaru's menu included Japanese adaptations of French dishes, which were considered a symbol of modernity and sophistication among the Japanese (Ishige 2001: 155–67, Cwiertka 2006: 23).[6] The eclectic combination of Japanese and Western food was a common practice in Japan at *okonomi-shokudō*, or "all-you-like restaurants." Located on the top floors of Japanese department stores, these restaurants served up a selection of *washoku* (Japanese), *yōshoku* (Western), and *chūka* (Chinese) favorites to attract affluent diners. For example, even during World War II, Tokyo's leading department store Mitsukoshi offered French and Chinese dishes alongside more traditional Japanese fare

(Cwiertka and Yasuhara 2010: 177–80). While Daimaru Hong Kong included both Japanese and Western dishes on its menu, it understandably stopped short of offering Japanized Chinese dishes in the Chinese food paradise.

Daimaru sourced both the ingredients used in its restaurants and the food items on sale in its supermarket from Japan. Prior to the arrival of Daimaru, Hong Kong had only one grocery store that specialized in Japanese food. This store, Fuji, was located in the district of Wanchai; it had Taiwanese management, and stocked items such as Kikkoman soy sauce, Ajinomoto flavor enhancer (MSG), and canned food (interview with Frankie Wu, Hong Kong, November 22, 2012). As mentioned above, in 1960, Daimaru became the first modern supermarket selling Japanese food products in the British colonial city. A 1966 Daimaru advertisement in the city's leading English-language paper lists the wide range of Japanese food items that were available to buy in its supermarket:

> Kobe beef and other ... TASTY JAPANESE FOOD available in fine range at Daimaru's Super Market
>
> Kobe sirloin, fillet, rump steaks; ham and fish sausages; fish rolls; salted pink salmon ...
>
> In tins: *sukiyaki*; seasoned crab meat, abalone, tuna, pink salmon, scallops, mackerel, Kobe beef; smoked and boiled oysters; roasted bean curd ...
>
> Seasoned and roasted *nori* (seaweeds)
>
> Assorted *arare* (rice crackers)
>
> Instant fried, vegetable noodles [sic.]
>
> Rice cakes, mixed pickles, fruit cocktails, pastes, jelly, dried fish, seasoned sea urchin ... and of course SAKE
>
> Try something different you may like them [sic].
>
> Hong Kong Daimaru[7]

While the variety of food products on offer was impressive, most items were canned, bottled or dried, with the exception of Kobe beef, cured meat, and salmon. The store's customers were mostly Japanese; but in 1968, not all of the territory's then 789 Japanese residents patronized the upscale supermarket. A postgraduate student at the University of Hong Kong, Takemichi Hara, who started his studies that year, recounts what Daimaru meant to him:

> Japanese food was out of reach for me. I was a very poor student, so for other Japanese [residents in Hong Kong], it probably wasn't so. Most Japanese [in the city in those days] were salarymen who worked for major trading houses. I missed Japanese food, but I simply couldn't afford it. Daimaru was the only place that stocked Japanese groceries, but it was not somewhere I could afford to shop.
>
> (Interview, Hong Kong, December 15, 2000)

Daimaru was also beyond the means of Hong Kong's working and lower middle classes who constituted the majority of the territory's population. This majority bought daily necessities in shops found on the ground floor of their housing estates (or apartment complexes), and fresh meat, fish, and produce in nearby wet markets. In preparation for Chinese New Year, parents might take their children to department stores that specialized in goods from Mainland China to buy new clothes and shoes, and festival foods (H-W. Wong 2003: 137), but this type of expenditure was reserved for special occasions. As sociologist Tai-Lok Lui (2001) puts it, "Shopping and consumption, beyond the purchase of daily necessities, were associated with a lifestyle beyond the reach of ordinary people" (Lui 2001: 30).

While the food items offered on Daimaru's supermarket shelves might still have represented an unthinkable luxury for most Hong Kongers in the 1960s, there was one Japanese food-related product in the store that was making an impact. The National rice cooker embodied the aspirations of a burgeoning Hong Kong middle class for a better quality of life. In Japan, the rice cooker's success was overshadowed by that of the "Three Sacred Treasures"—the black-and-white television, washing machine, and refrigerator emblematic of the American lifestyle that they saw featured in comic strips. They were considered the true icons of modern Japanese living, and the rice cooker was perceived as a minor, though useful, appliance targeted at *okusan-yōhin* (housewives). By contrast, in 1960s Hong Kong, the National-brand rice cooker was held in much higher regard; it was a product whose acquisition evoked the feeling that "we are not that poor any more" (Nakano 2009: 1–15).

In 1960, the number of National rice cookers imported into Hong Kong stood at just 100 a year; seven years later, in 1967, annual sales had increased to over 100,000. By the time the colonial government made primary school education compulsory in 1971, the Japanese rice cooker had become a standard appliance in most Hong Kong homes. In the 1970s, refrigerators took over from Japanese rice cookers as a mark of social status. Hong Kong families often placed their newly acquired refrigerator in the living room to show it off to their visitors (Nakano 2009:10–1). But these Japanese kitchen appliances rarely cooked or stored Japanese food, and several decades were to elapse before they were likely to do so.

Culinary adventure and Hong Kong's middle class

Japanese food began to make a real impact in Hong Kong when a new middle class emerged in the 1980s. As the manufacturing industry propelled Hong Kong's economy forward in the 1970s, the daily lives of the colony's working class started to change dramatically (Tsang 2004: 161–79). In fact, many of the factory owners and investors were Japanese, and the number of Japanese residents in the territory increased sixfold, from 1,156 in 1969 to 7,049 in 1979 (HKJC 2006: 71). Along with this increase, the number of Japanese restaurants also surged. However, this led to fierce competition, with restaurants vying not only for Japanese customers but also trained chefs—both Japanese and Chinese—whose numbers in the territory were severely limited. This situation led Japanese restaurant owners and their local, Hong Kong suppliers to establish *Honkon Nihon Ryōriten*

Kyōkai (Hong Kong Japanese Restaurants Association) in 1979 (HKJRA 2005: 23–4). One of its founding members was the very Frankie Wu whose career had started at Daimaru in 1960. By the late 1970s, Wu had invested in two Japanese restaurants that were positioned to attract an affluent Hong Kong Chinese clientele. He urged his fellow Association members to consider expanding its customer base from the territory's 7,000 Japanese expatriates to its 5,000,000 residents:

> I suggested [to my Japanese colleagues in the Association] that "we should not limit our customers to Japanese salarymen stationed in Hong Kong. Let's not compete with each other, but instead expand the pie for Japanese food." … If we serve good food, many Hong Kong people will come too.
>
> (NNA 2009)

Taking his cue from other Chinese entrepreneurs involved in the promotion of Japanese goods in Asia, Wu developed the market for Japanese haute cuisine by making the most of his versatile linguistic skills, cultural awareness, and ability to capitalize on transnational networks. Born in Beijing, he moved to Tokyo when he was four years old and received a Japanese university education before coming to Hong Kong. He honed his business skills while working for Hong Kong Daimaru, and further expanded his network during his over ten years with Cathay Pacific Airways. In addition to his native Mandarin, he speaks fluent Japanese, Cantonese, and English, and moves effortlessly in business and social circles, acting as an effective intermediary between Hong Kong and Japan. He was one of the first Chinese to run a successful Japanese restaurant keyed to the local population. At his Ozeki chain of restaurants, he lowered the cost of Japanese haute cuisine through localization—engaging local cooks under the supervision of a single Japanese head chef and employing local Cantonese-speaking waitresses who, unlike Japanese waitresses, were able to explain the menu to local patrons.

In 1981, Wu introduced Hong Kong's favorite dining style—the lunch buffet— to his Japanese restaurant, offering a spread of Japanese food at the bargain price of HK$85 (US$11) every Sunday (*Sing Tao Tour Magazine* 1981). The meal started with a sumptuous appetizer buffet that featured raw oysters rather than sashimi, which was both more costly and not yet popular with Hong Kongers. This was followed by a *teppan-yaki* grill, which, by then, was already a well-established subcategory of Japanese dining in the United States (Ishige *et al.* 1985: 227–38); see Figure 6.3. *Teppan-yaki* chefs cooked beef, shrimp, and vegetables in front of their customers with the theatrical effects made famous by John Belushi in his late 1970s *Saturday Night Live* skit. In Hong Kong, some Japanese master chefs questioned Wu's efforts to localize the Japanese restaurant business. But as he predicted, well-heeled Hong Kongers began to venture into his restaurants in increasing numbers (interview with Frankie Wu, Hong Kong, March 26 and November 22, 2012).

In 1984, the colony's public broadcaster RTHK produced a program entitled, "The Japanese Influence." The documentary argued that the growing influence

Figure 6.3 Ozeki restaurant advertisement featuring Teppan-yaki grill counters, circa 1981

of Japanese food on the lifestyle choices of Hong Kongers was not occurring in a vacuum but was rather indicative of the strong presence of Japanese investment in the territory and the popularity of Japanese products such as electric appliances, *anime* and *manga*, and teenage idols like Masahiko Kondo and Akina Nakamori. The program also pointed to a growing number of Hong Kong tourists who had experienced Japanese food during their trips to Japan:

> Japanese food was more expensive than other foods in Hong Kong, because most of its ingredients had to be transported to Hong Kong by plane. And its sweet flavor didn't appeal to local tastes, but recently the price of Japanese food has become more or less the same as other foods. And because more Hong Kong people have been to Japan on holidays, they have grown to accept Japanese food. … Today, the Japanese restaurant business is expanding fast in Hong Kong. When this restaurant [Yamato] was first set up [in the early 1970s], there were only five Japanese restaurants in town; at the end of last year [1983], there were already thirty-four.
>
> (RTHK 1984)

Indeed, the number of visitors from Hong Kong to Japan jumped from 18,641 in 1974 to 55,542 in 1984, but this still represented just 1 percent of the population (JNTO 2008: 165). The territory's 34 Japanese restaurants barely figured on the dining landscape of an emerging middle class whose children were consumers of *anime, manga,* and teenage pop star memorabilia. It was the Japanese supermarket Yaohan, argues anthropologist Dixon Wong, that made Japanese food accessible to a new generation of Hong Kongers born and bred in the territory (H-W. Wong 2006: 164–5).

Yaohan was the first foreign supermarket-cum-department store to venture into Hong Kong's suburban shopping malls—away from the city center where Daimaru and other Japanese department stores had established themselves. The store opened in Shatin in December 1984—ten days before the Sino-British Joint Declaration was signed by British Prime Minister Margaret Thatcher and Chinese Prime Minister Zhao Ziyang—with the slogan, "Yaohan Has Everything You Want; Enjoyment for the Entire Family" (advertisement in *Oriental Daily*, December 9, 1984). Back in the 1970s, under the governorship of Sir Murray MacLehose, the government had embarked on its Ten-Year Housing Program and began development on several new towns built in the New Territories, away from the overpopulated urban areas. By 1985, the New Territories had absorbed 34 percent of Hong Kong's population (Lee 1999: 52). One such development was located in the district of Shatin, which was connected to the Kowloon peninsula by Hong Kong's first tunnel, the Lion Rock Tunnel. In addition to its residential blocks, Shatin New Town featured a giant shopping mall named "New Town Plaza" which was built directly above Shatin train station.

The early 1980s, however, were a time of political uncertainty and anxiety. Those who had fled poverty-stricken villages in China and whose family members had suffered hardship during the Cultural Revolution felt uneasy about their future under a communist regime (Carroll 2007: 196, S.-L. Wong 1997: 69–70). As a result, the developer of New Town Plaza had a hard time filling its retail spaces. Major retailers—local as well as international—were reluctant to take up a three-story shop space. Eventually, Yaohan, a regional Japanese supermarket with international ambitions, was able to secure it for a bargain price (H.-W. Wong 2006: 158–60). Unlike Daimaru, which was a household name, Yaohan was virtually unknown in Japan outside of Shizuoka, despite its branches in Singapore, Costa Rica, and California.

In Hong Kong, as was the case at its stores in California and New Jersey, Yaohan offered neatly packed fresh produce, meat and fish, frozen foods, snacks, and seasonings at an affordable price. Yaohan also introduced Japanese fast food to the territory, with sushi, *tako-yaki* octopus balls, and a Japanese adaptation of French crepes served in its food court. In addition, Yamazaki Bakery sold oven-fresh bread throughout the day, using ingredients that had all been imported from Japan. But one of the major differences between Yaohan's stores in the United States and Hong Kong was their customer base. While the US stores attracted mainly expatriated Asians, Yaohan's Shatin store, and the nine other branches that followed, appealed to Hong Kong's own emerging middle class.

Dixon Wong offers a unique theory on the meaning of shopping at Yaohan for Hong Kong and its people. Wong, a native Hong Konger who witnessed the rise of the modern Hong Kong lifestyle, argues that the shopping experience at Yaohan did not signify the Japanization of Hong Kong, but rather Japanese products and services facilitated the process by which "Chinese people" developed a second identity as "Hong Kong people" (H.-W. Wong 2003: 167–8).

Hong Kong is a city of immigrants, one where, in the mid-1970s, four out of ten of the city's residents had been born on the Chinese mainland. Many elderly people in particular were unwilling to think of Hong Kong as a permanent place of abode, preferring to see it as just a temporary refuge. For those whose parents and siblings remained across the border, Mainland China was still considered home. Hong Kong, however, offered a modern living environment and appealed to a younger generation aspiring to join the ranks of the middle class. The more young people modernized their lifestyles by purchasing Japanese goods, the more they felt they were distancing themselves from being "Chinese" or "mainlanders" and establishing a dual and overlapping identity as "Hong Kongers" (H.-W. Wong 2006: 163–4, see also Nakano 2009: 14–5).

Sushi: globalization of the seafood trade and food tastes

Yaohan supermarket stores operated in Hong Kong from 1984 to 1997, after which they were replaced by JUSCO (now AEON) and Seiyu (now Yata). During this period, Yaohan actively introduced relatively new and affordable ingredients presented in a Japanese cooking style and, in so doing, popularized a localized, Hong Kong version of Japanese food. Salmon sushi is one example of this. Today, when we visit the sushi section at any supermarket in the territory, display counters are overwhelmingly orangey-pink, unlike their counterparts in Japan, which feature a colorful mosaic of red tuna, white flounder, pinkish white prawn, yellow egg, and brown *anago* eel. In Hong Kong, salmon is consistently the most popular variety of fish for sushi and sashimi (Centre for Food Safety 2010: 45). It holds the place that is reserved for tuna in Japan, a staple of Japanese cuisine whose supply is sustained by ever-expanding global networks that link Tokyo's Tsukiji fish market with fishing grounds in Maine, Spain, and Croatia (Bestor 2000, 2004: 148–9).

The Japanese traditionally did not consume salmon raw. There is an age-old sashimi safety tip that goes, "Don't eat river fish raw because it is more likely to carry parasites [than sea fish]." In Japan, salmon, which spends part of its life in fresh water, was considered a river fish and thus unfit for raw consumption. However, in 1985, the Norwegian seafood industry backed by Norway's Fishery Ministry launched "Project Japan." The aims of the campaign were to overcome the Japanese reluctance to eat raw salmon and develop the market for North Atlantic seafood in Japan. The Norwegians organized a massive drive to promote seawater-farmed salmon for sushi, targeting importers, distributors, supermarket chains, and restaurants. Bjørn Eirik Olsen, the former fish attaché to the Norwegian ambassador in Japan who oversaw market research for Project Japan from 1986 to 1991, explains:

> Everybody said 'we do not eat raw salmon. … We had to really fight to introduce salmon into the market. … It took 15 years from when the first salmon went to Japan (in 1980) to the breakthrough for raw consumption in 1995.
>
> (*Nortrade.com* 2011)

By 1995, Norway had succeeded in exporting to Japan more than 5,500 tons of farmed salmon for raw consumption.

Project Japan had a profound impact on the way Hong Kongers defined sushi. When Yaohan opened its Shatin store in 1984, most Hong Kongers had reservations about eating raw fish, since consuming any kind of uncooked food was counter to Chinese food habits. Nonetheless, Yaohan stores set up sushi and sashimi counters in their supermarkets and food courts and started stocking raw Atlantic salmon. Such counters were among the few places where Hong Kong's new middle class had access to affordable sushi (H.-W. Wong 2006: 164).

In this new market for sushi, Atlantic salmon from Norway had a competitive advantage: it was far cheaper than the leanest parts of the popular bluefin tuna. According to the Food and Agriculture Organization of the United Nations' (n.d.) fishery statistics for the late 1980s, for example, Atlantic bluefin tuna from Spain was consistently twice as expensive as Atlantic salmon from Norway. This is because farmed salmon can be bred from fertilized eggs, while tuna can only be raised from young fish that are caught in the wild. By the 1980s, the farming techniques for salmon were well developed, whereas those for tuna were still being perfected at university research labs—an endeavor that continues to this day. These farming practices guaranteed a stable, year-round supply of salmon. Furthermore, the salmon were raised under strict control in marine rather than fresh water, which significantly eased traditional safety concerns. As a result, unlike the Japanese who had to overcome their traditional beliefs about freshwater fish, Hong Kongers did not attach any stigma to raw salmon. Once the fish was harvested, advanced refrigeration allowed it to be transported chilled rather than frozen from Norway to Hong Kong, ensuring better flavor and texture. In addition, the rich taste of Atlantic salmon appealed to Chinese consumers. In Japan, Norwegian producers promoted their salmon to Japanese intermediaries by emphasizing the similarity of its texture to that of prized *toro* (fatty tuna), but for Hong Kong's first-time sushi eaters, salmon sushi was simply tasty.

In this way, raw salmon, which started its journey eastward as a substitute for *toro* in 1980s Japan, became the star of the sushi set in Hong Kong. Yaohan may not have been the first store to introduce raw salmon to the territory's emerging middle class, but it certainly played a significant role in making this particular culinary adventure popular and affordable. Many among the older generation of Japanese still frown upon salmon sushi and sashimi, saying that they are not Japanese. Likewise, many among the older generation of Hong Kongers cannot bear the thought of chomping down on a piece of raw fish. Nevertheless, salmon sushi became a symbol of sophistication for a younger generation of Hong Kongers.

The 1980s sushi boom was not unique to Hong Kong, but rather a worldwide phenomenon. In southern California, for example, the number of sushi restaurants tripled between 1977 and 1980, from 39 outlets to 116, while the overall number of Japanese restaurants only doubled. Consequently, sushi replaced sukiyaki and tempura as the most prominent symbol of Japanese food in Los Angeles (Ishige *et al.* 1985: 131, 203). As the demand for sushi grew outside of Japan, the seafood trade began to expand its transnational networks. Anthropologist Theodore Bestor, writing on the flow of tuna to Tokyo's Tsukiji market, notes that, "Sushi's global popularity as an emblem of a sophisticated cosmopolitan class more or less coincided with a profound transformation in the international role of the Japanese fishing industry" (2000: 57). However, as sushi became more readily available in Hong Kong—a city lying 1,800 miles southwest of Tsukiji—it was not only the international role of the Japanese fishing industry that was evolving: the Norwegian fishing industry also played a significant part in this process. In the following decades, Norwegian raw salmon would go on to define sushi in other cities in Asia.

Ramen and Gyōza: from China to Japan and back again

Hong Kong's economy continued to grow and by 1993 its per capita GDP had surpassed that of its colonial master, the United Kingdom. As the territory's new middle class grew more affluent, Hong Kong entrepreneurs began to invest in Japanese franchise restaurants that served moderately priced food. Hong Kong teenagers, who likewise had more money in their pockets, were to become their biggest customers. In the mid-1990s, these high school students generally headed to American fast food restaurants such as McDonald's, Kentucky Fried Chicken, and Wendy's after class to share snacks and chat with friends. In his edited volume, *Golden Arches East: McDonald's in East Asia*, anthropologist James Watson describes how McDonald's arrival in Hong Kong in 1975 corresponded with the emergence of a new class of affluent consumers in the territory:

> McDonald's take off ... paralleled the rise of a new class of highly educated, affluent consumers who thrive in Hong Kong's ever-changing urban environment. ... These new consumers eat out more often than their parents and have created a huge demand for fast convenient food of all types.
>
> (Watson 2006: 82)

For these Hong Kong teenagers, who had previously eaten their afternoon snacks at family-owned wonton noodle places, McDonald's sold more than food; it offered an "American" experience in "a clean, safe, air-conditioned, and reasonably quiet setting" (Watson 2006: 103). By the 1990s it functioned as a "youth center" for high school students whose afternoon snacks now consisted of hamburgers and fries.

In 1996, 21 years after McDonald's opened its first outlet in Hong Kong, Ajisen Ramen landed in the territory and began serving Japanese-style *ramen* noodles and *gyōza* dumplings, two food items that have their roots in China. In Japan, these "Chinese" dishes, which are often served together, much like hamburgers and french fries, became extremely popular after World War II, especially with working-class men, because they were cheap, fast, and filling (Solt 2014). By the end of the first decade of the twenty-first century, Ajisen Ramen became by far the most successful Japanese franchise restaurant in Greater China. Of its 725 overseas branches, 35 are located in Hong Kong and more than 600 in Mainland China, including three branches in Urumqi, the capital of Xinjiang Uighur

Autonomous Region. In 2010, Ajisen (China) reported net sales of HK$2,681 million (US$343.7 million) (Ajisen Holdings Limited 2010: 5), while in June 2011, the company's annual, reported domestic net sales totaled just ¥2.2 billion (US$27.2 million) (Ajisen Ramen n.d.).

The Ajisen Ramen empire was founded by a Taiwanese immigrant to Japan, Liu Yunxiang. The advent of *ramen* and *gyōza* in Japan is closely tied to mass cross-border mobility propelled by the country's territorial expansion to Taiwan, Manchuria, and China. The 15-year-old Liu arrived in Japan's southern island of Kyushu in 1940 in order to pursue his higher education (Shigemitsu 2010: 16–7). After graduating from the then Kumamoto Technical College (now Kumamoto University) in central Kyushu, Liu started a Chinese noodle manufacturing business under his adopted Japanese name, Takaharu Shigemitsu. When, in 1968, he opened his first *ramen* shop in Kumamoto, it had only eight seats. He eventually became one of the pioneers of Kumamoto-style *ramen* by developing a recipe for *tonkotsu* pork-bone broth that was inspired by that of a popular *ramen* shop in nearby Kurume city and to which he added a Taiwanese twist (Shigemitsu 2010: 19–23, 27–8). His noodles were rather thick and straight, presented in a big bowl, and topped with an egg boiled in broth, crunchy cloud ear mushrooms, and dark fried-garlic sauce. The resulting dish was far removed from the soup noodle dishes that were traditionally served up in China.

What is notable about Ajisen's transnational expansion lies in the fact that it was not initiated by the company's Japanese management; rather, it took a Hong Kong Chinese entrepreneur to fully realize its overseas ambitions (Ng 2006: 303). Twenty-seven year-old Ricky Cheng had become a fan of *ramen* while studying in Japan in the late 1980s, and saw the market potential of these Japanized Chinese noodles. Most Japanese regarded, and continue to regard, *ramen* as "Chinese," because they only became an everyday food item after World War II. Even today, *soba* and *udon* noodles are served at Japanese diplomatic banquets, but not *ramen*, since they are still largely considered to be an imported dish. Perhaps it took a Chinese eye to see that, over the decades, *ramen* had evolved into a distinctly Japanese dish. Cheng found out about Ajisen's franchise operation in Taipei, called up the, by then, 71-year-old Shigemitsu, and proposed forming a partnership to open an Ajisen shop in Hong Kong (Shigemitsu 2010: 71).

It was Cheng who chose the shop's location in one of Asia's most expensive commercial districts. The first Hong Kong Ajisen was located in Causeway Bay, a major shopping destination with four upscale Japanese department stores—Daimaru, Matsuzakaya, Mitsukoshi, and Sogo. The monthly rent for the 60-seat restaurant was HK$170,000 (US$21,800). The company's Japanese management was taken aback by the high rent because a bowl of *ramen* cost just HK$30 (US$3.85) and the shop would have to sell more than 10,000 bowls a month to break even (Shigemitsu 2010: 88). But Cheng's business sense prevailed. Soon after the shop opened in August 1996, a popular Chinese-language weekly, *Next Magazine* (1996), reported that Ajisen's business hours had been extended until one in the morning because the customers "kept coming in droves," and advised its readers to arrive after 10 p.m. to avoid queues. Young Hong Kongers flocked to get a taste of these new "Japanese-style" soup noodles, undeterred by the fact that the Japanese themselves actually considered the dish to be Chinese.

Many Hong Kong teenagers were aware that *ramen* and *gyōza* were different from the noodles and dumplings that were served in Hong Kong through their exposure to Japanese television programs, which were screened on local channels and widely available on pirated disks. Since the 1970s, Japanese *anime* and TV dramas had been dubbed into Cantonese and become mainstream programing. In the 1980s, *manga* comic books were also widely available in Chinese. Japanese *anime, manga*, and TV dramas often featured scenes of everyday life in Japan, including depictions of food and mealtimes. One such example is the 1996 TV drama *Long Vacation*, which proved a phenomenal success with the younger generation in Japan; in 1997, pirated versions of the series on VCD (a lower-resolution cousin of the DVD) made it a cult hit in Hong Kong (Iwabuchi 2004, Nakano 2002). In practically every episode, heartthrob Takuya Kimura could be seen venturing to a neighborhood Chinese restaurant for dinner and eating *ramen* noodles out of a far bigger bowl than the one customarily used for wonton noodles in Hong Kong. The show raised curiosity about *ramen* among young Hong Kongers—especially women, who wondered what Kimura's favorite noodles tasted like.

Separately, starting in 1988, Hong Kong's most popular Chinese-language channel, TVB Jade, began screening a series of *anime* programs that featured talented chefs, such as *Mister Ajikko, OH! My Konbu*, and *Cooking Papa*. Just like the popular, live-action cooking show *Iron Chef*, many of these *anime* stories revolved around challenges and battles, turning the cooking process into entertainment. By watching these shows, Hong Kong children became familiar with the types of ingredients used by Japanese chefs and how they seasoned their broth and chopped their vegetables. In this way, Hong Kong teenagers learned more about Japanese cuisine through their consumption of popular culture than they did through their actual consumption of Japanese food. Eventually, however, armed with this visual knowledge of Japanese culinary habits, young Hong Kongers ventured into Ajisen, and similar, moderately priced Japanese eateries, to experience what they had seen on screen.

Ajisen Ramen significantly lowered the average age of Japanese food consumers in Hong Kong. In the mid-1990s, the territory's Japanese restaurants were still serving predominately haute cuisine, such as tempura, sukiyaki, and sushi, all of which had acquired the label of "traditionally Japanese food."[8] Although some of these restaurants listed *ramen* and *gyōza* on their menu, they were almost afterthoughts (HKJRA 2005: 32). One precursor to *ramen* was Japanese instant noodles. These were invented by another Taiwanese immigrant to Japan, Wu Baifu, who is better known by his Japanese name of Momofuku Ando. His company, Nissin Foods, which is responsible for Top Ramen and Cup Noodles, introduced the Demae Iccho brand to Japan in 1968 and to Hong Kong a year later. Instant noodles topped with ham or spam and a fried egg soon became an extremely popular breakfast item at the local *cha chaan teng* diners, which served an eclectic mix of affordable food. But *ramen* with freshly made noodles and soup were beyond the means of ordinary schoolchildren. The arrival of Ajisen Ramen in 1996, which offered a bowl of *ramen* for less than US$4, soon attracted a loyal following among high school students who had previously spent their afternoon hours in American fast food chains. Joyce Leung, who was a high school student in 1997, recalls that when she went to Ajisen, she usually spent HK$40 to 60 (US$5.1 to 7.7) sharing a big bowl of noodles and side dishes with her classmates:

> Eating at Ajisen Ramen was slightly pricier, when compared to McDonald's meals which were all under HK$20 and wonton noodles which were around HK$10 to HK$20 something only. … My classmates and I usually ordered some *ramen* noodles and other appetizers such as sushi, *gyōza*, stuffed chicken wings, deep-fried chicken gristle, and salad and shared among us. … To me, Ajisen Ramen offered a new kind of food, because it served hot meals with good visual presentation and always came with a cup of green tea. And the unlimited—and free—tea refilling service did keep us there eating and chatting longer and longer. Besides, it was a new kind of place because after adding Ajisen Ramen to our list of eateries, we did not have to always stick to local noodle shops, American fast food shops, bakeries, and sandwich places for chitchat. We had one more option to choose from.
>
> (E-mail interview, January 27, 2012)

As had been the case with McDonald's, for these Hong Kong high school students Ajisen was more than a place to fill an empty stomach. The aesthetic presentation of its dishes, clean tables and utensils, bowls and plates sporting stylish patterns, the red apron and bandana worn by its waiters and waitresses, and the unlimited green tea refill service all contributed to a novel experience for these young Hong Kongers.

The popularity of *ramen* meant that *gyōza*, which were often ordered as an accompaniment and were themselves a Japanese adaptation of *jiaozi* dumplings from Manchuria, also became fashionable. *Jiaozi* were not an original feature of southern Chinese cuisine, but Hong Kong had plenty of *jiaozi* eateries that were run by immigrants from Beijing and Shandong. Although tasty and affordable, Hong Kongers considered the boiled dumplings—with their fatty, minced pork filling and chewy dough—"heavy" and "fattening." A typical *jiaozi* restaurant had no décor to speak of; customers were seated on plastic stools and the wait staff usually consisted of middle-aged men and women from northeastern China. By contrast, the *gyōza* dumplings served by Ajisen were smaller in size, encased in a thinly rolled skin and pan-fried until a golden crust formed on the bottom. Young Hong Kongers found *gyōza* lighter than *jiaozi*, and they began to order them as a snack or side dish rather than as a main. It was not only the taste of crispy *gyōza* that appealed to Hong Kongers, but also the stylish presentation that set them apart from *jiaozi*. Ajisen's *ramen* and *gyōza* added a touch of class and exoticism to the more prosaic noodle and dumpling, and Hong Kong's high school students began eating their way to cosmopolitan sophistication.

Eating one's way to cosmopolitan sophistication

In the 1990s, young Hong Kongers began to cross borders more frequently, thereby expanding their culinary horizons. Their travel destinations became more varied: in addition to the obligatory visits to see their relatives in Mainland China, they now undertook leisure trips to Thailand, Taiwan, and Japan, often on group tours. Having grown up with Japanese *anime, manga,* and TV dramas, the younger generation found the idea of a five-day tour package to Tokyo, Kyushu, and Hokkaido attractive. It was also more affordable. The number of Japanese tourists to Hong Kong had increased dramatically before the 1997 handover, but had suffered a significant drop immediately afterwards. Airlines were therefore eager to fill their seats, and this caused cut-throat competition among Hong Kong tour agencies, all desperate for local business (Shiozawa 2001: 44). As a result, Japan became a posh, yet accessible, dining and shopping destination for Hong Kongers. The number of annual visitors from Hong Kong to Japan, which hovered around 150,000 in the early 1990s, grew rapidly, reaching 250,000 in 1997, 500,000 in 2008, and 745,800 in 2013 (JNTO 2008, 2011, 2014). A number equivalent to approximately 10 percent of all Hong Kong residents visited Japan in 2013; and most consumed Japanese food more than once during their stay. Since 1996, Hong Kong has consistently ranked in the top five sources of visitors to Japan, after South Korea, Taiwan, China, and the United States, each of which has a far larger population than the territory. It is probably safe to say that Hong Kong has the highest concentration of non-Japanese people who have sampled Japanese food in Japan.

In fact, eating Japanese food is a highlight for Hong Kong tourists. Their source of restaurant information goes far beyond the Michelin guides for Tokyo or Osaka. Hong Kong's local magazines, television and radio programs, and even infotainment on double-decker buses, constantly feature dishes from popular restaurants in Japan as if these establishments were located in a neighboring suburb rather than a four-hour plane ride away. Wherever possible, Hong Kongers go for Japanese food that is not offered in the territory and available at a bargain price. They queue outside the hottest *ramen* places in Tokyo, Sapporo, and Fukuoka. They head to Tsukiji fish market to sample fresh cuts of tuna, *uni* sea urchin, and *amaebi* shrimps. They fly to Hokkaido for juicy *kegani* crabs. They hit the food halls of department stores after 6 p.m. to buy marked-down assortments of sushi and other delicatessen items. When Hong Kongers head home, they take advantage of the territory's liberal import policy and hand-carry boxes of Japanese strawberries, peaches, and grapes.

But the Hong Kongers' Japanese culinary adventure is not limited to *ramen,* raw seafood, and fruit. They also buy food items from around the world that the Japanese have adapted and reinvented, and given their own twist too; these include food products that originated in Europe, long held as a model of cosmopolitan sophistication by the Japanese. Just like *ramen* and *gyōza,* Japanized European food, particularly sweets and snacks, is making its way to Hong Kong as "Japanese food." Hong Kongers stand in line at bakeries in Tokyo or Osaka for freshly baked *baumkuchen*, a layered ring cake that was introduced to Japan by German prisoner-of-war, Karl Joseph Wilhelm Juchheim, who was captured in Qingdao, China, in 1915 (Juchheim n.d.). Nearly a century later, *baumkuchen* is far more popular in Japan than in its native Germany, especially since 2007 when a deluxe version with select ingredients became a hit at the renovated Daimaru Tokyo. Young Hong Kongers think of *baumkuchen* as Japanese, not German.[9]

Another example is a Japanese adaptation of the French *langue de chat* cookie with white chocolate called *Shiroi Koibito* (White Love), which is a favorite gift item with Hong Kong tourists. Since 1976, the luxury cookies have been produced in Sapporo and are marketed predominantly in Hokkaido as part of its branding exercise—few downtown Tokyo stores carry them other than during special Hokkaido fairs. However, over the last 15 years the cookies have become so popular with Hong Kong and Taiwanese tourists that stacks of their gift boxes are found at 12 locations in Tokyo Narita International Airport, ready for sale (Ishiya. n.d.). Another Hokkaido brand that tourism has turned into a household name in Hong Kong is ROYCE', which is known for its velvety "raw chocolate." The company has gone even further with the opening of sales counters at Hong Kong's most successful high-end supermarket chain, city'super, in 2002 (ROYCE' n.d.).

Japanese residents in the territory came up with the city'super concept in the 1990s to cater to Hong Kong's changing lifestyle. The upmarket megastore specifically targets the growing number of upper-middle- and upper-class Hong Kongers with its wares sourced from around the world but showcased with a distinctive Japanese flavor. It stock-keeps 15,000 units of gourmet food, wine, and kitchenware, and 12,000 units of stationery, personal care products, and household goods. The first city'super opened its doors in December 1996 in the 43,000 sq. ft. (3,994 m²) basement of a luxury shopping mall in Causeway Bay. It was headed up by Masashi Ishikawa, the former store manager of Seibu Hong Kong, a Japanese department store that had operated in the territory since 1990. When, in 1996, Seibu's Tokyo management made the decision to sell the Hong Kong operating rights to entrepreneur Dickson Poon, Ishikawa left the company along with six other Japanese staff members. Together, they began to plan a new store based on their years of retail experience in Hong Kong (interview with Masaaki Ogino, Hong Kong, March 13, 2012).

Japanese department stores in Hong Kong had often struggled to find the right target market, and due to Causeway Bay's soaring rents, Daimaru, Matsuzakaya, and Mitsukoshi would all eventually close down their operations in Hong Kong; only Sogo would remain, in name, after selling its operating rights to a Hong Kong corporation. But Ishikawa and his team had a clear target: products at city'super were to be visibly high end, showcased in a stylish and sleek setting, with Stan Getz or Miles Davis playing in the background. They aimed to not only cater to Hong Kongers daily needs but also "enhance the quality of their lives" by helping them fulfill their aspirations (city'super n.d.). Seeking financial support for the project, Ishikawa turned to Japanese fashion entrepreneur Masaaki Ogino, who had been based in Hong Kong since 1966, manufacturing and exporting high-end knitwear mainly to Japan. In 1986 he had brought Hong

Kong's first Prada boutique to the Peninsula Hotel, and in 1993 financed the luxury brand Anteprima, which would become famous for the woven wirebags designed by his wife Izumi (NNA 2001). After listening to Ishikawa's presentation, Ogino fell in love with the idea of targeting the territory's "middle-to upper-class" and agreed to inject ¥500 million (approximately US$4.5 million) into the city'super project in 1996 (interview with Masaaki Ogino, Hong Kong, November 28, 2011).

The result is a transnational supermarket that carries "traditional" Japanese food alongside items that appeal to sophisticated cosmopolitan consumers. City'super carries salmon and tuna sashimi, a variety of Japanese curry sauce, and an extensive selection of fresh produce, including prized *amaou* strawberries. It houses a Japanese-French bakery, a patisserie and deli, and a food court that offers a mix of a dozen international cuisines, including ramen. It also carries a large selection of wines, cheeses, olive oils, oysters, and prosciutto ham. Ishikawa would tell his buyers, "Bring the best products from around the world. Don't be tempted by the cheap and affordable" (interview with Masaaki Ogino, Hong Kong, March 13, 2012). The formula worked so well in Hong Kong that city'super would add three more megastores between 1996 and 2005. The fourth and latest store is in Shatin's New Town Plaza, the shopping mall where Yaohan supermarket first made an impact in 1984 on Hong Kong's emerging middle-class. Anthropologist Sidney Mintz reminds us that eating a particular food is not only a fulfilling experience but also "a form of self-identification and of communication" (Mintz 1996: 13). Young Hong Kongers are adventurous eaters and over the past two decades they have been eating their way to a transnationally indexed sophistication. The consumption of "Japanese" food contributed to the defining of this new Hong Kong middle class and distinct Hong Kong identity.

However, there is one more twist to the story. City'super's version of sophistication is crossing borders again, and making its way to other Chinese cities via Hong Kong. There are currently six city'super stores in Taiwan and two in Shanghai. One more store is set to open in Shanghai in 2014. By the time Norwegian salmon makes its way to the city'super store in Shanghai and combines with rice to become sushi, it will no longer be possible to tell whose sophistication its Chinese consumers aspire to.

Notes

1 The research described in this chapter was supported by a grant from the Research Grants Council of the Hong Kong Special Administrative Region, China (Project No. HKU 750711H). I greatly benefited from editorial advice from Georgina Challen and Andrew McNaughton. I would also like to thank Janet Boland, Kota Ohashi, and Elizabeth Sinn for their insights.

2 These categories include restaurants that have since closed down, as the site does not indicate the status of restaurants for categories with entries exceeding 500.

3 The consumption of Japanese snacks is a favorite research topic among Hong Kong students for their term papers. In their on-line surveys collecting impressions of Japanese snacks, adjectives such as "refined," "expensive," "delicious," "trendy," "high quality," and "cute" come to the fore. See, for example, www.my3q.com/research/penguin_jas/70908.phtml (accessed March 2012).

4 The Imperial Hotel in Hong Kong has no relationship with the Imperial Hotel in Hibiya, Tokyo.
5 Shin Osaka Hotel became Osaka Royal Hotel in 1965.
6 Daimaru Advertisement in *Wah Kiu Yat Po* [Overseas Chinese Daily], October 4, 1960. In its coffee shop Daimaru served Japanized Italian pasta and other Western light fare.
7 Daimaru advertisement in the *South China Morning Post*, December 28, 1966.
8 In fact, traditional Japanese food often reflects foreign influences. For example, tempura, the undisputed star at Japanese restaurants in the territory since 1960, is an adaptation of the deep-fried dishes of Portuguese missionaries in the sixeenth century (Harada 2005: 140–2).
9 Sogo Hong Kong, a Japanese-style department store now owned by a Hong Kong company, Lifestyle International Holdings Limited, introduced a sales counter for baumkuchen in its basement in March 2012.

References

Bestor, T C. 2000. How Sushi Went Global. *Foreign Policy* 121 (Nov/Dec): 54–63.
——2004. *Tsukiji: The Fish Market at the Center of the World.* Berkeley: University of California Press.
Carroll, J. M. 2007. *A Concise History of Hong Kong.* Hong Kong: Hong Kong University Press.
Centre for Food Safety. 2010. *Hong Kong Population-Based Food Consumption Survey 2005–2007 Final Report.* The Food and Environmental Hygiene Department of the Government of the Hong Kong, SAR. Available at: www.cfs.gov.hk/english/programme/programme_firm/files/FCS_final_report.pdf (accessed February 2012).
Consulate General of Japan, Hong Kong, 2013. Honkon Sōryōjikan Kankatsu-nai Hōjinsū [Japanese Nationals in Hong Kong]. Available at: www.hk.emb-japan.go.jp/jp/docs/houjin_statistics.pdf (accessed May 2014).
Cwiertka, K. J. 2006. *Modern Japanese Cuisine: Food, Power, and National Identity.* London: Reaktion.
Cwiertka, K. J. and M. Yasuhara. 2010. Beyond Hunger: Grocery Shopping, Cooking, and Eating in 1940s Japan. In *Japanese Foodways, Past, and Present*, E. C. Rath and S. Assmann, eds. Urbana: University of Illinois Press.
Daimaru. 1967. *Daimaru Nihyakugojyūnen-shi* [Daimaru 250 Year History]. Osaka.
Food and Agriculture Organization of the United Nations. n.d. FishStat Plus. Available at: www.fao.org/fishery/statistics/software/fishstat/en (accessed February 2012).
Harada, N. 2005. *Washoku to Nihon Bunka: Nihon Ryōri no Shakai-shi* [Traditional Food and Japanese Culture: Social History of Japanese Cuisine]. Tokyo: Shogakukan.
Hong Kong Japanese Restaurants Association (HKJRA). 2005. *Nijyūgo-shū-nen-kinenshi* [A Twenty-five-year History]. Hong Kong.
Hongkong Japanese Club (HKJC). 2006. *Honkon Nihon-jin Shakai no Rekishi* [A History of the Japanese Community in Hong Kong]. Hong Kong.
Ishige, N. 2001. *The History and Culture of Japanese Food.* London: Kegan Paul.
Ishige, N., S. Koyama, M. Yamaguchi, and S. Ekuan.1985. *Rosu Anjerusu no Nihonryori-ten: Sono Bunkajinruigakuteki Kenkyū* [Japanese Restaurants in Los Angeles: Cultural Anthropological Research]. Tokyo: Domesu Shuppan.
Iwabuchi, K., ed. 2004. *Feeling Asian Modernities: Transnational Consumption of Japanese TV Dramas.* Hong Kong: Hong Kong University Press.
Japan External Trade Organization (JETRO). 2002. Nōrinsuisanbutsu Bōeki Enkatuka Suishin Jigyō: Nihonshokuhin Yushutsu Sokushin Seminar Jisshi Hōkokusho [Report on a Seminar Aimed at Promoting Exports of Japanese Food Products Under the Earmarked Project to Promote Trades of Agricultural and Marine Products]. Tokyo.

——2012. *Honkon Shōhisha no Nihon Shokuhin ni Taisuru Ishikichōsa Hōkoku-sho* [Report on a Hong Kong Consumer Survey on Japanese Food]. Available at: www.jetro.go.jp/world/asia/hk/reports/07000835 (accessed March 2012).

Japan National Tourism Organization (JNTO). 2008. *Hōnichi Ryokō Yūchi Handobukku Sōgōhen 2007–2008* [Handbook for Further Promotion of Inbound Tourism to Japan]. Tokyo.

——2011. "Visit Japan" Jigyō Kaishi-Iraiikou no Hōnichi-kyaku no Suii [Statistics on Inbound Visitors Since the Launch of the "Visit Japan" Campaign]. Available at: www.jnto.go.jp/jpn/downloads/vjc2003_2010.pdf (accessed March 2012).

——2014. Press Release: Visitor Arrivals for December 2013. Available at: www.jnto.go.jp/jpn/news/data_info_listing/pdf/pdf/140117_monthly.pdf (accessed May 2014).

Lee, J. Z. 1999. *Housing, Home Ownership, and Social Change in Hong Kong*. Aldershot: Ashgate.

Lui, T-L. 2001. The Malling of Hong Kong. In *Consuming Hong Kong*, G. Mathews and T-L. Lui, eds. Hong Kong: Hong Kong University Press.

Ministry of Agriculture, Forestry, and Fisheries of Japan (MAFF). 2007. Kaigai Nihonshoku Resututoran Suishō ni Tsuite [Recommendations for Japanese Restaurants Outside of Japan] (also in English). Available at: www.maff.go.jp/j/shokusan/sanki/easia/e_sesaku/japanese_food/index.html (accessed April 2012).

——2014. *Nōrinsuisanbutu Yushutunyu Gaikyō 2013* [An Overview of International Trade: Agricultural, Forestry, and Fishery Products, 2013]. Available at: www.maff.go.jp/j/tokei/kouhyou/kokusai/pdf/yusyutu_gaikyo_13.pdf (accessed May 2014).

Mintz, S. 1996. *Tasting Food, Tasting Freedom: Excursions into Eating, Culture, and the Past*. Boston, MA: Beacon Press.

Nakano, Y. 2002. Who Initiates a Global Flow? Japanese Pop Culture in Asia. *Visual Communication* 1(2): 229–53.

——2009. *Where There Are Asians, There Are Rice Cookers: How "National" Went Global via Hong Kong*. Hong Kong: Hong Kong University Press.

Next Magazine. 1996. La Mian mi Ling [Ramen, Secret Order]. August 16.

Ng, W-M. 2006. Imaging and Consuming Japanese Food in Hong Kong, SAR, China: A Study of Culinary Domestication and Hybridization. *Asian Profile* 34 (4): 299–308.

NNA. 2001. Ajia Nihon-jin Gunzō: Ogino Maaki San, Honkon [Japanese in Asia: Mr. Masaaki Ogino, Hong Kong]. Available at: http://nna.jp/free/interview/gunzou/gunzou10.html (accessed May 2014).

——2009. Honkon VIP Intabyū: Go Ho-shun San [Interviews with VIPs in Hong Kong: Mr. Frankie Wu]. Available at: http://nna.jp/free/interview/040709_hkg/key_person 41.html (accessed April 2011).

Nortrade.com, 2011. Norway's Introduction of Salmon Sushi to Japan. The Norwegian Trade Portal. Available at: www.nortrade.com/sectors/articles/norways-introduction-of-salmon-sushi-to-japan/ (accessed April 2011).

RTHK. 1984. *Hong Kong Connection: The Japanese Influence*. July 30.

Shigemitsu, K. 2010. *Chūgoku de Ichiban Seikoushiteiru Nihon no Gaishoku-cheen wa Kumamoto no Chiisama Rāmen-ya Datte Shittemasuka?* [Do You Know that the Most Successful Japanese Restaurant Chain in China Started from a Small *Ramen* Eatery in Kumamoto?] Tokyo: Diamond-sha.

Shiozawa, I. 2001. Chūgoku Henkan-go no Honkon no Ryokō Shijyō Bunseki to Hōnichi Ryokō ni Kansuru Kōsatsu [Analysis of the Hong Kong Tourism Market After the Handover to China and Observations Regarding Hong Kong Travelers to Japan]. *Osaka Meijyō University Bulletin* 1: 39–50.

Shiraishi, T. 2000. *Umi no Teikoku* [Maritime Empire]. Tokyo: Chukyo Shinsho.

Sing Tao Tour Magazine. 1981. Wo Sou Chiguo de Riben Liaoli [Japanese Food that I have Tried].

Solt, George. 2014. *The Untold History of Ramen: How Political Crisis in Japan Spawned a Global Food Craze.* Berkeley: University of California Press.

South China Morning Post. 2011. 25pc of City's Japanese Restaurants May Go Bust. April 4.

Tateishi, Y. 1997. *Sanwa Ginkō Honkon Shiten* [Sanwa Bank Hong Kong Branch]. Tokyo: Kodansha.

Tsang, S. 2004. *A Modern History of Hong Kong.* Hong Kong: Hong Kong University Press.

Watson, J. L., ed. 2006. *Golden Arches East: McDonald's in East Asia* (second edition). Stanford, CA: Stanford University Press.

Wong, H-W. 2003. 1970 zhi 1980 Niandai de Xinxing–Chengzhang yu Fazhan [Shun Hing in the 1970s and 1980s: Growth and Development]. In *You le Sheng Pai "Dian Fan Bao" Er qi* [Selling Japan in Hong Kong], K. Refsing, Y. Nakano, and H.-W. Wong, eds. Hong Kong: Hong Kong University Press.

——2006. *Ba Bai Ban de Jue qi yu Xiang Gan She Hui Bian Qian* [The Success of Yaohan and the Social Changes of Hong Kong]. In *Ribenwenhua zai Xianggan* [Japanese Culture in Hong Kong], P.-T. Lee, ed. Hong Kong: Hong Kong University Press.

Wong, S-L. 1997. Issues Paper from Hong Kong. In *Migration Issues in the Asia Pacific*, P. Brownlee and C. Mitchell, eds. Wollongong, NSW: APMRN Secretariat.

Company websites

AEON Stores (Hong Kong). n.d. Available at: www.aeonstores.com.hk/ (accessed May 2014).

Ajisen Holdings Limited (China). 2010. *Annual Report 2010.* Available at: http://202.66.146.82/listco/hk/ajisen/annual/2010/ar2010.pdf (accessed March 2012).

Ajisen Ramen (Japan). n.d. Available at: www.aji1000.co.jp/ (accessed February 2012).

city'super. n.d. Available at: www.citysuper.com.hk/corp_profile.php (accessed February 2012).

Ishiya. n.d. Available at: www.ishiya.co.jp/ (accessed May 2014).

Juchheim. n.d. The History of Juchheim. Available at: www.juchheim.co.jp/company/history/ (accessed May 2014).

Okashi Land. n.d. Available at: www.okashiland.com/ (accessed May 2014).

ROYCE'. n.d. Available at: www.royce.com/contents/english_shop/ (accessed May 2014).

Yamazaki Bakery. n.d. Available at: www.yamazaki.hk/ (accessed May 2014).

7 Immigration, nationhood, and transnationalization in industrialized East Asia

John D. Skrentny and Jack Jin Gary Lee[1]

Long known for emigration, the industrialized states of East Asia have begun to play a significant new role in the world as destinations for immigration. The East Asian approaches to immigration, however, have some notable features, with transnational regional effects. Focusing primarily on Japan and South Korea but making comparisons with other industrialized countries as well, we identify three key dynamics in this process.

First, we show the role of migrant labor in increasing transnationalization.[2] The most advanced countries in East Asia are increasingly joining Western countries in their reliance on foreign labor in both low- and high-skilled labor markets. The reliance at the low end is driven by changes in native workforces, which are becoming both smaller and more educated. Notably, however, the low-skilled migration also drives a regional transnationalization, as it remains overwhelmingly intra-Asian and short term. That is, it is very difficult for low-skilled labor migrants to gain permanent residence or citizenship, and visas are invariably of only a few years duration. Lacking family reunification opportunities, these migrants are not likely to settle illegally.

Second, we explore the important role of ethnic return migration in the region. Because it is enabled if not also encouraged by state policy, this migration has important implications for transnationalization in each state. Ethnic return migrants do not easily gain citizenship and most likely see advantages to the lower cost of living in their sending states; this is particularly so in the event of a recession in their host states. Therefore, many if not most return home.

Third, East Asian states have created marital migration as the primary path for low-skilled migrants who are not ethnic return migrants to settle. This has introduced cultural diversity into the intimate setting of family life, as tens of thousands of men, particularly in rural areas, are importing brides from less wealthy Asian countries, particularly Vietnam, the Philippines, and China. However, because these brides cannot bring family members and because they come from poorer countries and have incentives to send remittances home, marital migration also brings a transnational regional dynamic to several East Asian states. Drawing on Oishi's (2005) scholarship on the labor migration of women, we propose that this phenomenon has helped to establish a "culture of migration" within sending communities, whereby local marriage and labor markets in both sending and receiving states are shaped by the prospect of marriage migration. We conclude by highlighting the complex interplay of the nation and the transnational effects created by exclusionary immigration policies in the East Asian region.

Throughout, we show how the transnational dynamics are mostly unintended consequences of Asian immigration policies directed toward preserving social order, minimizing costs, and preserving or strengthening the nation. We make no claim that these processes are unique. States everywhere make immigration policy according to perceived national interests, and patterns of transnationalization are found in other regions, such as Europe and North America, and also across regions. What may distinguish the East Asian patterns of transnationalization are that they result from a less favorable array of rights and freedoms. While all states make immigration policies according to their national interest, they balance these with migrant rights in different ways. Migrants to East Asia face greater structural constraints to their mobility due to the more exclusionary nature of the policies that regulate migrants' families and their settlement. By regulating immigration, policymakers implicitly reveal their understandings of the boundaries of their respective nations and enact conceptions of nationhood (Brubaker 1994, Fitzgerald 1996). Yet they also show their linkages with other states in the region, and their plans for their own preservation and growth. By limiting opportunities for family reunification and settlement, the East Asian immigration policies reveal a fragile and defensive stance toward the nation, as their exclusionary policies aim to forestall "potentially disruptive" cultural diversity.

East Asian states do not succeed in preserving some presumed ethnic homogeneity (as in the cases of Japan and South Korea), nor does their particular mix of ethnicities remain unchallenged (as in the case of Singapore and Taiwan). Immigration is remaking these nations, particularly as thousands of "multicultural children" are born as a result of marital migration. At the same time, the prohibitions on migrant settlement and family reunification give incentives for regional transnationalization as well as regional integration. By structuring the mobility of migrants, state policies facilitate circular migration[3] and, without intending it, foster the acceptance of migration within sending communities. Despite the increasingly complex controls imposed by states, we may thus observe a growing set of transnational dynamics that are reshaping the nation in East Asia.

Low-skilled migrant labor: transnationalization through circular migration

One can discern a protectionist model of nationhood and the consequent incentives for transnationalization in the low-skilled migrant labor policies of Japan and South Korea as well as other industrialized East Asian states. Despite variations, these policies share a basic similarity: they limit migrant workers in ways that are highly protective (relative to Western states) of the fiscal, economic, and social needs of the various Asian host states. Put another way, the rights of migrant workers are very limited. Most notably and distinctively—except in the case of some co-ethnic migrants as discussed in the following section—low-skilled migrants working in Asia are not allowed to settle or bring spouses or children with them. Migrant workers settled or living with children in East Asia are exceptions to the norm.

The lack of settlement opportunities or family reunification rights may have various causes, but the fact that there are opportunities for settlement in Europe and the US as well as the fact that family reunification for spouses and children is taken for granted in Europe and in the US while restricted throughout Asia suggests that policy-makers in Asia do not want to offer these opportunities. No sending state, interest group, or political institution has had the leverage and desire to change what in the short term may be an economically sound policy (Seol and Skrentny 2009a). They protect national labor markets by seeking to minimize migrant workers' stay and, by restricting family entry, they make it less likely that migrant workers will overstay their visas or remain in the country if they lose their job—thus less likely to depress wages of native workers. Moreover, by not admitting the children of migrants, the restriction of family rights protects the state's social welfare outlays and thus also protects taxpayers because impacts on schools and health services are minimized.

Another notable feature of Asian labor migration, particularly in South Korea and Japan, is its expression of ethnic or nationality preferences (Freeman and Mo 1996; more on this, see following section). Many of the migrants who play key roles in the economy in Japan and South Korea are ethnic return migrants, so assessing the national origins actually overstates ethnic diversity (see Table 7.1). For example, in South Korea the most numerous migrant group is made up of Korean Chinese, who typically speak Korean. However, other East Asian states express different national interests in the management of migrants' ethnic or national backgrounds. While Japan and Korea have formulated policies that allow for Japanese and Korean populations in South America and China, respectively, to return and fill low-skilled labor positions, this is not the case in the other major migrant-receiving states like Singapore and Taiwan. For complex reasons related to ethnic preferences and economic ties, the former has adopted a policy approach that admits culturally similar Malaysian workers together with other Asian low-skilled workers from "non-traditional sources" in South and Southeast Asia (Kaur 2006). In contrast, the latter has restricted co-ethnics from mainland China due to political concerns over its sovereignty, relying instead on Southeast Asian workers to fill shortages of low-skilled labor (Tseng 2004). Even without ethnic return migration, the ethnic diversity that labor migration has brought to industrialized Asian states remains bounded by its intra-regional orientation. Migrants from Africa, a major source of migrants to Europe for example, remain very rare. This phenomenon also reflects regional political and economic ties that have shaped the cross-border movement of labor (Seol and Skrentny 2004, Tseng 2004).

Although Japan has always had multiple ethnic groups as a result of its colonial practices (Lie 2001) and also hosts growing numbers of foreigners, it resembles South Korea and not European states in not allowing family reunification and migrant settlement, particularly for low-skilled foreigners (Peach 2003). South

Table 7.1 Migrant origins in East Asia

Japan (2009) 2,186,121		South Korea (2009) 1,168,477		Taiwan (2010) 419,086	
China	680,518 (31.1%)	China (*Joseonjok*)	377,560 (32.3%)	Indonesia	142,849 (34.1%)
N. and S. Korea	578,495 (26.5%)	China	177,522 (15.2%)	Vietnam	86,048 (20.5%)
Brazil (*Nikkeijin*)	267,456 (12.2%)	USA	122,659 (10.5%)	Philippines	73,262 (17.5%)
Philippines	211,716 (9.7%)	Vietnam	90,931 (7.8%)	Thailand	67,442 (16.1%)
Peru (*Nikkeijin*)	57,464 (2.6%)	Japan	47,718 (4.1%)	Japan	10,202 (2.4%)

Sources: Immigration Bureau of Japan 2010a, Korea Immigration Service 2010, National Immigration Agency, Taiwan, Republic of China 2010.

Korea has adopted some of Japan's immigration control policies; for example, Korea's initiation of its "5-year plan against illegal immigration" in 2008 followed a similar plan implemented in Japan from 2003 to 2008 (Korea Immigration Service 2009: 75–6, Shipper 2008: 50). However, unlike South Korea, Japan has maintained its formal policy stance of not admitting low-skilled migrants despite continuing pressure from civil society and major industrial groups (also see Yamanaka 2010).

Japan offers no work permits or visas to low-skilled workers. Foreigners who take up manufacturing, agricultural, or service jobs in Japan come on special visas as industrial "trainees" to work in the Technical Intern Training Program and are not officially workers. Ostensibly, they are in Japan to learn skills valuable to multinational companies that also operate in their homelands. While Japan's admission of trainees as *de facto* "guest workers" may be traced to the Technical Development Plan that the Ministry of Labor adopted in 1971, policy-makers expanded this source of labor in terms of the number of trainees allowed per firm and the number of eligible firms and industries in the early 1990s (Bartram 2005: 115, Shimada 1994: 70). Foreigners on student visas also do low-skilled work in Japan (Liu-Farrer 2011, Shipper 2008).

Furthermore, Japan reserves settlement and family visas for professionals and specialty occupations only (with the exception of family members of ethnic Japanese who had previously emigrated, as discussed in the following section).[4] Not surprisingly, there has been relatively little research published in English on migrant settlement or permanent migrant communities in Japan; scholarship has focused instead on various short-term or isolated migrants such as entertainers, migrant wives, and international students (see, for example, Faier 2009, Liu-Farrer 2011, Parreñas 2010, 2011, Shipper 2002, 2008). One study of "migrants and their children" discusses only the children of migrants who had children with Japanese nationals (Terasawa 2000).

These legal constraints on migrant settlement for low-skilled migrant workers are backed up by a state that has the capacity to enforce its immigration laws. As Shipper (2002) argued, illegal Asian workers "cannot form a permanent community" due to their fear of immigration raids. For instance, he observed that:

> When a close-knit community of several thousand Thais was formed in Tsuchiura-shi in the Ibaraki Prefecture in the early 1990s, the Immigration Office conducted several raids that effectively dissolved the local Thai community. Thereafter, Thais were afraid to come together in large numbers, fearing that they would again be an easy target for raids.
>
> (Shipper 2002: 46)

Similarly, as Seol and Skrentny (2009a: 609) discuss, evidence from field research on international migrants in East Asia reveals how Chinese migrants' awareness of such punitive measures in Japan have shaped their decisions regarding migration with or without authorization, leading some of them to prefer destinations in

Europe over Japan. Such perceptions may be related to the reduction of illegal migration in Japan. Japanese policy-makers noted that the creation of stricter enforcement measures resulted in the steady decrease in illegal migration from a peak of 300,000 in 1993 to 92,000 in 2010 (Ministry of Justice, Japan 2010: 15).

Although officially available, settlement and family visas are also rare in South Korea and, like Japan, mostly involve cases that are not likely to lead to significant migrant settlement. According to Justice Ministry regulations, dependent family visas are available only to certain classes of professionals and specialty occupations, such as artists and athletes, and ethnic Koreans from developed countries. Similarly, permanent resident visas are limited to professionals and specialty occupations with the visa decision ultimately being based on the discretion of the Justice Ministry. Not surprisingly, these individuals are relatively few in number and mostly from developed states.

Low-skilled workers originally came to South Korea as part of the Industrial Technical Training Program (ITTP), which was modeled on Japan's trainee program, and similarly designed to meet low-skilled labor needs. The ITTP restricted the rights and wages of migrant workers so much that many found better opportunities as illegal workers (Seol and Skrentny 2004). To introduce more effective controls on the labor conditions and mobility of foreign workers, Korean policy-makers enacted and began to enforce the Employment Permit System (EPS) Act in 2004 (Seol and Lee 2011). Notably, the Korean state's policy change occurred amidst political contention over the recognition of migrant rights. Yamanaka (2010) argues that Christian churches and other civil society advocates, who had staged intensive public campaigns for the recognition of foreign labor as workers, were instrumental in the replacement of the ITTP, which was finally abolished at the end of 2006, by the EPS. However, except for the few that called for amnesty for undocumented workers, the pro-migrant groups did not press for family reunification or migrant settlement (Seol and Skrentny 2009a: 600–1). According to the EPS Act, low-skilled migrants may come in on a work permit that allows a stay of up to three years and can be extended once, without provision for family unification or settlement (Ministry of Government Legislation, Republic of Korea 2010). Consequently, the number of foreigners holding permanent resident or dependent family member visas is small (relative to Europe) with developed states well represented.

The lack of migrant settlement among the low-skilled in South Korea may be further evidenced by the particular policies that policy-makers have enacted in the face of different policy problems. For instance, the Korean response to the onset of the 1997 Asian financial crisis included an amnesty for undocumented migrant workers in 1998. Rather than allowing legalization opportunities, this amnesty only lifted penalties for visa overstayers to encourage their voluntary repatriation, resulting in the departure of more than 53,000 undocumented workers (roughly one-third of the estimated undocumented population) (Lucas 2005: 242, Seol and Skrentny 2004). This was accompanied by a similarly sharp decrease in the number of foreign trainees in the same period. As Lucas

(2005: 243) observed, labor migration in South Korea offered "considerable flexibility to the host country," since the sharp dip in the stock of undocumented workers and trainees in 1998 was subsequently followed by a rebound in 1999 as economic conditions recovered.

Finally, another way to highlight probable transnational ties from circular migration is with population statistics: the number of foreign children in schools can be an indicator of current or incipient migrant settlement. By this measure, South Korea is not a country of settlement for migrant workers and their families. As Lee (2014: 178–9) reports, in 2010, there were only 1,748 children of migrant workers attending elementary, middle, and high schools in South Korea. While this figure omits most of the children of undocumented migrant workers (less than 20 percent of the over 17,000 children of undocumented migrant workers of school age were enrolled in school in this period), even a high estimate of the total number of children of migrant workers of school age would still be less than 4 percent of the estimated total number of migrant workers (556,746) in 2010. The highly limited settlement of migrant workers and their families may be directly contrasted with the growing presence of marriage migrants and their children in South Korea: there were 30,040 children of international marriages studying in elementary, middle, and high schools, the majority of whom (78.6 percent) were enrolled in elementary schools (Lee 2014: 177).

The numbers from Japan are similar. Japan's Ministry of Education, Culture, Sports, Science and Technology (2011) reported that, in 2010, there were 28,511 foreign children who required special Japanese language instruction in Japanese schools (excluding higher education institutions) in 2010. While this figure does not include foreign children who do not need Japanese language instruction, the latter group includes the children of long-term residents or special permanent residents who are descended from Koreans and Taiwanese displaced during World War II and may not be a sound indicator of migrant settlement as a result (Green 2013: 13). More importantly, the small number of such students relative to the registered foreign population in 2010 (2,134,151) (Immigration Bureau of Japan 2011) suggests that migrants to Japan, like those to Korea, do not bring family members or have children because they do not intend to stay. Instead, they maintain ties with their homelands for eventual return.

While we have stressed the relative lack of settlement by migrant labor and pointed to its implications for the transnational movement of low-skilled persons within Asia, our claim here is not that patterns of transnationalization and regionalism are unique and may not be found in other regions like Europe.[5] Europe's migration patterns clearly reveal regional integration (Van Selm 1999). Our point is that these dynamics are of a different nature to those in Asia and shaped by exclusionary state policies. This corroborates Cornelius and Tsuda (2004: 16), who observe that policy convergence has been occurring on a regional scale. Importantly, despite the restrictions imposed on the settlement of low-skilled labor migrants in East Asia, we observe a set of transnational activities mostly constituted by the circular and regular flows of migrants between sending and receiving nation-states in the region.

Ethnic return migration: transnationalization through "hierarchical nationhood"

East Asian policy-makers have not considered national membership to be coterminous with territory, nor do they consider it to be an equalizing status. Instead, the people of the nation encompass those citizens within the territory, and also co-ethnics who live abroad and are citizens of foreign states and their descendants. When they come to the ancestral homeland as "ethnic return migrants," they do not simply replenish nations—they remake them. This is true because ethnic return migrants have in various mixtures characteristics of both their original sending state and their adopted homelands. At the same time, these differences are exacerbated because neither citizens nor policy-makers typically consider co-ethnic foreigners to be equal to citizens. While immigration policy recognizes these individuals' co-ethnicity, and places them closer to the nation and above foreigners from different backgrounds, it also limits their rights and excludes them from some of the core aspects of membership. These states thus maintain a "hierarchical nationhood" (Seol and Skrentny 2009b) in which policy and public attitudes show both preferences and national closeness but also exclude and maintain a system of unequal membership.

In Japan, the largest group of co-ethnic foreigners, the *Nikkeijin*, is the ethnic Japanese from South America. Japanese emigration to Brazil began in 1908 and continued, interrupted by the world wars, until the 1950s (Herbert 1996). Japan began to receive large numbers of ethnically Japanese return migrants from this region in 1989. Their migration increased rapidly and they numbered about 325,000 in 2010 (see Table 7.1). Most are from Brazil, which is home to about 1.2 million ethnic Japanese. Peru is the next largest sending state, and considerably smaller numbers arrived from Argentina, Paraguay, and Bolivia (Cornelius 1994). The majority are second and third generation, and are consequently culturally Latin American, with limited Japanese speaking ability (Tsuda 2003). Though usually well-educated white collar workers in Latin America, in Japan they typically do blue-collar work, especially in manufacturing, which remains attractive due to wage differentials with their home countries (Cornelius 1994).

Preferential admission policy regarding the *Nikkeijin* began in 1990 (Herbert 1996, Mori 1997). In its revision of Japan's immigration policies in 1990, the Ministry of Justice crafted a residential status that allowed anyone with Japanese ancestry, with no geographical distinctions but up to the third generation, unrestricted access to the Japanese labor market. Japanese ancestry was determined through links to a family registry system, which is common in East Asia. The Justice Ministry began to issue three-year "long-term resident" visas that are renewable and are similar to permanent residency (Cornelius 1994, Yamanaka 1993). As suggested above, the law led to an immediate influx of the *Nikkeijin* and employers began replacing other migrant workers with these ethnic Japanese (Yamanaka 2004). Even though the revised law recognized the *Nikkeijin* as long-term residents by virtue of their familial ties, there were no preferential policies to actively promote their naturalization. Neither were there policies designed to ease adjustment or help to settle the *Nikkeijin*. In 2009, in the context of the global economic downturn and increased unemployment among the *Nikkeijin* and their strained ability to afford housing and education for their children, the Japanese government set up the Council for the Promotion of Measures for Foreign Residents. The Council introduced a set of ameliorative measures including employment assistance, vocational training, housing, and educational support, but also the option of voluntary repatriation (Roberts 2012: 52; for more on this, see concluding section).

The rationale for the overall *Nikkeijin* policy is apparently economic, though official statements imply that other goals are also at stake. While the policy served to supply cheap labor to small and medium-sized companies in Japan, Yamanaka (1993) reports that official documents from 1989 emphasize concerns with forestalling ethnic diversity. The *Nikkeijin* were desirable because policy-makers believed Japanese economic development was aided by its ethnically and linguistically homogenous population. They assumed, according to documents, that the *Nikkeijin* "would be able to assimilate into Japanese society regardless of nationality" (quoted in Yamanaka 1993: 9). Through co-ethnic guest workers, Japan could continue its economic development with minimal social disruption. Policy-makers ignored the fact that the *Nikkeijin* were in fact very different culturally. In this, the policy continued a Japanese tendency to conflate Japanese ethnicity or race with Japanese culture, which justifies the preference for those of Japanese descent, regardless of origins, over those with Japanese culture but of different descent (Lie 2001, Yoshino 1997).

South Korea's ethnic preference policy is more complex than Japan's, though it similarly gives preferences to ethnic Koreans unavailable to other foreigners. The primary overseas Korean communities include the approximately two million *Joseonjok*, ethnic Koreans who live in China, and a smaller group, the *Goryeoin*, who number about 800,000 and are more scattered throughout Russia, Kazakhstan, and Uzbekistan. Koreans have lived in China in large numbers since the late nineteenth century, with most arriving during the Japanese occupation of Korea, 1905–45. As with the *Goryeoin* and a much smaller number of Koreans who went to Hawaii and later California (Schmid 2002), many of the *Joseonjok* were fleeing Japanese oppression or plotting Korean independence. The Japanese also forcibly sent many Koreans to China to cultivate the land (Lee 1986, Piao 1990).

Ethnic Koreans, especially the *Joseonjok*, began to return in the late 1980s. After an initial period of indecision, South Korea avoided giving the *Joseonjok* free access to the labor market comparable to what the *Nikkeijin* enjoy in Japan. In addition, South Korea separated them from ethnic Koreans in the West by creating provisions for the *Joseonjok* to participate in the ITTP (Seol and Skrentny 2004). The government gave the *Joseonjok* the largest quota in the program, separate from other Chinese workers, and originally ordered them to be paid higher wages. Even after the replacement of the ITTP by the EPS in 2007, they remain the largest source of foreign labor and the largest group among undocumented workers.

In 2002, policy-makers created another program for importing *Joseonjok* labor. Under the Employment Management Program for Overseas Ethnic Koreans (*Chuieop Gwanri Jedo*), overseas Koreans over the age of 40 and with family (cousins or closer relatives) in South Korea would receive special two-year visas to work in the labor-starved service industry, especially restaurants, cleaning companies, and nursing facilities (not as nurses, but as "caregivers"); construction was added later. Employers could hire up to ten overseas Koreans provided they showed they could not find workers domestically (Seol and Skrentny 2009b).

Another policy giving preference to foreign co-ethnics came in 1999's "Law of Entry and Status of Overseas Koreans (*Chaeoe dongpo*)," or the Overseas Koreans Act. The law defined *Chaeoe dongpo* as "Korean citizens who live abroad in order to get the citizenship of the resident country and overseas Koreans who had South Korean citizenship in the past and their descendents." This definition excluded both the *Joseonjok* and the *Goryeoin* because they had left the peninsula before the establishment of South Korea. Those classified as *Chaeoe dongpo* were entitled to register as "domestic residents" if they wanted to stay longer than 30 days. This status gave rights that made the *Chaeoe dongpo* almost equal to Korean citizens, such as in banking, owning property, medical insurance, and pensions.[6] On the other hand, the law prohibited the *Chaeoe dongpo* from unskilled manual work. The state's recognition of this transnational linkage aimed to secure economic benefit from the migration of skilled labor of Korean ancestry—there were no cultural or language tests.

The Ministry of Justice, which drafted the law, originally intended it to apply to all overseas Koreans, but this plan faced opposition from outside and inside the South Korean state. First, both Chinese and Russian governments resisted the Korean state's transnational grab, expressing the concern that the law would compromise the loyalty of their *Joseonjok* and *Goryeoin* citizens. Second, some policy-makers feared the economic and social problems that a mass influx of unskilled *Joseonjok* would cause. Third, there was a national security concern that North Korea might use the allowance "as a route for infiltration, thereby causing immediate security threat."[7] After three *Joseonjok* appealed to the Constitutional Court on their exclusion, the National Assembly eliminated the requirement of prior linkage to the South Korean state in 2004. However, because the law retains its prohibitions on unskilled labor, it offers few opportunities for ethnic Koreans in East Asia.

A final Korean policy creating transnational links to co-ethnics abroad deals with North Koreans. The South Korean constitution defines North Koreans as part of its own polity; technically, they are not foreigners at all (Lee 2003). Indeed, the main group of refugees that Korea accepts are those from North Korea,[8] and because of their lack of familiarity with a capitalist economy, they are a burden on the state, requiring extensive settlement packages and adjustment. However, though their numbers are growing, they are still very few (under 25,000 in 2012) (Ministry of Unification, Republic of Korea 2014).

The rationale for co-ethnic preference in South Korean policy appears similar to that of Japan: providing needed labor or skills for economic development with minimal disruption of Korean society and the Korean labor market. The policies all bring economic benefits and at almost no cost. The trainee program was ostensibly for transferring skills to foreign workers, though that rarely happened. According to Lim (2002:19), South Korea preferred *Joseonjok* trainees because they would "pose less of a threat to South Korea's tight-knit, homogenous society." The service-job visa for the *Joseonjok* was also justified as an aid to this group (allowing them opportunities to work in a relatively high-wage economy), but obviously the Korean economy has benefited. The Overseas Koreans Act also stated a nominal "helping" goal by explaining that one of the purposes of the act is to aid ethnic Koreans' adjustment to their countries of residence, and in fact Korean Americans lobbied for it (Park and Chang 2004). However, the law's goals of economic growth through targeted ethnic transnationalism was stated explicitly in several places in the law itself and in the Constitutional Court opinion striking down part of the act's exclusion of the *Joseonjok*. It stated that the law's purpose was "to promote globalization of the Korean society by encouraging more active participation of ethnic Koreans living abroad in all spheres of the Korean society" and that "[t]he Act aims to encourage investment in Korea by simplifying regulations" on business dealings.

In summary, Japan and South Korea promote an ethnic transnationalism by recognizing co-ethnicity across borders and even oceans, and migrants have utilized these opportunities in great numbers. At the same time, limitations on ethnic return migrants' rights encourage them to return home rather than settle. *Joseonjok* and *Nikkeijin* migrants generally do not show the same interest in settling in the ancestral homeland as do ethnic return migrants to Europe, many of whom enjoyed immediate or preferential paths to citizenship (Seol and Skrentny 2009b). Like the *Nikkeijin*, of whom only about 30–40 percent intend to stay in Japan (Kajita 1998: 127, Kuwahara 1998: 371–2), most *Joseonjok* migrants prefer to simply work in South Korea and use those earnings to increase their buying power in China (Choi 2001, Seol and Rhee 2005). They thus engage in circular migration, as do other low-skilled migrants, maintaining ties with their homelands even while remaking their host states.

Marital migration: transnationalization through international marriage

The primary challenge to East Asian nationhood, and another dynamic for regional transnationalization, comes from Asian women who migrate to East Asian states in order to marry men who were not able to find partners domestically. South Korea and Japan, as well as other Asian states such as Taiwan and Singapore, have allowed these often poorly educated young women the right to settle permanently. Though many are actually ethnic return migrants, many are not, and these states have established policies that sacrifice the putative purity of the nation in order to ensure the reproduction of future generations, particularly in rural areas where tradition dictates that the eldest son stays to manage the farm, while women have fled to pursue greater opportunities in the cities.

The terms of marriage migrants' social and political integration have been conditional upon their fulfillment of their roles as wives, mothers, or daughters-in-law of citizens. This has shaped East Asian nations' multicultural transitions, particularly so for those states that have claimed to be mono-ethnic, such as Japan and Korea.

Despite the nascent public discourse on multiculturalism and the adoption of "passive multicultural" provisions, however, policy-makers in Japan, Korea, and Taiwan have remained resistant to the idea of the ethnic diversity of the nation (Kim and Oh 2011; for Japan, see also Iwabuchi in this volume). Notably, they have designed policies to ensure that the full inclusion of foreign wives in their host societies, including naturalization, is based on their acquisition of the language and cultural skills of the host society. As a measure to offset the forming of ethnic enclaves, marriage migrants are typically barred from bringing any family members, except for dependent children they may already have. Integration policies, in this regard, are not based on the recognition and incorporation of cultural diversity. Even in the case of Singapore, which has been a multicultural nation-state since independence, marriage migration has yet to alter the official racial categories of CMIO (Chinese, Malay, Indian, Others). Nevertheless, we recognize the remaking of nationhood in East Asia through marriage migration. In the face of assimilationist integration and naturalization policies, marriage migration has brought about the development of transnational activities that tie together families as well as the marriage and labor markets of the sending and receiving nation-states.

The rise in international marriages in East Asia since the early 1990s has been closely associated with the establishment of international trade and capital flows within the region. It has consisted mainly of men from more developed countries marrying women from developing countries in East and Southeast Asia. Based on available estimates, Jones and Shen (2008) state that Taiwan (32 percent), Singapore (17 percent), Korea (14 percent) and Japan (5 percent) had the highest proportion of international marriages (out of all marriages) in East and Southeast Asia in 2005. However, the majority of these marriages were marriages between persons of the same ethnicity, e.g. marriages between *Joseonjok* women and Korean men.

In South Korea, the increase in international marriages began in 1992 with the normalization of relations with China (Lee 2008). Since then, marriages between *Joseonjok* women and Korean men have accounted for the largest proportion of international marriages in Korea. Initially, these marriages were promoted by local governmental groups who introduced Korean farmers to *Joseonjok* women. Similarly, state-arranged marriages had become a relatively widespread (and well-known) phenomenon in Japan by the late 1980s mostly due to the shortage of brides in rural areas (Nakamatsu 2003, Shipper 2008). This initial wave of international marriages contrasts with the privately arranged (through commercial brokers or social networks) marriages that have characterized international marriages in East Asia since the late 1990s. Like labor migration, marriage migration has had a strong regional orientation. Jones and Shen (2008) identify China, Vietnam, the Philippines, and Indonesia as the major countries of origin of marriage migrants in Taiwan, Korea, Japan, and Singapore.

The legal status and rights of foreign spouses in South Korea has been the subject of several policy changes, marking a tentative but gradual progression towards greater economic and social inclusion (Lee 2008). One of the first changes was the granting of F-2 residence visas in 2002, which allowed marriage migrants to seek employment. In 2005, marriage migrants who had not been naturalized could apply for permanent residency after two years of residence. One key policy change affected the right to settlement of foreign wives. Previously, a foreign wife had to return to her country of origin (without her children) if she divorced her husband during the first two years of marriage. This was changed in 2003 such that a foreign wife could extend her residence visa and apply for naturalization if 1) her husband was deceased or missing, 2) they had separated or divorced because of her husband's actions, or 3) she had been the caregiver of their children or his parents. Despite this change, the legal status of the foreign wife was still defined through her past or present duties as a wife (especially with the second and third conditions). Lastly, foreign wives and their families were included in the social security system in 2007.

The gradual inclusion of marriage migrants has constituted the primary pathway for immigration to remake nationhood in the major migrant-receiving Asian states. In South Korea, the official adoption of multiculturalism as a policy was institutionalized through the Plan for Promoting the Social Integration of Migrant Women, Biracial People, and Immigrants, or the "Grand Plan," as announced on 26 April 2006 (Kim 2007, Lee 2008). The plan identified the Ministry for Gender Equality and Family as the main coordinating agency for a set of social policies aimed at the comprehensive support and protection of foreign wives and their children, and at increasing Koreans' acceptance of a multicultural society. The Korea Immigration Service's (2009) First Basic Plan for Immigration Policy echoes the "Grand Plan" in its section on "High-quality Social Integration." Notably, in both plans, the provision of social rights (mostly in the form of social services) only extends to foreign wives and their multicultural children. No other groups were named as targets of the proposed policies.

Despite the Korean state's efforts at integration, many non-Korean foreign wives have not naturalized. Korean policy-makers have identified migrants' lack of language and cultural skills as a source of the problem, citing, for example, the relatively low rates of success of Cambodian (20 percent) and Vietnamese (18.5 percent) marriage migrants in their applications for naturalization (Korea Immigration Service 2009: 46). The basis of their concern is not rights of migrants but, similar to the rationales for their labor and ethnic return migration policies, the minimization of disruption: "The failure of immigrants through marriage to adapt to Korean society undermines the foundation of families and incurs major social costs" (Korea Immigration Service 2009: 46).

Japan's treatment of female marriage migrants has been similar to South Korea's gradual integration of "multicultural families." In Japan, the admission and settlement of foreign wives have been conditional upon their status as the spouses of Japanese nationals. This was reinforced by a 2009 amendment to the Immigration Control and Refugee Recognition Act. It introduced a provision [see Article 22–4(1)(vii)] that made the residence of foreign spouses revocable if they do not "engage in the activities of a person with a status under a spouse of a Japanese national … for six months or more while residing in Japan" (Immigration Bureau of Japan 2009). Therefore, even though marriage migrants possess more rights (such as the right to work and full access to the national health care system) than ethnic return and labor migrants, their lack of citizenship nevertheless leaves them in a precarious state (Shipper 2008: 50–1).

In their implementation of naturalization policy, similar to South Korean practices, Japanese policy-makers have expected marriage migrants to assimilate despite the fact that there is no such requirement in the Nationality Law. This has been reinforced by the perceptions and attitudes shared by marriage migrants and their Japanese families. Faier (2009) argued that Filipina wives and the rural families that they have married into have evaluated their moral and social standing in their families and community in relation to the Japanese ideal of being a *ii oyomesan* (good bride and daughter-in-law). Critically, conformity with this cultural ideal has facilitated marriage migrants' acquisition of permanent residency and citizenship because of the way immigration bureaucrats have investigated applications for residency and citizenship.[9] In this regard, Parreñas (2011: 178–9) noted that the Filipina wives of Japanese men often distinguished themselves as "'real' members of Japanese society" from their co-ethnic brethren, particularly those working under the legal status of "entertainers" in hostess bars, due to their more privileged social and legal status.

Framed in cultural terms, marriage migrants' attainment of social and legal status in Japan demonstrates the importance of socio-cultural assimilation to their settlement and incorporation. As a whole, these social and political practices highlight the centrality of the culture of the nation and the family in structuring the settlement of foreign wives. However, Faier (2009) observed that the effective performance of the cultural ideal of *ii oyomesan* also allowed Filipina wives to achieve economic and political benefits that could help them better support their families in the Philippines. This points to the series of transnational practices that marriage migration makes possible, and to the fact that the study of marriage migration cannot be limited to its occurrence within the host society alone. For one, the phenomenon of marriage migration, like all forms of migration, occurs in both sending and receiving communities. And, second, the extent of the nation-state's control of marriage migrants and their practices is necessarily limited by the fact that their social actions and interests often cross the nation's borders.

To put it differently, Japanese policy-makers' emphasis on the socio-cultural integration of foreign wives does not preclude the continuation of transnational practices by those who view socio-cultural integration as a pragmatic means to securing greater social, political, and economic gains in both sending and receiving communities. The same may be said of foreign wives in South Korea whose fulfillment of their social and cultural roles as wife, daughter-in-law, and mother of Korean nationals would allow them to secure residency and, eventually, citizenship. In turn, this grants them greater security in their engagement in cross-border activities that help sustain their natal families in their country of origin.

The implications of marriage migration on regional transnationalization in East Asia may be also illustrated by its impact on sending communities. Bélanger and Tran (2011) document the impact that marriage migration has had on gender and familial relations within sending communities in southern Vietnam, from where most Vietnamese marriage migrants who left for South Korea and Taiwan originated. They found that the status of migrant wives in their natal families increased because of their financial contributions to their families. In addition, families that have had the experience of marriage migration seemed more willing to consider marriage migration as an option for their younger daughters. These findings highlight how the interests of marriage migrants may not be well understood if framed only in terms of their integration into the host society. They also reveal the increasing ties that link the marriage markets in both sending and receiving communities.

Since its development in the early 1990s, international marriages have gained greater acceptance as more men and women have crossed borders in search of marital partners. We note that the increasing migration of women from developing Asian countries as wives mirrors the increasing mobility of women as labor migrants. As Oishi (2005) noted, the increasing social acceptance of women's cross-border movements in sending communities indicates a "culture of migration." Despite this similarity with labor migration, the transnational practices linked to marriage migration have a greater potential to create long-term transnational connections within the region because foreign wives may settle and are even expected to integrate as members of the nation.

Prospects for transnational connections and regional integration

We have discussed how East Asian policies governing labor migration, ethnic return migration, and international marriages have expressed policy-makers' distinct understandings of nationhood. The forestalling of family reunification, migrant settlement, and racial diversity demonstrate the commitment of East Asian states to form multi-ethnic societies that are distinct from the European and North American approach. As Manuel Castells (1998: 308) has observed with regards to the industrialized states of East Asia, "the process of development has been, and is, enacted by parallel nationalisms, which are absolutely not ready to downplay their identity." Our comparative analysis of immigration policies has, likewise, pointed to the effect of policy-makers' conceptions of nationhood in creating exclusionary policies geared toward social order that nevertheless remake the nation.

East Asian states have developed policies that allow for needed migrant labor but have also sought to protect the nation from the perceived social and cultural disruption brought about by immigrants. Ironically, such a defensive approach to policy-making may in turn encourage regional transnationalism and integration. Indeed, these policies have fostered circular migration and transnational ties between migrants and their homelands, and they have encouraged states to cooperate in order to manage migration.

In limiting the ability of low-skilled migrant workers to stay for long periods and settle, receiving states like South Korea and Japan have facilitated the circular migration of low-skilled migrant workers between certain sending and receiving states. For example, in the case of the Korea's Employment Permit

System (EPS), guest workers are allowed one extension of their work contracts and they may not return immediately on new contracts after their final departure. Even the *Joseonjok* face a similar situation as they are granted five-year, multi-entry visas that only allow them to stay in Korea continuously for up to three years, unless requested otherwise by their employers.

In comparison, Japan's immigration policies are even more restrictive since they still maintain the principle of not admitting low-skilled foreign workers despite their presence as "trainees." Research shows that restrictive visa policies have given rise to different patterns of migration among Filipina women employed in Japan's nightlife industry depending on their individual trajectories (Faier 2009, Parreñas 2010, 2011). The vast majority of them have not settled because of the short stays allowed by "entertainer" visas (six months); within this group, some have been able to return to Japan one to two more times, making them circular migrants. An analogous pattern may be observed for the *Nikkeijin*, even though they qualify as "long-term residents" in Japan.

The circulation of migrants between states also indicates the underlying trans-national networks (as mediated by kin and/or labor recruitment agencies) that have shaped a "culture of migration" in the sending countries. As Oishi (2005), drawing from Massey *et al.* (1993), defines it, migration becomes an accepted part of a sending community's practices and values as the younger generation begins to accept, idealize and follow the migratory paths of its family members. In our view, circular migration highlights the distinct transnational connections and "culture of migration" that have been conditioned by the restrictive immigration policies within migrant-receiving states. These transnational connections are thus different from the transnationalism of settled diasporas, which are simultaneously invested in both sending and receiving states. Given the limitations on their mobility, circular migrants maintain a greater identification with and loyalty to their homelands (Parreñas 2010).

Though Japan and South Korea have policies designed to attract ethnic return migrants, it is not the case that they have sought to encourage permanent stay for the low-skilled among them. This may give incentives for them to engage in transnational practices. For example, during the 2008 global economic downturn, the Japanese state encouraged the *Nikkeijin* to return to their countries of origin by creating a voluntary return program that provided financial support for the departure of the *Nikkeijin* and their families. According to one official source, as reported in McCabe *et al.* (2009), this program has received 13,188 applications (11,329 approved) from a population of about 350,000 *Nikkeijin* between April and October 2009, with the majority being Japanese Brazilians. In contrast, McCabe and her colleagues show that only about 5400 migrants applied for a Spanish voluntary return program (4100 approved) of a total eligible migrant population of about 1.2 million. However, as they state, the actual rate of return may be even higher in Japan; one study reports that the number of registered foreigners from Brazil decreased by 49,511 persons (16 percent) between 2008 and 2009 (Roberts 2012: 53). As such, the ethnic return migration of the *Nikkeijin* may be more circular than permanent, as is the case with the *Joseonjok* in Korea.

Marriage migrants, on the other hand, have engaged in transnational practices while negotiating their settlement and naturalization in their host societies. Like labor migrants, they have sent remittances back to their countries of origin. The main difference is that state policies have allowed them to settle and gain citizenship based on the fulfillment of their social and cultural roles as the wives, mothers, and daughters-in-law of citizens. Being immigrants, their mode of transnationalism is different from temporary labor and ethnic return migrants. Also, the "culture of migration" that marriage migration creates in sending communities—whereby women view foreign men from more developed countries as ideal prospective partners—may foster the creation of greater and more sustained cross-border linkages within the region despite restrictive immigration policies. Even so, as we have argued, marriage migration is still shaped by state policies that seek to preserve the social and cultural boundaries of the nation.

In this chapter we have discussed three different forms of migration (labor, ethnic return, and marriage) and their implications for transnationalization in relation to the two largest migrant-receiving states of East Asia, Japan and South Korea, but what of other states in the region? Comparisons with two other industrialized, migrant-receiving states in the region, Singapore and Taiwan, are illuminating. Though operating in very different contexts (Singapore is a former British colony and a multi-ethnic state, while Taiwan exists with a continuous sovereignty threat from China's irredentist aspirations), both share with Japan and Korea highly restrictive policies toward low-skilled migrants that similarly appear to lead to regionally oriented, transnational practices.

In terms of labor migration, both Singapore and Taiwan have enacted work permit programs that admit low-skilled foreigners for work in several industries without rights to settlement or family reunification; this leads guest workers to engage in circular migration instead. There are also similarities in marriage migration patterns since foreign wives have increasingly settled in Singapore and Taiwan due to the bride shortages faced by less-educated men who have struggled to find marriage partners in their local society. Because of their ability to settle, marriage migrants from Vietnam in particular have become increasingly visible in Singapore and Taiwan. This has introduced greater ethnic diversity into their mostly Chinese multicultural societies. One key area of difference, however, lies in the domain of ethnic return migration. Singapore lacks a large emigrant population and Taiwan has national security concerns regarding the mainland Chinese. Neither therefore provides preferences for ethnic return migrants to enter and work as low-skilled workers.

This suggests that Japan and South Korea, as well as Singapore and Taiwan, exemplify how state policies, while protective of nationhood and the nation's perceived interests, have also fostered an unintended set of transnational practices by guest worker, ethnic return migrants, and marriage migrants. The incentives for transnationalization created through the prohibition of settlement and family reunification contrast with European patterns, where family reunification rights have led to significant migrant settlement (for a detailed comparison, see Lee and Skrentny forthcoming). Further research may examine the role of sending state policies and their interactions with migrants as well as the policies of migrant-receiving states. One possible area of further investigation is the role of inter-state relations in structuring transnational activities. To conclude, we offer a brief discussion of the emergent role of bilateral agreements between Asian states in shaping the region's transnationalization.

Restrictive immigration policies within industrialized Asia have engendered a distinct form of international cooperation within the region. Unlike Europe, where the European Union acts as an international institution that facilitates the free movement of goods and persons between its member states, no equivalent institution or policy has emerged in Asia. While the Asia-Pacific Economic Cooperation (APEC) and the Association of Southeast Asian Nations (ASEAN) have existed as possible platforms for regional cooperation on migration issues, they have only developed regional agreements aimed at the mobility of business and skilled persons (Chia 2006). For instance, APEC has set up the APEC Business Travel Card Scheme to ensure the smooth passage of business visitors into participating states, while the discourse over the creation of the ASEAN Economic Community only envisions free movement for skilled labor. This lack of regional coordination over the mobility of low-skilled migrant workers reflects the greater influence wielded by migrant-receiving states, which have "asymmetric policies" towards skilled and low-skilled labor migration, over the formulation of regional bodies and agreements (Chia 2006: 364). In this regard we identify an alternative avenue towards regional integration in the bilateral agreements and negotiations between sending and receiving states.

Bilateral agreements have been a significant component of the labor importation schemes in Japan, South Korea, and Taiwan. Japan has been most restrictive. For instance, while Japan agreed to accept nurses and caregivers from 2008 because of its Economic Partnership Agreements (EPAs) with Indonesia and the Philippines, its designation and admission of care-workers as relatively skilled labor migrants has been very limited in magnitude, numbering only in the hundreds. Foreign care-workers are expected to pass a national examination in either nursing or caregiving that is administered in the Japanese language in order to stay beyond their three-year training period; not surprisingly, the passing rates have been low (Roberts 2012: 55). Hence, like other foreigners, the vast majority of care-workers return home after their practical training in Japan. Within this context, even though Japan has agreed to a similar agreement with Vietnam, with India and Thailand to follow, it is unlikely that these EPAs signal Japanese policy-makers' openness to the official importation of foreign labor. Instead, as Oishi (2005: 42) points out, the admission of care-workers from abroad should be seen as a concession within the negotiations of free trade agreements that would serve Japanese interests in trade and investment.

We contrast the limited nature of EPAs to the use of bilateral agreements to manage low-skilled labor migration in South Korea and Taiwan. Bilateral cooperation and infrastructure is a key component of Korea's Employment Permit System, allowing the state to oversee and control the recruitment and subsequent return of guest workers. To date, South Korea has signed "memoranda of understanding" with 15 countries (all within Asia) to supply low-skilled labor under the E-9 visa or the H-2 Working Visit Visa (for ethnic Koreans) (Ministry of Government Legislation, Republic of Korea 2010). In the eyes of the Korean state, the maintenance of these agreements may be made dependent upon the successful return of guest workers to their home countries (Skeldon 2009). Another dimension of these bilateral agreements over labor mobility is the potential role they play in international diplomacy, which is a particularly acute problem for Taiwan. As Tseng discusses, the Taiwanese state has selected source countries in its guest worker scheme according to "the degree of support given to state's interests in international political forums" (Tseng 2004: 113).

As these cases demonstrate, bilateral agreements are ultimately subject to national interests and they may be instrumental in articulating states' responses to political, economic, and social concerns; such as the access to foreign markets (Japan), the avoidance of illegal immigration (Korea), and recognition in the international system (Taiwan). The precedence of the nation-state's interests in the crafting of these bilateral agreements highlights the competitive nature of this nascent mode of regional integration. Nevertheless, as Skeldon (2009: 20) notes, these bilateral agreements are still "in their infancy," and may "become more open to design, monitoring and implementation within some common regional or multilateral facility."

The future trajectories of migration policy, transnationalization, and regional integration in East Asia are far from clear. The low birthrates in the region and the ensuing shrinkage in the national workforces will put pressure on these states to increase immigration to keep their economies growing and their pensions funded. Will they tip their balance away from national interests and more towards the rights of migrants and more institutionalized regional transnationalism, like the European approach? Whether or not they can address demographic challenges through circular migration and without family reunification and settlement—and more significant challenges to conceptions of nationhood—will be a question of great significance in the next decades.

Notes

1 Jack Jin Gary Lee would like to acknowledge the support provided by the Tan Kah Kee Foundation. We thank Satoko Kakihara and Yusuke Mazumi for timely advice on our referencing of Japanese-language sources.
2 As an initial point of departure, we refer to "transnationalism" as consisting of the "trans-state social action," or cross-border activities, that migrants engage in (Waldinger and FitzGerald 2004). Going beyond, we demonstrate how these practices result in changes in the social organization and the national demographic profile of both sending and receiving countries despite state controls.
3 Following Parreñas (2010), we define circular migrants as short-term migrants who are involved in temporary stints of employment abroad and maintain strong loyalties and ties to their sending societies. In addition, we understand circular migration as a social fact that primarily consists of the circulation of labor and ethnic return migrants between sending communities and receiving states.
4 Article 50 of Japan's Immigration Act allows the Ministry of Justice to issue permits for special permission to remain at the discretion of the minister and based on

humanitarian considerations. In some instances the ministry has issued permits to entire immigrant families. This is not a mass amnesty, however, and not a settlement or family reunification policy. The numbers are very limited: from 2003 to 2006, for example, the ministry has given permits to not more than 30 persons in any year (Immigration Bureau of Japan 2010b).

5 For a historical overview of migration and its implications for transnationalization in Europe, see Lucassen 2005. For transnational patterns in marriage migration, see Beck-Gernsheim 2007.

6 Originally, in the enactment process, allowing dual citizenship was considered, but it was excluded because of issues with military conscription, taxation, and social sentiments.

7 Act on the Immigration and Legal Status of Overseas Koreans Case (13–2 KCCR 714, 99Hung-Ma494, November 29, 2001) (http://english.ccourt.go.kr/home/english/decisions/mgr_decision_view.jsp?seq=284&code=5, accessed January 2011).

8 While North Koreans are recognized as refugees in public discourse, they are legally defined as "residents escaping from North Korea." See the Act On The Protection And Settlement Support Of Residents Escaping From North (Act No. 10188, March 26, 2010) (http://elaw.klri.re.kr/eng_service/lawView.do?hseq=20154&lang=ENG, accessed May 2014).

9 Their investigation could entail interviews with the applicant's family and their neighbors with regards to her role in the family.

References

Bartram, D. 2005. *International Labor Migration: Foreign Workers and Public Policy*. New York: Palgrave Macmillan.

Beck-Gernsheim, E. 2007. Transnational Lives, Transnational Marriages: A Review of the Evidence From Migrant Communities in Europe. *Global Networks* 7(3): 271–88.

Bélanger, D. and G. L. Tran. 2011. The Impact of Transnational Migration on Gender and Marriage in Sending Communities of Vietnam. *Current Sociology* 59(1): 59–77.

Brubaker, R. 1994. Nation as Institutionalized Form, Practical Category, Contingent Event. *Contention* 4(1): 3–14.

Calavita, K. 2004. Italy: Economic Realities, Political Fictions, and Policy Failures. In *Controlling Immigration: A Global Perspective* (second editions), W. A. Cornelius, T. Tsuda, P. L. Martin, and J. F. Hollifield, eds. Stanford, CA: Stanford University Press.

Castells, M. 1998. *End of Millenium. The Information Age: Economy, Society and Culture* (Vol. 3). Malden, MA: Blackwell Publishers.

Chia, S.Y. 2006. Labor Mobility and East Asian Integration. *Asian Economic Policy Review* 1(2): 349–67.

Choi, W-G. 2001. The Korean Minority in China: The Change of its Identity. *Development and Society* 30(1): 119–41.

Cornelius, W. A. 1994. Japan: The Illusion of Immigration Control. In *Controlling Immigration: A Global Perspective*, W. A. Cornelius, J.F. Hollifield, and P. L. Martin, eds. Stanford, CA: Stanford University Press.

Cornelius, W. A. and T. Tsuda. 2004. Controlling Immigration: The Limits of Government Intervention. In *Controlling Immigration: A Global Perspective* (second edition), W. A. Cornelius, T. Tsuda, P. L. Martin and J. F. Hollifield, eds. Stanford, CA: Stanford University Press.

Faier, L. 2009. *Intimate Encounters: Filipina Women and the Remaking of Rural Japan*. Berkeley: University of California Press.

Fitzgerald, K. 1996. *The Face of the Nation: Immigration, the State and the National Identity*. Stanford, CA: Stanford University Press.

Freeman, G. P. and J. Mo. 1996. Japan and the Asian NICs as New Countries of Destination. In *International Trade and Migration in the APEC Region*, P. J. Lloyd and L. S. Williams, eds. Melbourne: Oxford University Press.

Green, D. 2013. Education of Foreign Children in Japan: Local Versus National Initiatives. *Journal of International Migration and Integration*, published online, 20 July 2013. Available at: http://link.springer.com/article/10.1007%2Fs12134–013-0299-z (accessed May 2014).

Herbert, W. 1996. *Foreign Workers and Law Enforcement in Japan*. New York: Kegan Paul International.

Immigration Bureau of Japan. 2009. Immigration Control and Refugee Recognition Act (provisional translation). Ministry of Justice. Available at: www.immi-moj.go.jp/english/newimmiact/pdf/RefugeeRecognitionAct01.pdf (accessed January 2011).

——2010a. Kokuseki (Shusshinchi) Betsu Gaikokujin Tōrokushasū no Suii. [Estimates of Registered Foreigners by Nationality (Place of Birth)]. Ministry of Justice. Available at: www.moj.go.jp/content/000049970.pdf (accessed January 2011).

——2010b. Zairyū Tokubetsu Kyoka Sareta Jirei oyobi Zairyū Tokubetsu Kyoka Sarenakatta Jirei ni tsuite [Regarding Cases of Special Permission for Residence Granted as well as Cases of Special Permission for Residence not Granted]. Ministry of Justice. Available at: www.moj.go.jp/NYUKAN/nyukan25.html (accessed July 2008).

——2011. *Immigration Control Report 2011*. Ministry of Justice. Available at: www.moj.go.jp/content/000081971.pdf (accessed May 2014).

Jones, G. and H. Shen. 2008. International Marriage in East and Southeast Asia: Trends and Research Emphases. *Citizenship Studies* 12(1): 9–25.

Kajita, T. 1998. The Challenge of Incorporating Foreigners in Japan: "Ethnic Japanese" and "Sociological Japanese." In *Temporary Workers or Future Citizens*, M. Weiner and T. Hanami, eds. New York: New York University Press.

Kaur, A. 2006. *International Migration in Malaysia and Singapore since the 1880s: State Policies, Migration Trends and Governance of Migration*. Armidale, NSW: University of New England Asia Centre.

Kim, H.-R. and I. Oh. 2011. Migration and Multicultural Contention in East Asia. *Journal of Ethnic & Migration Studies* 37(10): 1563–81.

Kim, H. M. 2007. The State and Migrant Women: Diverging Hopes in the Making of "Multicultural Families" in Contemporary Korea. *Korea Journal* 47(4): 100–22.

Korea Immigration Service. 2009. *The First Basic Plan for Immigration Policy: 2008–12*. Gwacheon, Korea: Ministry of Justice.

——2010. *KIS Statistics 2009*. Gwacheon, Korea: Ministry of Justice.

Kuwahara, Y. 1998. Japan's Dilemma: Can International Migration be Controlled? In *Temporary Workers or Future Citizens*, M. Weiner and T. Hanami, eds. New York: New York University Press.

Lee, C. 2003. "Us" and "Them" in Korean Law: The Creation, Accommodation and Exclusion of Outsiders in South Korea. In *East Asian Law: Universal Norms and Local Cultures*, A. Rosett, L. Cheng and M. Y. K. Woo, eds. New York: Routledge Curzon.

Lee, C-J. 1986. *China's Korean Minority: The Politics of Ethnic Education*. Boulder, CO: Westview Press.

Lee, H-K. 2008. International Marriage and the State in South Korea: Focusing on Governmental Policy. *Citizenship Studies* 12(1): 107–23.

Lee, M-K. 2014. Multicultural Education in Republic of Korea: Social Change and School Education. In *Korean Education in Changing Economic and Demographic Contexts*, H. Park and K-K. Kim, eds. Dordrecht: Springer Verlag.

Lee, J. J. G. and J. D. Skrentny. Forthcoming. Korean Multiculturalism In Comparative Perspective. In *Multiethnic Korea? Multiculturalism, Migration, and Peoplehood Diversity in*

Contemporary South Korea, J. Lie, ed. Berkeley: Institute for East Asian Studies, University of California, Berkeley.

Lie, J. 2001. *Multi-Ethnic Japan*. Cambridge, MA: Harvard University Press.

Lim, T. 2002. The Changing Face of South Korea: The Emergence of Korea as a "Land of Immigration." *Korea Society Quarterly* 3(2/3): 16–21.

Liu-Farrer, G. 2011. *Labour Migration from China to Japan: International Students, Transnational Migrants*. New York: Routledge.

Lucas, R. E. B. 2005. *International Migration and Economic Development: Lessons from Low-Income Countries*. Northampton, MA: Edward Elgar Publishing.

Lucassen, L. 2005. *The Immigrant Threat: the Integration of Old and New Migrants in Western Europe since 1850*. Urbana: University of Illinois Press.

Massey, D. S., J. Arrango, G. Hugo, A. Kouaouci, A. Pellegrino, and E. J. Taylor. 1993. Theories of International Migration: A Review and Appraisal. *Population and Development Review* 19(3): 431–66.

McCabe, K., S. Y.-Y. Lin, H. Tanaka, and P. Plewa 2009. Pay to Go: Countries Offer Cash to Immigrants Willing to Pack Their Bags. *Migration Information Source*. Available at: www.migrationinformation.org/Feature/display.cfm?ID=749 (accessed December 2011).

Ministry of Education, Culture, Sports, Science and Technology, Japan. 2011. Nihongo Shidō ga Hitsuyō na Jidō Seito no Ukeire Jōkyō nado ni kansuru Chōsa, Heisei 20 Nendo [Survey of the Admission of Young Students that Require Japanese Language Instruction, 2010]. Available at: www.e-stat.go.jp/SG1/estat/List.do?bid=000001034469&cycode=0 (accessed May 2014).

Ministry of Government Legislation, Republic of Korea. 2010. *Non-professional Employment (E-9) Visa Holders' Employment Procedure*. Available at: http://oneclick.law.go.kr/CSM/OvCnpRetrieveP.laf?csmSeq=501&ccfNo=3&cciNo=2&cnpClsNo=1 (accessed December 2011).

Ministry of Justice, Japan. 2010. *Basic Plan for Immigration Control: 4th Edition (provisional translation)*. Available at: www.immi-moj.go.jp/seisaku/keikaku_101006_english.pdf (accessed December 2011).

Ministry of Unification, Republic of Korea. 2011. Major Statistics in Inter-Korean Relations. Available at: http://eng.unikorea.go.kr/index.do?menuCd=DOM_000000204003000000 (accessed May2014).

Mori, H. 1997. *Immigration Policy and Foreign Workers in Japan*. New York: St Martin's Press.

Nakamatsu, T. 2003. International Marriage through Introduction Agencies: Social and Legal Realities of "Asian Wives" of Japanese Men. In *Wife or Worker: Asian Women and Migration*, N. Piper and M. Roces, eds. Lanham, MD: Rowman and Littlefield.

National Immigration Agency, Taiwan, Republic of China. 2010. Wai Qiao Ju Liu Ren Shu Tong Ji [Statistics of Foreign Residents]. Available at: http://iff.immigration.gov.tw/public/Attachment/13168381366.xls (accessed May 2014).

Oishi, N. 2005. *Women in Motion: Globalization, State Policies, and Labor Migration in Asia*. Stanford, CA: Stanford University Press.

Park, J.-S. and Paul Y. Chang. 2004. Contestation in the Formation of National and Ethnic Identities in Global Context: The Case of the Overseas Koreans Act. Paper presented at the conference on *Korean Identity: Past and Present*. Yonsei University, Seoul.

Parreñas, R. S. 2010. Homeward Bound: The Circular Migration of Entertainers Between Japan and the Philippines. *Global Networks* 10(3): 301–23.

——2011. *Illicit Flirtations: Labor, Migration, and Sex Trafficking in Tokyo*. Stanford, CA: Stanford University Press.

Peach, C. 2003. Contrasts in Economic Growth and Immigration Policy in Japan, the European Union and the United States. In *Global Japan: The Experience of Japan's New*

Migrant and Overseas Communities, R. Goodman, C. Peach, A. Takenaka, and P. White, eds. New York: Routledge.

Piao, C. 1990. The History of Koreans in China and the Yanbian Korean Autonomous Prefecture. In *Koreans in China*, D.-S. Suh and E. J. Shultz, eds. Honolulu: Center for Korean Studies, University of Hawaii.

Roberts, G. 2012. Vocalizing the "I" Word: Proposals and Initiatives on Immigration to Japan from the LDP and Beyond. *ASIEN* 124(July): 48–68.

Schmid, A. 2002. *Korea Between Empires, 1895–1919.* New York: Columbia University Press.

Seol, D.-H. and Y.-J. Lee. 2011. Research Note: Recent Developments and Implications of Policies on Ethnic Return Migration in Korea. *Asian and Pacific Migration Journal* 20(2): 215–31.

Seol, D.-H. and H. C. Rhee. 2005. Oeguk Gukjeok Dongpo Goyong yi Guknae Nodongsijang e Michineun Sahoe Gyeongje Jeok Hyogwa Bunseok [Employment of Overseas Ethnic Koreans in Korea and its Socioeconomic Effects on Korean Labor Market]. Gwacheon, Korea: Ministry of Labor.

Seol, D.-H. and J. D. Skrentny. 2004. South Korea: Importing Undocumented Workers. In *Controlling Immigration: A Global Perspective* (second edition), W. A. Cornelius, T. Tsuda, P. L. Martin, and J. F. Hollifield, eds. Stanford, CA: Stanford University Press.

——2009a. Why Is There So Little Migrant Settlement in East Asia? *International Migration Review* 43(3): 578–620.

——2009b. Ethnic Return Migration and Hierarchical Nationhood: Korean Chinese Foreign Workers in South Korea. *Ethnicities* 9(2): 147–74.

Shimada, H. 1994. *Japan's "Guest Workers": Issues and Public Policies.* Tokyo: University of Tokyo Press.

Shipper, A. W. 2002. The Political Construction of Foreign Workers in Japan. *Critical Asian Studies* 34(1): 41–68.

——2008. *Fighting for Foreigners: Immigration and its Impact on Japanese Democracy.* Ithaca, NY: Cornell University Press.

Skeldon, R. 2009. *Managing Irregular Migration as a Negative Factor in the Development of Eastern Asia.* Asian Regional Programme on Governance of Labour Migration. Working Paper no. 18. Bangkok: ILO Regional Office for Asia and the Pacific. Available at: www.ilo.org/wcmsp5/groups/public/–asia/–ro-bangkok/documents/publication/wcms_105108.pdf (accessed January 2011).

Solidarity Network with Migrants Japan. 2007. *Living Together with Migrants and Ethnic Minorities in Japan: NGO Policy Proposals.* Tokyo.

Terasawa, K. 2000. Labor Law, Civil Law, Immigration Law and the Reality of Migrants and Their Children. In *Japan and Global Migration: Foreign Workers and the Advent of a Multicultural Society*, M. Douglass and G. S. Roberts, eds. Honolulu: University of Hawaii Press.

Tseng, Y.-F. 2004. Politics of Importing Foreigners: Foreign Labour Policy in Taiwan. In *Migration between States and Markets*, H. Entzinger, M. Martiniello, and C. W. de Wenden, eds. Burlington, VT: Ashgate.

Tsuda, T. 2003. *Strangers in the Ethnic Homeland: Japanese Brazilian Return Migration in Transnational Perspective.* New York: Columbia University Press.

Van Selm, J. 1999. Regional Integration and Rights of Migrants: Europe and Asia. *European Journal of Migration & Law* 1(2): 215–28.

Waldinger, R. and D. FitzGerald. 2004. Transnationalism in Question. *American Journal of Sociology* 109(5): 1177–95.

Yamanaka, K. 1993. New Immigration Policy and Unskilled Foreign Workers in Japan. *Pacific Affairs* 66(1): 72–90.

——2004. Citizenship and Differential Exclusion of Immigrants in Japan. In *State/Nation/Transnation: Perspectives on Transnationalism in the Asia-Pacific*, K. Willis and B. S. A. Yeoh, eds. New York: Routledge.

——2010. Civil Society and Social Movements for Immigrant Rights in Japan and South Korea: Convergence and Divergence in Unskilled Immigration Policy. *Korea Observer* 41(4): 615–47.

Yoshino, K. 1997. The Discourse on Blood and Racial Identity in Contemporary Japan. In *The Construction of Racial Identities in China and Japan*, F. Dikötter, ed. Honolulu: University of Hawaii Press.

Imaginaries

8 Single women and cosmopolitan re-imaginings of gendered citizenship in Shanghai, Hong Kong, and Tokyo[1]

Lynne Y. Nakano

Women are marrying later throughout the world, but most noticeably in East Asia's large cities. The median age of marriage for women is 29.7 in Tokyo (Ministry of Health, Labor, and Welfare 2009), 29 in Hong Kong (Census and Statistics Department, HKSAR 2013a), and 29.9 in Shanghai (Chinese Women's Research Network 2011). In Japan, in the 30 to 34-year-old age range, as many as 34 percent of women are single (National Institute of Population and Social Security Research 2012), and in Tokyo, an astonishing 40 percent of women in this age group are single (Tokyo Metropolitan Government 2012). In Hong Kong, the figure is 39 percent (Census and Statistics Department, HKSAR 2013a). In Shanghai, the percentage of single women between the age of 30 and 34 remains relatively low at 4.5 percent in 2010 but has nearly doubled since 2000 (Chiu 2013).

This demographic shift to later marriage or indefinite singlehood is surprising given that marrying and having a family continue to be seen as the primary ways for women to contribute to their societies. How do single women in East Asia's largest cities view their contribution to society given that they are not forming families through marriage? This chapter argues that despite differences in the ways that their societies structure gendered citizenship through state policies and social expectations, single women in metropolitan East Asian cities have much in common regarding the ways in which they imagine their life courses to be transnationally located and grounded in values of individual achievement and fulfillment.

My analysis focuses on expressions of citizenship among single women in the cities of Shanghai, Hong Kong, and Tokyo. I chose Hong Kong and Tokyo because I am familiar with these cities having lived in both places for many years, and because these cities have large numbers of single women and late ages of first marriage. I added Shanghai to the study in 2009 because the age of first marriage rose sharply in the city and throughout China in the 2000s. All three are global cities (Sassen 1991) as they have experienced shifts in locations of production, expansion of international financial transactions, and class and spatial polarization. As regional and global centers, they attract women from surrounding areas, are hubs of higher education, and are used as stepping stones by women to move to other global cities.

Over ten years I interviewed over thirty women in each city; in total more than one hundred women. These women tended to be highly educated, as over half were university graduates, and a few had graduate degrees. Women with university degrees worked in a range of white-collar roles as, for instance, accountants, editors, financial analysts, and managers. Slightly less than half were high-school educated and worked as clerks in stores or offices. The sample also included independent business owners, a university professor, a free-lance editor, and an unemployed woman looking for work. All of the informants earned enough to be able to spend on themselves for consumptive pleasures such as meals out, clothes, and, in many cases, domestic and international travel. Their incomes allowed them to choose not to marry and to explore personal interests. They were relatively mobile: about half had lived in more than one city or town in order to pursue education or work opportunities. In Shanghai, through snowball sampling, I met local Shanghainese women as well as women from other regions in China, such as Hubei, Guangzhou, and Anhui provinces. In Hong Kong, I met local Hong Kongers and women from Tokyo, Nagoya, Kyushu, Tohoku, and Shanghai. In Tokyo, I met Tokyo natives and women from other prefectures in Japan.

In exploring gendered citizenship in these three cities, my focus is not on how women support the state and its citizenship projects, but how they imagine and articulate their contribution to their societies. The study of single women in three cities provides an ideal setting to consider how women's identities are situated in local contexts and shaped by transnational networks and globally circulating ideas. As mentioned, the single women in this study had high levels of education and were able to earn their own living. They were able to travel in their own country and overseas and gather ideas from a cosmopolitan "cultural supermarket" made available through the internet, travel, books, and other media (Mathews 2000). Their consumer, travel, and online experiences generate imaginings of possibilities that transcend nation-specific contexts. I follow Arjun Appadurai's (1996: 31) argument that the imagination plays a critical role in global processes, not as mere fantasy or escape, but as a form of agency. Transnational flows are, however, controlled and directed by states and local societal contexts (Ong 1999). States shape women's opportunities for education and work as well as related cultural practices through their policies of population reproduction. Cultural and societal practices constitute the local context through which women experience regional and transnational opportunities and construct their imaginings of a meaningful life as citizens. In the following, I first discuss the state and societal contexts and then move to the description of single women's projections of their choices and commitments in three arenas: education and employment, marriage, and leisure. I conclude by reflecting on the reimaginings of gendered citizenship among single women in East Asia.

The state and gendered citizenship

With long lifespans and low fertility rates, governments worry about maintaining their society's labor force, tax base, and social security provisions. All three societies included in this study have large percentages of elderly in the population, over eighty years of life expectancy for women, and low fertility rates. In 2012,

Japan had the oldest population in the world, with 24 percent of the population over the age of 65 (Ministry of Internal Affairs and Communications, Statistics Bureau 2013). In Shanghai in 2012, nearly three-and-a-half million or 25 percent of the total registered population were 60 years or older. The figure is expected to rise to 28 percent by 2015 and will represent one third of the city's population by 2020 (Lu 2012). Of the three cities, Hong Kong's population is the youngest, with only 13 percent of the population 65 years and older in 2012, but the percentage is expected to rise to 30 percent by 2041 (Census and Statistics Department, HKSAR 2012a). Fertility rates in the three cities are among the lowest in the world. Shanghai residents are required to comply with China's one-child policy, but the city's fertility rate of 0.7 per woman is much lower than the national average of 1.5 (Cai 2012), and significantly lower than the birthrate of 2.1 that is normally given as the rate necessary to reproduce a population. Birthrates in Hong Kong have also been extremely low, falling to 0.9 in 2004 and then rising slightly to 1.3 in 2012 (Census and Statistics Department, HKSAR 2013b). The fertility rate in Japan has fallen steadily over several decades, from 3.65 in 1950 to 1.41 in 2012 (Ministry of Internal Affairs and Communications, Statistics Bureau 2013).

In Japan, opinions are divided on how to address the issue of social reproduction, with some hoping that women will have more children. In 2007, the Japanese minister of health at the time, Hakuo Yanagisawa, infamously described Japanese women as "birth-giving machines" and commented that "all we can do is ask them to do their best per head" (McCurry 2007). Others in Japan urge that the government reform its immigration and naturalization policies, which have been relatively closed to migrants throughout the postwar period (see Skrentny and Lee in this volume). These people want the government to lower immigration standards and abolish quotas to allow migrants to enter Japan to help reproduce the population and maintain economic growth. A third group, a minority, suggests that Japan's population be allowed to shrink and the Japanese people learn to embrace a slower-paced and less materialistic life (Kashiwazaki and Akaha 2006).

In contrast to the Japanese government's resistance, the Hong Kong and Shanghai governments openly rely on migrants to rejuvenate the population. As a Special Administrative Region within China with a population just over seven million, Hong Kong maintains control of its own borders, regulates immigration from foreign countries, and controls immigration from mainland China, its largest source of immigrants. In 2010, for example, 43,000 mainlanders joined their families in Hong Kong in a One-Way Permit scheme, which imposes a daily entry quota of 150 persons (Information Services Department, HKSAR 2010: 416). The Hong Kong government launched a Quality Migrant Admission Scheme in 2006 for mainland Chinese with specialized or high-level skills to settle in Hong Kong without first securing an offer of employment. A second scheme, Capital Migrant Admission Scheme, admits people who have made major capital investments in the territory. The number of people who apply and are accepted through these programs, however, has remained relatively small, as fewer than 10,000 were granted admission to Hong Kong in this way in 2010 (Information and Services Department, HKSAR 2010: 418).

Unlike Hong Kong, which maintains control over its borders, the Shanghai government cannot prevent millions of migrants from around China from living and working in the city. According to the national census conducted in November 2010, Shanghai is home to 8.98 million non-locals, accounting for 39 percent of the city's 23 million residents (Jia 2011). The city government of Shanghai controls city resources through the *hukou*, a residence registration system that provides registered residents with essential social services such as access to education in local schools, subsidized medical care, pensions, and eligibility to apply for subsidized public housing. In 2002, the Shanghai government introduced a system of residence permits that would allow skilled professionals to apply for a *hukou* after seven years of residence. Very few *hukou*, however, have been allocated in this way (R. Li 2011).

Beyond policies on population and migration control, women's role in societal reproduction is often intimated in political discourse. In Japan, although politicians calling upon women to have babies for the nation—like the Yanagisawa instance mentioned above—is frowned upon, conservative segments nevertheless associate having a family and bearing children with patriotism and good citizenship. In Hong Kong, where China's one-child policy does not apply, political leaders occasionally exhort Hong Kong women to produce babies to maintain the territory's population and economic vitality. For example, in a 2005 radio address, Hong Kong Chief Executive Donald Tsang urged every family in Hong Kong to have three children (*China Daily* 2005). Such pleas are not common, however, as it is believed that immigration from mainland China will solve Hong Kong's manpower needs. Hong Kong women face less public pressure to marry and bear children than women in Japan, while their role as family carers is nevertheless confirmed. In Shanghai, where the one-child policy applies and the city government protects resources through the residence registration system, single women face enormous pressure not from the government but from their families, which expect daughters to marry and have the one child they are allotted, as I discuss in greater detail below.

Societal context of gendered citizenship

Women's sense of citizenship is closely linked with the educational and employment opportunities available to them and interacts with societal views and norms on success, marriage, and gender roles. The following section outlines these conditions in each city.

Tokyo

Women's educational levels in Tokyo and in Japan as a whole have risen greatly in recent decades, but gender tracking continues in higher education. Since the 1970s, girls have outnumbered boys in high school enrollment, and women's attendance at four-year universities and two-year junior colleges has risen tremendously; in 1990, women accounted for only 15 percent of enrollment in four-year universities, and by 2009 the figure had risen to 44 percent. Women's levels of education in Tokyo are the highest in Japan, with 60 percent of women aged 30 to 44 having a junior college or a four-year university education. Gender tracking in higher education in Japan remains pronounced however; 44 percent of those enrolled in four-year universities are women, whereas in two-year junior colleges they make up the 90 percent of those enrolled (Ministry of Education, Culture, Sports, Science and Technology 2012).

Although labor force participation rates among Japanese women have increased, women continue to temporarily leave the workforce after childbirth, work in primarily lower-paid part-time work, and remain underrepresented in management positions. In Tokyo in 2010, 76 percent of women aged 25 to 34 were in the workforce, but the figure drops to 67 percent among women aged 35 to 44 as they leave the workforce to care for young children, and rises to 71 percent of among women aged 45 to 54 as their children enter middle and high school (Tokyo Metropolitan Government 2011). A national survey found that as many as 43 percent of women who gave birth between 2000 and 2004 had quit their jobs upon childbirth (Gender Equality Bureau 2011). With the decline of the "lifetime employment model," the percentage of women working full-time has decreased, from 68 percent in 1985 to 46.5 percent in 2008 (Gender Equality Bureau 2011). This has meant less job stability and lower earnings. In 2010, women working full-time earned 69 percent of male workers' earnings, and women working part-time earned only 48 percent of full-time male workers' earnings. Women remain excluded from top leadership positions; only 10 percent of businesses have women working in the position of section chief or above, and women comprised only 2 percent of national government ministry directors, and 17 percent of positions at university at the rank of lecturer and above (Gender Equality Bureau 2011).

In 2009, the average monthly income of Tokyo households that included at least one wage earner was ¥598,723 (US$7,796), but the cost of living in Tokyo is high, as the average monthly household expenditure was ¥339,130 (US$4,412) (Tokyo Metropolitan Government 2009). For single women, standards of living may depend on whether or not they live with their parents. Single women who live with their parents may have considerable resources to spend on leisure consumption, while single women who live on their own face far more financial difficulties given the high prices of housing and utilities (Yamada 1999). An important trend since the 1990s has been the increase in the numbers of single women who decide to live and work overseas, especially during their late twenties through their early forties. Ministry of Foreign Affairs (2011) statistics show that in 2010, 1.14 million Japanese, a record number, lived overseas, with women slightly outnumbering men: women comprised 52 percent of Japanese nationals overseas. The exodus of women from Japan, at least temporarily, may be due to the lack of opportunities for advancement and the male-dominated employment structures in Japan (Kelsky 2001).

There is not much consensus in popular views of single women's position in Japan. Surveys show that the vast majority of women wish to marry.[2] They also show women are slightly more likely to disagree than agree with the view that women must remain in the home and men must work outside (Cabinet Office, Government of Japan 2012). Popular literature emphasizes the importance of remaining true to one's principles and becoming economically self-reliant. In her bestselling book, *The Distant Cry of Loser Dogs*, author Junko Sakai (2003) argues that single women are stronger and truer to themselves than women who marry, as she contends that many women enter marriage primarily for security and self-protection. According to Sakai, single women become "losers" as they age because they struggle in the labor market while married women rely on the social status and financial support of their husbands. In contrast to the argument that single women are "parasites" living off their parents, an argument that became widely repeated following the publication of the book, *The Age of Parasite Singles*, by sociologist Masahiro Yamada (1999), some single women's literature defended their contributions to society by pointing out that single women give money to their families, take care of their parents, and earn an independent living. Takayo Yamamoto's (2001) book, *Not a Parasite*, is an example. Much of this popular literature fiercely endorses the values of independence and individual ability and makes the point that the individual rather than the family should be considered as the basic unit of society.

Hong Kong

Like Japan, educational levels and workforce participation rates of women in Hong Kong have also risen significantly in recent decades. In 2012, women constituted 53 percent of enrolment in post-secondary degree institutions compared to only 33 percent in 1987 (Census and Statistics Department, HKSAR 2013a: 67). In 2011, labor force participation rates peaked for women aged 25 to 29 at 86 percent, and remained over 70 percent for those aged 30 to 44 (Census and Statistics Department, HKSAR 2011). Labor force participation rates were even higher for never-married women; over 90 percent in the 25- to 45-year-old age group were working in 2010, compared to slightly more than 60 percent for the same age group of married women (Hong Kong Women's Commission, HKSAR 2011). Again, not unlike Japan, in spite of their high levels of education and labor force participation, women in Hong Kong comprise only 18 percent of legislators, 32 percent of top-ranked civil servants, and 10 percent of board membership of the top fifty Hang Seng Index-listed companies (Ko 2010).

The range of income levels and expenditures is great in Hong Kong. The Gini coefficient, which measures income differentials, was .475 in 2011, indicating that Hong Kong has one of the largest gaps between rich and poor in the world (Census and Statistics Department, HKSAR 2012b). The median domestic monthly income for households in 2012 was HK$20,000 (US$2,670) (Information Services Department, HKSAR 2013). The Hong Kong government offers significant amounts of subsidized housing, with 29 percent of the population living in subsidized public rental units and 17 percent living in subsidized units that they have purchased (Information Services Department, HKSAR 2013). However, few other social security services are publicly provided; families tend to rely on one another for childcare, elder care, loans, living arrangements, and shared financing of education, investments, and home purchases.

Such strong family reliance shapes expectations regarding women's societal role. In Hong Kong, marriage is not as important indicator of a woman's "success" as in Shanghai and Tokyo. Instead, contribution to the family is critical to being considered a successful and ethical person. For single women, the family to which she contributes need not be the family that she creates through marriage, but may be her natal or extended family: her parents, brothers and sisters, and nieces and nephews. Perhaps because of the understanding that single women have duties within families even if they do not marry, there seems be less pressure for women to marry in Hong Kong compared with the other two cities.

Furthermore, women in Hong Kong are often said to be disadvantaged in the marriage market, as large numbers of Hong Kong men have found romantic partners from mainland China in recent years. In 2006, for example, 39 percent of Hong Kong men's marriages involved women from mainland China. But few Hong Kong women marry mainland men; only 6.3 percent in 2005 (Census and Statistics Department, HKSAR 2011). The rise in Hong Kong men's romantic engagements with mainland women is due to the increase in opportunities for Hong Kong men to live and work in mainland China and wealth differentials that allowed Hong Kong men to serve in culturally expected roles as financial providers. Women outnumber men in Hong Kong by a margin of 12 percent; a disadvantage for women looking for marriage partners, as also commented on by the media. Among single people, however, men outnumber women. In 2012, in the 30- to 34-year-old age group, 53 percent of men were never married, compared to 40 percent of women; in the 35- to 39-year-old age group, 32 per-cent of men were never married compared to 22 percent of women; and in the 40- to 44-year-old age group, 23 percent of men were never married compared to 18 percent of women (Census and Statistics Department, HKSAR 2013a: 38–41). This suggests that both Hong Kong women and men are unwilling or unable to marry, further contributing to the societal pressure on single women to be the caregiver in the broader family.

It is worth noting that in Hong Kong, single women's experiences differ according to their age. Women born in the 1950s through the early 1960s grew up in relative poverty and in families with many siblings. These women left school early and worked in factories to contribute to family finances. Often, they helped to pay for the education of younger siblings. Women born after the 1970s benefitted from the growing wealth of the then British colony and had access to education due to changes in the British government's policy which made six years of primary and three years of secondary education in government-subsidized schools become compulsory. Migration in and out of Hong Kong also increased opportunities for Hong Kong women to gain an education, as women went overseas for university and postgraduate degrees, often in places close to where family and friends had settled.

Single women have a visible presence in Hong Kong popular culture; a wealth of widely consumed popular media, television, magazines, and internet forums, generate everyday and popular conversations about them. TVB, one of Hong Kong's two main Cantonese-language television broadcasters, has produced a series of highly popular primetime documentaries since 2009 such as *Gang Nam Jiang Nu* (Hong Kong Men Talk about Women), *Gang Nu Jiang Nam* (Hong Kong Women Talk about Men), *Zhongnu Gaobai* (Middle-aged Women's Announcements), and *Touting Namren Xin* (Eavesdropping on Men's True Thoughts). These programs have created new vocabulary referring to single women and men, such as *gang nu* (Hong Kong woman), *zhong nu* (middle-aged woman), and *gang nam* (Hong Kong man). The programs tend to reproduce stereotypes of Hong Kong women as selfish, shallow, brand-obsessed, critical of men, unreasonable, and demanding. Men are stereotyped as immature, obsessed with computer games, comics, and Japanese pornography, unattractive, and having low career potential. Much of the discussion is in the form of a "battle of the sexes" dialogue in which women are featured criticizing Hong Kong men followed by programming showing men criticizing Hong Kong women. The gendered stereotypes suggest that some women and men experience frustration in dating and finding an appropriate person to marry. In this mud-slinging, however, women rather than men are generally targeted. While men are criticized for being unsuccessful in their careers, the implication in this stereotyping is that Hong Kong women have become educated, independent, and successful in their careers, yet are unable to marry and are thus unfulfilled. We can conclude that Hong Kong society remains deeply ambivalent about women's financial independence, and expects that women continue to maintain primary responsibility for caring for a family.

Shanghai

Overall standards of living have risen dramatically in Shanghai in the 2000s. The average annual income for Shanghai urban residents (CN¥26,675 [US$4,227] in 2008) is approximately three times lower than that in Hong Kong and ten times lower than that of Tokyo, but represents a 100 percent increase from the previous decade for Shanghai residents. Also, the cost of living in Shanghai is low—average annual expenditure in 2010 was about CN¥19,500 (US$3,095) (Shanghai Municipal Government 2011). Education levels for both women and men in Shanghai are low compared to those of Hong Kong and Tokyo, but on the rise nevertheless. In 2010, approximately 20 percent of women between the age of 16 and 54 held a post-tertiary degree, up from about 10 percent from the previous decade (Shanghai Municipal Government 2011). More importantly, across China, women accounted for 50 percent of students enrolled in university, 50 percent of students enrolled in MA programs, and 35 percent of students enrolled in PhD programs (Ministry of Education of the People's Republic of China 2012a). Further, the Chinese government has encouraged overseas study since its open-door policy in the 1970s, and between 1978 and 2003, 700,200 PRC citizens have studied overseas (Ministry of Education of the People's Republic of China 2012b). In Shanghai and even more so in the rest of China, however, large gaps in educational levels among women remain, with 20 percent of women between the age of 15 and 64 having an elementary school level education or less and nearly 60 percent with a middle school education or less (Shanghai Municipal

Government 2011). While labor force participation rates for women are high (68 percent for the ages between16 and 64), as in the other cities, women earn roughly two-thirds that of the average male earner and are still underrepresented in leadership positions. Women comprise 34 percent of management positions (J. Li 2011), 23 percent of the members of the National People's Congress (National People's Congress of the People's Republic of China 2013), and only 6 percent of the members of the Chinese Academy of Sciences (Chinese Academy of Sciences 2014). On the whole however, increasing levels of education, work opportunity, and income provide young women in Shanghai with opportunities that were not imaginable for women of their mothers' generation.

In Shanghai under the one-child policy, most young adults are only children, and as such they are their parents' only hope for having a grandchild. In Shanghai and across China, expectations of universal marriage are strong, and parents are often involved in helping their adult children to find partners by arranging meetings with *xiangqin* (potential spouses). Women in Shanghai and in other Chinese cities often appreciate this help, in part because they have a narrow window of opportunity to find an appropriate partner. High school students and sometimes even university students are not encouraged to date (*China Daily* 2003), and yet at the age of 22 or 23, women are expected to be securing a potential husband so that a marriage may take place before the woman reaches the age of 27.

In Shanghai's environment of rapidly changing socio-economic conditions, the idea that everyone should take opportunities to be successful is widely felt. Success for a woman means getting a good education, a good job, marrying a financially stable and loving husband, and then having a child who repeats the process. Housing is expensive in Shanghai, yet most women and their families expect that the groom and his family provide housing for the newly married couple.[3] This puts pressure on men to own property if they wish to marry. In the past, newlyweds often lived with the husband and his parents, but this has been changing as more brides prefer to maintain an independent household. Family size has thus been shrinking. The average household size in Shanghai is now 2.49 per household, down 0.3 percent since 2004 (Shanghai Municipal Government 2011).

Even though the percentage of single women in China's big cities is not as nearly high as in Tokyo or Hong Kong, new vocabulary to describe such women has nevertheless entered the Chinese language. In popular parlance, single women over the age of 30 are commonly described as *shengnu*, meaning "leftover women." The word "leftover" suggests that single women are unwanted by men, but according to the *Baidu Baike* (the mainland Chinese equivalent of Wikipedia), the phrase also suggests that these women have a high educational level, high income, and high intelligence, and remain "stuck" in singlehood because they are too choosy when searching for a spouse.[4] In 2011, Shanghai TV Arts and Culture Channel capitalized on public interest in the trend with the broadcast of a 24-part mini-series, *Shengnu de Huangjin Shidai* (The Golden Age of Leftover Ladies). The drama depicts the love lives of two beautiful, successful career women in their early thirties who search for husbands after their mothers threaten to set them up on arranged dates. In 2010, the state television broadcaster, China Central Television, aired the 25-episode drama, *Da Nu Dang Jia* (Aging Daughter Should Get Married), which follows the love life of a 33-year-old school teacher whose family members decide to devote themselves to arranging her marriage. In these popular media, marriage is portrayed as a way of achieving personal happiness and a way of satisfying filial duty. As in the case of Hong Kong, we can see the anxiety that the price of women's success in education and work is that women become unwilling or unable to marry. Worry about the risks of obtaining a higher education can also be seen in the phrase that has been circulating among highly educated women, *di san zhong* (third kind of human being). The phrase refers to the idea that women with PhD degrees are neither women nor men, but a third category of human being. In other words, the phrase warns that highly educated women become "freaks" who will not be accepted by men as marriage partners and who thus cannot enter the mainstream life paths of marriage and family.

To recapitulate, while all three societies under consideration offer substantially improved educational opportunities for women and increased rates of women's employment, political and social pressures that encourage women to marry and care for families are still present. Public commentary and popular media frequently target singlehood for women as being more problematic than singlehood for men, even though men are more likely than women to remain single in all three societies. Such negative commentary on single women reflects the biases and anxieties in society about women's growing individuality and autonomy.

Imaginaries of life projects

Even while confined by state policies and societal expectations that enforce a gendered role, my research shows that single women increasingly construct their life projects around the notions of gender equality, individuality, self-determination, self-fulfillment, and the pursuit of happiness and love. These life projects converge across metropolitan cities as women negotiate and locate their choices within transnationally affirmed trajectories and universalistic values.

Education and employment markets

Women I interviewed saw themselves as located within transnational education and employment markets, regardless of whether or not they actually study or take jobs overseas. Their choices of where to study were embedded in transnational hierarchies in which degrees from top schools in Asian cities could be used to move to better schools in other Asian cities or in the West. For women in Hong Kong and China, top universities in the United States stood at the apex of the educational hierarchy. Hong Kong is a stepping stone for students from mainland China who want to eventually study for a PhD in the United States. One informant originally from Shanghai, for example, received a scholarship to study at a second-tier university in Hong Kong. From there she transferred to a first-tier university in Hong Kong, which led her to study for a master's degree at a first-tier university in the UK, and she plans to return to the UK for her PhD. Japanese women were less concerned with studying at a top university in the United States as the Japanese education market is more focused on national universities in Japan. Nonetheless, some Japanese women expressed interest in studying overseas. A Japanese woman in her forties spoke of getting an MBA in the United States as a missed opportunity. She felt that if she had done so, she might be a manager rather than a technician. Studying overseas was within the realm of the imagination of possibilities for women in all three cities, even if they were not in a position to take advantage of these opportunities.

Taking part in transnational education and employment markets is based on the ideals of individual achievement and self-fulfillment, and it requires mobility, time, and capital. The marriage market, on the other hand, penalizes women who accumulate experiences of mobility and who spend too much time in education or developing a career. Women I interviewed thus attempted to negotiate the opportunities in the educational and employment markets while minimizing damage to themselves in marriage markets.

I asked Miao, a 26-year-old PhD student from Shanghai who was studying at a university in Hong Kong, about how obtaining the PhD affected her hopes for marriage. She said:

> It is totally disadvantageous! Many people think that a man should earn more than a woman. If the man has a PhD, then his target would be a woman with an MA or below. People think men should have a higher socio-economic status so that the relationship can be more stable.

Miao planned to finish her PhD as soon as possible and return to Shanghai to get married. She expected that her parents would arrange *xiangqin*, or meetings with a view to marriage, to help her find a suitable person. Some women and men who planned to study overseas talked about finding someone to marry before they left China. Marriage was a greater problem for women than for men, however, because women face earlier marriage deadlines. In Hong Kong, marriage deadlines for women were not clearly agreed upon, although some women who were eager to marry became anxious if they had no prospects by the age of 30. In Japan, women talked about 30 as a critical year, although women also pushed this deadline up as they aged and remained single. In Shanghai, women hoped to marry by age 27, and many felt that 30 was the upper limit for a woman to marry well. In other words, women navigated educational markets with care as they kept in mind the requirements of local marriage markets.

Even more than education, success in the job market is closely tied to the ability to be mobile, and generally greater mobility brings greater rewards in the market. Many of the women I met had moved from one city or town to another at least once for work or education. In Hong Kong and Shanghai, moving up in one's career meant women should be willing to travel around mainland China and Asia. In Japan, women on the management track expected to be posted to different cities in Japan or overseas. By moving to pursue a more interesting career, some women needed to sacrifice relationships with boyfriends and endanger their chances of marrying.

Kathy, a woman from Wuhan whom I met in Shanghai, emphasized that she did not want to be a *nuqiangren* (superwoman). Rather, she just wanted her life to be a little more interesting, and she wanted to fully explore the possibilities available to her. She said:

> I don't want great achievement. I just want to make my life more comfortable. I like change. I like to try different things. When I was young, I had a dream to go abroad, to see other parts of the world besides China. I want to have a wide view [of the world].

Kathy had moved to Shanghai the year before I met her after getting a job as a computer technician at one of China's largest banks. In coming to Shanghai, she had left behind a boyfriend and a job as a university lecturer in a small city. She said:

> As time went by, I realized that [the life I was leading] was not what I wanted. I could tell what I would look like after 20 years there. My life would not change greatly. I wanted to see what else I could achieve. That was the great challenge for me. I decided to leave my boyfriend and my family. I would come here to work all by myself. It was the first time I left my homeland. It took courage to do what I did.

Kathy hoped that her boyfriend would join her in Shanghai, but instead, several months after our interview, her boyfriend broke up with her, and Kathy decided that she preferred to marry rather than pursue her dream of living in Shanghai. She found a new boyfriend in Guangzhou, and planned to move there to be with him. Although she gave up her dream of pursuing a career, she did not step too far away from her "courageous" path, choosing a move to another wealthy "cosmopolitan center" over moving back to her hometown, a second-tier city in China's hinterlands.

Venturing overseas for work can create an even bigger hurdle in marriage markets. A 33-year-old woman from Nagoya who worked as a flight attendant and lived in Hong Kong said that Japanese men she met in Tokyo physically recoiled from her when they heard that she lived in Hong Kong, and she had been rejected in an *omiai* (arranged meeting for the purpose of marriage) when the prospective marriage partner, a school teacher in her home town, learned that she lived in Hong Kong. She said:

> I was rejected by the man before we even met! The man read about my background and said that it would be a waste (*mottainai*) [for someone like him to be with me]. In Aichi [prefecture], if you've lived overseas or had a career, some people will start to look at you differently.

Expectations that women should be less experienced and less mobile than men help to explain why men with international experience were desirable on the marriage market according to women I met, but women with international experience quickly found out that they did not have the same desirability when they tried to marry.

Marriage markets

In the marriage market, women I interviewed looked for partners who possessed individual attributes that would inspire "love," such as the ability to understand feelings, maturity, a sense of humor, and conversation and social skills. They also considered the impersonal criteria of age, educational and income level, and social background. In using the word "market" to describe women's experience and imagination of marriage possibilities, my approach is similar to that of Constable (2003: 120), who asks "how love and emotion are intertwined with political economy through cultural logics of desire." Marriage markets are markets in the sense that local but increasingly universalistic cultural logics, with their emphasis on love and feelings, shape expectations and imaginations of what social, economic, and personal qualities a potential spouse might possess.

Studies show that a majority of people in China believes that a good marriage should be based first on impersonal criteria such as the man's income and ability to provide housing. A survey reported in the *Chongqing Morning Post* found that 70 percent of respondents felt that a man should possess an apartment before he be considered as a marriage partner and 80 percent of respondents felt that only men with salaries exceeding CN¥4000 (US$634) a month deserve to have relationships with women (Gao 2012). As such, getting married commonly involves arranged meetings and explicit exposure of the individual's assets at the start of courtship. A man's assets generally include his educational background, income, and possession of an apartment, while a woman's assets are beauty, youth, and gentleness of character. Some women quipped that to marry in Shanghai, a man must have *chezi, fanzi, piaozi* (a car, house, and money).

Women who are looking at impersonal criteria are more willing to consider arranged meetings and local markets. Miao, the Shanghai woman studying for her PhD in Hong Kong mentioned earlier, said this about arranged meetings:

> This is the most common way and the most secure. From the start we can know a lot about their background, family, education, and career. After being set up for an introduction, the only thing left is for us to meet and see if we get along. This is an especially good method for local Shanghai people. Their relatives can ask their colleagues if they know someone of a similar age.

That being said, she would clearly not marry just anyone who had a good education and career. She had recently rejected two well-educated young men, one an assistant professor, because she felt that they were not interesting, lacked social skills, and did not inspire any feelings of attraction.

Although arranged meetings to help people find marriage partners remain common in Shanghai, such practices appear to be declining in other East Asian cities. Arranged meetings were common in Hong Kong a generation ago, but my Hong Kong-born informants nearly unanimously felt that such meetings today were in very poor taste. In Japan, arranged marriages have steadily declined. In 1935, 69 percent of all marriages were reported to be the product of *omiai* (arranged meeting). In 1970, the figure fell to 45 percent, and by 2005 only 6 percent of marriages were reported to be a result of an *omiai* (National Institute of Population and Social Security Research 2006: 3). A 43-year-old Tokyo woman explained her experience of *omiai*:

> My parents made me go, and the whole time I was saying, "no, no, no." It was a little disrespectful to the man, because I went there thinking "no." But the men who come to *omiai* are never any good. I would try my best to keep up the conversation but he would have nothing to say.

She explained that she had had 16 unsuccessful *omiai*:

> None of the men were the type I could love. It's very difficult for me to find someone that I love, and if I don't love him, I'm not interested so there's no point.

Even in Shanghai, where arranged meetings are common, some women expressed their dislike of the idea, describing it as "strange" or "unnatural." Two friends made these comments:

ANNA: I tried *xiangqin* (arranged meeting) just to stop my mother from bothering me. I tried a few times. I didn't expect much and didn't get much. It's not my style.
MIFENG: I wouldn't try *xiangqin* because I'm romantic. My heart keeps on beating. I don't like to be embarrassed. I don't want to meet someone [just to get] married. I want to love first. I want to be in love and be loved.

Women in Hong Kong and Shanghai who believed in romantic love tended to also believe in a single person, described as "the one" or "Mr Right," using the English terms. Japanese women used the phrase *ii hito* (a good or appropriate person), often stating that they hoped that fate would bring them to their match. Marriage in all three societies, but particularly in Shanghai and Hong Kong, was seen as an end result based on a combination of fate and individual effort.[5]

As mentioned earlier, age was an important factor that shaped women's position in local marriage markets. Marriage deadlines, or the idea that beyond a certain age, women will be too old for the marriage market persists in all three societies, but most strongly in Shanghai and across China. Thirty-three-year-old Sharon in Shanghai said:

> When I was 20 my aunt took me aside and said, find a never-married man from a decent family like ours. A few years later she said, it's okay if he is a widower but not divorced. If I talked to her again, I think she would say, just get married—anyone is okay.

Women saw their value in local marriage markets falling in this way as they aged. Yet many understood that they were still considered attractive by Western men and had value in an international market. A 33-year-old Japanese woman living in Tokyo said, "The first thing that Japanese men ask is, 'How old are you?' Western men never ask me that." This woman had given up on finding a Japanese partner and was actively searching for a Western husband by frequenting Roppongi, the bar district popular among foreign men in Tokyo.

Even women who have never left their own society compared men in their society with men in other societies. A Tokyo woman, for example, said that she could never marry a Japanese man because they cannot meet her expectations. She said:

> I believe that men should be superior to women (*dansonjohi*). I think that a man should know a lot of things. If he doesn't know something then I'd think, "Why doesn't he know about that?" He should know more than me. That's why it's hard to date a Japanese man. If the man is a foreigner, I'd understand that he doesn't know something about Japan. But if he's a Japanese man, I'd think, "He's Japanese so why doesn't he know about that?"

Interestingly, she not only used transnational positioning to articulate her choices, she also evoked the traditional view of "man's superiority" to explain her nontraditional choices—a foreign man or indefinite singlehood.

Whether women decided to choose a partner from the neighborhood or from across the world, one common thread in the interviews was that they viewed marriage as a personal decision and maintained that they had the right to choose a partner based on criteria of their own making. They privileged their own choice of partner and the timing of their marriage over the preferences of their parents—a clear expression of their individuality.

Leisure markets

The leisure markets were an area through which the women I interviewed had opened themselves up to interacting with the broader world and the vast choices this world has to offer. They had access to choices of leisure pursuits through the internet, television, books, and other media in what Gordon Mathews (2000) calls a global cultural supermarket. Women I met felt that they could pursue these options if they had the money and the time. My informants were fans of Korean dramas, Hong Kong pop stars, Formula One racing, and world-class international downhill skiing competitions, among other things, and some indeed traveled the world to pursue these interests.

Single women are probably in a better position to enjoy leisure markets than most other segments of the population, including men and married women. They may have greater access to leisure markets than men in large part because women are marginalized from top-tier and highly paid work, giving them more freedom to use their time away from work. Single women may also have disposable income, especially if they live with their parents and can thus save on utilities and housing expenses. A 37-year-old clerk who lived with her parents in Tokyo contributed ¥50,000 (US$488) per month for household expenditures, leaving plenty of salary to spend leisure consumption. She used her income to travel to Canada several times a year. She said:

> My married friends tell me that they are envious when they hear that I go to Canada and do whatever I want to do. They say, "You shouldn't marry." They don't think I should marry because I'd lose my freedom. None of my friends who are married say that they are glad that they married. Of course they have their own things that are good, such as children and they seem happy, but I don't feel envious of them at all.

A 33-year-old Shanghai woman, an executive at a Japanese firm who also lived with her parents, immensely enjoyed her leisure activities. She said:

> My favorite thing to do is travel. I've been to Europe, France, Italy, Switzerland, Germany. I was really moved; it stirred my heart to see French architecture. I've been to almost everywhere in China. I want to see all the places in China, and then see the whole world. I went to Hokkaido last year. I read at least one book a month. I like psychology—these are popular now—cooking books, and novels. I like to see films six times a year, often with my mother. There is not enough time! Every year I have 15 days paid leave so I have to plan carefully.

Like many women, she described leisure as a way of opening her eyes to the world and developing a more sophisticated self. She shared her travel experiences and impressions with her friends in a travel blog. Although this woman told me that she wanted to marry, she was also unwilling to give up traveling, which would make finding an appropriate partner difficult. Women understood that they had to choose between leisure and marriage, and those deeply involved in leisure consumption found little appeal in marriage.

Some women linked leisure to personal growth and reflection. A Shanghai woman told me that to understand how Shanghai women felt, I should read American author Elizabeth Gilbert's bestselling memoir, *Eat, Pray, Love* (2010) that chronicles Gilbert's travels to Italy, India, and Bali to discover herself after leaving her husband. A 34-year-old Shanghai woman told me that she decided to leave Shanghai to work and travel overseas following a breakup with her fiancé, a French national. She said, "I needed to exile myself and drift around in order to let it go. I needed to travel to find myself—it was my reflection period." She worked in India for several months before traveling to Hong Kong, Japan, and New York. A few informants in all three societies spoke of leaving their home society to travel to the West or India as a way of escaping the pressures to marry or a failed relationship, and coming back refreshed and better able to face their problems.

While most women joined leisure activities for the sheer joy, pleasure, and relief that they brought, some even found ways to link leisure with the support and care of others. Some Hong Kong women traveled with their parents and paid for them, as single women in Hong Kong generally earn more than their parents. One Hong Kong woman explained that her life purpose was to make others happy, but in order to do so, she needed to first make herself happy by traveling. For these women, leisure and travel were not simply asserting their individual choices and refusing the pressures of their own societies, but also for bettering themselves as persons and citizens.

Reinterpreting gendered citizenship

The ideas of responsibility and living a meaningful and fulfilling life were dominant motives in the narratives of single women regarding self worth. Women I interviewed emphasized responsibility for their own lives by getting an education, earning their own living, and attempting to achieve their own potential. But they also saw such action as their contribution to society, thus as confirmation of their good citizenship.

In Tokyo, women defined their financial independence as a significant contribution. One woman explained how she had taken responsibility for managing her own education, career, and finances. She decided at an early age that she would not rely on her family, whose primary message to her was that she should marry as soon as possible. Instead, she used her own savings to study English at a community college in the United States. She bought a condominium apartment in Tokyo and was studying for an accounting degree in her spare time. She had a Canadian boyfriend but was not sure if she wanted to marry him. She emphasized self-reliance as a key life value rather than reliance on her natal family or on a romantic partner.

In Hong Kong, women emphasized their contribution to their immediate families. As mentioned, some women born in the 1950s and 1960s were eldest daughters who had sacrificed their own education to earn an income for their families. These women had left secondary school at age 15 or 16 and had gone to work in factories to send their younger siblings to school in Hong Kong and overseas. They may not have consciously sacrificed their own opportunities to marry for their families, but may have understood that marriage would have limited their ability to earn money for their families. As adults, they remained close to their natal families. Some continued living with their parents or their brothers' families into their forties and fifties, and were actively involved in raising their nieces and nephews.

Searching for broader meaning and direction in life was a motivating factor for many women I met. Women commonly spoke of following their dreams and living a good life as a way of contributing to society. The woman mentioned earlier, Kathy, who moved from Wuhan to Shanghai, explained:

> Marriage is no longer the only way for women. Women value career and want respect from men and from society. Being happy is the most important thing. Some can be happy as a housewife. Some think they can devote themselves to society … . I think people should try their best to do challenging things, to improve themselves. If I stayed home in Wuhan, life would

have been easier. Shanghai brings many chances and new things. I have to live by following my heart.

Kathy expressed a view shared by many other women; that in being single they have taken a more difficult but nobler path as they tried to achieve own potential and lead a meaningful life.

A handful of women had clear mission statements for their lives, as in the case of Erica, a confident and attractive 42-year-old manager who worked in the education sector in Hong Kong. She said:

> My purpose in life is to pursue happiness while making a contribution to society. It is important to be involved in society and to do something that is meaningful. When I worked in PR [public relations], in the mass media, I tried to close the gap between business and society. In higher education, I try to help students and their families to live more meaningful lives.

Erica added that everything she does in her life must comply with her motto of achieving happiness through service. In her life plan, marriage does not have a place. She explained that many people, especially her parents, had tried to convince her to marry, but she felt that she was happiest and most satisfied without a boyfriend or husband, which permitted flexibility in her schedule and relationships.

Having a clear life mission was not common, but in general the single women I interviewed were unambiguous about justifying their "extraordinary" paths of life on moral grounds of being good and worthy. They saw the contribution of their life choices in terms of gendered citizenship roles of good daughters serving their parents, women making others happy, and dutiful individuals serving society and the greater good of humanity as a whole. But by taking the responsibility for these choices and actively pursuing them for self-realization and fulfillment, they also showed awareness of transnational frameworks and vocabularies that affirm and allow their individuality.

Conclusion

Women's lives are shaped by the societies in which they live; their governments provide opportunities and restrictions, and social contexts provide norms and values through which people make sense of the world. The one-child policy in China powerfully shapes women's choices, family formation, and social expectations. Children and family heirs become more important, and parents place greater pressure on their daughters to marry and bear a child. Japan's essentially closed immigration policies are based on the assumption that women must take responsibility for social reproduction, thus shaping the tenor of public discussion that links marriage and fertility to citizenship. In Hong Kong, women's rising levels of education and income, combined with expectations that men should be more educated than women in romantic relationships, has led to contradictions in which highly educated women are unable to find appropriate partners. In all three societies, social structures and norms operate on assumptions that women and men are happiest in heterosexual unions in which women are primary family caregivers and men are the superior income earners.

That being said, single women living in metropolitan, global East Asian cities past the age of 30 are choosing not to marry in large numbers. As my research reveals, remaining single in most cases is not based on a single decision. Instead, women find themselves single as they make a series of decisions to reject "inappropriate" matches and as they proceed to engage the opportunities available to them. They see themselves as individuals located within a range of markets; local, regional, national, and transnational. Women maneuver in these markets with the aim of achieving happiness, success, love, and self-fulfillment, and find ways to link individual achievements to others in their company, society, nation, and beyond. In this way, with rhetoric mild and familiar, single women are pointing to their accomplishments in education, work, and in their personal lives, and urging that these—rather than marriage and family—serve as the criteria by which their citizenship is valued.

Notes

1 Substantial parts of the work described in this chapter were supported by funding from the Research Grants Council of the Hong Kong Special Administrative Region, China (Project No. CUHK4018/02H). The research was also made possible by a 2001 Summer Grant for Research and a 2001–2 direct grant awarded by the Chinese University of Hong Kong. I thank Moeko Wagatsuma and Chan Yim Ting for their assistance in conducting this research.

2 In a 2005 national survey conducted by the Ministry of Health and Welfare (2006), 90 percent of single women aged 18 to 34 stated that they wanted to marry at some point in their life. Only 5.6 percent stated that they did not plan to marry at all. Furthermore, 19 percent of single women stated that their ideal life course was to marry and become a full-time housewife, while 33.3 percent said they wanted to marry and temporarily leave the workforce while caring for their children, and 30 percent said that they wanted to marry and remain in the workforce.

3 In January 2012, the average price of property was CN¥19,336 (US$3,060) per square meter (Shanghai Municipal Government 2011), but the average annual income was CN¥26,675 (US$4,280), making it almost impossible for a young man to afford to buy an apartment on his salary alone.

4 http://baike.baidu.com/view/404328.htm (accessed January 2012).

5 Women commonly used the word *yuanfen* (fate) in Chinese or say *en ga areba* (if we are fated to meet) in Japanese to describe their understanding that finding the right person was a matter of fate or destiny. Some women used this idea to explain why they did not want to actively search for a partner. Chinese women also pointed out that *yuanfen* combines the elements of both fate and effort. There was a great range in the degree of effort involved in finding a partner, from total passivity to actively meeting people. Common activities included participating in commercial and noncommercial matchmaking dinners, commercially organized speed dating, registering in matchmaking companies, joining online chatting and matchmaking sites, joining hiking or other activity groups where men were likely to appear, going to bars and clubs, and asking friends and relatives to arrange meetings and blind dates. A new word, *konkatsu* has emerged in Japan in recent years, describing women's efforts to seek a spouse (*kekkon katsudo*), mimicking the word for job seeking (*shushoku katsudo*).

References

Appadurai, A. 1996. *Modernity at Large: Cultural Dimensions of Globalization*. Minneapolis: University of Minnesota Press.

Cabinet Office, Government of Japan. 2012. Danjo Kyodo Sankaku Shakai Ni Kansuru Yoron Chosa, Heisei 24nenban. [Public Opinion Survey Regarding Cooperative Planning for a Gender Equal Society, 2012 edition]. Available at: www.gender.go.jp/policy/men_danjo/pdf/basic/siryo1_1.pdf (accessed June 2014).

Cai, W. 2012. Concern Over Shanghai Having the Lowest Birthrate. *Shanghai Daily*, April 27. Available at: www.shanghaidaily.com/Metro/education/Concern-over-Shanghai-having-lowest-birth-rate/shdaily.shtml (accessed June 2014).

Census and Statistics Department, HKSAR. 2011. Women and Men in Hong Kong: Key Statistics. Available at: www.censtatd.gov.hk/hong_kong_statistics/gender/marr_fert_and_family_con/index.jsp (accessed May 2011).

——2012a. *Hong Kong Population Projections 2012–2041*. Available at: www.statistics.gov.hk/pub/B1120015052012XXXXB0100.pdf (accessed June 2014).

——2012b. Census and Statistics Department Announces the Results of the Study on Household Income Distribution in Hong Kong. Available at: www.censtatd.gov.hk/press_release/pressReleaseDetail.jsp?charsetID=1&pressRID=2965 (accessed June 2014).

——2013a. Women and Men in Hong Kong: Key Statistics. Available at: www.censtatd.gov.hk/hong_kong_statistics/gender/marr_fert_and_family_con/index.jsp (accessed June 2014).

——2013b. Monthly Digest of Statistics: The Fertility Trend in Hong Kong, 1980–2012. Available at: www.statistics.gov.hk/pub/B71312FA2013XXXXB0100.pdf (accessed June 2014).

China Daily. 2003. Dating a Tricky Game for University Women. August 27. Available at: www.chinadaily.com.cn/en/doc/2003-8/27/content_258799.htm (accessed June 2014).

——2005. Hong Kong Administration Suggests Three Children per Couple. February 22. Available at: www.chinadaily.com.cn/english/doc/2005-02/22/content_418419.htm (accessed June 2014).

Chinese Academy of Sciences. 2014. Scientists. Available at: http://english.cas.cn/Sc/ (accessed June 2014).

Chinese Women's Research Network. 2011. Shanghai Sustains Late Marriage Trend. January 27. Available at: http://en.wsic.ac.cn/academicnews/2095.htm (accessed January 2012).

Chiu, J. 2013. Unlucky in Love ... or Just Left Out of the Market. *South China Morning Post*, March 4. Available at: www.scmp.com/news/hong-kong/article/1173765/unlucky-love-or-just-left-out-market (accessed June 2014).

Constable, N. 2003. *Romance on a Global Stage: Pen Pals, Virtual Ethnography, and "Mail Order" Marriages*. Berkeley: University of California Press.

Gao, Q. 2012. 70% of Women Require House Before Marriage. *China Daily*, January 5. Available at: www.chinadaily.com.cn/china/2012-01/05/content_14386646.htm (accessed June 2014).

Gender Equality Bureau, 2011. Women and Men in Japan: Facts and Figures. Cabinet Office, Government of Japan. Available at: www.gender.go.jp/english_contents/pr_act/pub/pamphlet/women-and-men11/pdf/1.pdf (accessed June 2014).

Hong Kong Women's Commission, HKSAR. 2011. *Hong Kong Women in Figures, 2011*. Available at: www.women.gov.hk/download/research/HK_Women2011_e.pdf (accessed December 2011).

Information Services Department, HKSAR. 2010. Hong Kong Year Book 2010. Available at: www.yearbook.gov.hk/2010/en/index.html (accessed April 2011).

——2013. Hong Kong: The Facts. Available at: www.gov.hk/en/about/abouthk/factsheets/docs/population.pdf (accessed June 2014).

Jia, F. 2011. Policies Change as More Arrive. *Shanghai Daily*, May 4.

Kashiwazaki, C. and T. Akaha. 2006. Japanese Immigration Policy: Responding to Conflicting Pressures. *Migration Immigration Source*, November 1. Available at: www.migrationinform ation.org/feature/display.cfm?ID=487 (accessed June 2014).

Kelsky, K. 2001. *Women on the Verge: Japanese Women, Western Dreams*. Durham, NC: Duke University Press.

Li, J. 2011. Women Hold 34 Percent of Senior Management Positions in China. *People's Daily Online*, March 8. Available at: http://english.people.com.cn/90001/90778/7312330.html (accessed June 2014).

Li, R. 2011. Migrants Failed by Cities' Efforts to Mitigate Unfairness of Hukou System. *South China Morning Post*, February 14. Available at: www.scmp.com/article/738143/migrants-failed-cities-efforts-mitigate-unfairness-hukou-system (accessed June 2014).

Lu, F. 2012. Baby Boom Boosts City's Aging Population. *Shanghai Daily*, March 30. Available at: www.shanghaidaily.com/Metro/society/Baby-boom-boosts-citys-aging-population/shd aily.shtml (accessed June 2014).

Mathews, G. 2000. *Global Culture, Individual Identity: Searching for Home in the Cultural Supermarket*. New York: Routledge.

McCurry, J. 2007. Japanese Minister Wants Birth-giving Machines, AKA Women, to Have More Babies. *The Guardian*, January 29. Available at: www.theguardian.com/world/2007/jan/29/japan.justinmccurry (accessed June 2014).

Ministry of Education, Culture, Sports, Science and Technology. 2012. Statistics. Available at: www.mext.go.jp/english/statistics/ (accessed June 2012).

Ministry of Education of the People's Republic of China. 2012a. Number of Female Students of Schools of All Levels and Types. Available at: www.moe.edu.cn/publicfiles/business/htmlfiles/moe/s6208/201201/129613.html (accessed January 2012).

——2012b. The Overall Situation of Studying Abroad. Available at: www.moe.edu.cn/publicfiles/business/htmlfiles/moe/s3917/201007/91574.html (accessed January 2012).

Ministry of Foreign Affairs. 2011. Kaigai Zairyu Hojinsu Chosa Tokei [Annual Report of Statistics of Japanese Nationals Overseas]. Available at: www.mofa.go.jp/mofaj/toko/tokei/hojin/11/pdfs/2.pdf (accessed December 2011).

Ministry of Health, Labor, and Welfare. 2006. Kekkon To Shussan Ni Kansuru Zenkoku Chosa [National Survey on Marriage and Childbirth]. Available at: www.mhlw.go.jp/shingi/2006/09/dl/s0929–6b2.pdf (accessed February 2012).

——2009. Konnin. Heisei 21nen Jinko Dotai Tokei Geppo Nenkei No Gaikyo [Annual Overview of Monthly Statistics on Population Trends 2009]. Available at: www.mhlw.go.jp/toukei/saikin/hw/jinkou/geppo/nengai09/kekka4.html (accessed June 2014).

Ministry of Internal Affairs and Communication, Statistics Bureau. 2013. *Statistical Handbook of Japan 2013*. Available at: www.stat.go.jp/english/data/handbook/c0117.htm (accessed June 2014).

National Institute of Population and Social Security Research. 2006. Dai13sai Shussan Doko Kihon Chosa. Kekkon To Shussan Ni Kansuru Zenkoku Chosa [The 13th Basic Survey on Birthrate Trends. National Survey on Marriage and Births]. Available at: www.ipss.go.jp/ps-doukou/j/doukou13/doukou13.pdf (accessed June 2014).

National Institute of Population and Social Security Research 2012. Population Statistics of Japan. Nuptiality, Population by Marital Status. Available at: www.ipss.go.jp/p-info/e/psj2012/PSJ2012.asp (accessed June 2014).

National People's Congress of the People's Republic of China. 2013. New National Legislature Sees More Diversity. February 27. Available at: www.npc.gov.cn/englishnpc/news/Focus/2013–02/27/content_1759084.htm (accessed June 2014).

Ong, A. 1999. *Flexible Citizenship: The Cultural Logics of Transnationality*. Durham, NC: Duke University Press.

Sakai, J. 2003. *Makeinu No Toboe* [The Distant Cry of Loser Dogs]. Tokyo: Kodansha.

Sassen, S. 1991. *The Global City: New York, London, Tokyo*. Princeton, NJ: Princeton University Press.

Shanghai Municipal Government. 2011. Shanghai Residents Still Top of Income Table. Available at: www.shanghai.gov.cn/shanghai/node27118/node27818/u22ai70742.html (accessed June 2014).

Tokyo Metropolitan Government. 2009. Tokyo Statistical Yearbook, 2009. Available at: www.toukei.metro.tokyo.jp/tnenkan/2009/tn09q3e014.htm (accessed January 2012).

——2011. Tokyo Statistical Yearbook. Population and Households (2011). Available at: www.toukei.metro.tokyo.jp/tnenkan/tn-eindex.htm (accessed June 2014).

——2012. Tokyo Statistical Yearbook. Population and Households (2012). Available at: www.toukei.metro.tokyo.jp/tnenkan/tn-eindex.htm (accessed June 2014).

Ko, V. 2010. Hong Kong Women Struggling to Close the Gender Gap. *South China Morning Post*, December 16. Available at: www.scmp.com/article/733499/hk-women-struggling-close-gender-gap (accessed June 2014).

Yamada, M. 1999. *Parasaito Shinguru no Jidai* [The Age of Parasite Singles]. Tokyo: Chikuma Shobo.

Yamamoto, T. 2001. *Nonpara: Parasaito Shinai Onnatachi No Honto* [Nonparasites: The Real Situation of Women Who Choose Not to Become Parasites]. Tokyo: Magajin Hausu.

9 The changing transnational imagery of "good nation" and the Ainu in Japan

Kiyoteru Tsutsui

This chapter examines how the changing transnational imagery of "good nation" shaped politics around the Ainu, an indigenous people in Japan. In much of the debate about minority politics, observers tend to assume that the root causes of injustices against minority groups lie in local society, whether it is racial bigotry in people's minds or discriminatory policies by the local government. For those individuals who bear the brunt of those injustices on a daily basis, a link between their hardship and transnational imagery of "good nation" might seem trifling. However, recent scholarship in comparative historical sociology and global and transnational sociology has uncovered that transnationally legitimated models of treatment of minorities can have transformative impact on local minority politics (Soysal 1995, Tsutsui and Shin 2008). When international frameworks legitimate domination of minority groups, the government's main approach might be repression, exploitation, or even genocide. When broader models encourage assimilation, the government might fancy itself a paternalistic benefactor to minorities, providing minimal welfare in exchange for cultural submission. When transnational human rights norms promote self-determination of minorities, minorities become empowered into activism for more rights. Consequently, the state might reluctantly give in and abolish discriminatory laws. Even in this case, minority discrimination may not completely disappear; it tends to persist in informal social realms. In all these scenarios, minorities face injustices, but in very different forms. What was a blatant aggression against minorities turns into an arrogant imposition of majority culture and then more subtle social discrimination.

Drawing on interviews and archival data, this chapter examines such transformation of politics around the Ainu since Japan's modernization in the late nineteenth century. Throughout this period, the transnationally located conceptions of "good nation" have informed the Japanese government's policy toward Ainu as well as the Ainu's political orientation. In the first few decades of modern Japan, based on social Darwinist views of the Ainu, the government colonized Ainu lands and characterized the Ainu as "a dying race" and "savages to be civilized." Dispossessed of material resources and their traditional life styles, most Ainu had no choice but to become subordinates within Imperial Japan and live on what little welfare it offered. Soon thereafter, with the rise of concerns that the Ainu's deplorable living conditions might bring embarrassment to Japan in the international community, provision of minimal welfare and efforts toward assimilation began. In the post-World War II period, the government adopted the ideology of homogenous Japan and pushed the Ainu more forcefully into assimilation. Ainuness was shunned not only by the mainstream Japanese but also by the Ainu themselves, and Ainu culture was on display only within the confines of tourist industries and anthropological research. Correspondingly, the government claimed that the Ainu have been completely assimilated into mainstream Japanese society. Since the 1970s, however, inspired by the global indigenous rights movement and domestic leftist/anti-colonial activism, the Ainu slowly transformed themselves into a proud indigenous people and have actively mobilized politically to achieve significant successes. The government was hard-pressed to continue its denial of the Ainu's existence, acknowledging them as an indigenous people in 2008. Thus, reflecting changes in the dominant approach to ethnic minorities among the nations of the "developed world," the Japanese government's approach to the Ainu has shifted from colonial domination through cultural assimilation to finally cultural autonomy/multiculturalism. While the level of cultural autonomy for the Ainu is still quite limited, respect for Ainu culture is beginning to take root in contemporary Japan. This dramatic change, I argue, was possible because transnationally legitimated understandings of "good nation" shifted during this period from a dominant colonial power through an assimilationist nation-state to a diverse multicultural community. Table 9.1 summarizes these shifts as well as key Ainu-related events and serves as a guide to the historical examination below.

Theoretically, this study seeks to connect the literature on globalization, which tends to highlight the impact of global forces on local changes, and social movement studies, which tend to emphasize the role of social movements in producing political changes. The former has demonstrated that transnational models of proper majority-minority relationships can reconfigure local political dynamics to encourage mobilization by previously underprivileged groups and produce relevant policy changes (Brysk 2000, Keck and Sikkink 1998, Risse, Ropp, and Sikkink 1999, Soysal 1995, Tsutsui 2004). The latter, on the other hand, highlight the bottom-up processes through which local activists strategically use global institutions to advance their movements (della Porta, Kriesi, and Rucht 1999, Guidry, Kennedy, and Zald 2000, Ron 1997). Building on these studies, as well as those that more explicitly examine the negotiated and mediated nature of the impact of global forces on local politics (Goodale and Merry 2007, Liu 2006, Tarrow 2005, Tsutsui and Shin 2008), but examining a longer time span than most empirical studies, this chapter demonstrates that transnational models influenced Ainu politics throughout the history of modern Japan.

The Ainu in premodern Japan[1]

The Ainu today are descendants of people who have inhabited northern parts of Japan for thousands of years. In prehistoric times, the Ainu ancestors, known initially as Emishi and then Ezo since the late twelfth century, lived all over the

Table 9.1 Chronology of Ainu activism and changing transnational imagery of "good nation"

Year	Ainu-related events	The dominant transnational imagery of "good nation"
1869	Hokkaido established as a prefecture	From colonial domination to imperialistic "civilizing" assimilation
1899	Former Aborigines Protection Act enacted	
1946	Hokkaido Ainu Association established (it is seen as distinct from its prewar namesake)	National self-determination/Culturally homogenous nation-state
1961	Hokkaido Ainu Association changes its name to Hokkaido Utari Association	
1974	Visits to indigenous communities abroad	Diverse multicultural polity/ Multiculturalism
1980	The first country report to the UN Human Rights Committee by the Japanese government	
1984	Hokkaido Utari Association proposes a new law that would replace the Former Aborigines Protection Act	
1986	Prime Minister Nakasone comments that "Japan is a homogeneous nation" Hokkaido Utari Association sends an appeal to the UN Center for Human Rights	
1987	The Japanese government acknowledges the Ainu as a distinct group at the UN Working Group on Indigenous Populations First participation in the UN Working Group on Indigenous Populations by the Ainu	
1991	The Japanese government acknowledges the Ainu as an ethnic minority group in its third report to the Human Rights Committee	
1992	Director of the Hokkaido Utari Association gives a speech at the UN event celebrating the UN Decade of Indigenous Peoples	
1997	The Ainu Cultural Promotion Law enacted	
2008	The Japanese government officially recognizes the Ainu as an indigenous people	

border areas between what are now Japan and Russia. They shared some similar cultural and physical characteristics but were not a homogenous ethnic group, and the designation of Emishi/Ezo simply meant "barbarians" vis-à-vis the "civilized" mainland Japanese. Some of the Ainu ancestors once lived in the Tohoku area, the northernmost part of mainland Japan, but they kept being pushed northward by central Japanese governments throughout history and moved into a big northern island known today as Hokkaido.

The history of the Ainu in premodern Japan resembles that of many ethnic groups in the world that were at economic and military disadvantage. They suffered a series of military expeditions by the central government to conquer the areas, and were forced to move out of their original habitat. Their economic relations with the mainlanders became increasingly exploitative over time, to the point that they have very little economic autonomy. They had to accept a subject status after several failed uprisings, and by the end of the eighteenth century lost the capacity to wage large-scale rebellion. At least until the mid-nineteenth century, however, they maintained relatively autonomous life style—culture, customs, and way of life. Their main interaction with the mainlanders was economic, and while they were economically subjugated, the mainlanders did not aggressively try to change their culture, out of contempt more than respect. This changes in the Meiji period.

Colonial expansion and Ainu subjugation from the Meiji Restoration to World War II, 1867–1945

In this period, colonialism was in vogue among major Western powers, and it was their incursion into the Pacific that prompted the fall of Tokugawa rule and the restoration of the emperor as ruler of the Japanese nation. The Meiji Restoration in 1867 ended the feudal era in Japan. Following the Western model of "good nation," the Meiji government would seek nation-building at home and colonial expansion abroad, which soon engulfed the Ainu lands in the north. The Meiji government adopted an official policy of building up "a rich country with a strong army" to fend off Western powers that threatened to colonize much of Asia and also to demonstrate to the world that Japan was a legitimate and powerful modern nation. This policy turned Japan into a colonial power itself and its colonial expansion would eventually build the Great East Asia Co-Prosperity Zone. In this process, Hokkaido, where most Ainu lived by the mid-nineteenth century, became Japan's first testing ground for its colonial ambition, along with Ryuku (Okinawa).

As the new Meiji government embarked on its nation-building project, its tentacles soon reached the Ainu. With its superior modern military, the Meiji government pushed the surviving Tokugawa faithful further and further to the north and defeated them at the Goryokaku castle in Hokkaido. The government immediately established the Colonial Commission (*kaitakushi*) to develop Hokkaido in July of 1869. Two months later, under the newly implemented prefecture system, the Meiji government officially named the area "Hokkaido," signaling formal incorporation of the area into the Japanese state.

This swift move reflected the Meiji government's concern about the northern territories. The territorial boundaries were still fluid during the era of colonialism, despite
treaties with the Russian government. Thus, the Meiji government needed to quickly
consolidate its control over Hokkaido in order to prevent Russian incursion ino
the northern lands.[2] Reflecting this concern about the territorial integrity in the
north, the envoy at the Colonial Commission was soon given ministerial status in the
government and gained a great deal of autonomy in Hokkaido affairs. The government appointed Kiyotaka Kuroda as the head of the Colonial Commission; he
was a heavyweight in Meiji politics who would become the second prime minister in
1888. Hailing from the Satsuma domain in southern Japan, Kuroda had some
experience in dealing with the Ryukyu area, the southernmost islands of Japan that
were under Satsuma's control but had significant cultural autonomy. He implemented policies to develop Hokkaido into an area of agricultural and fishing
production and a source of natural resources for industrialization of Japan. He
recruited as his advisor Horace Capron, the second US secretary of agriculture
who had experience of dealing with Native Americans in the United States, luring
him with a salary greater than that of the prime minister of Japan (Siddle 1996: 56).
Capron and Kuroda reapplied their policy formula to Hokkaido, which was to
develop an efficiency-oriented industrial system that paid little attention to the welfare
of indigenous peoples. This was a typical approach to minority groups in new territories among "advanced" nations of the time, and as an emerging modern nation,
the Meiji government followed what it thought was the internationally accepted
model of "good nation," learning directly from a policy maker from a Western power.

The government coupled this development policy with a legal system that made
Ainu Japanese citizens. Ainu individuals now had to assume family names, and
gained the same legal status as any Japanese. In this regard too, the Japanese
government adopted the Western ideal of equality of all citizens before the law.

In reality, however, Ainu's living conditions quickly deteriorated. Released
from the feudal system, the Ainu became free workers in the new industrializing
economy. However, as many workers from the mainland moved to Hokkaido in
this period, the new economy left many Ainu unemployed. The government also
confiscated their traditional lands, giving them to new settlers from the mainland.
As capital from the mainland entered in earnest from the 1890s, the mainlander
population increased dramatically, pushing the Ainu further to unwanted and
unproductive areas. These immigrants from the mainland exploited natural resources in Hokkaido ruthlessly, and quickly depleted the bountiful natural resources that
sustained Ainu lives, especially deer and fish. To make matters worse, the Meiji
government, believing the Ainu to be a backward people in need of enlightenment,
outlawed most of their traditional practices, including the use of hunting traps and
poisoned arrows. Deprived of their fishing and hunting grounds and with their most
effective hunting devices banned, Ainu had difficulty sustaining their livelihood.

Faced with the deepening plight of the Ainu, the government attempted some
remedies for them. After a few short-term welfare measures, the government
passed the Hokkaido Former Aborigines Protection Act (*Hokkaido Kyuu Dojin Hogo Hou*)
in 1899, which was the most comprehensive Ainu policy of the Meiji government.

A document that discusses reasons for the act clarifies the prevalent views on Ainu among political elites at the time:

> [the plight of the Ainu] is a natural outcome of the superior winning and the inferior losing out. Nonetheless, the former aborigines are equal subjects before the Emperor, and we cannot ignore their plight and not take measures to address them.
>
> (Quoted in Kato 2007: 47)

In addition to some provisions about social welfare for the Ainu, the act had two main pillars. The first was to turn the Ainu into farmers. This policy did not help the Ainu much, because the Ainu (especially Ainu men) were not used to farming and because much of the land given to them was not very fertile. In addition, unscrupulous Japanese merchants deceived many Ainu and took their lands at virtually no cost. The second pillar of the act was to "educate" the Ainu and make them loyal subjects of the emperor. Despite some discriminatory treatment of Ainu children at schools, the teaching of patriotism and loyalty to the emperor was as extensive as in any other Japanese classrooms. The effect of this education was evident in the school essays of Ainu children, who expressed their undying support and admiration for the imperial house.

The Former Aborigines Protection Act exemplifies a transition in Japanese government's approach from colonial domination to welfare state assimilation. In this, Japan closely followed what was regarded internationally acceptable. Assimilationist approach was the order of the day for nations across the Western world, which developed expansive forced assimilation programs toward their own indigenous minorities in the name of "civilizing" them. From the beginning, the Japanese policy developed in tandem with their relationship with the Western world. In addition, the government was motivated to provide some remedies for the Ainu, for two reasons. First, it is important to note that the Meiji government's main diplomatic goal was to abolish unequal treaties that the Western countries had imposed on them in the mid-nineteenth century. For that purpose, the government had to convince Westerners that Japan was a civilized nation worthy of equal treatment. Concerned about its reputation in international society and in line with its broader modernization quest, Japan sought to present itself as a "good nation" by adopting an official policy of all citizens being equal before the law. The government initially focused on development of the colonized lands and paid little attention to Ainu welfare, but soon legislated the Former Aborigines Protection Act to provide the Ainu with minimal welfare. As lifting of travel restrictions for foreigners was approaching, the government feared that if Westerners observed Ainu's impoverished lives first-hand, they might think that Japan was still an uncivilized country (Oguma 1998). Second, another growing concern was that oppression of an ethnic minority at home might make the government look hypocritical, when in the international arena the government was criticizing Western nations for their racial discrimination (Ogasawara 2001). Japan had been making proposals to include provisions about racial equality in international documents, most notably at the Paris Conference after World War I, but had been denied by other colonial powers, which practiced blatant discrimination. Japan's colonial rule was no less oppressive, but its official policies, used to justify its colonial expansion, were that everyone in the Japanese Empire was equal under the emperor. Because of this official stance, Ainu's deepening plight was of concern to Japanese elites.

Ainu individuals, on the other hand, struggled in dire living conditions and were unable to organize much sustained political mobilization. The Former Aborigines Protection Act was not a result of activism by the Ainu; few had an identity as Ainu people outside their local communities, and there was only one known case of Ainu individuals speaking out for the Ainu before the act (Siddle 1996: 114–15). It was mostly progressive groups of Japanese and missionaries from abroad who rallied for the act.

In the Taisho era (1911–26), waves of democratic movements reached Hokkaido and provided impetus for some Ainu political mobilization. Ainu indignation found outlet in the form of novels (e.g. Tokusaburou Takekuma and Yamabe Yasunosuke) and poetry (e.g. Hokuto Iboshi, Yayeko Bachelor, and Takeichi Moritake), and some limited grassroots ethno-political activity emerged. In 1926, *Kaiheisha*, arguably the first Ainu organization, was founded in Asahikawa, Hokkaido, directly influenced by the establishment of *Suiheisha*, the renowned Burakumin movement organization founded in 1922 (Osaka Jinken Rekishi Shiryou Kan 1993). The Ainu could relate to the discrimination the Burakumin had been through as a former outcast group, and were inspired by their political awareness and activism to fight for equality and freedom. In 1930, the first Hokkaido-wide Ainu organization, the Hokkaido Ainu Association (*Hokkaido Ainu Kyokai*), emerged. This organization, however, received support from the local government, and was deemed a government tool to assimilate Ainu into mainstream society.[3] While Ainu mobilization achieved some modest success, such as compelling the government to revise the Former Aborigines Protection Act in 1937, this emergent fervor for political mobilization was dampened by Japan's embarking upon 15 years of international warfare. As with other political activities in Japan, Ainu protests faced increasing levels of repression during the war.

In this period, colonial domination and then "civilizing" assimilation characterized the government's approach to the Ainu. Most Ainu were barely able to keep their heads above water and had little choice but to adopt the ideology of modernization and progress that the Japanese Empire advocated and to depend on the minimal remedies that the government provided. With few exceptions, Ainu leaders, who rose to prominence on mainland Japanese terms, emphasized the importance of education and assimilation. Although some of them expressed pride in their Ainu heritage, few advocated cultural autonomy or ethnic distinction. Few Ainu deemed their culture as something to be proud of or protected. Given that contemporary frameworks of minority-majority relations did not offer much to encourage cultural autonomy or political self-determination by indigenous peoples, the Ainu had limited access to resources they could draw upon for their political mobilization (other than the Burakumin movement in Japan).

The early post-war period, 1945–early 1970s

The immediate postwar period, starting in August 1945, was a chaotic time. After the defeat, Japan lost its colonies but retained Hokkaido as its territory.[4] The Ainu were hopeful that they would see their marginalized status improve in a new democratized Japan. Energized by this hope, they were very active in the first few years after the end of the war. In 1946 they formed the first truly Ainu-wide organization, the Hokkaido Ainu Association (*Hokkaido Ainu Kyokai*), which is still to date the largest and most influential Ainu organization. It had the same name as the prewar Ainu organization established in 1930 and carried over some members, but was considered a distinct entity because of the long period of dormancy of the prewar namesake. Unlike its predecessor, the new Ainu association had the support of the vast majority of Ainu people and included Asahikawa Ainu, who did not participate in the prewar association. Ainu were active in asserting their cultural differences as they claimed themselves as "the only different race in our country" and "an indigenous people" (Mukai 1948: 4) and called for Ainu solidarity and collective uprising (Ogawa 1948). Furthermore, some Ainu individuals ran for office in the first national election for the House of Representatives (Lower House) and in regional elections for Hokkaido governor and Hokkaido prefectural assembly seats. None of these Ainu won the elections but their campaigns marked an important chapter in Ainu history.

However, as Japan regained its independence in 1951 and gradually reclaimed its status as an international power, Ainu activities fizzled out. Because of the loss of its overseas territories, postwar Japan shifted its ideological stance on ethnic/racial diversity from a multi-ethnic/racial empire to a culturally homogenous nation-state. This was in many ways in line with the broader trends of the time, as prescribed by the newly founded United Nations and its various conventions. A "good nation" was no longer expected to have overseas territories and undermine local populations' rights to self-determination; rather, it was supposed to stay within the boundaries of cultural similarities and become a homogenous nation-state. Massive waves of decolonization worldwide in the following two decades further confirmed and enhanced the principle of self-determination of culturally bounded nation-states. Stripped of its colonies, Japan's own cultural homogeneity policy put immense pressure on the Ainu to curtail assertion of any cultural distinctiveness. Entering the 1950s, larger Japanese society began to "reverse course," shifting away from a thorough purge of prewar elites, and conservative elements in Japan regained their prominent position. This shift further contributed to the Ainu's marginalization. As many Japanese were enthused by the miraculous economic growth of the 1950s and 1960s and the myth of homogeneous Japan captured the nation's psyche, the Ainu quickly became a forgotten group in mainstream Japanese society. The government's view was captured in the following claim in its report to the International Labor Organization in 1953 regarding the Convention Concerning the Regulation of Certain Special System of Recruiting Workers:

> In the course of the Second World War, Japan lost all its dependent territories. As a result there no longer exist in Japan either workers belonging to

or assimilated to the indigenous populations of the dependent territories, or to the dependent indigenous populations of the home territories.

(Teshima 1990: 58)

In this context, many Ainu felt ambivalent about claiming distinct ethnicity of the Ainu people vis-a-vis the mainstream Japanese. The assimilationist ideology that the government had promoted had a hold on them, and claims for a distinct Ainu identity became submerged in grassroots cultural/literary activities. Consequently, most Ainu chose the path of least resistance, trying to "pass" as Japanese in mainstream Japanese society.

In addition to the societal pressure to assimilate, many Ainu faced economic hardship, as an increasing number of non-Ainu individuals flooded traditionally Ainu-dominant townships and forced many Ainu to leave their hometown to earn a living (Emori 2008: 522). For better economic opportunities, assertion of Ainu identity was detrimental. Moreover, the largest and only Hokkaido-wide Ainu organization, the Hokkaido Ainu Association, was functioning virtually as a wing of the Hokkaido government, and internal cohesion among Ainu began to evaporate due to infighting, with some members criticizing leaders of "selling out" to powerful politicians (Ogasawara 2001: 213). Considering these factors, it is not surprising that little political mobilization by Ainu emerged in this period.

Symbolizing this changing zeitgeist, the Hokkaido Ainu Association changed its name to the Hokkaido Utari Association (*Hokkaido Utari Kyokai*) in 1961, because many members felt that "Ainu" was a discriminatory term used to cast them in a negative light (Ogasawara 2001: 214). "Utari" has a neutral meaning of "friend" or "comrade" in the Ainu language, but the term "Ainu," meaning "human," does not have any intrinsic negative connotation within Ainu society either. The name change reflected the severe discrimination against the Ainu, and demonstrates that most Ainu had little ethnic pride and thought that assimilation was the most desirable path for them. In the first volume of the association's new periodical, *Senkusha no Tsudoi* (henceforth SNT), which began publication in 1963, a board member, Hiroaki Kita, called for "eliminating any ethnic identity once and for all" (SNT 1963, 1: 27). While Kita is a non-Ainu individual, the fact that a statement like this appeared in the first volume of an official publication of the Utari Association speaks volumes. Ainu's own writings in the same volume walk a tightrope, claiming Ainu identity and pride modestly but trying not to be too assertive about Ainu rights and anti-discrimination activism (SNT 1963, 1: 33).

The domestic political environment slowly shifted in the 1960s and 1970s. In this period of much political contention, influenced by student activism in the West, college students in Japan led the leftist movement, challenging the US–Japan Security Treaty specifically and Japan's conservative establishment generally. Minority issues constituted a part of the anti-colonialism rhetoric of the time. Inspired by the civil rights movement in the United States, Burakumin activism grew particularly stronger in this period. That in turn encouraged other minority movements in Japan, including hitherto dormant Ainu activism.

A particularly important occasion for the Ainu came in 1968, the year that marked the One Hundredth Anniversary of the establishment of Hokkaido as well as the centennial of the Meiji Restoration. The ceremonies surrounding the Meiji centennial drew many criticisms from leftist activists for their lack of recognition of imperialist expansions of modern Japan. As these Japanese activists criticized the sanitized version of Japan's modern history propagated on the occasion, their critical eyes turned to the colonization of Hokkaido in the Meiji period. Finding no mention of Ainu in Hokkaido's One Hundredth Anniversary events, some of these Japanese activists extended their radical activism to Hokkaido and engaged in various acts of vandalism and violence. For instance, in 1972, the name of the governor of Hokkaido was erased from the monument built in remembrance of the Shakushain Uprising (the Ainu rebellion against Japanese authority on Hokkaido between 1669 and 1672), which was erected as a part of celebration of the anniversary but was controversial due to the lack of input by the Ainu. In 1976, an incident with the heaviest casualties took place when the Hokkaido regional government building (*Docho*) in Sapporo was bombed, killing two people and injuring over 90. These acts were carried out by radical leftwing Japanese activists and had little Ainu involvement. In fact, many Ainu groups including the Hokkaido Utari Association made statements to dissociate themselves from these violent acts. Nonetheless, as the events were reported widely and constantly in the media, they politicized the marginalization of Ainu, and exposure to the news reports likely awakened the ethnic, if not the indigenous, identity of many Ainu.

Growing Burakumin activism had a more direct impact on Ainu politics. Burakumin issues were less well known in Hokkaido than in mainland Japan, but their heightened activism in this period publicized the persistent discrimination nationally through protest activities and publications. Many Ainu learned of Burakumin issues and found many similarities in their experience of marginalization in Japanese society, from substandard living conditions and educational achievements to social discrimination at school and workplace and in marriage and employment markets. For example, a newly published Ainu periodical featured an article by an Ainu individual who was "surprised to learn that there is such a thing as unemancipated Buraku" and found in Burakumin's struggles so much in common with "the living conditions and environment that I have been in." She further argued that, on learning about Burakumin activism, she was "strongly encouraged and told myself that ... we Ainu can form such a liberation league ... and we should do that to eliminate discrimination from this world" (*Hoppogun*, Vol. 1, 1970, quoted in Emori 2008: 526–7).

Directly and indirectly, the season of contentious politics in Japan energized Ainu individuals, especially the young generation, into various forms of collective mobilization. First, several small groups that focused on studying Ainu history and culture and challenging their subjugated status were formed by Ainu individuals. The Ainu Liberation League (*Ainu Kaiho Domei*) (1972), the Tokyo Association of Ainu (*Tokyo Utari Kai*) (1972), the Yai Yukara (By Ourselves) Ethnic Studies Group (*Yai Yukara Kenkyukai*) (1972), the Reed Society (*Ashi no Kai*) (1972) and the

National Conference for Conversations about Ainu (*Zenkoku Ainu Kataru Kai*) (1973) were some of the main groups that emerged in this period (Siddle 1997).[5] Second, Ainu publications gained momentum. Publication of the Utari Association's official periodical, *Senkusha no Tsudoi* (SNT) resumed in 1971 after over eight years of dormancy; the aforementioned new Ainu periodical, *Hoppogun*, started publication in 1970; and a monthly news magazine called *Anutari Ainu* (We the Humans) was published in 1973 led by young Ainu women. Third, direct action challenging Japanese authorities increased. In 1972, The Ainu Association's Ishikari branch (which soon changed its name to Sapporo branch) filed a complaint to the Hokkaido Broadcasting Company, a major television station, regarding the discriminatory depiction of Ainu in its drama show (Emori 2008: 527–30). The TV station apologized for the show and promised to change its content so as not to offend Ainu. Also in 1972, on the occasion of a joint conference of the Japanese Anthropological Association and the Japanese Ethnological Association in Sapporo focusing on Ainu, the leader of the Ainu Liberation League challenged the conference on the ground that the anthropologists were examining Ainu remains without Ainu consent. Then in 1973, Ainu workers participated in a May Day protest for the first time, waving a newly designed Ainu national flag (Emori 2008: 533).

These emergent collective actions by Ainu marked a departure from the long-standing assimilation model. They were carried out mostly by young Ainu who may have been members of the Hokkaido Utari Association but were not satisfied with the association's leadership. The association, on the other hand, was still reluctant to support political activities that would openly challenge government authorities. Although the networks that the association provided facilitated many of the collective actions informally, the association's leaders, coming from relatively wealthy background and linked with government elites, were mostly conservative and preferred the assimilation model.

In sum, collective pride was re-emerging among some politically conscious young Ainu, laying the basis for Ainu-wide social movements to come, but at this stage it did not rise to the level of sustained social movements with coherent goals. Most Ainu were dependent on governmental welfare programs and continued to seek assimilation to avoid discrimination in their daily lives. The association had generally collaborative, and often dependent, relationships with the Hokkaido government and was not eager to jeopardize that relationship by challenging its authority aggressively, especially since its alliance with the government was a main source of its power in Ainu communities. Even the politically active Ainu did not have effective frames to appeal to many Ainu and indicate why they could and should claim more rights, much less convince the Japanese public that the Ainu deserved special rights because of their distinct historical background. The Japanese government continued to promote the myth of homogeneous Japan, especially as Japan rose on the international scene as an economic superpower. Neither was there much political pressure on Japan internationally to modify this stance, as the culturally uniform nation-state model still held wide acceptance. Thus, the Ainu did not have a viable alternative to assimilation. However, as a new model of "good nation" spread across the globe and influenced both the government and the Ainu over the following few decades, Ainu politics took a new turn, leading ultimately to official acceptance of the Ainu as an indigenous people in 2008.

Growing interaction with indigenous peoples abroad since the early 1970s

The new era of Ainu politics dawned when the emerging international indigenous rights movement reached Ainu in the late 1970s and set in motion sustained and organized Ainu activism. Ainu's first official international encounter was with China. In 1974, mediated by a Japan Socialist Party politician, the Hokkaido Utari Association sent a delegation of 15 members to various parts of China, including autonomous minority regions. The delegation was impressed by the Chinese government's dealing with minority groups, crediting it to the socialist system (SNT 1975, 8: 3). The second delegation to China, also composed of 15 members but including many younger Ainu, visited in 1976. Official and unofficial delegations of Hokkaido Ainu then visited China in 1976, 1977, 1978, and 1983 (SNT 1976, 12: 9; SNT 1978, 17: 7; SNT 1979, 20: 6; SNT 1984, 35:4). Ainu also invited Chinese contingents to Hokkaido in 1976, 1979, and 1981 (SNT 1976, 11: 7; SNT 1979, 21: 7; SNT 1982, 29: 4), giving them a warm reception.

Ainu leaders visited other parts of the world as well. In 1976, a group of young Ainu artists performed a modern dramatized version of Ainu epics as part of a UNESCO cultural festival in Paris (SNT 1976, 11: 10). In 1978, a 12-member Ainu delegation led by the director of the Hokkaido Utari Association traveled to the North Slope Autonomous Region in Alaska, invited by the mayor of Barrow. The Ainu delegation learned about self-governance, education policy, and financing autonomous activities through tax revenue from natural resources such as oil (Siddle 1997: 36–9). The Ainu were impressed by the degree of autonomy that the Inuit enjoyed and also found many commonalities in their history and culture. The two groups issued a joint statement confirming the common heritage of Inuit and Ainu (SNT 1978, 19: 7–10). Soon after, in September of 1978, an Ainu culture study group visited Canada and engaged in cultural exchange with indigenous peoples (SNT 1979, 20: 6). In May of 1981, an Ainu representative attended the World Conference of Indigenous Peoples in Canberra, Australia, joining about a thousand delegates from 21 countries (Siddle 1997: 39). In 1983, an Ainu individual made a speech at the UN Hammasjold Auditorium as part of ongoing efforts to launch the UN Year of Indigenous Peoples, which materialized ten years later (Atuy 2002). In 1984, an Ainu contingent also visited four Scandinavian countries for exchange with the Sami, an indigenous people in the region.

The Ainu's interactions with indigenous peoples abroad were a product of a larger trend of growing indigenous rights movements that emerged in the 1960s as an offshoot of the movement for decolonization and anti-discrimination. The UN officially started working on indigenous peoples' issues in 1971 when the Economic and Social Council passed Resolution 1589; this recommended that the

Sub-Commission on Prevention of Discrimination and Protection of Minorities of the UN Commission on Human Rights appoint a special rapporteur to investigate the plight of indigenous peoples and propose measures to address them. The Sub-Commission appointed José R. Martínez Cobo from Ecuador to this post. His report is known as the Cobo report and served as the legitimating document for many subsequent indigenous rights movements. On the basis of the Cobo report, the Working Group on Indigenous Populations (WGIP), the first major UN forum for indigenous peoples, was established in 1982 under the UN Commission on Human Rights. Subsequent development in the promotion of indigenous rights by the WGIP and other international institutions, which culminated in the 2007 adoption of the Declaration on the Rights of Indigenous Peoples, would change the transnational model of "good nation"; instead of cultural homogeneity, acceptance of cultural diversity and protection of minority cultures, particularly those of indigenous ones, became an important component of a "good nation."

In this rising tide of global indigenous rights activism, many indigenous peoples began traveling abroad to build greater solidarity with indigenous peoples in other countries. It was in the context of this global movement to change the understanding of a "good nation" that the Ainu's interaction with indigenous peoples abroad intensified. Many of these interactions were on the basis of cultural exchange. The end outcome, however, was that Ainu leaders got exposed to global indigenous rights movements and learned about more advanced minority and indigenous rights policies in the US, Canada, China, and elsewhere. These countries granted indigenous groups a significant degree of autonomy, and the Ainu were encouraged to claim more rights in Japan.

For instance, in his report on a trip to Alaska, Tadashi Kaizawa, who made many of the international visits in this period, stated that he was "envious" of the autonomy the Inuit enjoyed in economic affairs and the success Inuit children had achieved in education and employment. And he was especially struck by the comment by the mayor of Barrow, an Inuit, that "if we remain dependent on the government, we will always be second or third-class citizens" (SNT 1978, 19: 10). Another Ainu activist who participated in many of these trips spoke of a culture shock he experienced at his visit to an indigenous community in Canada in 1978:

> To my complete amazement, when I stepped out of the gate at the Vancouver airport, I was greeted by a group of indigenous people performing their tribal dance in their traditional costume. It was shocking to me that an indigenous people could exhibit its traditional culture with such pride in a highly modernized setting of an international airport.
>
> (Interview May 18, 2003)

Seeing the way the Canadian tribe proudly exhibited their culture and preserved their way of life in their community, he and other Ainu delegates realized that the Ainu needed greater autonomy and more protection of their traditional culture. Through these international experiences he came to realize that his Ainu heritage was something to be proud of, not something to run away from. He and many other Ainu, especially those at an impressionable age, learned to be proud of their indigenous heritage and were inspired to challenge their marginalization. These Ainu individuals would lead Ainu activism for decades from this period.

The impact of international activities on Ainu activism from the late-1970s

Inspired by these international encounters, Ainu leaders brought back a resurgent pride to their local community and reinvigorated political activism. From this period, Ainu activism has involved a higher proportion of the Ainu people, not just a handful of activists, placed Ainu issues on the national, not just the local Hokkaido, stage, and sought Ainu indigenous rights, not just more welfare benefits. Some early manifestations of the new approach among the Ainu can be seen in the political campaign for a seat in the national parliament in 1977 by an Ainu activist with substantial international experience (SNT 1979, 21: 3), the Hokkaido Utari Association's submission of complaints to the Ministry of Education about textbook portrayals of Ainu people in 1982 (SNT 1983, 32: 7), and similar complaints to the Hokkaido governor, the head of the Committee on Education, and the Association of School Teachers of Hokkaido among others about a high school teacher's derogatory comments about Ainu in 1983 (SNT 1984, 34: 6). The Utari Association's shift away from the assimilationist approach to Ainu indigenous rights culminated in the 1984 adoption of the draft New Ainu Law (as it was termed). The Utari Association set up a special committee and spent two years working on the draft, which was adopted in May of 1984 at the association's general assembly (SNT 1985, 40: 7). Now it had become the association's official goal to get the assimilationist 1899 Former Aborigines Protection Act abolished and a new law passed that protected Ainu human rights and their cultural traditions as an indigenous people.

The Former Aborigines Protection Act had been revised a few times in the postwar period (1946, 1947, and 1968) and several provisions had been deleted. Nevertheless, primarily because this was for a long time the only social welfare policy specifically for the Ainu, the Utari Association was consistently opposed to the abolition of the act, arguing that the act provided what little safety net there was for the Ainu. As recently as 1970 the association had voted unanimously against abolition of the Former Aborigines Protection Act. Within about ten years the association had reversed this approach, largely because of the international experiences that Ainu had accumulated in this period. What they learned from interacting with and observing the lives of indigenous peoples abroad had significant bearing on the new policy proposal. The draft New Ainu Law had six main components:

(1) Securing basic human rights for and eliminating discrimination against the Ainu;
(2) The right to political participation including government-guaranteed seats for Ainu representatives in the national Diet and local assemblies;

(3) Promoting education and preservation of Ainu culture and education to eliminate discrimination against the Ainu;

(4) Provision of necessary means for agriculture, fishery, forestry, manufacturing and trading by the Ainu;

(5) Establishing the Ainu Independence Fund, run by the Ainu themselves with the original money provided by the Japanese government, to ensure that the Ainu will be able to participate fully in political, economic and cultural life;

(6) Establishing consultative organs, consisting of Ainu representatives, relevant ministers, congressmen and experts, under Prime Minister and in Hokkaido.

(SNT 1984, 37: 4–6; Tsunemoto 2002)

These main components mirrored the rights that indigenous groups in other countries enjoyed or demanded. In the arguments that motivated these policy demands there were clear references to indigenous rights movements in North America, Australia, and New Zealand, as well as to the Civil Rights Movement in the US (Siddle 1997: 35–8). While few Ainu expected this proposal to become law immediately, it was remarkable for Ainu to be taking the initiative to demand rights beyond minimum welfare, given their history of dependence on the government. This proposal would make its way from the Utari Association to the Hokkaido local government and then to the national government in the next dozen years, materializing into the Ainu Cultural Promotion Law in 1997, as I examine below.

While Ainu activism was also influenced by the Buraku liberation movement, the largest minority movement in Japan that was already a powerful movement (SNT 1977, 15: 2), there is little doubt that Ainu international experiences transformed Ainu ethnic identity and ignited indigenous pride among them. Global indigenous rights movement enabled Ainu to find their indigenous brothers and sisters, who had experienced the same colonization and domination and faced the same issues of loss of traditional culture and land. An alliance with these other indigenous groups made intuitive sense and the language of indigenous rights exactly fitted what the Ainu needed. Consequently, the Ainu made concrete policy proposals to the Japanese government, demanding indigenous rights. As the legitimacy of Ainu activism grew with the framing of their issues in terms of indigenous rights—which already had substantial global currency—and as the Utari Association officially supported and promoted these activities, many new Ainu individuals joined the movement. A leading Ainu activist today, who joined the movement around this time, reflected on this period:

I was hiding my Ainu heritage and was trying to pass as mainstream Japanese, and was pretty successful at that. Hearing about and then meeting with leading Ainu activists of the time, and then participating in minority rights conferences in Japan and abroad, I came to appreciate my Ainu heritage and grew convinced that I should be proud of it and work to protect it.

(Interview May 25, 2005)

Ratification of the covenants and appeal to the UN Center for Human Rights

Around the same time that the Ainu's interaction with other indigenous groups intensified in the 1970s, the Japanese government ratified the International Covenant on Civil and Political Rights (CCPR) and the International Covenant on Economic, Social, and Cultural Rights (CESCR) in 1979. Ratification of these treaties, particularly that of the CCPR, would change the political dynamics for ethnic minorities in Japan, opening up new political opportunities for them and legitimating their claims for more rights. As a state party to these core human rights treaties, Japan had to follow the model of "good nation" they prescribed. Particularly important for minority politics was Article 27 of the CCPR. When a country ratifies the CCPR, it is required to submit its first report within a year, and subsequent reports are due every five years. In the reports, the government has to account for its domestic practice regarding each of the provisions in the treaty, including ethnic minority rights as specified in Article 27:

> In those states in which ethnic, religious or linguistic minorities exist, persons belonging to such minorities shall not be denied the right, in community with the other members of their group, to enjoy their own culture, to profess and practise their own religion, or to use their own language.

Then, the Human Rights Committee, the monitoring body of the CCPR, reviews the reports and makes further inquiry or recommendations for improvement to the government.

The Japanese government submitted its first mandatory report to the Human Rights Committee in 1980. In the report, the government claimed, regarding Article 27, that "ethnic minority groups, as defined in this Covenant, do not exist in Japan" (CCPR/C/10Add.1 1980). When questioned by committee members about the existence of groups such as the Ainu, the government representative maintained:

> [S]ince the Meiji restoration in the nineteenth century, establishment of a rapid communication system had made the differences in their way of life indiscernible. The Utari were (sic) Japanese nationals and treated equally with other Japanese.

(CCPR/C/SR324 1981)

The government essentially claimed that the Ainu had been completely assimilated into Japanese culture. As astounding as this statement sounds today, it did not create much uproar at the time. Some newspaper reporters alerted the Utari Association and tried to elicit comments, but the association made no official response and the news story was buried under other stories. The person at the Utari Association who dealt with the media inquiry recalls:

We certainly did not like the statement, but did not quite know what to make of it, primarily because we did not recognize the significance of this (reporting) system (in the Human Rights Committee) or the statement there. We were also not fully prepared to make strong claims about Ainu being a distinct ethnic minority.

(Interview May 11, 2002)

This turn of events (or non-event) reflects both the social environment in Japan, where perceived cultural homogeneity was touted as a major source of its economic success, and the persistent trepidation among many members of the Utari Association about departing from the assimilationist path they had been on. The first few years of the 1980s were a transition period for the Ainu, from the dependent relationship on the government to demands for the new law in 1984, and many Ainu still feared that challenging the government would have negative consequences for their social welfare. For this reason the Ainu passed up this political opportunity to challenge the government. However, the report was to resurface in six years.

In 1986, then Prime Minister Yasuhiro Nakasone stated that "Japan is a homogeneous nation, and the homogeneity enables the high level of intelligence, which is difficult in an ethnically diverse country such as the US" and that "blacks, Puerto Ricans, and Mexicans and so forth lower the national intelligence level in the US while that is not a problem in Japan" (Liberal Democratic Party National Seminar [*Jimintou Zenkoku Kenshukai*], September 22, 1986). These comments immediately triggered a lot of criticism in the United States and aggravated the already strained US–Japan relationship. In Japan, the Ainu were the first to react to the comments, and other ethnic groups, such as Korean and Chinese residents in Japan, followed. Nakasone elaborated on his point:

I don't think there is any discriminated ethnic minority in Japan, as long as we're talking about those with Japanese nationality, and I believe that our report to the UN to that effect is correct. … I have thick eyebrows and beard, which indicates to me that I have a good deal of Ainu blood in me.

(House of Representatives, October 21, 1986)

In contrast to the situation in 1980, the Hokkaido Utari Association had begun to challenge the government with the draft New Ainu Law in 1984, and was trying to push the government to accept the proposal. For Ainu leaders seeking opportunities to propel their movement to the national level, Nakasone's comments presented "a one-in-a-million opportunity" (interview May 11, 2002). They filed protest letters to Prime Minister Nakasone, other members of the cabinet, and relevant politicians, and organized protest events in Hokkaido and Tokyo, urging Nakasone to correct his views and acknowledge that Japan is not an ethnically homogenous nation. In its protest letter to Nakasone and others, the association referred specifically to the 1980 statement in the report to the Human Rights Committee and demanded that the government change its view officially (SNT 1987, 43: 11). Ironically,

Nakasone's reference to the UN report in the quote above reminded the Ainu of the earlier government report to the UN.

Seeing the unremorseful response from Nakasone, the association held an emergency board meeting in November 1986 and decided to appeal to the UN in addition to protesting domestically (SNT 1987, 43: 9). Since this was the first time Ainu would appeal to the UN, Ainu leaders needed help in submitting a letter. An international nongovernmental organization based in Japan called the Citizens' Diplomacy Center (*Shimin Gaiko Center* [SGC]) and a Japanese official at the UN Center for Human Rights in Geneva, Yo Kubota, provided critical assistance in this process. The SGC had already developed ties with the Utari Association and suggested that it appeal to the UN through the 1503 procedure of the UN Commission on Human Rights.[6] Seeing that the leaders of the association were still hesitant about going over the government's head to the UN, the SGC helped put them in touch with Kubota. Kubota convinced them of the utility and legitimacy of the procedure and, with his and SGC's guidance, the Utari Association sent a letter to the UN Center for Human Rights on November 25 of 1986 (interview November 26, 2004). The letter reported the government's position on ethnic minorities in Japan and appealed to the UN to examine and discuss the notion of ethnic homogeneity in Japan claimed by the government in its first report to the UN Human Rights Committee (SNT 1987, 44: 6–8). An acknowledgement of the receipt of the letter was mailed to the association on December 10 with a promise of referring the matter as classified to the Human Rights Committee and the Sub-Commission on Prevention of Discrimination and Protection of Minorities and the relevant (Japanese) government. This was a standard response from the Center for Human Rights but it seemed to the Utari Association that the UN was taking their appeal very seriously and promising careful examination of the case.

While the appeal to the Center for Human Rights did not lead to any official condemnation, the publicity these international activities generated pressured the Japanese government into quickly acknowledging the Ainu as "a distinct group" at the UN Working Group on Indigenous Populations (WGIP) in 1987, which greatly encouraged the Ainu to continue their global activism. The government representative stated that "the Japanese government does not claim that Japan is 'a monoethnic state,' nor does it deny the existence of Ainu people" (SNT 1987, 45: 3). Ainu representatives were in attendance when this statement was made. The 1987 WGIP was their first official participation in international human rights forums in person. This trip to Geneva was also mediated by the SGC; a SGC member, who was working at the WGIP as an intern, encouraged and facilitated Ainu participation in it (SNT 1987, 45: 2). Since then, the Ainu have continued their involvement in UN indigenous rights/minority rights activities, participating regularly in virtually all UN indigenous rights forums.

Thus, the government report to the Human Rights Committee in 1980 created an entry point for the Ainu to engage with the UN human rights system. With the Nakasone gaffe in 1986 as a trigger, the Ainu started using the UN system and continued its engagement over the next two decades.

Increasing domestic mobilization and international activities toward a new Ainu law

Taking advantage of the momentum generated by their foray into international human rights forums, Ainu kept pressuring the Japanese government to pass new legislation for the Ainu. They pressed on in the international arena, participating in all major UN indigenous rights forums from 1987. In addition, in 1992, the Director of the Hokkaido Utari Association, Nomura Giichi, made a historic speech at the UN General Assembly, which boosted the association's and the Ainu movement's credibility in Japan and in the world. Alongside these international activities, Ainu representatives continuously invoked the need to abolish the Former Aborigines Protection Act and for a new law to be passed. Their presence at these forums and other indigenous groups' support for them gave much credence to Ainu's indigenous status and made it difficult for the government to dismiss their claims.

Domestically too, the Utari Association organized numerous conferences and demonstrations on the streets to promote a new Ainu law (SNT 1990, 52: 1–4; SNT 1993, 58: 5), and filed many petitions to politicians, political parties, ministries, and Hokkaido local governments (SNT 1988, 46: 1–3; SNT 1988, 48: 1–3; SNT 1989, 49: 4; SNT 1992, 57: 2–3; SNT 1993, 58: 5). Their domestic mobilization intensified especially in the few years leading up to the Year of Indigenous Peoples, and many of these events had an international flavor. For example, in 1991 the Utari Association invited the chair of the UN Working Group on Indigenous Populations, Erica Daes, and other international human rights officials to Japan. These guests observed Ainu lives in Hokkaido and participated in the General Assembly of the Utari Association. Daes made a speech to promote the rights of Ainu as an indigenous people, arguing that "the Ainu have the right to enjoy respect and fundamental human rights as an indigenous people" (SNT 1992, 57: 3–4). In 1992, Ainu gathered around the national Diet building in traditional costume to appeal to the government for new Ainu legislation. The appeal mentioned the upcoming Year of Indigenous Peoples specifically and urged the Japanese government to pass a new law for the Ainu during that year (Emori 2008: 582). In 1993, the Year of Indigenous Peoples, a number of events about the Ainu were organized in Japan, with guests from other indigenous peoples. One of the biggest events was the Nibutani Forum 1993, which took place in Hokkaido in August, with indigenous peoples from the US, Canada, Sweden, the Philippines, and South Africa (Ainu Nibutani Forum Organizing Committee 1994). Many of the participants in the Nibutani Forum, including the indigenous peoples from abroad, took part in a demonstration supporting a new Ainu law in Sapporo; about 350 people gathered. Another major event took place in September in Hokkaido and Tokyo, which celebrated the Year and promoted a new Ainu law with the Nobel Peace Prize-winner and UN Honorary Ambassador for the Year of Indigenous Peoples, Rigoberta Menchú. Menchú's visit, as well as Daes's, became possible because Ainu representatives participated in the UN activities and approached them about the possibility of a trip to Japan. Menchú visited an Ainu village in Hokkaido and was welcomed by Ainu songs and dances. She also gave a speech in Tokyo at an event promoting a new Ainu law. Thanks to these events, by the end of August of 1993, the association succeeded in collecting 265,415 signatures in support of a new law, which it submitted to Prime Minister Hosokawa Morihiro in November (SNT 1993, 60: 1–5, 9–10).

As Ainu's political mobilization was intensifying, the 1984 draft New Ainu Law was making its way from the Utari Association's boardroom through the Hokkaido government to the national Diet. As soon as the draft was adopted by the association in 1984, the association petitioned the Hokkaido government, the Hokkaido Mayors' Association, and major political parties to pass a new law on the Ainu and abolish the Former Aborigines Protection Act. In response, in December of 1984 a deliberative body under the governor, the Utari Affairs Council (*Utari Mondai Konwa Kai*), was set up. This council was initially composed of 15 members, including five Ainu representatives; later it was increased to 20 members, including seven Ainu representatives. After much deliberation regarding the problems of the Former Aborigines Protection Act and examination of indigenous rights policies in other countries, such as the United States, Australia, and New Zealand, the council submitted to the governor a report entitled "On a New Law on Ainu People (*Ainu Minzoku ni Kansuru Shinpou Mondai ni tsuite*)" in March of 1988. The report recommended that the Japanese government abolish the Former Aborigines Protection Act and enact a new Ainu law. Thanks to the rising tide of Ainu activism in this period and the presence of Ainu representatives in the council, the council report kept all but one of the items from the 1984 Ainu proposal. The one item that was dropped was the provision to secure government-guaranteed seats for the Ainu in the Diet and local assemblies. It was considered this clashed directly with constitutional provisions mandating the equality of voting rights. The report even acknowledged that "it is a self-evident fact that the Ainu were indigenous to Hokkaido" and that "'indigenous rights' can be an important basis for 'New Ainu Law'," although "the concept of 'indigenous rights' has not been clearly defined in law" (SNT 1988, 47: 6–7).

The Utari Association welcomed this report, and in August of 1988 the governor requested the Japanese government that the contents of the report be examined and translated into law. In response to this request, the Japanese government established the Committee for Examining a New Law on the Ainu (*Ainu Shinpou Mondai Kentou Iinkai*) in 1989. This committee's task was simply to discuss whether a new law on the Ainu was needed or not. The committee consisted of representatives of ten relevant ministries, and their bureaucratic debates did not lead anywhere.

In the meantime, due to sustained domestic and international pressures generated by Ainu activism, the Japanese government was forced to change its approach to the Ainu in international political forums. First, as discussed above, it had to acknowledge the existence of the Ainu as "a distinct group" at the WGIP in 1987. The government even made an attempt to justify its remedial policy, and asserted that it had spent ¥30.9 billion for the welfare of the Ainu people between 1974 and 1986 and that the Former Aborigines Protection Act functioned to protect the rights of the Ainu. Then, in its third report to the Human

Rights Committee in 1991, the government clearly stated that the Ainu were "an ethnic minority group." While the government stopped short of recognizing the Ainu as an indigenous people, this was a significant achievement for the Ainu. It further encouraged their political mobilization and convinced them of the utility of international political opportunities. Transnational discourse on ethnic rights, particularly indigenous peoples' rights, was increasing dramatically around the same time: many international conferences on indigenous peoples were held, 1993 was designated the UN International Year of the World's Indigenous People, and 1994 was the beginning of the UN International Decade of the World's Indigenous People. These global trends presented a new model of "good nation" to Ainu and the Japanese government alike and provided impetus for the government to address issues around the Ainu.

Reflecting this changing approach and helped by a new ruling coalition that included the Socialist Party, the Japanese government picked up the matter of the New Ainu Law again. In March 1995, Chief Cabinet Secretary (*Naikaku Kanbou Choukan*) Kouzou Igarashi, a Diet member in the Socialist Party, set up a private advisory body, the Conference of the Experts on the Measures for the Ainu People (*Utari Taisaku no Arikata ni Kansuru Yuushikisha Kondankai*). The conference was initially composed of six members (with a seventh member added later), whose occupations ranged from anthropologist and historian to former Supreme Court judge and Hokkaido governor. It was fortunate for the Ainu that political turmoil in Japan left the Socialist Party in power during this period, and Igarashi, who had formerly been mayor of Asahikawa, Hokkaido, and had worked extensively on Ainu issues in the course of his political career, was in a position of power. The problem with the conference, however, was that it had no Ainu representative, unlike the Hokkaido Council established in 1984.

The conference submitted a report in April 1996, recommending that the old laws on the Ainu be replaced by a new one intended to protect Ainu culture. The report had five main components:

(1) The history and culture of Ainu people
(2) The evaluation of Hokkaido Utari welfare measures
(3) Debates about indigenous rights in the UN
(4) New policy proposals
(5) The treatment of the Former Aborigines Protection Act.

It is notable that the third part of the report was devoted entirely to the debates in the UN, indicating the extent to which the Japanese government was concerned about its international reputation and following the transnational model of "good nation." Substantively, however, the report was far from what the Utari Association originally called for. While the report acknowledged that the Ainu lived in the northern part of Japan prior to the mainland Japanese (*Wajin*) expansion, it stopped short of recognizing the Ainu as an indigenous people, avoiding the term "indigenous" so that the rights that might come with indigenousness would not become an issue. More importantly, the report essentially proposed continuing the existing welfare measures for Ainu, and its only new policy proposal was the promotion of Ainu culture. Thus, the six key demands of the 1984 proposal were stripped down to five as the draft went through the Hokkaido Council, with the demand for special seats for the Ainu in the Diet and local assemblies dropped, and then the conference report further cut four of those remaining demands, keeping only cultural promotion.

Despite the shortcomings, the Utari Association accepted this proposal, and the Ainu Cultural Promotion Law (officially the Law for the Promotion of Ainu Culture and the Dissemination and Advocacy of Knowledge in respect of Ainu Traditions) became law in May of 1997.[7] The Hokkaido Former Aborigines Protection Act was abolished at the same time. The law established the Center for Ainu Culture Promotion, with a budget intended to promote and protect Ainu culture and traditions, and it gave rise to various new cultural activities. Ainu leaders fully recognized that the law was not satisfactory, but given the history of missed opportunities and the need for a new law, they accepted it as a positive step.

The law was, nonetheless, a significant milestone for Japanese minority rights, since it recognized for the first time in the post-World War II period that a culture that was distinct from mainstream Japanese culture existed in the country and that it was a culture worth investing government money in to protect. Many saw the law as a first step to multicultural Japan. While multicultural Japan remained an ideal rather than an accepted reality among the Japanese, the Japanese government's approach had certainly changed substantially by this time. Following the law's provision that the government establish a guideline for policies on the promotion of Ainu culture, Prime Minister Hashimoto laid out the main principles of the policies soon after the law was enacted. In them, he acknowledged that Ainu inhabited Hokkaido prior to the Wajin, and claimed that the Ainu's rich culture and tradition should be shared with the whole world (Emori 2008: 588–9). What the Japanese government worked hard to hide from international attention in the Meiji era has now become something it wants to proudly share with the world.

Recognition as an indigenous people

While the Japanese government had recognized the Ainu as an ethnic minority in 1991 and acknowledged the Ainu's distinct culture with the Ainu Cultural Promotion Law in 1997, it had yet to offer recognition of the Ainu as an indigenous people. The next step for Ainu activism was to gain that recognition. There were already a few signals that such recognition was forthcoming. One of them was the judgment in the Nibutani Dam case of 1997.

The Nibutani area in Hokkaido has a high concentration of Ainu (about 80 percent of the population is said to be Ainu) and includes lands that are important for traditional Ainu culture and livelihoods. When the government decided to build a dam in that area and started buying the land for it, all but two Ainu agreed to sell their land. Negotiations with the two remaining Ainu landowners failed, and in the end the local government forcibly took away their holdings and started building the dam. The two Ainu whose lands were forcibly confiscated, Shigeru Kayano and Tadashi Kaizawa, sued the government, making an argument for their indigenous right to "Mother Earth." The dam was finished in 1996 and began its operation soon thereafter. The lawsuit was still pending, and the verdict did not come until March of 1997. The court found the forceful confiscation of the lands of the Ainu owners illegal. But since the dam had already been completed, the court did not order the government to return the land. More significant for Ainu politics was that the verdict recognized, for the first time, the Ainu as an indigenous people. The judge referred directly to the International Covenant on Civil and Political Rights, pointing out that the Ainu were an ethnic minority group as described in Article 27 of the Covenant and that the government ought to have taken special measures to protect their culture and livelihood as an indigenous people. The judge went on to define indigenous peoples as:

> social groups that continue to maintain their own culture and identity as a minority group that has different culture and identity from the majority group of a state since before that state's rule reached that minority group's areas of residence ... Ainu lived in Hokkaido before our state's rule reached Hokkaido, with their own culture and identity ... and despite the economic and social damage they suffered since they were incorporated to Japan, they continue to maintain their own culture and identity. Therefore they fall under the category of "indigenous peoples."
>
> (Abe 2004: 41)

The Nibutani case was in the judicial branch, and the executive branch also seemed willing to acknowledge the Ainu as an indigenous people. On May 7, 1997, one day before the passing of the Ainu Cultural Promotion Law, seven leaders of the Utari Association visited then-Prime Minister Ryutaro Hashimoto, Cabinet Secretary Seiroku Kajiyama, and other cabinet members in the Prime Minister's Office. They told the seven Ainu that there was no question that the Ainu were an indigenous people and promised that "when the UN Declaration on the Rights of Indigenous Peoples gets adopted, the Japanese government will promptly accept it and adhere to it, and examine implementation of policies to comply with it, observing relevant international trends" (Abe 2004: 47). Thus, the Ainu's welfare was directly tied to the international politics of indigenous peoples. For Ainu to achieve any more progress, such as recognition as an indigenous people and legislation covering the remaining key demands in the 1984 draft New Ainu Law, the adoption of the Declaration on the Rights of Indigenous Peoples at the UN was essential.

The drafting of the Declaration on the Rights of Indigenous Peoples took more than a decade due to opposition by major powers such as the US, Canada, Australia, and New Zealand. Even before 1997, Ainu had focused on the Declaration since the Japanese government repeatedly cited a lack of international consensus on the definition of indigenous peoples as the reason for its unwillingness to acknowledge Ainu indigenousness. Now that their movement's progress was even more directly tied to the Declaration, Ainu acted vigorously to promote it, participating in the working group on the draft every year. The UN Declaration was adopted in 2007 with the Japanese government voting in favor, as Prime Minister Hashimoto had promised. The Utari Association moved swiftly to urge Diet (parliament) members from Hokkaido to form a nonpartisan group, the Committee of Diet Members to Think about the Establishment of Ainu's Rights (*Ainu Minzoku no Kenri Kakuritsu wo Kangaeru Giin no Kai*), which sponsored a resolution to recognize the Ainu as an indigenous people. Former Liberal Democratic Party politicians who had strong ties with the Utari Association, such as Muneo Suzuki (New Party Daichi) and Yukio Hatoyama (Democratic Party of Japan), played leading roles in this process, but current LDP politicians were members as well (SNT 2008, 113: 7). Lobbying by the Utari Association to promote the resolution worked through this Committee.

International factors were also at work. Japan's Universal Periodical Review at the Human Rights Council, which was a new mechanism of the newly established UN human rights body that replaced the Commission on Human Rights, took place in May of 2008. During the review the Japanese government was questioned about the Ainu and was pressured to recognize them as an indigenous people. It was also helpful that a G-8 summit was about to take place in Hokkaido in the summer of 2008; the government likely feared protests by Ainu which would embarrass the host government by showing them not to be a legitimate member of the "good nation" circle. With all these domestic and international pressures mounting, on June 6, 2008, the resolution to recognize Ainu's indigenousness was unanimously passed in the Japanese Diet. The legislative branch finally recognized the Ainu as an indigenous people, and the group that was considered "a dying race" several decades ago has officially earned the title of an indigenous people of Japan. Subsequently, the Ainu themselves have demonstrated to the world that they have fully restored their pride in Ainuness. On April 1, 2009, the Hokkaido Utari Association reclaimed its original name, the Hokkaido Ainu Association.

Conclusion

The foregoing has demonstrated how "a dying race" has become "an indigenous people" in modern Japan. The changing transnational model of "good nation" played a major role in enabling this transformation. From the Meiji Restoration to World War II, the predominant model allowed major colonial powers to mercilessly engulf various peoples in the periphery into their colonial empires while administering assimilationist policies in the name of civilizing them. The Japanese government did exactly that to the Ainu. Weakened by a history of aggression by mainland Japanese and overwhelmed by the modern technologies that the Japanese government possessed, the Ainu were largely powerless to resist the incursions and lost much of their land and culture. After World War II, colonial expansion became discredited and the nation-state that contains culturally homogeneous populations became the more legitimate transnational model.

The government assumed that Ainu would gradually become part of the homogenous Japanese nation and did not develop any special policies for them apart from welfare provision. Mired in the prevalent myth of homogeneous Japan, many Ainu tried to assimilate into mainstream Japanese culture and "pass" as Japanese. This situation changed from the late 1970s as the era of global human rights dawned and the transnational model slowly shifted from assimilation to multiculturalism. Starting in the 1970s, the influence of international human rights instruments and growing interaction with indigenous peoples in other countries catapulted the emerging Ainu activities into large-scale social movements. Exposure to global human rights activities in general and indigenous rights movements in particular provided Ainu activism with a focus and vocabulary to move beyond dependence on the government to seek proactive measures to restore their lost lands and traditions. International human rights institutions and organizations provided new political opportunities and important international allies, both of which were critical for the rise and subsequent success of Ainu social movements. New political opportunities became available as Japan became involved in the growing international human rights regime, ratifying key human rights treaties and participating in international human rights institutions. Ainu activists found allies in indigenous peoples and human rights organizations abroad as well as Japanese human rights activists, or "rooted cosmopolitans" (Tarrow 2005), who were affiliated with the United Nations or international NGOs.

I note that local Ainu activists laid the foundation for the resurgence of Ainu pride, but transnational influences propelled their movement into a powerful force that the government could no longer ignore or easily co-opt. The Japanese government, facing pressures on both the domestic and international front, slowly shifted its approach to the Ainu, aligning itself with the emerging global norms about indigenous rights. It accepted the Ainu as a distinct group in 1987, an ethnic minority in 1991, and finally an indigenous people in 2008. Following the increasingly legitimate multicultural model of "good nation," the Japanese government acknowledged Ainu culture as distinct from mainstream Japanese culture and yet worthy of protection by the government. While many of the Ainu demands outlined in the 1984 draft New Ainu Law remain unfulfilled and discrimination against Ainu has not completely disappeared, the strides that the Ainu have made in the past few decades are remarkable.

This chapter located the trajectory of Ainu activism and its gains within the progressive incorporation of minority rights into the transnational model of "good nation," as legitimated by the broader human rights frameworks, in the postwar period. This is not to overlook the fact that in many parts of the world governments continue to violate minority rights with relative impunity. Even in Japan, where the government has been relatively more responsive to international pressures to improve minority rights, the widespread understanding of the nation has yet to embrace multiculturalism (see Iwabuchi in this volume). Other minorities such as the Burakumin and Koreans in Japan have also earned some hard-fought gains by engaging human rights discourses and activism (Tsutsui and Shin 2008), but geopolitics, complicated by the collective memory of Japan's colonial history, continues to generate tensions in majority-minority relations in Japan (Tsutsui 2006, 2009; see also Dudden, Selden in this volume).

Future research should further examine how different types of minority groups might use transnational models differently, and how different types of countries might incorporate them differently. Such cross-national comparative research would complement historical studies like this one to present a comprehensive picture of the impact of transnational models on local politics.

Notes

1 The brief description in this chapter does not do justice to the richness of Ainu history, and interested readers are advised to peruse Emori (2008), Howell (2005), Ogasawara (1997, 2001), and Siddle (1996, 1997).
2 Many Ainu were in the border areas between Japan and Russia by then, and as successive wars and peace treaties with Russia changed the ownership of these areas, the Ainu were pushed back and forth and many tragic situations of ethnic diaspora and separation ensued.
3 In protest at this, the Ainu in the Asahikawa area did not participate in the organization.
4 It did lose some of the surrounding islands, and those Ainu who lived there were separated from their relatives in Hokkaido.
5 Even in the early 1960s, influenced by the emerging leftist movements in Japan, a few groups that sought to improve Ainu lives, such as the Society for the Study of Ainu Issues (*Ainu Mondai Kenkyukai*) (1963) and the Young Utari Society (*Peure Utari no Kai*) (1964), emerged. While there were some young Ainu members, these organizations were largely composed of non-Ainu Japanese students pursuing their anti-colonialism agenda (Siddle 1996: 162).
6 Adopted in 1971, the ECOSOC resolution 1503 made it possible for individuals to seek remedy for systematic violations of human rights by appealing to the UN Commission on Human Rights.
7 Before the law was enacted, a cabinet resolution of June 27, 1997 specified that the scope of the Ainu Cultural Promotion Law was limited to Hokkaido, and only municipalities within Hokkaido could plan and enact the law's execution. Thus, the rights of Ainu living outside of Hokkaido to receive benefit from the law were severely limited (Abe 2004: 44, Uemura 2004: 232).

References

Abe, Y. 2004. Ainu Minzoku no Hukken Undo [Movements to Regain Rights by the Ainu]. In *Gurobaru Jidai no Senjuuminzoku* [Indigenous Peoples in the Age of Globalization]. M. Fujioka and K. Nakano, eds. Kyoto, Japan: Horitsu Bunkasha.
Ainu Nibutani Forum Organizing Committee. 1994. *Gathering in Ainumoshir, the Land of the Ainu: Messages from Indigenous Peoples in the World.* Tokyo: Yushisha.
Atuy. 2002. *Ore ha Tamashii wo Dezain Suru* [I Design Souls]. Sapporo: Hokkaido Shimbunsha.
Brysk, A. 2000. *From Tribal Village to Global Village: Indian Rights and International Relations in Latin America.* Stanford, CA: Stanford University Press.
della Porta, D., H. Kriesi, and D. Rucht. 1999. *Social Movements in a Globalizing World.* New York: St. Martin's Press.
Emori, S. 2008. *Ainu Minzoku no Rekishi* [The History of the Ainu]. Urayasu, Japan: Sofukan.
Goodale, M. and S. E. Merry. 2007. *The Practice of Human Rights: Tracking Law Between the Global and the Local.* Cambridge: Cambridge University Press.

Guidry, J. A., M. D. Kennedy, and M. N. Zald, eds. 2000. *Globalizations and Social Movements: Culture, Power, and the Transnational Public Sphere*. Ann Arbor: University of Michigan Press.

Howell, D. L. 2005. *Geographies of Identity in Nineteenth-Century Japan*. Berkeley: University of California Press.

Kato, T. 2007. Rinri to Senjuuminzoku Ainu no Jinken [Research Ethic and the Human Rights of the Indigenous People, the Ainu]. In *Gendai Bunkajinruigaku no Kadai* [Issues in Contemporary Cultural Anthropology], T. Irimoto and T. Yamagishi, eds. Tokyo: Sekai Shiso Sha.

Keck, M.E. and K. Sikkink. 1998. *Activists Beyond Borders: Advocacy Networks in International Politics*. Ithaca, NY: Cornell University Press.

Liu, D. 2006. When Do National Movements Adopt or Reject International Agendas? A Comparative Analysis of the Chinese and Indian Women's Movements. *American Sociological Review* 71(6): 921–42.

Mukai, Y. 1948. Zendou Utari Shoshi ni Tsugu [Addressing All Utrai in Hokkaido]. *Kita no Hikari* 1: 4–6.

Ogasawara, N. 1997. *Ainu Sabetsu Mondai Dokuhon* [A Book on Issues around Ainu Discrimination]. Tokyo: Ryokufu Shuppan.

——2001. *Ainu Kin-Gendaishi Dokuhon* [A Book on Modern and Contemporary History of Ainu]. Tokyo: Ryokufu Shuppan.

Ogawa, S. 1948. Ainu Kyokai Sonritsu no Shushi to Shimei [The Intentions and Missions of the Establishment of the Ainu Association]. *Kita no Hikari* 1: 6–10.

Oguma, E. 1998. *"Nihonjin" no Kyoukai–Okinawa, Ainu, Waiwan, Chousen, Shokuminchi Shihai Kara Hukki Undou Made* [The Boundaries of Japanese: Okinawa, Ainu, Taiwan, Korea, from Colonial Occupation to Return Movement]. Tokyo: Shinyosha.

Osaka Jinken Rekishi Shiryou Kan (Osaka Human Rights History Archive Center). 1993. *Kindai Nihon to Ainu Minzoku* [Modern Japan and Ainu People]. Osaka.

Risse, T., S. C. Ropp, and K. Sikkink, eds. 1999. *The Power of Human Rights: International Norms and Domestic Change*. Cambridge: Cambridge University Press.

Ron, J. 1997. Varying Methods of State Violence. *International Organization* 51(2): 275–300.

Siddle, R. 1996. *Race, Resistance and the Ainu of Japan*. London: Routledge.

——1997. Ainu: Japan's Indigenous People. In *Japan's Minorities: The Illusion of Homogeneity*, M. Wiener, ed. London: Routledge.

SNT (*Senkusha No Tsudoi*), various years. Periodical of the Hokkaido Utari/Ainu Association.

Soysal, Nuhoğlu Y. 1995. *Limits of Citizenship: Migrants and Postnational Membership in Europe*. Chicago, IL: University of Chicago Press.

Tarrow, S. 2005. *The New Transnational Activism*. Cambridge: Cambridge University Press.

Teshima, T. 1990. ILO 169 gou Jouyaku no Seiritsu to Nihon [The Adoption of ILO Treaty 169 and Japan]. *Buraku Kaiho Kenkyu* 77: 45–69.

Tsunemoto, T. 2002. Constitutional and Legal Status of the Ainu in Japan: A National Report. *International Academy of Comparative Law*. Available at: http://courseweb.edteched.uottawa.ca/IACLindigenousminorityrights/JapanTsunemoto.htm (accessed May 2012).

Tsutsui, K. 2004. Global Civil Society and Ethnic Social Movements in the Contemporary World. *Sociological Forum* 19(1): 63–88.

——2006. Redressing Past Human Rights Violations: Global Dimensions of Contemporary Social Movements. *Social Forces* 85(1): 331–54.

——2009. The Trajectory of Perpetrators' Trauma: Mnemonic Politics around the Asia-Pacific War in Japan. *Social Forces* 87(3): 1389–422.

Tsutsui, K. and H. J. Shin. 2008. Global Norms, Local Activism and Social Movement Outcomes: Global Human Rights and Resident Koreans in Japan. *Social Problems* 55(3): 391–418.

Uemura, H. 2004. "Senjuuminzoku no Kokusai 10 Nen" ga Umidashita Kibou, Genjitsu, soshite Gensou [The Hope, Reality, and Illusion that "the Decade of Indigenous People" Produced]. In *Gurobaru Jidai no Senjuuminzoku* [Indigenous Peoples in the Age of Globalization], M. Fujioka and K. Nakano, eds. Kyoto: Horitsu Bunkasha.

10 Japan's place in the world

Transformations of national imaginings of geography

Alexis Dudden

Sovereign territory is a critical national institution and international law is the means for its institutionalization (Meyer et al. 1997). It also has sanctity in regionalization projects. Regardless of whether the European Union is a good or bad idea or whether it has a chance of succeeding, one of the most important preconditions for a state's entry into a regional union is the absence of border disputes. To be sure, there are occasional instances of border friction among EU members—to say nothing of open and closed borders within Europe as far as immigration is concerned. Yet from a macro perspective and despite, and I would argue in part because of, existing international laws, the situation could not look more different in Asia, especially Northeast Asia. From China's refusal to recognize Taiwan as a separate entity to the painful, protracted way of life that is the Korean War, Asia is rife with big-ticket border problems. A number of scholars pointedly argue that the Cold War has never ended in this region, largely because the era's wars were always "hot" here, now nervously held in check in many places and persisting in living memory throughout the region (Dirlik 1993, Kwon 2010).

Noticeably, in the midst of this state of affairs, Japan—theoretically the most stable place in the region—has promulgated a surprising new map of itself during the past two decades, which in many ways exacerbates the country's plentiful border disputes that have lingered since the collapse of its empire in 1945 (see Figure 10.1).

In many ways, the new map of Japan, published in 2011 by the Japanese Coast Guard, clearly represents an ideal: should Japan be able to assert uncontested control over all the islands that it claims as its sovereign territory—which would include the Northern Territories/Kurils, Takeshima/Dokdo, and Senkaku/Diaoyutai—and define far-flung reefs as islands (particularly Okinotorishima), then this lumpy circle with its misshapen donut hole would in fact define Japan as the "sixth largest nation in the world." At the same time, uneasily for hopes of a Northeast Asian regional community, for many Japanese, especially policymakers, this map is far more than ideal; it is the current representation of the nation. Its definition of Japan's borders is in line with how teachers are instructed to teach schoolchildren about Japanese sovereignty over disputed islands and military troops are charged with guarding the islands as integral national territory.

In a region rife with high-stakes territorial disputes, such as the conflict on the Korean Peninsula or tensions over Taiwan and Tibet, the expression "island

208 *Alexis Dudden*

Figure 10.1 Japan Coast Guard Map, 2011
Source: Japan Coast Guard 2011: 1.

disputes" may appear to suggest that Japan's border contests are somewhat inconsequential. At the same time, all of Japan's disputes taken together mean that, except for the Pacific Ocean to the east, the nation's borders are entirely up for grabs. Noticeably, since the mid-1990s, there has been a newly energized focus on the part of Japanese state leaders to maximize the shape of Japan within Northeast Asia.

The following pages consider various aspects of island disputes by revolving around a series of linked questions: What are Japan's boundaries, its national edges? How are these edges shaped and energized by the workings of the ocean regime as it has unfolded since the end of World War II?

Answers to these questions stem from how international law attempts to define territorial boundaries and how it interacts with the endless historical debates over Japan's attempts to control Asia between roughly 1870 and 1945, the time period that comprises the substance of the history on which these very same laws rely on to legitimate present-day borders and sovereignty. This focuses attention at once both within Japan and in surrounding countries on conflicting understandings of national space and time: on divergent ways of interpreting the involved history to describe the present and hoped-for future place of the nation within the region.

The chapter remains squarely centered on Japan because while each nation in Northeast Asia has its own serious border disputes, Japanese leaders and policy-makers appear to be going beyond other countries by drawing increasingly rigid borders with the country's surrounding neighbors. By pursuing a policy of all-or-nothing possession of the islands to nervously mark Japan's borders to the north, west, southwest, and south—uncontested ownership of these territories would unequivocally grant Japan a far larger space on the planet than what many might currently imagine as the country's shape—Japan would seem to have the most to win or lose. For this reason it provides a convenient gaze to the making and unmaking of transnational trajectories in the region.

Island disputes

As is well known, the 1951 Treaty of Peace with Japan (the San Francisco Treaty) named new, post-empire physical limits for the Japanese nation—the space on the planet that Japan would henceforth inhabit.[1] Article 2 of the treaty is most associated with this moment, and its terms, intentionally or not, left vague ultimate control over the Kurils/Northern Territories, Dokdo/Takeshima, and the Senkaku/Diaoyutai, among other places. These main groups of islands together total roughly 5050 square kilometers and form the bulk of Japan's island disputes, alongside the question of whether Okinotorishima in the far south constitutes an island or a reef (sovereignty is not debated) and who has ultimate control over Okinawa's air, water, and land.

Two things bind island disputes to the San Francisco Treaty: first, its imprecision; and, second, and more to the point, its failure to award reparations. The countries that control Northeast Asia's disputed territories contend that the treaty made their ownership clear; Japan argues differently, using the treaty document to contend that its inspecificity means that the territories are indeed Japan's. The Japanese government strives to separate the wartime reparations issue from contemporary territorial matters, yet its continued reluctance to pay such reparations—which sits uncomfortably with the international expectations of national self-reflection and owning up to past human rights violations—infuriates many in the countries repudiating Japan's claims to the islands, especially China and Korea. The resistance of Japanese government to making amends to those who suffered under Japanese rule and war in the past is highly entangled with the islands row. In this light, the territorial disputes have become the non-negotiable means by which to continue the charge for reparations.

In the simplest terms, the islands in question are the indeterminate remnants of Japan's once vast empire as well as of the international treaty process itself. To begin with, there have been numerous disagreements since the San Francisco Treaty came into force between Japan, Russia, the Koreas, China, Taiwan, and the United States over all of the disputed islands, as well as countless agreements and conventions regulating rights of passage, use of natural resources, and military bases (Hara and Jukes 2009, Rozman 2000, Yoshizawa 2009). Sketches of fishing limit lines surrounding the islands contested between Japan and South Korea as well as lighthouse positions, for example, comprise most of the appendix material of the 1965 Treaty of Basic Relations between Japan and the Republic of Korea (Selden 2011).

During the past decade or so, however, the stand-offs over these islands have changed in tenor and intensity. Although state-to-state discussions have maintained a rough stasis vis-à-vis fishing lines and gas and oil drilling, public outcries over recurrent clashes have become increasingly entangled in the history problems and apology politics rotating around them. The international regime of ocean and ocean resource control, particularly the United Nations Convention of the Law of the Sea (UNCLOS), plays greatly to this state of affairs. Island disputes demonstrate at once that the UNCLOS, which came into force in 1994 and subsequently expanded, is oblivious to Northeast Asia's particular terrain or modern history; equally important, it would seem that the convention provides an opening for Northeast Asian nations to renew issues festering from the eras of empire, war, and occupation.

The Law of the Sea is clear: scientific measurements determine possible expansion, and history, custom, and convention determine who owns what. Notably, however, lawyers and not scientists make the final decisions about what constitutes certain dimensions of the sea floor among other things, leaving the law far more open-ended than the sediment that science measures. The rulebook for the law's most recent component—national extensions to the continental shelf—acknowledges that claiming underwater domains is a relatively new process; a variety of disagreements could arise. The text states that should concerns arise about extending national limits, "[n]eighboring coastal States may also need to be approached during the process of elaborating a submission to the Commission on the Limits of the Continental Shelf (CLCS)" (United Nations, Division for Ocean Affairs and the Law of the Sea 2006, Section VIII: 2).

On November 12, 2008, the Japanese government made its formal request to the United Nations that the international community recognizes pieces of Japan's national shape in line with the "New Maritime Nation" that the Coast Guard envisions (The Foreign Ministry of Japan, Department of Oceanic Affairs 2008). On October 1, 2009 the United Nations' CLCS chairman announced the committee's receipt of the Japanese submission; shortly thereafter, Chinese and South Korean delegates submitted protest notes. At the end of April 2012, Japanese sources connected with the submission leaked news to the *Asahi Shimbun* among other news sources that the United Nations would rule in Japan's favor. The next day, the Chinese press roundly disagreed: "Did not;" "Did so" would seem to define the moment. Clearly, international route is not a neutral process in allocating underwater domains and associated resources.

And reactions come not only from neighboring states but from their citizens too. Waves of protests and boycotts of Japanese businesses and products were launched both in China and Korea during 2012 and 2013. The 2014 annual opinion poll conducted by the Asan Institute for Policy Studies in Seoul discovered that South Koreans overwhelmingly regard the island clash with Japan the "biggest obstacle to the development of Korean-Japanese relations," averaging at just above 42 percent across the spectrum in both age and ideological leaning categories, with textbooks coming in second at roughly 33 percent and "comfort women" at just under 14 percent (Jiyoon et al. 2014: 23).[2] Not coincidentally, as age has increasingly taken survivors of the well-known touchstones of the region's unending history problems, public clamor for control over the islands has supplanted focus on the survivors and moved the islands to the center of the history wars.

A signal difference between the island issues and the other components of the history problems, such as the Nanjing massacre or the forced sexual slavery system, is that the islands themselves have very little human history at stake.[3] As such, the islands themselves offer relatively blank fields on which to battle the past in the present. They are importantly free of problems such as collaboration or complicity, which complicate pure "us versus them" versions of the past articulated in the other history problems. The island disputes allow all those who engage in the debates enormous liberties with the categories of historical perpetrator and victim, among other things. The Japanese, for example, can much more easily become victims in telling the islands' history—"We were robbed!"—than when trying to explain away the atrocities Japanese troops committed in Nanjing. As a result, the islands now stand as the pre-eminent objects and markers with which to claim the contested past for the future of the region.

Japan's hardening boundaries

The earthquake and tsunami of March 2011 (3.11 hereafter), and the subsequent nuclear crisis, is monumental and will color transformations of Japan's place in the world at least for the foreseeable future (Kingston 2011). Instructively, it would appear thus far that Tokyo's official claims for Japan's boundaries have not simply remained the same as before March 2011, but that they have hardened. Here the words "Tokyo" and "official" refer specifically to publicly available Japanese government documents, and in this instance examples include white papers from the ministries of Education and Defense as well as Foreign Ministry policy statements. Especially because the cataclysmic events of 3.11 created the possibility, at least in historical terms, for Japan's leaders to reflect about repositioning the nation in practical and metaphorical terms, it is noticeable that when taken together government statements reveal a hardened Japan vis-à-vis the rest of Northeast Asia. By "hardened" I mean more than simply "the rise of the right." It is perhaps most productive to understand Japan's rigidity at the beginning of the twenty-first century in terms of how the centrist doctrine incorporates claims and issues that throughout much of the post-1945 era located and defined the rallying cries of the nation's extremist voices. In other words, official Japan has in many ways neutralized once radical claims into the mainstream view. Tokyo's claims over the islands Japan disputes with its neighbors are all the more fraught, therefore, trapped in this mix which also incorporates post-3.11 vulnerabilities and anxieties.

On March 30, 2011, Japan's Ministry of Education released its middle school textbook review advising teachers throughout Japan to instruct children that, among other things, the small islands dotting Japan's north, west, and southwest were called "the Northern Territories," "Takeshima," and the "Senkaku" and were "Japanese territory" over which Japan alone had "sovereignty." With this review, the proportion of approved geography, civics, and history textbooks containing these names and claims rose from 43 percent in 2008, the previous round of screening, to 66 percent.[4] The same reviewing guidelines were later introduced for elementary school social studies textbooks as well.[5]

At the time, many in the region were shocked, though not so much by Japan's repetition of its officially stated prior position; rather, many were stunned that while Japan was openly in a state of crisis and actively receiving a tremendous outpouring of neighborly goodwill from the very countries with which it had its island disputes—as much as $4 million had already come from a single fundraising event in Taiwan, with $10 million from a similar telethon in South Korea and even $750,000 from North Korea—Tokyo would proceed forward in such a seemingly obdurate manner (Penney 2011).

Then, on August 2, 2011—roughly four months after daily radiation readings for Tokyo and the northeast region of Japan overnight became as regular as the weather map in the country's major newspapers—the new "Defense of Japan" guidelines took effect. Each of Japan's surrounding countries voiced displeasure over how the ministry envisaged Japan's future handling of disputes over the very same islands that the Ministry of Education had earlier in the year called "Japanese territory." China's spokesman took most umbrage because the guidelines named China "assertive" (*koatsuteki*) with regard to how it was handling its own territorial claims in the South China Sea, while declaring for the first time that Japanese forces would "respond to attacks on Japan's offshore islands by quickly deploying mobile units to prevent and reject invasion" (Ministry of Defense, Japan 2011: 10). The National Defense Program Guidelines released in 2014, which outlines policies for the next ten years, reiterated the same view (Ministry of Defense, Japan 2014: 6, 8).

In comparison, the approach of Japan's Ministry of Foreign Affairs to the islands would seem a bit out of step. By definition the shaper of Japan's place in the world and the bureaucratic organ responsible for addressing diplomatic standoffs (the level at which the island tensions remain), the Foreign Ministry exerts tremendous influence over what goes on. However, in contrast to the ministries of Education and Defense's global statements on islands as "sovereign/ offshore territory," the Ministry of Foreign Affairs has continued to categorize each dispute in a bilateral fashion, regardless of their increasingly apparent interconnections.[6] Undoubtedly, this approach works best with regard to Okinawa and US relations, managing to keep questions of control and sovereignty over those islands on a separate plane of existence and generally from much of the discussion of the history problems writ large. Within Japan's more immediate Northeast Asian context, however, this country-to-country approach falters. The Foreign Ministry's policy statements erase the historical totality of the long-vanished Japanese empire, all the while insisting that history legitimates Japan's sovereignty over the islands today even though it was the course of the Japanese empire that initially marked all these islands as under Japanese sovereign control.

The Foreign Ministry's approach suggests, however, that deeper matters are at play, since its policy writers are ultimately responsible for engaging Japan's actions with other nations in ways that accord to international norms. In ministry statements, references to international law appear in abundance. And here lies the under-appreciated feature of island disputes. The remaining part of the chapter, therefore, steps outside the confines of the island disputes that we can see on the ocean's surface in Northeast Asia to briefly introduce how the United Nations Convention on the Law of the Sea fits in, and especially its rules regarding the limits of the continental shelf. Such rules, while affirming the primacy of transnational defini-tions over seabed and ocean floor beyond national imaginings, also lend themselves to reworking national histories and revivifying national claims.

The transnational ocean regime

Broadly speaking, in the mid- to late nineteenth century, when Japanese thinkers and officials engaged Japan in the terminology and practice of international law, the substance and bulk of this law revolved around controlling land, specifically states and their possessions (Dudden 2006, chapter 2). Of course, certain provi-sions in the law governed things that happened at sea: incidents involving pirates, accidents between ships, as well as international law's subset preoccupation with timing legitimate artillery fire from ship to ship or onto enemy land (Wheaton 1836). During the first half of the twentieth century, developments in submarine cable technology among other things energized legal thinking in terms of what these inventions would entail for sovereign ownership of territory and rights of passage (Finn and Yang 2009). That said, through the end of World War II and through the writing of the San Francisco Treaty, international law remained conceptually grounded onshore.

At the outset of the twenty-first century, international law's focus and concerns have shifted and lie decidedly with the world's oceans: what's in them, what's under them, and how they might be controlled. Given the customary nature of inter-national law, there is a historical moment that sparked the change we see coded into practice today. On September 28, 1945, in keeping with United States' unilateralist swagger at that time, President Harry Truman single-handedly rejected the long-standing and still-prevailing seventeenth-century concept of the Freedom of the Seas and declared in Presidential Proclamation No 2667 that:

> the Government of the United States regards the natural resources of the subsoil and the sea bed of the continental shelf beneath the high seas but contiguous to the coasts of the United States as appertaining to the United States, subject to its jurisdiction and control.
>
> (Quoted in United Nations, Division for Ocean Affairs and the Law of the Sea 2006, Section I: 14)

Suffice it to say that other nations in the world paid attention to Truman's announcement that the United States just got even bigger. Similarly to the way that other countries responded to the news that the United States would not "share" nuclear weapons by developing their own, a number of "coastal states" (as the law names nations with watery edges) followed suit and declared their nation's respective expansion into the sea.

Also comparable to the international history of nuclear weapons profusion, a number of private and public voices clamored via United Nations' mechanisms to demand some sort of control—lest there be no fish or oil left in oceans—and in 1958, in Geneva, United Nations representatives convened the first Conference on the Law of the Sea. Simultaneously, those concerned not simply with ordering regimes in the present but with environmentally sustainable futures—beginning with Arvid Pardo, Malta's Ambassador to the United Nations—called for a "legal order for the seas and oceans [to] facilitate international communication, and ... promote the[ir] peaceful uses ... , the equitable and efficient utilization of their resources, the conservation of their living resources, and the study, protection and preservation of the marine environment," bringing the United Nations Seabed Commission into being and making its concerns part and parcel of the Law of the Sea (United Nations, Division for Ocean Affairs and the Law of the Sea n.d.). In 1982, representatives of 60 nations signed the law into being, and in 1994 the UN General Assembly adopted it as the global norm.

Japan, China, South Korea, and Russia are among the 165 states together with the European Union that have ratified the convention, while the United States and North Korea have not (as of 2013). More important, though, is noticing how nationally aggrandizing impulses to expand entwine here with an awareness that the earth and its resources are finite. Those fearing a loss in potential profit quickly developed the concept of the "exclusive economic zone (EEZ)," whose regulations grant accredited nations an additional 200 miles of ocean beyond the Law of the Sea's 12-mile free edge given to all (United Nations, Division for Ocean Affairs and the Law of the Sea 1997, Part V: 40–49). Environmentally minded legal thinkers such as Arvid Padro declared EEZs a travesty that would eventually deplete the world's oceans to nothing more than a little seaweed.

Since the 1990s, when EEZs became standard operating procedure, the ocean's contents have become increasingly more visible, generating even more desire for further "exclusive" national ownership of what lies within. The practice of the "extended continental shelf" has appeared in international law whose provisions can add up to an additional 150 miles on top of the 200 additional EEZ miles some nations are fortunate enough to claim as their own.

Looked at differently, laws and practices governing exclusive economic zones and continental shelf areas grant sovereign rights to the nation claiming them—rights that are both "exclusive (even if the coastal State does not explore … or exploit them) … and independent from occupation"—as well as jurisdiction over all aspects of marine life and activity therein (United Nations, Division for Ocean Affairs and the Law of the Sea 2006, Section I: 22). Legal notions of the EEZ and the extended continental shelf take the fundamentals of nineteenth-century international law's ideas about sovereignty—in terms of possessing land to control the people and resources inscribed therein—and blend them into the most contemporary submarine technologies that have made previously unseen worlds increasingly knowable, desirable, and profitable. The United Nations' 2006 *Training Manual For Delineation of the Outer Limits of the Continental Shelf Beyond 200 Nautical Miles* makes this abundantly clear:

> Historically, the seabed and subsoil lying beyond the territorial sea—due to their relative inaccessibility—had been the object of only sporadic economic activities … . Over time, scientific and technological and technical advances led to the discovery of substantive mineral resources (oil and gas in particular) underwater and an economically viable prospect for their future exploration. As a result of these developments, States practice became increasingly shaped by the interest of coastal states to affirm their rights to the continental shelf beyond the territorial sea.
>
> (United Nations, Division for Ocean Affairs and the
> Law of the Sea 2006, Section I: 13)

According to the law, these rights are there for the taking but not de facto presumed, which allows anyone to exploit the resources not yet "properly" claimed. The Training Manual explains what interested parties must do to define this extra space within their nation's edges and is, thus, even more specific about what's at stake:

> The resources to be derived from the continental shelf are enormous and, in the future, the shelf area will be the main source of world oil and gas supplies. Offshore oil production in the year 2000 was estimated at 1.23 billion tons, and natural gas at 650 billion cubic meters. The effect of the provisions of UNCLOS on the continental shelf is that practically all seabed oil and natural gas resources will fall under the control of coastal States. Therefore, recognized outer limits of the continental shelf will provide legal certainty for the coastal State to exercise its sovereign rights over those natural resources.
>
> (United Nations, Division for Ocean Affairs and the
> Law of the Sea 2006, Section VIII: 2)

Noticeably, the authors of the UN's Convention decided that for their purposes science was useful up to a point: good for determining undersea topographies with precision and for locating resources yet ineffective in determining just how far a nation could go without competition. Accordingly, the law declares that the "legal" continental shelf is not the same as the "scientific" continental shelf: it is broader (United Nations, Division for Ocean Affairs and the Law of the Sea 2006, Section I: 2, 4, 5–6). Thus, the Law of the Sea takes man-made maps into the deep sea, mixing together as international legal practice geography's divide over science and humanities to create a contested map of the earth's sea floor.

History and water rules

Granted, the island disputes cannot be isolated to Japan's own doing, and certainly not from its broader Asia-Pacific context (see Selden in this volume). Both China and South Korea have fortified their positions about islands since 2012, China even escalating militarily. Yet Japan's continued act to will away the nation's past, at odds with transnational norms of "proper membership" in world polity, appears to be doing great disservice to the possibility of calm resolutions to present-day contentions (Barkan 2000, Dudden 2008).

For all practical purposes, Northeast Asia's island disputes generate head-on collisions because the international law ultimately relies on "history" to judge ownership. The problem remains that the history involved in Japan's possession of these islands during the first half of the twentieth century remains obfuscated at the highest levels of politics in Japan, leaving neighboring countries at the beginning of the twenty-first century wondering what Japan thinks the rest of the world fails to understand about who lost the war, let alone empire.

The EEZ and extended continental shelf features of the Law of the Sea make difficult anything other than a winner-take-all approach to the matters. While the law relies on technical and scientific measurements in delineating what the ocean has to offer and what the outer limits of continental shelf should be, it leaves it to history, custom, and convention to determine legal ownership. When disagreement exists, the law advises that "neighboring coastal Sates may also need to be approached." The problem is of course that disagreement exists at each turn, with Japan at the center having the most to win or lose and history being far from a neutral record. Should history be part of determining ownership today, all sides involved must allow history to be what it is: messy, open-ended, and indeterminate—lest they squander remaining opportunities to craft mutually agreeable and productively stable boundaries for the future stability of the region.

It is important to understand that the idealized nationscape that the Japanese government envisions reflects the Japanese government's determination to maximize legitimate use of the United Nations Law of the Sea, not some wild, expansionistic dreams. It would be misguided to see Japan's island politics as evidence, for example, of hidden desires among its leaders to rekindle long-gone megalomaniac passions. At the same time, it is significant to note that Japan's legitimate use of current international law is guiding the nation's steps, much as it did in the late nineteenth and early twentieth century when Japan established its protectorates, spheres of influence, and annexed territories on the Asian mainland. Questions about what is going on today, therefore, should focus on the international law itself, and its functioning, as well as examining how Japan and other nations approach the law.

Notes

1 Treaty of Peace With Japan, September 8, 1951, San Francisco, California, USA. Available at: www.taiwandocuments.org/sanfrancisco01.htm (accessed April 2014).
2 It is worth noting that the poll also revealed strong support for improving Korea–Japan relations, a near majority (49.5 percent) of the South Korean public favoring a Korea–Japan summit, and a similar number (50.7 percent) supporting the signing of the General Security of Military Information Agreement (Jiyoon et al. 2014: 17).
3 This includes the Northern Territories/Kurils which count as the only truly sustainably inhabited of all of the islands in question.
4 All the regional papers featured articles on this topic. See *Asahi Shimbun* and *Japan Times*, March 30 and March 31, 2011, as well as *Hankyoreh* and *Korea Herald*, March 30–31, 2011.
5 *Japan Times* and *China Daily*, April 4, 2014.
6 During the past decade, the Foreign Ministry has devoted much time and resources to these disputes, reworking earlier statements through publication and distribution of elaborate multi-lingual brochures. See for example: www.mofa.go.jp/region/asia-paci/ takeshima/index.html (accessed April 2014); www.mofa.go.jp/region/europe/russia/ territory/pamphlet.pdf (accessed April 2014).

References

Barkan, E. 2000. *The Guilt of Nations: Restitution and Negotiating Historical Injustices*. Baltimore, MD: The Johns Hopkins University Press.
Dirlik, A., ed. 1993. *What Is in a Rim? Critical Perspectives on the Pacific Region Idea*. Boulder, CO: Westview Press.
Dudden, A. 2006. *Japan's Colonization of Korea: Discourse and Power*. Honolulu: University of Hawaii Press.
——2008. *Troubled Apologies among Japan, Korea, and the United States*. New York: Columbia University Press.
Finn, B. and D. Yang. 2009. *Communication Under the Seas: The Evolving Cable Network and Its Implications*. Cambridge, MA: MIT Press.
Hara, K. and G. Jukes, eds. 2009. *Northern Territories, Asia-Pacific Regional Conflicts and the Aland Experience: Untying the Kurillian Knot*. Abingdon: Routledge.
Igarashi, A. 2010. *Nihon Seiji ron* [Japanese Politics]. Tokyo: Iwanamishoten.
Japan Coast Guard. 2011. Japan Coast Guard Annual Report 2011 [Kaijō Hoan Repōto 2011]. Tokyo: Japan Coast Guard.
Jiyoon, K., K. Friedhoff, K. Chungku, and L. Euicheol. 2014. *Challenges and Opportunities for Korea-Japan Relations in 2014*. Asan Public Opinion Report. Seoul: The Asan Institute for Policy Studies. Available at: http://en.asaninst.org/challenges-and-opportunities-for-korea-japan-relations-in-2014/ (accessed April 2014).
Kingston, J., ed. 2011. *Tsunami: Japan's Post-Fukushima Future*. Washington, DC: Foreign Policy.

Kwon, H. 2010. *The Other Cold War*. New York: Columbia University Press.

Meyer, J. W., J. Boli, G. M. Thomas, and F. O. Ramirez. 1997. World Society and the Nation-State. *American Journal of Sociology* 103(1): 144–81.

Ministry of Defense, Japan. 2011. National Defense Program Guidelines for FY 2011 and Beyond. Available at: www.tr.emb-japan.go.jp/T_06/files/National_Defense_Program_FY2011.PDF (accessed April 2014).

——2014. National Defense Program Guidelines for FY 2014 and Beyond. Available at: www.mod.go.jp/j/approach/agenda/guideline/2014/pdf/20131217_e.pdf (accessed April 2014).

Ministry of Foreign Affairs, Japan, Department of Oceanic Affairs. 2008. Japan's Submission to the Commission on the Limits of the Continental Shelf. Tokyo: MOFA.

Penney, M. 2011. Outpouring of International Support for Japan. *The Asia-Pacific Journal* March 21. Available at: http://japanfocus.org/events/view/55 (accessed April 2014).

Rozman, G. 2000. *Japan and Russia: The Tortuous Path to Normalization, 1949–1999*. New York: St Martin's Press.

Samuels, R. J. 2008. *Securing Japan: Tokyo's Grand Strategy and the Future of East Asia*. Ithaca, NY: Cornell University Press.

Selden, M. 2011. Small Islets, Enduring Conflict: Dokdo, Korea-Japan Colonial Legacy and the United States. *The Asia-Pacific Journal* 9(17/2), April 25. Available at: www.japanfocus.org/-mark-selden/3520 (accessed April 2014).

United Nations, Division for Ocean Affairs and the Law of the Sea. n.d. The United Nations Convention on the Law of the Sea: Historical Perspectives. Available at: www.un.org/Depts/los/convention_agreements/convention_historical_perspective.htm (accessed May 2014).

——1997. *The United Nations Convention on the Law of the Sea*. New York: United Nations Publications.

——2006. *The Law of the Sea: Training Manual for Delineation of the Outer Limits of the Continental Shelf beyond 200 Nautical Miles and for Preparation of Submissions to the Commission on the Limits of the Continental Shelf*. New York: United Nations Publications.

Wheaton, H. 1836. *Elements of International Law*. New York: Carey, Lea and Blanchard.

Yoshizawa, F. 2005. *Sengo Nikkan Kankei: Kokko Seitoka Koho wo Megutte* [Postwar Japanese-Korean Relations: On Negotiations for Normalization of Diplomatic Relations]. Tokyo: Cranebook.

Possibilities

11 Generational shift in a transnational world

Civic orientations of Taiwanese youth

Ly-Yun Chang and Tony Tam

In 2011, an influential magazine in Taiwan, *Commonwealth*, published a special issue on the topic of "Civic Education: From Me to Us." The special issue was a reaction to a finding in the report of the 2009 International Civic and Citizenship Study (Schulz et al. 2010). The report showed a discrepancy between the level of civic knowledge and the level of civic engagement among Taiwanese students: an exceptionally high level of knowledge but a disappointingly low level of engagement.[1] Not surprisingly, the special issue attempted to address the question of how to nurture the next generation of citizens to become "responsible, not-indifferent, knowing when and how to respect others, and think critically"—as most basic principles of a democratic society. Such concerns are not specific to Taiwan. Since 2000, public attention to identifying proper civic norms and the teaching of democratic citizenship has gained ground in education throughout the world (Soysal and Wong 2007).

While the public debate on appropriate civic norms is fierce, studies focusing on Taiwanese youth's orientations toward civic norms are scarce. The empirical focus of our chapter is exactly this: to present a portrait of the civic orientations of Taiwanese adolescents and analyze the forces that are currently shaping such orientations. We draw on unique data from the Taiwan Education Panel Survey[2] (TEPS hereafter), a national panel survey of representative samples of high school students and their parents and teachers since 2001. The adolescents under this study are the 1988–89 birth cohort. The data include vignette-style questions designed to elicit information on the civic orientations of students and their parents. Together with standard data on family background and exceptional data on school contexts, we are able to profile adolescent civic orientations in one major East Asian society and examine the possible interaction of transnational dynamics with the formation of such civic orientations.

The 1988–89 birth cohort offers a particularly useful vantage point for addressing our research question. This is a generation that was born right after the lifting of martial law and arrived at adolescence when Taiwanese society had opened up transnationally. In the two decades since then, Taiwanese citizens witnessed the transformation from a society under martial law to one open to the world, with democratic elections, and a wide range of transnational connections. This generation of Taiwanese adolescents grew up in a milieu of family, peers, and institutions whose cultural practices were more diverse and more dynamic than ever before. Mediated by diffuse mass media, transnational cultural frameworks and practices are shaping the values and outlooks of adolescents, just as are their parents, schools, and peers who are part of the pervasive socializing environment of adolescents.

Although we are interested in examining the interplay between local contexts (family and school) and transnational dynamics in the formation of civic orientations, we realize that this is a difficult challenge. The influence of transnational frameworks, particularly through global mass media, is highly decentralized and diffuse. Families, schools, and peers do not exist in a vacuum. Global media influence is intertwined with the influences of the family, school, and peers. Such influence may multiply rapidly through social contagion dynamics. We thus take a combination of direct and residual approaches to assessing the extent to which the family, school, peers, and diffuse mass media account for the variation in adolescent responses to civic scenarios. While we have multiple indicators for the influences of the family, school, and peers on civic orientations, we interpret the unexplained variation as a crude estimate of the cumulative impact of the global mass media. In a way, the estimate is a conservative one because the measured influences of the family, school, and peers arguably mediate some of the media influence. In interpreting our findings, we also reflect on the challenges that Taiwan currently faces in building a coherent civic culture.

A vignette study

We recognize that the list of "desirable" civic orientations can be arguably long, and might differ across time and space. Given the availability of the TEPS data, we examine responses to hypothetical scenarios related to five civic norms: integrity, caring, responsibility, justice, and public goodness. The following seven scenarios were designed by TEPS to elicit the civic normative orientations of a respondent while minimizing social desirability bias. The scenarios are all about how a respondent deals with her immediate environment; as such they reveal the respondent's choice of conduct in a civic situation. Specifically, student respondents were asked what they would most likely do when they were faced with the following seven scenarios:

(1) your classmate asks you to show him/her the answers while taking an examination (integrity);
(2) your classmates have voted for a place for a graduation trip that is later found to be inaccessible for one classmate because of physical disability (caring for the disabled);
(3) you are provided with the option of cutting down old trees or replanting them somewhere else (though half the trees might die after replanting) for the construction of a new building on campus (caring for environmental sustainability);
(4) you find a stray dog on campus (caring for animals);

(5) as a prefect,[3] you discover while patrolling that your best friend has violated school rules and you are the only person to know (responsibility);

(6) you find that one of your classmates, who used to be unfriendly to you, was unjustly treated and you are the only person to know (justice);

(7) you find that in one of the restrooms on campus was smeared (public good).

For none of the scenarios are the proposed answers a matter of right or wrong (see Table 11.1). The answers reflect competing orientations toward five civic norms. For instance, in the graduation trip scenario, choosing "go with the voting result" indicates preference for democratic resolution of differences, while choosing "propose another place" suggests preference for taking care of the disabled class-mate. The old trees scenario solicits preferences toward environmental preservation and economic development. The scenarios regarding the unjustly treated classmate, smeared toilet, and stray dogs assess whether the students are willing to put aside personal interest for the sake of achieving justice, pay a price to keep a public facility clean, or take the trouble to care for a destitute animal. For the scenarios of cheating in an examination and one's best friend breaking a rule, the answers reflect a unidimensional measure of the degree of integrity and respect for one's official duty of enforcing rules, respectively. Comparable scenarios were asked of the parents.

For each scenario we can code a response as reflecting indifference or compliance to a civic norm. For instance, we code a response as indifferent when a respondent chooses to ignore the norm against cheating on an examination, an assigned responsibility, an unjustly treated classmate, a smeared toilet on campus, and a stray dog; when the respondent refuses to put aside their own choice of location for the graduation trip in order to facilitate a disabled classmate to join; or when choosing a new building at the expense of old trees. In contrast, we code a response as compliant when a respondent refuses to cooperate in cheating, puts aside their interest by proposing to change the trip destination for the disabled class-mate, preserves old trees, fulfills responsibility, speaks for the unjustly treated classmate, and does something about the smeared toilet and the stray dog on campus. The respondent could take a third position: situation-contingent—that is, one's response would be contingent on the specific details of a situation, or a middle ground between compliance and indifference. For instance, in the scenario of cheating in the examination, a situation-contingent response could depend upon the academic subject, who was involved, and the risk of getting caught. In the scenario of old trees versus new building, a middle-ground approach would be to transplant the old trees even if the survival chance is about 50 percent. In the scenario of the smeared toilet in a public restroom, a middle-ground approach would be to notify the custodian.

Orientations toward civic norms: a profile

To provide a large sample perspective, we analyze the responses from two cross-sectional representative samples of the 1988–89 birth cohort in 2003 and 2007 when they were in Grade 9 and Grade 12. Table 11.1 presents the distributions

Table 11.1 Descriptive statistics of civic orientations in Grade 9 (2003) and Grade 12 (2007)

	New	Grade 9 in 2003		Grade 12 in 2007	
	Code[1]	Raw[2]	Recoded[2]	Raw	Recoded
Cheating in examination					
Show him/her the answers	1	5.57	5.57	9.76	9.76
Depends on who's asking	2	21.92	42.71	25.85	58.10
Depends on risk of being caught	2	14.58		21.81	
Depends on what subject	2	6.21		10.44	
Definitely refuse	3	51.72	51.72	32.14	32.14
N		18,630		18,797	
Graduation trip					
Go with the voting result	1	29.11	29.11	68.41	68.41
Report to teacher	2	40.63	40.63	6.03	6.03
Propose to choose another place	3	30.26	30.26	25.56	25.56
N		18,441		18,773	
Old trees verses a new building					
Remove the trees	1	4.17	4.17	7.21	7.21
No comment	2	14.93	41.47	12.73	60.75
Move the trees to another place	2	26.54		48.02	
Keep the trees	3	54.36	54.36	32.05	32.05
N		18,572		18,764	
Stray dog on campus					
Do nothing	1	23.12	28.13	22.71	27.05
Expel it on your own	1	5.01		4.34	
Depends	2	34.56	34.56	32.43	32.43
Report to the school	3	23.06	37.32	29.22	40.52
Take care of it	3	14.26		11.30	
N		18,660		18,762	
Classmate who is unfriendly but unjustly treated					
Do nothing	1	26.89	26.89	39.81	39.81
Tell your teacher in private	2	34.36	49.38	40.46	40.46
Tell your classmates in private	2	15.02			
Tell your teacher and classmates right away	3	23.73	23.73	19.73	19.73
N		18,553		18,787	
Patrolling violated school rules					
Do nothing	1	10.25	10.25	10.78	10.78
Keep no record, but private warning	2	42.80	62.11	43.88	69.76
Depends	2	19.31		25.88	
Keep a record of the violation	3	27.63	27.63	19.46	19.46
N		18,656		18,789	
Smeared toilet					
Leave it alone	1	48.07	48.07	46.04	46.04
Inform the custodian	2	10.33	10.33	5.86	5.86
Flush it	3	41.59	41.59	48.10	48.10
N		18,424		18,796	

Notes
[1] 1 = indifferent, 2 = "situation contingent," and 3 = compliant.
[2] Raw refers to original coding, while recoded is coding representing three types of orientations toward civic norms.

of the original answers and the recoded answers of the TEPS students in Grade 9 and Grade 12. The civic orientations of the 1988–89 birth cohort suggest that this is a generation with poor civic compliance, a lack of consensus, and a preference for situation-contingent responses.

First of all, compliance is low. As one can tell from the distributions in Table 11.1, the percentage of civic compliance among students in Grade 9 (age 15 in 2003) ranges between 23 percent and 54 percent. Fifty-four percent of the students would prefer "keeping the old trees," while slightly over 52 percent would definitely refuse to cooperate when being asked to cheat on the examination. About 42 percent would take the trouble to flush the smeared toilet and 37 percent would take care of the stray dog on campus. For the scenario of the graduation trip, 30 percent would propose another trip destination in order to allow the disabled classmate to join. For the scenario of a school prefect discovering her best friend breaking a rule, only about 28 percent would dutifully keep a record of the violation. As for the scenario of an unjustly treated classmate, about 24 percent would immediately speak out for the classmate who was unfriendly to them.

Consensus is also low. The responses reveal a strong diversity of orientations toward civic norms, resulting in the absence of absolute majority responses in most of the scenarios. When there is a majority in two of the scenarios, the majority is only slightly over half of the students: the preference for preserving old trees over having a new building (54 percent) or refusing to assist a classmate with cheating in an exam (52 percent). In addition, a sizable fraction of responses is situation-contingent. For the scenario of cheating on an exam, about 43 percent of the responses were situation-contingent: 22 percent were contingent on who the classmate is, 15 percent on the risk of being caught, and 6 percent on the course subject. For the scenario of patrolling violated school rules, 62 percent is situation-contingent: over 42 percent of the respondents would privately warn their best friend without filing a record of the incident while 19 percent indicated that their action would depend upon the circumstance. A substantial proportion of students took a middle-ground position on the environmental issue. Over 40 percent chose moving the tree to another place even if the survival rate is not high, while 15 percent indicated no preference at all.

The 1988–89 birth cohort in Grade 12 (aged 18 in 2007) presents the same major patterns of orientations toward civic norms. For better illustrating the similarities and differences for the 1988–89 birth cohort at two time points (in grade 9 and grade 12), visual presentation is offered in Figures 11.1a and 11.1b. The most distinct response shifts were a substantial decline in civic compliance and a substantial increase in situation-contingency. As the adolescent generation went through more years of schooling, they became even less compliant with civic norms. They were more inclined to choose to move the old trees for a new building even though the survival rate was low. Moreover, they were more inclined to take into account who made the request, about which subject, and the risk of being caught when being asked to cheat in an examination. Similarly, they were more likely to take into account the situation when finding out the rule-breaking was committed by their best friend.

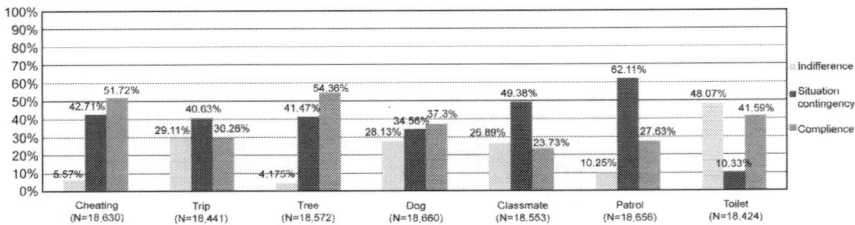

Figure 11.1a Descriptive statistics of the responses toward seven civic scenarios for the 1988–89 birth cohort in Grade 9 (2003)

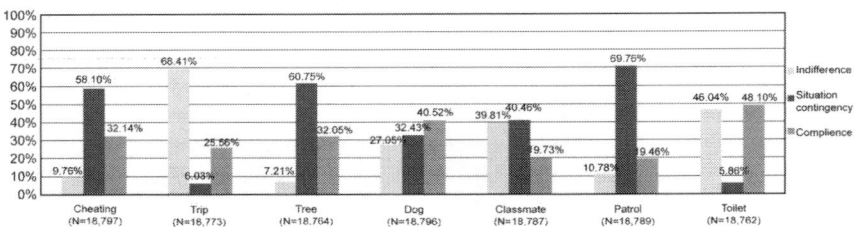

Figure 11.1b Descriptive statistics of the responses toward seven civic scenarios for the 1988–89 birth cohort in Grade 12 (2007)

Students' response toward the scenario involving the graduation trip presented a somewhat different pattern. In Grade 12, students were more reluctant to sacrifice their majority preference of trip destination in order to accommodate the disabled classmate. Over 68 percent of them preferred following what had been voted for, at the expense of the disabled classmate. In Grade 9, only 29 percent indicated this preference. Although the change may be read as a reflection of a growing commitment to deliberation by democratic decision-making, our informal empiricism suggests that the commitment of Taiwanese adolescents to democratic decision-making was formed early and remained stable. Democracy is a fundamental value that permeates discourses in school and diffuse media. However, caring for the disabled is a less fundamental value and likely contingent on the situation. So we believe the findings suggest that students in upper secondary school were less willing to attend to the needs of a disabled classmate, rather than more committed to democratic decision-making.

In summary, according to the size and direction of response shifts across seven scenarios, we found a rise in indifference and a rise in situation-contingent responses. Taiwanese adolescents were less inclined to comply with civic norms as they got older. It is hard to overemphasize that this finding is opposite to the prediction of prior research on the age profile of moral development (Eisenberg *et al.* 2009, Hart and Carlo 2005). Theories of psychological development do not anticipate this finding of declining compliance as the adolescents become older.

Generational shift

Although the profile of civic orientations among the 1988–89 birth cohort reveals some interesting changes between age 15 and age 18, more fundamental for the purpose of this chapter is to assess whether there is any generational shift as Taiwanese society opens up to global cultural flows. This is a difficult question because of its obvious data requirement. Fortunately, TEPS offers data not only on the civic orientations of Taiwanese adolescents but also on those of their parents.[4] Comparable questions were asked of adolescents and their parents. This unique design greatly simplifies the data analysis necessary for substantive inference.[5] Even though we cannot directly compare two generations while they were adolescent, TEPS does provide us with an opportunity to address the following substantive question: How do the civic orientations of the child (the adolescent generation) compare to those of their parents (the adult generation) in a given year? Is there a generational gap or shift?

The parent–child comparisons were possible across six scenarios, not seven, because TEPS did not find a comparable way to measure the orientation of the parents toward responsibility. We cross-classify the recoded responses of the students and their parents across the six scenarios at two points in time. We examine the civic orientations of all parent–child pairs according to three broad categories: parent–child consistent, child more civic compliant than parent, and child less civic compliant than parent. Both the second and third categories reflect generational differences. Differences may take place in either or both directions.

Table 11.2 presents the six percentage distributions over the three categories of parent-child comparison. The percentage of parent-child consistency ranges from a low of 24 percent and a high of 53 percent in 2003 (and 23 percent and 55 percent in 2007). More telling are the differences between parent and child. Among the six civic scenarios for which data for both students and their parents were available, parents showed more compliance to civic norms than their children by caring for the disabled, by being willing to speak up for the unjustly treated neighbor even though the neighbor was not so friendly, and by being more responsive to vandalized roads and homeless dogs in their neighborhood. This pattern was found for both time points, i.e. when the children were 15 and 18 years old. There are two exceptions. The first relates to cheating. Parents were less concerned with cheating in an election than their children were with cheating on an exam. It is likely that the political culture in Taiwan is a factor here—divisive national identities (for independence vs. unification) and party preferences have been heated issues in almost every election since democratization at local and national level. It is common that political ideologies overshadow candidates' integrity in elections; personal integrity thus yields to political preference. The second exception involves environmental preservation. When there was inconsistency, students were more inclined to take a middle-ground approach while their parents were more inclined to opt for the construction of a new building at the expense of old trees.

Table 11.2 Comparisons of the civic orientations of parents and children in Grade 9 (2003) and Grade 12 (2007)[1]

	Examination	Graduation trip	Old tree	Stray dogs in campus	Unjustly treated classmate	Smeared toilet
	Integrity	*Caring for the disabled*	*Caring for environment*	*Caring for animal*	*Justice*	*Public good*
Grade 9 (Age 15 in 2003)						
Parent–Child consistent	24%	36%	53%	42%	37%	28%
Child more compliant	63	23	28	23	23	26
Child less compliant	13	41	19	35	41	46
N	18,473	18,298	18,464	18,559	18,528	18,222
Grade 12 (Age 18 in 2007)						
Parent–Child consistent	23	32	55	39	38	27
Child more compliant	59	12	34	26	22	33
Child less compliant	18	56	12	35	40	39
N	18,581	18,576	18,571	18,602	18,584	18,506

Notes
[1] Each column label highlights a specific scenario and the civic norm being assessed. The scenario "patrol" is not available for parents.

Overall, the comparisons with the parental generation suggest that the new adolescent generation has become relatively more indifferent to civic norms, especially in the cases of compassion for the disabled (over favoring their own choice) and justice. The profile of civic orientations also hint that students' choice of conduct is much more situation-contingent than their parental generation's. Individual pursuit is evident in their responses, shaped by contexts, persons, and risks involved.

The role of the family, school climate, and peer influence in the formation of civic orientations

The generational gap we find between Taiwanese adolescents and their parents stands in stark contrast to the conventional wisdom. The prevailing view holds that the family is the primary site and parents are the principle agents for children learning respect for rules and regulations, responsibility, and care for others (Mustillo, Wilson, and Lynch 2004). The school is also expected to cultivate civic norms among the young generation and transmit society's core values through official curricula and school practices (Eccles and Roeser 2011, Tye 2003). However, our findings suggest otherwise. Not surprisingly, the academic literature and public policy discourse have long focused on family and school when looking at the formation of adolescent civic orientations. On the other hand, we find strong peer influence—another commonly emphasized source of pressure on adolescents. Because peers are often exposed to the same diffuse mass media, peer contagion is a likely mediator and amplifier of the cultural frameworks and practices that spread across national boundaries. With a nationally representative survey at hand, we have the opportunity to further substantiate our interpretation by evaluating the importance of family, school climate, and peer influence.[6]

To assess family influence on adolescent civic orientations, we draw on the results of Model 2 in Table 11.3.[7] Parental education and family income, two major indicators of socioeconomic status, were found not consistently powerful in predicting students' civic orientations. Students whose parents received more education have less respect for integrity and assigned responsibility but are more willing to attend to the public good. Students from higher-income families were more indifferent to the civic norms of integrity, responsibility, justice, public goodness, and caring for animals. Students whose parents were more compliant with civic norms were themselves more inclined to compliance. But the sizes of the influences are limited. Table 11.3 reinforces this observation by showing that the estimated declines in civic compliance from Grade 9 to Grade 12 are much larger than the effects of parental compliance in two scenarios, modestly larger in two other scenarios, and weaker only in two of the six scenarios. These contrasts are quite remarkable. The cumulative influence of parents from birth to adolescence is no match for the declines in children's civic compliance that took place over a short span of three years.

To evaluate the role of school climate, we draw on the results of Model 3 (Table 11.3). The results show that school climate also has a limited effect on the formation of civic orientation. Specifically, we examined both general characteristics and also specific aspects of school climate.[8] Students in public or private schools, in academic or vocational tracks, or in schools in urban or non-urban areas were not different from each other regarding civic orientations. While some aspects of school environment predicted students' tendency toward civic scenarios, the direction and size of these effects were not observed consistently across different aspects of school environment or across different civic scenarios.

Given the limited family and school effects on civic orientations of the adolescents, the strength of peer effects in Model 3 is striking. We found that peer effects were evident in shaping adolescents' civic orientations.[9] Students with more civic-compliant classmates tended to be more prone to civic compliance. Strong positive peer effects were consistently observed across seven civic scenarios. Strong peer effect also accounted for the rise of civic indifference.

The local and transnational influences on civic orientations

The peer influence on adolescents' civic orientations is not surprising. With adolescence, the social space that youth accesses broadens, enhancing peer connections and increasing exposure to new ideas and life habits. However, peer influences do not exist in a vacuum; they are shaped through broader cultural contexts and practices. The 1988–89 birth cohort grew up in an era of material affluence and an information explosion. The lift of the ban on censorship and surveillance regarding freedom of speech in 1988 was a historic moment for the development of the mass media industry in Taiwan. A report based on surveys of internet users by Taiwan Network Information Center (TNIC) reveals that broadband users

Table 11.3 Summary of sources of influence on civic orientations in Grade 9 and Grade 12

	Examination	Graduation trip	Old trees	Stray dog on campus	Unjustly treated classmate	Violated school rules[1]	Smeared toilet
Base Model							
Difference between Grade 9 and Grade 12	-0.463***	-0.667***	-0.475***	0.094***	-0.250***	-0.173***	0.115***
Model 2=Base Model + Family Characteristics							
Difference between Grade 9 and Grade 12	-0.469***	-0.672***	-0.381***	0.070***	-0.241***	-0.177***	0.121***
Parental education	-0.010***	-0.002	-0.003	0.008	-0.008	-0.010***	0.008***
Family income	-0.064***	-0.016	0.000	0.027***	-0.018*	-0.038***	-0.018*
Parental civic compliance	0.144***	0.084***	0.320***	0.202***	0.195***		0.049***
Model 3 = Model 2 + School Characteristics + Peers' Civic Compliance							
Difference between Grade 9 and Grade 12	-0.196**	-0.304*	-0.292	0.030***	-0.235***	-0.058***	0.112***
Academic tracking	0.031	-0.041	-0.046	0.103*	0.027	0.048	0.054**
Urbanized location	-0.027*	0.003	-0.010	0.010*	0.011	-0.001	0.023
Public school	-0.078	-0.011	-0.064	-0.036	0.015	-0.033	0.027*
School_Happy	0.041***	-0.036**	0.065***	0.054*	-0.077	0.070***	0.073**
School_Fair	-0.036	0.063***	-0.197**	-0.008	-0.025***	-0.002	0.010
School_Caring	0.001	-0.085*	0.073*	0.029***	-0.014	0.016	0.108***
Peers' civic compliance	1.753***	1.681***	1.369***	1.427***	1.414***	2.078***	2.056***
N	34,114	33,950	34,094	34,201	34,163	34,383	33,802

Notes

* p < 0.05, ** p < 0.01, *** p < 0.001

[1] The scenario "patrolling violated school rules" is not available in parents' questionnaire.

reached 17.53 million in 2012, constituting 77.7 percent of the total population—an increase from 61 percent in 2004 (the earliest statistics available, TNIC 2012). A staggering 1.6 million (57.7 percent) of the population under 12 use the internet regularly. Close to 100 percent of the population aged between 12 and 34 report that broadband use constitutes a major part of their daily life. They use the internet for entertainment and shopping. Market researchers have long recognized the remarkably similar entertainment and consumption habits of young people all over the world (Kjeldgaard and Askegaard 2006). Consumerism promotes lifestyles that exemplify individualism, emancipation from social constraints, self-entitlement, and value relativism. More broadly, the 1988–89 birth cohort came into adolescence when individualistic expressions of self were legitimated and fostered through a variety of institutional and cultural sites, from consumption and entertainment to pedagogical and human rights ideologies. Such broader frameworks, commonly associated with the West, have made their presence widely felt in Taiwan and East Asia in the last two decades.

The parental generation experienced a very different Taiwan. The 1949 retreat of the Kuomintang (KMT hereafter) regime from Mainland China to Taiwan fundamentally reshaped the political, social, and economic development of Taiwan as a modern society. With the enactment of martial law (1949–87), the state exercised tight control over the infusion and dissemination of information, knowledge, cultural meanings, and political thoughts domestically and from abroad. Basic civil rights, including the freedom of speech, travel, and association and assembly, were curtailed under martial law. The KMT regime's concern was with status legitimacy, identity-building, and economic survival. Its cultural, educational, and language policies were to a large extent formulated to avoid the "ill impact" of foreign thoughts, culture, and values and the dispersion of such information within the island. Books, music and movies, TV programs, and radio broadcasting were heavily censored and under tight control. For instance, a policy of "triple censors" on the number of newspapers, the number of pages for each issue, and the number of printing each day was applied to the newspaper industry from 1950 on (C. C. Lee 1993). Television entered family living rooms from 1956; however, TV stations and their programs were under tight surveillance by the so-called "triple alliance": the KMT party, military force, and the state (C. C. Lee 2009, Peng 2012).

Amid such strict control, there were nevertheless different carriers of diverse ideologies, cultural meanings, and symbols. Along with ethnic Taiwanese (Minnan) music, which became a symbol for anti-authoritarianism and independence, Western popular culture entered Taiwan through American military forces, beginning in 1950, carrying not only the dream of an affluent life but also reflections on war and human rights. This exposure also served to stimulate reflections about the loose connection of the dominant teachings in school to the lands and the people in local society. An equally important channel of dissemination of such ideals was the large number of college graduates who went to the United States. Strict restrictions on overseas travel made studying abroad the easiest way to leave the country for college graduates before 1979, when the ban on traveling abroad was lifted. Government statistics indicate that about 20 percent of college graduates went abroad using student visas in 1950 (Ministry of Education 2011). The percentage rose to and remained around 30 percent for about 15 years until 1965, and then dropped to a level of 20 percent because of the expansion of higher education in Taiwan (the enlarged denominator).

From the 1970s on, as the "returning elites," these US-educated professionals contributed significantly not only to the economic growth miracle but also to the profound sociopolitical transformation of Taiwan. The rapid, export-oriented economic growth led to increased social mobility and greater flows of information in society. The returning elites had plenty of exposure to the Western world and free access to information. They introduced the progressive ideas and values of the times to college students and the general public. Among the returning elites were professors at major universities. Many also served as opinion leaders by regularly writing for newspapers and magazines, advocating not only for democracy and human rights but also for social safety nets for children, the elderly, and the disabled. The lifting of martial law in 1987 is widely interpreted as an accommodative response to the strong social and political public demands and grassroots social mobilization of the 1970s and 1980s (M. K. Chang 1994, Ho 2010).

Thus, even though the parental generation grew up under martial law and strict authoritarian control, they were never completely cut off from broader cultural frameworks. State control turned out to be extremely limited, especially from the early 1970s when Taiwan's economic expansion began. The parental generation did engage with the pluralistic framework of moral concerns and orientations that diffuse globally. The anti-authoritarian, anti-establishment worldview of the parental generation prepared the ground for a diversely shaped and individual-oriented normative framework for their children.

Challenges for building a civic culture among Taiwanese adolescents

In the past few decades Taiwan has experienced profound political and social changes as a result of increasing economic affluence, ongoing democratization, and the opening up of the country socially and culturally to the world scene. Within the context of cross-strait tensions in postwar Taiwan, the dominant political ideology used to emphasize national loyalty and strong traditionalism with a code of conformist conduct. These features of the reigning ideology were also the salient components of moral education (Liu 2002, Yang 1994). The education reform of the 1990s critically challenged this old foundation of civic curriculum and demanded major revisions (Chiu 1997). The ideological components were thus excluded from the curriculum with the 1998 Guidelines (implemented fully by 2004). Since then, the Taiwanese elementary and high school curricula has gone through significant structural changes, showing greater concern with issues involving the development of individuality and critical thinking among students. In line with global educational trends, the revised curricula highlight a strong social science orientation, adopting notions of human rights, democracy, gender equality, multiculturalism, and environmental awareness (Chou and Cheng 2010, A.C.M. Lee 2004; for similar curricular developments in Japan and China, see Soysal and Wong in this volume). The teaching of Taiwanese history and society, the globalizing world, and the inculcation of core values of civic society were included as part of citizenship education (M. K. Chang 2009, Sung and Chen 2008). Overall, a more diversified and social science–oriented civic education replaced the traditional civic education that emphasized moral values and official ideology. School education now endorses a citizenship model based on reflective, autonomous, and democratic individuals.

While the education reform of the 1990s had broad-based grassroots and scholarly support, heated public debates were also widespread following the official launch of the education reform. Drawing on educational theories centered on child development, educational and social scientists wrote commentaries and book-length reports to warn that the abrupt and wholesale deregulation tendency recommended in the 1996 Executive Yuan Consulting Committee's Report on Education Reform was grossly premature. The proposed educational reform had overlooked the necessity of putting in place the many prerequisites for a successive shift to a pedagogical approach that emphasizes individuality and critical thinking (Fan 2004, Huang 2003). Concerned scholars argued that the new pedagogical approach had sidelined the teaching of moral and civic values that are central to the formation of civil society (Wang 2006).

These concerns are not a local conservative backlash against the encroaching influence of global culture. Frontline teachers and parents often lament the lack of a coherent framework to teach civic norms and values. They are increasingly frustrated with the difficulty of teaching what is right and wrong. The infusion of individual autonomy, pluralism, and the deregulation tendency in education were partly the result of the parental generation's struggle against the KMT regime in postwar Taiwan. The notions of democracy, freedom, equality, human rights, and self-reflexivity—notions closely linked to the Western value system but now globally dominant—carried strong implicit criticism of the KMT regime and established conventions (Lin 2003). The longstanding salience of politics in postwar Taiwanese society significantly enhances the centrality of these values as higher order compared to those of responsibility, caring, and collective good.

The intense pressure of competing for academic advancement constitutes an additional formidable barrier to the teaching of civic norms in schools. Similar to other East Asian countries, competition pressure confronted by students, parents, school administrators, and teachers is the foremost challenge for Taiwanese educational policy-makers. Despite the extension of compulsory schooling from six years to nine years in 1968, the expansion of upper secondary education in the 1980s, and the expansion of higher education in the late 1980s, such pressure persists. Cram schools have grown phenomenally since 1980. Fierce competition for academic advancement creates a culture of time use in which students, parents, and school administrators allocate time only to activities that are expected to lead to better performance in school entrance examinations. School activities are accordingly organized around preparing students for gaining admission to the best schools. Civic education is deemed not crucial for academic advancement. Irrespective of whether it was designated as a required test subject, civic education remains peripheral to the curriculum and instruction for compulsory and upper secondary education. The 1990 education reform and efforts to revise the civic curriculum failed to alter the peripheral nature of civic education. Both teachers and students treat the course content as knowledge to be acquainted with rather than strongly relevant to one's personal development and future success in life (Chiu 1996, Hung 2006, Jiang 2005). Anecdotal stories report the common practice of converting time slots for civic curriculum into extra time slots for teaching mathematics, English, or sciences. School administrators widely recognize that the interest of the school is to be disengaged from rather than fully engaged in civic education. Not surprisingly, then, school proves to be an ineffective socializing agent in the formation of coherent civic orientations among adolescents.

The concerns about schools' failure to foster civic norms notwithstanding, the second decade of the twenty-first century saw a wave of civic movements, whose core was constituted by young people who were disillusioned by failing democratic politics in Taiwan and who "want their voices heard" (Sui 2014). Social media, expectedly, played a significant role in the organization of these civic movements against a range of issues from construction of nuclear power plants to "autocratic" governmental decision-making and in defense of freedom of speech, and helped galvanized public sympathy and intense international attention. Young activists demonstrated their organizational and political skills in various forms of civil disobedience, mobilizing widespread marches, sit-ins, and occupations. At the same time, public concern was raised regarding "uncivic" aspects of the movements, such as uncompromising demands, disjointed consensus, and the lack of respect by the leadership of movements of diverse views among the participants. All this suggests that Taiwan still faces the challenge of balancing the varying forces of cultural and political change in order to build a democratic and just society supported by a civic culture that is both locally and globally located.

Notes

1 According to the 2009 International Civic and Citizenship Study Report, adolescents in several East Asian countries (South Korea, Taiwan, and Hong Kong) have more civic knowledge but engage less in civic activities than their Western counterparts. Taiwanese students ranked fourth among the thirty-eight participating countries in terms of civic knowledge, but are next to last in terms of civic engagement: more than 65 percent do not report any civic activity outside of school.

2 The Taiwan Education Panel Survey project (2001–8) collected data on representative samples of students of two birth cohorts. For our purposes, we draw on the 1988–89 birth cohort. A representative sample of this cohort was surveyed when they were in 7th and 9th grades in 2001 and 2003, respectively (L. Y. Chang et al. 2009). Another representative sample of the 1988–89 birth cohort was surveyed in 2005 and 2007 when they were in 11th and 12th grades, respectively. Since TEPS

employed a multi-stage cluster sampling technique, weights were used to calculate the population parameters (Tam 2005). The sample size of each survey was around 20,000.

3 It is a common practice in schools in Taiwan that students take turns serving as school prefects to enforce rules and regulations. The assigned responsibility is usually for about half an hour before classes start in the morning and again after school ends. The prefects stand in public spaces with a noticeable badge.

4 TEPS does not offer such data on the parental generation in their adolescence; we are unaware of any such data from any other society either.

5 By matching children with their own parents, our intergenerational comparisons are always based on people who share many contextual conditions such as home environment, neighborhood, economic well-being, socioeconomic status, and resources. Therefore, when detecting any generational shift in the civic orientations of the parent and child generations, we do not have to worry too much about shifts that might have arisen from intergenerational changes in the physical environment and standard of living.

6 For this analysis we appended the data on the 2007 sample to that on the 2003 sample. To estimate change across grades, a variable "Wave" (G12 = 1) was included. The coefficients of Wave were the estimated difference between Grade 9 and Grade 12. The estimated difference can be interpreted as a change in the response patterns of the respondents from lower secondary to upper secondary. The estimated coefficients were derived in each of the seven civic conduct scenarios, controlling for sex and cognitive ability. A negative coefficient represents a tendency away from compliance with civic norms (and a positive coefficient vice versa). The baseline model included the core variable Wave and the controls (sex and cognitive ability). The second model added family variables for estimation, while the third model added school context and peers' civic conduct compliance. The change of Wave coefficients across models provides information regarding whether students' change in responses has to do with the effects of family, school, or peer influences. Tables on the analysis of individual scenarios were not presented here for simplicity. Table 11.3 presents results from model estimations for individual scenarios.

7 Findings in this section were derived from a series of model estimations, including family, school, and peer variables. Parents' civic orientation was measured as one of the parents' responses to similar civic scenarios albeit in different contexts than those for students. Parental education was coded as father's or mother's education, whichever was higher. Logged family income (monthly) was used in the analysis.

8 Please refer to Endnote 6 for model specification. School characteristics referred to whether school was on an academic track or not (academic = 1), school sector (public = 1), and school location (urban = 1). School environmental indicators included students' assessment of whether school was 1) a happy place, 2) fair in dealing with various matters, 3) caring for the students, and 4) consistent. The answer categories ranged from 1 to 4, indicating strongly disagree to strongly agree, respectively. According to the sample design of the TEPS, 30 to 120 students from 2 to 8 classes, depending upon the size of the school, were selected randomly from each school for survey. Students from a total of 332 lower secondary schools and 261 upper secondary schools and junior colleges were surveyed four times during the period between 2001 and 2007. Mean scores on the three climate items were derived for each school to construct school-level climates. Higher score implies a positive assessment that students had of their own school.

9 Please refer to Endnote 6 for model specification. The percentage of students within each school who were civic-compliant was used to indicate peers' orientation toward seven scenarios. Means ranged between 0.179 and 0.582, and standard deviations between 0.079 and 0.156. The measure for peer civic compliance was based on all respondents in each school.

References

Chang, L. Y., T. Tam, P. Y. Kuan, M. L. Yang and L. Y. Wang. 2009. Taiwan Jiaoyu Changqi Zhuizong Ziliao, 2001–2007: Zhixing Baogao Ji Xushu Tongji [Taiwan Educational Panel Surveys, 2001–2007: Project Report and Descriptive Statistics]. Taipei: Institute of Sociology, Academia Sinica.

Chang, M. K. 1994. Minjian Shehui, Ziyuan Dongyuan Yu Xin Shehui Yundong – Taiwan Shehui Yundong Yanjiu De Lilun Zhixiang [Civil Society, Resource Mobilization and New Social Movements; The Theoretical Direction of Social Movement Research in Taiwan]. *Xianggang Shehui Kexue Xuebao* [Hong Kong Journal of Social Sciences] 4: 33–66.

——2009. Zai Tan Gongmin: Fansi Gaozhong Gongmin Yu Shehui Xin Kegang Zhi Dingding [Civic Education Revisited: Reflecting on the Making of New Course Outline for High School "Civics and Society"]. *Gongmin Yu Daode Jiaoyu* [Bulletin of Civic and Moral Education] 20: 1–31.

Chiu, H. Y. 1996. Guozhong Shisheng Dui Gongmin Yu Daode Jiaoyu Yijian Zhi Fenxi [Analysis of the Attitude of High School Teachers and Student toward the Course of Citizenship and Morality]. *Guoli Bianyiguan Tongxun* [Newsletter of the National Institute for Compilation and Translation] 9(4): 36–47.

——1997. Shehui Jieceng, Wenhua Rentong Yu Yinyue Xihao [Social Stratification, Cultural Identification, and Musical Preference]. In *Jiuling Niandai De Taiwan Shehui* [Taiwanese Society in the 1990s], L. Y. Chang, Y. H. Lu, and F. C. Wang, eds. Taipei: Institute of Sociology, Academia Sinica.

Chou, P. I. and M. C. Cheng. 2010. Peiyu Haizi Chengwei Quanqiu Gongmin Ma? Cong Quanqiu Jiaoyuguan Dui Guoxiao Shehui Jiaokeshu De Lunshu Fenxi [Will Our Children Become Global Citizens? Discourse Analysis on Social Studies Textbooks in Taiwan's Elementary Schools from the Perspective of Global Education]. *Taiwan Minzhu Jikan* [Journal of Taiwan Democracy] 8: 2–41.

Eccles, J. S. and R. W. Roeser. 2011. Schools as Developmental Contexts during Adolescence. *Journal of Research on Adolescence* 21(1): 225–41.

Eisenberg, N., A. Sheffield Morris, B. McDaniel, and T. L. Spinrad. 2009. Moral Cognitions and Prosocial Responding in Adolescence. In *Handbook of Adolescent Psychology*, R. M. Lerner and L. Steinberg, eds. New York: Wiley & Sons.

Fan, H. H. 2004. How is Professional Dialog Possible when Teachers are Outwardly Compliant but Inwardly Unsubmissive? *Research on Applied Psychology* 21: 63–66.

Hart, D. and G. Carlo. 2005. Moral Development in Adolescence. *Journal of Research on Adolescence* 15(3): 223–33.

Huang, K. W. 2003. *Shei Zhuonong Le Jiaogai?* [What Is Wrong with Educational Reform?]. Taipei: Yin-Kar Pub.

Ho, M. S. 2010. Understanding the Trajectory of Social Movements in Taiwan (1980–2010). *Journal of Current Chinese Affairs* 39(3): 3–22.

Hung, C. H. 2006. Reflection and Prospect of the Civic Education in Taiwan. Paper presented at the Cross Strait Conference on Civic Education, June 16–17, University of Hong Kong, Hong Kong.

Jiang, Y. H. 2005. Gongmin Linian Yu Gongmin Jiaoyu [The Conception of Citizenship and Education for Citizen]. *Tongshi Jiaoyu Jikan* [Quarterly Journal of General Education] 12 (1): 27–44.

Kjeldgaard, D. and S. Askegaard. 2006. The Globalization of Youth Culture: The Global Youth Segment as Structures of Common Difference. *Journal of Consumer Research* 33(2): 231–47.

Lee, A. C. M. 2004. Changes and Challenges for Moral Education in Taiwan. *Journal of Moral Education* 33(4): 575–95.

Lee, C. C. 1993. Taiwan De Guangbo Dianshi Lantu [Blueprint for Taiwanese Television Broadcasting]. In *Jiegou Guangdian Meiti: Jianli Guangdian Xin Zhixu* [Deconstructing Broadcasting: Building up a New Order], R. Zheng, ed. Taipei: The Orange Society.

——2009. Taiwan Chuanmei Yu Minzhu Biange De Jiaoguanghuying: Meijie Zhengzhi-jingjixue De Beilun [The Interaction between Taiwanese Media and Democratic Progress: The Paradox of Media's Political Economy]. In *Taiwan Chuanmei Zai Jiegou* [Re-deconstructing Taiwanese Media]. Taipei: Foundation for Excellence of News Media.

Lin, Y. S. 2003. Lun Taiwan Minzhu Fazhan De Xingshi, Shizhi, Yu Qianjing: Wei Jinian Yinhaiguang Xiansheng Shishi San Shi San Zhounian Er Zuo [On the Form, Substance, and Prospect of Democratic Development in Taiwan: In Memory of Hai-Kwan Yin]. In *Ziyou Zhuyi De Fazhan Yu Yiti: Ziyou, Pingdeng, Yu Shehui Zhengyi, Yinhaiguang Jijinhui Huiyi Lunwen Ji* [Development and Issues of Liberalism: Conference Proceeding of the Hong Kong Yin Foundation Conference on Liberty, Equality, and Social Justice], H. Y. Chiu, C. H. Ku, and, Y. H. Chin, eds. Taipei: Kuen Gan Pub. Co.

Liu, M. H. 2002. Civic Education at the Crossroads: Case Study of Taiwan. In *Civic Education in the Asia-Pacific Region: Case Studies Across Six Societies*, J. J. Cogan, P. Morris, and M. Print, eds. New York: Routledge Falmer.

Ministry of Education. 2011. Education Statistics. Available at: http://english.moe.gov.tw/lp.asp?CtNode=11429&CtUnit=1345& BaseDSD=16&mp=1 (accessed June 2014).

Mustillo, S., J. Wilson, and S. M. Lynch. 2004. Legacy Volunteering: A Test of Two Theories of Intergenerational Transmission. *Journal of Marriage and Family* 66(2): 530–41.

Peng, Y. B. 2012. Zouguo Bainian: Zhonghuaminguo De Meiti Yu Shehui [Media and Society of the Republic of China: A Hundred Year History]. Paper presented at the Conference on the Centenary of the Republic of China, Taipei.

Schulz, W., J. Ainley, J. Fraillon, D. Kerr, and B. Losito. 2010. ICCS 2009 International Report: Civic Knowledge, Attitudes and Engagement among Lower Secondary-school Students in 38 Countries. Amsterdam: International Association for the Evaluation of Educational Achievement (IEA).

Soysal, Nuhoğlu Y. and S. Y. Wong. 2007. Educating Future Citizens in Europe and Asia. In *School Knowledge in Comparative and Historical Perspective: Changing Curricula in Primary and Secondary Education*, A. Benavot and C. Braslavsky, eds. New York: Springer.

Sui, C. 2014. What Unprecedented Protest Means for Taiwan. *BBC News*, March 26. Available at: www.bbc.co.uk/news/world-asia-26743794 (accessed April 2014).

Sung, P. F. and L. H. Chen. 2008. Quanqiu Jiaoyu Zhi Mailuo Fenxi Jian Ping Taiwan De Quanqiu Jiaoyu Yanjiu [Making Sense of Global Education with Comments on Taiwan's Global Education Research]. *Kecheng Yu Jiaoxue Jikan* [Quarterly of Curriculum and Instruction] 11(2): 1–26.

TNIC (Taiwan Network Information Center). 2012. A Survey of Broadband Usage in Taiwan: A Summary Report. Available at: www.twnic.net.tw/download/200307/20120709e.pdf (accessed May 2014).

Tam, T. 2005. Sampling: Taiwan Education Panel Survey 2001. Taiwan Education Panel Survey Project, Technical Report No. 3. Taipei: Institute of Sociology, Academia Sinica.

Tye, K. A. 2003. Global Education as a Worldwide Movement. *The Phi Delta Kappan* 85(2): 165–68.

Wang, H. L. 2006. Cong "Jiu Nian Yiguan Shehui Xuexi Lingyu" Guan Kui Taiwan Gongmin Shehui Zhi Weilai: Shi Lun Qunti Shenghuo De Dangdai Kunjing

[Contemporary Predicaments of Group Life: View of the Future of Taiwan's Civil Society via the Grade 1–9 Social Study Curriculum]. *Taiwan Shehuixue Kan* [Taiwanese Journal of Sociology] 36: 1–64.

Yang, Y. 1994. *Jiaoyu Yu Guojia Fazhan: Taiwan Jingyan* [Education and National Development: Taiwan's Experience]. Taipei: Guiguan Tushu.

12 Cultural citizenship and prospects for Japan as a multicultural nation

Koichi Iwabuchi

The first decade of the twenty-first century has witnessed the decline of multiculturalism as a policy and social aspiration to promote a fair recognition and equal treatment of cultural difference. As Ang (2009: 18) argues, "The world over, 'multiculturalism' has now lost its power to appeal to our imagination." This does not mean that the dynamics of people crossing national borders and cultural diversity within national borders are diminishing. On the contrary, they have been becoming even more active, multifaceted, and intricate. But such a "dynamic, hyper-diverse reality can no longer be captured by the singular term 'multiculturalism' with its rather static connotation of coexisting but mutually exclusive cultural communities" (Ang 2009: 19). More decisively, the decline of multiculturalism is pushed by the rise of intense national border control regimes and attempts to reclaim national integration. Multiculturalism has been under strong attack and critical scrutiny, especially after September 11, 2001, as it is considered divisive, detrimental to national unity, and harmful to national security. This rhetoric of national crisis amplifies people's longing for a secure and peaceful community to live in and their sense of anxiety; anxiety that has been provoked by the speed and scale of change and instability brought about by the mobility, interconnection, and encounters of money, people, and ideas under the processes of globalization.

Stuart Hall distinguishes multicultural questions from multiculturalism. Multiculturalism is "the strategies and policies adopted to govern or manage the problems of diversity and multiplicity, which multicultural societies throw up" (Hall 2000: 209). While policy issues are vital for the advancement of multicultural politics, a project that we imperatively need to engage with involves the multicultural questions: questions of "how people from different cultures, different backgrounds, with different languages, different religious beliefs, produced by different and highly uneven histories, live together and attempt to build a common life while retaining something of their 'original identity'" (Hall 2000: 210). The demise of multiculturalism does not erase the significance of multicultural questions but makes it necessary to develop a better conceptual tool, one that engages more people and institutions in tackling those questions. Cultural citizenship or cultural dimensions of citizenship is one such academic endeavor, which, in its inception in the Euro–American context, criticized legal formulations of citizenship that overlook cultural spheres of membership and belonging. Now the concept adopts broadly cosmopolitan perspectives to address injustices emanating from the cultural diversification of societies across the globe. The recent "cultural turn" of citizenship in political thought as well as the "citizenship turn" of critical studies of culture shows a transdisciplinary convergence in the reconsideration of the sociocultural inclusion of diverse citizens and their substantive participation in and belonging to society by going beyond both a right-based liberal approach and mosaic-like identity politics. Emphasizing self-reflexive learning processes for fostering cosmopolitan dialogue, this convergence aims to create a more inclusive public space in which hitherto marginalized voices are justly heard and commonly shared.

While multiculturalism has come under serious criticism in many Western societies, the management of growing multicultural situations has come to be increasingly officially discussed in East Asian countries such as Japan, South Korea, and Taiwan, though the term multiculturalism is not always used. In those countries, in addition to long-existing racial and ethnic minorities, the number of foreign-national residents, migrants, and "mixed blood" younger people has notably increased due to labor migration and international marriage in the last two or three decades (see Skrentny and Lee in this volume). Although postwar Japanese governments have been consistently reluctant to develop a policy that permits more migrants, the number of foreign nationals residing in Japan has been increasing since the late 1980s, when the strong Japanese economy attracted many migrant laborers. Due to a sharply declining birthrate and a rapidly aging population and with a strong push from industrial sectors, it has recently become urgent for Japan to take in more migrants to work as care workers for the aged and those who have special business skills to enhance Japan's economic strength. Accordingly, the Japanese government has been discussing the acceptance of more temporary workers from overseas. While the government still does not officially acknowledge Japan as an "immigrant country" and has not yet developed a substantial policy, an increasing number of migrants and intensifying cultural diversity are obviously vital social issues in the twenty-first century.

Japan's case, and the cases in South Korea and Taiwan too, poses an intriguing question: how to engage with the multicultural questions in a society that has not institutionally developed multiculturalism and related immigration policies at national level? In this chapter I examine this question by considering whether and how the conception of cultural citizenship, informed by cosmopolitan intellectual discourses and sensibilities, can be relevant to the consideration of multicultural questions in the Japanese context. Given that the Japanese government has refused to make immigration issues and multiculturalism a matter for the national policy agenda, support for migrants and ethnic minorities and the practices of citizenship have been increasingly occurring at local level. However, the cultural dimensions of citizenship have not been advanced in a way that counters a persistant essentialist definition of who Japanese citizens are. This is a rather urgent issue, as the Japanese government has recently become involved in pursuing a policy of "multicultural co-living" (*tabunka kyosei*) as a way of exploiting the significance of localities and avoiding the multicultural question as a national matter. I suggest that grassroots practices at local level are an important feature of

Japan's commitment to the multicultural question, but they should be combined with more effort to put forward a vision of Japan as a multicultural society that fairly recognizes and treats equally cultural differences. These considerations will highlight the issue of whether and how cultural citizenship can be realized without the institutional context that endangered its emergence as a model in the first place. I illustrate some limits of the conception of cultural citizenship developed in Western contexts, as well as the relevance of cosmopolitan perspectives that move beyond a deep-seated binary view of the nation and foreigners and advance currently existing practices of cultural citizenship in the localities.

Citizenship's cultural turn

Since the 1990s, studies of citizenship have paid a lot of attention to cultural dimensions. The notion of citizenship has been mostly concerned with issues of rights and duties in the political, civic, and social realms and within the framework of the nation-state (Marshall 1992 [1950]). The cultural dimension has not been much of a concern as culture is regarded as something particularistic while citizenship is conceived to be universal (Stevenson 2003a). However, as identity politics and recognition of cultural difference have become significant issues for social justice, researchers of citizenship in the field of political thought began turning their attention to cultural diversity and the identity of marginalized groups and their members (Isin and Wood 1999, Young 1990). This trend overlaps with a citizenship turn in the critical studies of culture in fields such as sociology, anthropology, and media and cultural studies. Those who had examined issues of identity, cultural differences, and marginalization moved to rethinking the empowerment of marginalized people by way of a cultural right for their voices and concerns to be fairly heard, shared, and understood in the public space. Rosaldo (1999) initiated such an approach with his study of Latino-Americans and others followed a similar path (e.g. Pakulski 1997, Stevenson 2003a, 2003b). Two trends became evident: the limits of identity politics and multiculturalism that tend to assume exclusive notions of culture and identity, and the mounting assault by the globally sanctioned neo-liberalism's market-driven individualization against the notion of a public good. Thus, linking critical studies of culture to actual social transformation and institutionalization that achieves a reconciliation of equality and differences has become a serious academic concern.

A basic tenet of cultural citizenship is that formal legal rights do not guarantee the full inclusion of people as proper members of society. Although their approaches differ at points, discussions of cultural citizenship in both political thought and in critical studies of culture attempt to make citizenship substantive by seriously considering the issues of culture, participation, and marginalization. Nick Stevenson makes this point clear:

> Cultural understandings of citizenship are concerned not only with "formal" processes such as who is entitled to vote and the maintenance of an active civil society, but whose cultural practices are disregarded. Cultural versions

of citizenship need to ask who is silenced, marginalized, stereotyped and rendered invisible.

(Stevenson 2003a: 23)

One early line of argument in this regard is exemplified by the work of Kymlicka (1996), who was concerned with minority groups' rights for their cultural differences to be treated fairly in society. However, taking seriously "the centrality of culture for an adequate understanding of citizenship" would urge us to go beyond the approach of "extending a more or less already established framework to include excluded or marginalized groups" (Delanty 2002: 64). The conception of culture in terms of a group right also tends to implicitly assume a static, clearly bounded notion of culture and reduce its internal complexity and intracultural connectivity to the relationship between cultures with fixed boundaries. Such a static, closed conception of culture and identity is easily co-opted by the state governance to control cultural diversity (Bhandar 2010). Vega and van Hensbroek argue that if we are concerned with the substance of citizenship, we should "take cultural citizenship to be a tool for understanding issues of cultural and social dominance rather than lack of rights … beyond the narrow agenda of liberal discourse on that subject" (Vega and van Hensbroek 2010: 249). As the issue at stake is less a minority group's differential rights conferred by existing institutions than "a more substantive integration of culture and politics," a dynamic and constructive conception of cultural citizenship as a process is necessary (Pawley 2008: 600). Such an approach does not regard the aim of cultural citizenship simply as the conferment of rights or status but aims to understand an entangled, mutually constitutive relationship between culture as symbolic and cognitive communication practices in everyday life and full inclusion as a citizen.

This approach to cultural citizenship stresses people's active "doing" by examining people's mundane practice of meaning construction and negotiation in terms of participation, belonging, and marginalization as citizens. Indeed, as Pawley (2008: 600) puts it, "Communicative cultural citizens cannot be made: they must do." Some scholars analyze this through access to media texts, especially the process of consumption of news media and entertainment as well as the production of and participation in internet communication. Some are concerned with people's right to know and the governmentality of popular media: how the media (mis)informs people of events and issues by treating them as consumers, not citizens, and not offering essential information about and understandings and explanations of the world we live in (Miller 2007). While the interest of such studies lies in the main in the regulation of media and cultural texts, a second line of research is more explicitly concerned with how people actively engage with various popular media and how this engagement is implicated in public participation. For scholars in this second group, the concern is less with the production and circulation of substantive knowledge than with people's negotiation with and use of media texts in everyday life (Hermes 2005, van Zoonen 2005). Nevertheless, both strands of research take seriously "people's doing" media culture for the realization of active and responsible citizenship.

Concerns with mundane practices of cultural citizenship are not limited to media-related ones. Urban space also abounds with such practices, negotiations, dialogue, and solidarity formed among people of diverse cultural backgrounds. While the city is a space in which neoliberalism forces articulate most prominently in terms of privatization of public space and widening of sociocultural division, looking into what is going on in the city is no less important for pondering possibilities of a new imagining of social relationships, which is significantly different from that of the nation (Donald 1999). The city and urban spaces can be considered as sites of "actually existing" cultural multiplicity and negotiation that are not easily grasped by methodological nationalism, and we are able to foster alternative social imaginings by closely examining urban dynamics in all their complexity. While the arbitrariness of the nation is well acknowledged, it tends be understood mostly in terms of a necessary fiction of abstract community, "as a community of fate, to be sustained in its essential unity through the course of historical time" (Robins 2000: 487). To grasp a different dimension of current society we need to "extend our cultural and political concerns from the national question to the urban question" as "the urban arena is about immersion in a world of multiplicity, and implicates us in the dimension of embodied cultural experience. ... The nation, we may say, is a space of identification and identity, whilst the city is an experiential and existential space" (Robins 2000: 489). Empirical examination of people's communicative practices at city/local level gives hints about the power and contradiction of the exclusivist national imagination and the complexity of living together in a multicultural society, thus providing a great source for learning how cultural citizenship is experienced and practiced (Stevenson 2003a: 58–60).

A "communicative cultural citizenship" is concerned with how people's communicative practices in everyday life are constrained by power relations but also show transformative competence against them (Pawley 2008: 600). Cultural citizenship is thus conceived as an ongoing process in which active citizens' cognitive practices engender new collective meanings and social transformations. Emphasized here is the view of cultural citizenship as a mundane dialogic process; in Stevenson's words, "an attempt to foster dialogue, complexity and communication in place of silence and homogeneity" (Stevenson 2003b: 345). Such a view dismisses the liberal claim of tolerance and moves toward a cosmopolitan dialogue based on a self-reflexive worldview that goes beyond dichotomized understandings of nation, culture, self, and other with fixed boundaries and a willingness to learn from one another (Stevenson 2003a, 2003b). Vega and van Hensbroek (2010) also see substantive content of citizenship in "citizens' capacity for civic virtue." What is required, they argue, is the cultivation of cultural capital—that is, the capacity to comprehend and converse with various subjects' interests and voices, including one-self. Endorsing a cosmopolitan approach to cultural citizenship, Delanty (2002, 2007) further conceptualizes cultural citizenship as a learning process in which people personally and collectively transform themselves and construct a more egalitarian democratic society through the "learning of the self and of the relationship of self and other." Hence the key concern of cultural citizenship is "less normative than symbolic and cognitive, since it is about the construction of cultural discourses" that aim to collectively advance self-reflexive reformation, learning, and dialogue (Delanty 2002: 64).

Cultural citizenship and its relevance to Japan's multicultural co-living

A concern with the substance of citizenship that pays critical attention to the cultural dimension is crucial for the advancement of multicultural questions. People's mundane practices, communicative dialogues, and learning processes are all important in going beyond the formal, nationalized understanding of citizenship. However, even if we agree that citizenship is not wholly about formal rights or membership in a political community, some crucial questions remain regarding its universal applicability, given its generalized, West-centered assumptions. The discussions of cultural citizenship implicitly assume that all citizens concerned (majority and minority) enjoy formal rights—political, civic, and social; what is missing is thus cultural recognition. However, how can the notion of cultural citizenship be applied and relevant to a society such as Japan, which has not officially developed an immigration policy and has no pre-existing institutions that deal with cultural diversity? In a society where citizenship is fundamentally equated with nationality based on *jus sanguinis* and differential exclusion is still the norm, the social, economic, and civic—if not political—aspects of citizenship are deemed more urgent matters than cultural ones. I do not wish to convey that cultural citizenship is not at all relevant in the Japanese context. Rather, Japan's case urges differentiated considerations of cultural citizenship, as I put forward in this chapter.

Despite representations of itself as homogenous, Japan has long been a multicultural and multiethnic nation. Before 1945, Japan was a renowned multiethnic empire, although with an obviously incongruous imperial ideology. After losing its colonies, however, and under the umbrella of US Cold War policy, Japan moved toward achieving economic development without seriously engaging with the aftermath of its imperial project, and reimagined itself as a racially homogenous nation (Iwabuchi 1994). No insignificant number of racial and ethnic minorities inhabit Japan's multicultural spectrum, including Korean and Chinese residents and indigenous Ainu people, as well as people of marginalized regions like Okinawa. The number of foreign-national residents is more than two million. Although their share of the total population is not high in comparison to that in many Western countries, if official figures included naturalized immigrants and ethnic minorities born with Japanese nationality, the size of the ethnic minority population would be much larger. Nevertheless, the government does not officially recognize Japan as a multiethnic, multiracial society—the exception being the recognition of Ainu as an indigenous people in 2008 (see Tsutsui in this volume)—and has not developed comprehensive policies to address ongoing inequality and discrimination against racial and ethnic minorities.

Related to this, the term *imin*, literally meaning immigration/immigrant, has not been used in official state policy agendas. When it is used, it refers to emigration—those Japanese nationals who leave for other countries, especially those who emigrated to Hawaii, California, and Latin American countries in the prewar era. In the postwar period, strict border control over ethno-inflow limited the number of people migrating into Japan, helping to establish a myth that Japan is not a country of immigration. However the situation changed significantly in the late 1980s. Attracted by the strong Japanese economy and yen, many people from Asia and Latin America (mostly Japanese Brazilians and Japanese Peruvians, descendants of those who emigrated in the early twentieth century) and other parts of the world entered Japan not just as tourists, expatriates or students, but also as workers and marriage migrants—in both urban and rural areas—who intended to live in Japan for a long time or permanently. Since then, the number of foreign national residents has nearly constantly increased in Japan, even though the collapse of the so-called bubble economy after the mid-1990s has dampened job opportunities for migrants. Currently, international marriage comprises about 5 percent of newly married couples each year and in Tokyo the percentage is around seven to eight. According to data from the Ministry of Justice's website, the number of foreign nationals living in Japan is about 2.13 million at the end of 2010, while it was 1.22 million as of 1991.[1] Despite the lingering financial and economic crisis that hit migrants' employment conditions and the March 2011 earthquake in Tohoku further discouraging those who would like to migrate, the gradual amplification of multicultural reality in Japan does not seem to be a short-term trend.

Furthermore, due to the sharp decline of the birthrate and consequent aging of the population, there is a major push factor to accept more migrants. This drastic change of social demography has not been experienced before in modern Japan, nor perhaps in its entire history; it encourages economic sectors to demand the further intake of labor forces from overseas. The demand is no longer limited to the so-called 3k (or 3d) jobs (*kiken, kitanai, kitsui* = dangerous, dirty, difficult) but also extends to nurses and caregivers for the elderly, as well as other skilled and managerial jobs. A 2000 report by the Department of Economic and Social Affairs United Nations Secretariat suggested the necessity for Japan to accept about 500,000 migrants every year for the next 50 years if Japan is to keep its economic activities intact (United Nations 2000). In 2008, some members of the Liberal Democratic Party then in government also proposed a more relaxed migration policy, looking at accepting ten million migrants (about 10 percent of the population) over the coming 50 years. Since 2006, the government has entered Economic Partnership Agreements (EPAs) with the Philippines, Indonesia, and Vietnam to bring in caregivers and has plans to expand these agreements. As in other Western countries, immigration, especially that of skilled migrants, has become an economic imperative in Japan.

Under these circumstances, the Japanese government became belatedly concerned with the administration of foreign nationals living in Japan. In 2005, the Committee for the Promotion of Multicultural Co-living was established by the Ministry of Internal Affairs and Communications of Japan, and in the subsequent year its report "Towards the Local Development of Multicultural Co-living" was submitted to the government. The report states the aim of multicultural co-living as follows: "People of various nationalities and ethnicities live as members of local communities by striving to mutually recognize differences and construct equal relationships." This initiative—encouraging and supporting local governments to offer appropriate services to foreign national residents, such as interpreting, language education, housing, and health care—was received as a positive first step in governmental involvement in the multicultural situation in Japan. Particularly important is the first official use of the term *seikatsusha/chiiki jumin* (residents of local communities), replacing the hitherto presumed notion that foreigners living in Japan were a social problem.

It should be noted that the government's multicultural co-living initiative still lacks substantial policies for immigration, social integration, and multiculturalism. A primary problem is that the government delegates actual support for and handling of foreign nationals living in Japan to local governments and NGOs/NPOs, and recognizes them simply as local residents, not as members of the nation. Multicultural co-living thus both lacks multiculturalism and fails to address the nation's multicultural questions. As such it raises an intriguing question as to whether and how cultural citizenship is pertinent in the absence of national policy and institutions for dealing with immigration and sociocultural integration. We find hints regarding this question in the widespread critique, by academics and activists alike, of the government's multicultural co-living policy, especially regarding how it came about and the way in which cultural aspects are superficially emphasized. As I discuss below, while such critiques attest to the significance of localities as sites where mundane practices of cultural citizenship are taking place even without national institutional arrangements, it also reveals the limits of such local initiatives in dealing with multicultural questions in the Japanese context.

Grassroots developments of multicultural co-living

The multicultural co-living policy has been much criticized by Japanese scholars as insubstantial, and its superficial emphasis on "multiculture" has been mistrusted. Its cheerful emphasis on harmonious co-living among groups of different cultures is questioned as a cosmetic celebration of multiculturalism without any change in the basic assumptions of national membership (Morris-Suzuki 2003). Multicultural co-living is considered just a sly policy to celebrate cultural diversity for the majority by the majority (Hatano 2006). This is suggestive of what Hage (1998) calls "multiculturalism of having," in which the dominant group can claim the power to control, tolerate, and consume cultural diversity in society without fundamentally changing the social structure. It is opposite to "multiculturalism of being," in which everyone fully recognizes cultural diversity as fundamentally constitutive of society and is responsible for self-reflexively changing their own view of self/other relations and transforming society in an inclusive manner. But, even worse, the cosmetic praise of multicultural co-living is believed to mask deeply structured discrimination. Policy discussion on multicultural co-living has not accompanied the development of related national policy regarding serious socioeconomic problems such as poverty and unemployment among migrant workers or their access to social security and health insurance. It is thus argued that multicultural co-living policy discourse, by glibly paying so much attention to culture and ethnicity, obscures social and economic predicaments that migrants face, which are more urgent than cultural issues (Kajita, Tannno, and Higuchi 2005).

The critiques also show a sense of distrust of the government's deployment of the term *kyosei*. The term *kyosei* was first advocated by various groups and social movements furthering the causes of feminism, the Ainu people, and *minamata* (mercury poisoning) from the 1970s. Thus *kyosei* has not just been a policy slogan but a practice developed at grassroots level. Later, especially since the late-1980s, *tabunka kyosei* was adopted in the absence of national policy by local government in places such as Kawasaki and Hamamatsu and by NGOs, nonprofit organizations, and citizens' groups to support the lives of migrants, foreign nationals, and ethnic/racial minorities who lack fundamental citizenship rights and access to social services. Furthermore, *tabunka kyosei* became a practice-driven watchword after the Great Hanshin-Awaji Earthquake of 1995 as citizens of different descent such as resident Koreans and Vietnamese worked together with Japanese communities to support the victims and revive the areas that had suffered. Paying attention to what is going on in the locality is thus crucial in the Japanese context as it reveals how grassroots-supporting activities and movements expanded citizenship for certain ethnic minorities and migrants in the absence of a national policy and institution. In an age of active migration and transnational ethno-flows, the rising number of residents with (or without) various kinds of legal status makes it imperative to detach citizenship from nationality. Turning to local residency is particularly important for going beyond the nationality-constricted notion of citizenship in Japan, which is rigidly defined by its essentialized equation with nationality, ethnicity/race, and language.

Localities are also significant sites in Japan for discerning how cultural citizenship is practiced through community participation and mundane negotiation over cultural differences. Here, too, culture-centered discourse about multicultural co-living is condemned for masking actual practices at local level. This view is put forward by Matsumiya and Yamamoto (2007), who argue perceptively that the central issue to be analyzed is not a cultural one (i.e. ethnicity and difference), as emphasized by the multicultural co-living discourse, but how migrants live as local residents. They stress the significance of examining actual interactions, not necessarily of a harmonious kind, between Japanese and foreign residents in local communities. No doubt, no small number of Japanese people have negative images of foreign residents and tend to be reluctant to live together with "cultural others" in the same community. However, Matsumiya and Yamamoto (2007) point to the discrepancy between the "consciousness level" and the "interpersonal reciprocal level." Japanese residents' dispositions do not straightforwardly direct their actual practices. There is in reality a space in which residents, Japanese or not, meet and try to work together to solve various problems that they are facing in everyday life.

Matsumiya and Yamamoto's (2007) argument is in line with that of Ang (2006), who defines the city "as lived physical and social space" in contrast to the nation as an abstract imagined community. Similarly to Robins (2000), Ang (2006: 33) distinguishes urban citizenship—"politics of presence" that "centers around the everyday pragmatic and affective dimensions of 'rights to the city'"—from national citizenship—"politics of representation" that is "generally defined in terms of a formal demarcation of national belonging (such as the possession of a passport and the ability to vote)." As she put it:

> While concepts of national citizenship are delimited in absolutist terms of inclusion and exclusion, urban citizenship encompasses the process of living with difference, rather than its negation, handling actual heterogeneity rather than imposing imaginary homogeneity or commonality.
>
> (Ang 2006: 39)

Politics of presence highlights how citizenship is actually practiced and negotiated in the urban space, which is beyond reach at the level of national representation.

This is not to entirely separate local/urban citizenship from national citizenship. National citizenship still has an unambiguously dominant governing power that affects local/urban citizenship, as I will comment on later. However, investigation of politics of presence urges us to rethink what it means to belong to society and how people learn to negotiate with each other over the issues of cultural differences. It also elucidates the actual process of learning cosmopolitanism through mundane actions. As Kwame Appiah (2010) argues, it is not the detached, elite kind of cosmopolitanism, but one that is rooted in local practices and promotes individual transformations of the perception of self-other relationships. Indeed, the "city is the place where cosmopolitan orientations are most likely to take root" (Stevenson 2003a: 60). Only as we examine local encounters do we realize how important daily interactions are in order for people to learn from each other how to live together. While actual encounters might be highly conflict-laden, "conversation doesn't have to lead to consensus about anything, especially not values: it's enough that it helps people get used to one another" (Appiah 2010: 85). Furthermore, Matsumiya and Yamamoto (2007) contend, a culture-centered view that puts too much stress on irreducible cultural differences and/or managing cultural diversity disguised as celebration would lose sight of the day-to-day practices of multicultural co-living as it does not adequately attend to how the "etiquette of co-living" has been mutually learned and formed.

Engaging with culture: beyond a bipolar view of Japanese and foreigners

I concur with the arguments put forward by the critics of government policy and discourse. In the absence of national policies and institutional arrangements, localities emerge as the vital context within which we can understand how the citizenship of migrants and ethnically marginalized people are expanded and multicultural co-living is actually practiced. It is, however, questionable whether grassroots-driven practices and support for multicultural co-living in localities are sufficient to fully tackle multicultural questions. To say nothing of nationality law and immigration policy, comprehensive nationwide programs are required to enhance respect for cultural diversity by way of multicultural education curricula and anti-racism legislation, as well as media services that reflect diverse voices. Since these programs are all tightly controlled by the state, a central question is whether and how the grassroots practices of multicultural co-living in localities could lead to compelling, and collaborating with, the government to develop such programs and what kind of critique is most needed for the actualization of this bottom-up transformation.

Put bluntly, what is generally left out in Japan's multicultural co-living—not just in governmental policy discussion but also in its critique and grassroots practices—is a full engagement with the issue of proper recognition of cultural diversity. While the government is rightly criticized for its futilely culture-centered vision that masks socioeconomic difficulties and discrimination and loses sight of ordinary negotiation processes, it is highly doubtful that multicultural co-living policy really puts "culture" center stage as the critics seem to assume. It needs to be reiterated here that the Japanese government lets localities deal with the issue of multicultural co-living as a local matter, thus subtly refusing to make the multicultural question a national issue. Downplaying this cultural dimensions of citizenship, I would argue, risks conflating cultural diversity with the state governance that desperately seeks to keep an essentialized notion of the "Japanese nation" intact.

Discussion of the multicultural co-living policy shrewdly evades the question of who Japanese citizens are—who are "proper" members of the nation—which leaves intact the rigid boundary between Japanese and foreigners. The government appears willing to assist local actors in creating a better social environment where foreign residents can live smoothly and nonthreateningly, but a new category of "local residents" does not indicate the inclusion of those with cultural differences as members of the national society. In this regard, we should note that there is an obvious continuity between the policy of multicultural co-living and that of the "local internationalization" policy in the 1990s. At that time, the national government also aimed to support local governments accommodate the increasing number of foreigners staying and living in their constituencies, but with the stated goal of advancing international cultural exchange within Japan. This bipolar recognition of cultural diversity in terms of Japanese and foreigners goes back even further, to the internationalization discourses of the 1970s and 1980s. As I have argued elsewhere (Iwabuchi 1994), the internationalizing aspiration of the government paradoxically evoked further national feeling and posturing, as it did not question but rather reinforced the clearly demarcated cultural boundaries between nationals and "foreign others." Multicultural co-living thus does not deviate at all from the long-standing dominant discourse of internationalism.

I would argue that a clearly demarcated distinction between Japanese and foreign also tends to be shared by local governments and NGOs/NPOs. As Kashiwazaki (2011: 50–4) notes, in contrast to their achievements in "the dissociation of an array of citizenship rights from the possession of Japanese nationality … the[ir] effort to redefine Japanese nationality is relatively weak." Criticizing exclusive nationalism, strong forces of assimilation, and the unequivocal association of nationality and citizenship in Japan, the *gaikokujin* (foreigner) category based on the assumption of Japanese as ethnically homogeneous is not much critically questioned. Some NGOs, such as Solidarity Network with Migrants Japan, have replaced the term "foreigner" with "migrant workers and citizens of foreign nations." However, a more serious interrogation of the definition of who Japanese citizens are is required first to advance fair recognition of wide-ranging cultural differences beyond a "foreigner" category. In relation to this, also overlooked are the cultural differences of those who have Japanese nationalities by birth or by naturalization. This is another serious neglect by the multicultural co-living policy discourse, which tends to focus on recent migrants and ethnic minorities of non-Japanese nationals. What is really pressing in the Japanese context is engagement with the fundamental "cultural" question of interrogating ethno-racial boundaries of who is "Japanese," promoting equal and respectful recognition of cultural diversity and reimagining Japan as a multicultural society in its full spectrum. Neglecting to make the multicultural question a national matter is the most crucial source of weakness of the multicultural co-living policy discussion in Japan.

Toward redefining the Japanese nation: cultural citizenship as cosmopolitan dialogue and learning process

While it seems that the recognition of Japan as a homogenous nation has become less plausible with the intensification of multicultural situations, migrants and even settled ethnic minorities are still regarded as "foreign residents," not as members of the Japanese nation; they are in but not of Japan. What is urgently required is moving the "cultural" to the forefront so as to transcend the exclusive imagination of the nation. As Charles Taylor (1992) argues, we need to ensure two kinds of equality to do justice to multicultural situations: equal dignity and equal respect. As the Japanese case shows, while some forms of citizenship rights have expanded in localities, though slowly and insufficiently, equal respect is manifestly yet to be achieved. This is not to underestimate the grassroots endeavor to take care of multicultural situations. Cultural citizenship in terms of mundane practices of multicultural co-living and negotiation over cultural difference is occurring in localities even in the absence of national policy and institutions and grassroots activities would in the long run lead to the heightening of the national consciousness about cultural differences within Japan and the development of immigration policy (Shipper 2008). However, grassroots practices need to be further developed into a national aspiration by distinctly promoting a society-wide project over the redefinition of who is a Japanese citizen, what are the multicultural questions that Japanese society needs to tackle, and how to create and share a democratic vision of Japan as a multicultural society. This is to take culture not just as ethnic differences or media products but more fundamentally as "a constitutive and transformative force in all areas of life" (Pawley 2008: 605). It is to take seriously people's "cultural existence, i.e., their involvement in meaning-making process in society" (van Hensbroek 2010: 322).

For this purpose I will return to the idea of cultural citizenship as a cosmopolitan dialogue and learning process, as outlined at the beginning of the chapter. Such a perspective can be juxtaposed with a state-managed citizenship project that is based on officially prescribed codes, categories, and values, as exemplified by citizenship education that has become a staple of state policy in the last decade or so across a range of countries (see Soysal and Wong in this volume). Cultural citizenship in a cosmopolitan perspective, in contrast, emphasizes an active learning process that allows for the possibility of inclusive and democratic recognition and relationship between the self and others. And such learning is dialogic in the sense of attending to various citizens' voices, self-reflexively conversing with oneself, and mutually relearning the relationship between the self and others (Delanty 2007, Stevenson 2003a).

Maybe more importantly, such personal learning is constructive in that it is fundamentally connected with and leads to the collective and institutional learning process. This is not simply a change in one's disposition and course of action. For the ongoing prose of dialogic learning to be relevant for the elimination of sociocultural injustice and inequality in the long run, the learning component of citizenship has to be understood "not just in individual terms but also as a medium of social construction by which individual learning becomes translated and coordinated into collective learning and ultimately becomes realized in social institutions" (Delanty 2002: 66).

The idea of cultural citizenship as a cosmopolitan dialogue and learning process is highly suggestive for Japan, where a comprehensive national policy and institutional arrangements for multicultural society have yet to be developed. Such a project will further advance already existing local movements and daily practices of cultural citizenship in localities towards a full engagement with the multicultural question as it will lay the social foundation for going beyond the deep-seated binary thinking of Japanese and foreigner. While cultural citizenship in Western societies aims to make legal formations of citizenship more substantive by paying attention to the cultural dimension of participation and belonging, the perspective of the cultural citizenship as a dialogic learning process in the Japanese context will transform grassroots practices from a substitutive to not-yet-realized national policy with a substantive national engagement, including a comprehensive policy and institutions that deal fairly with the multicultural question. The engagement with cultural citizenship in the West and in Japan appears opposite in terms of their direction, but they share the ultimate aim. However, Japan's case would be a much more challenging bottom-up construction of an inclusive configuration of citizenship.

How to translate the critical knowledge of cultural citizenship into an actual substantive learning process remains an urgent task for everyone concerned. We researchers have to strive for practicing everyday cultural citizenship at various levels and sites of society by critically integrating the empirical and the aspirational and by collaborating with various social actors outside of schools and universities, in order to further develop already existing multicultural co-living, conviviality, and cosmopolitan dialogue and to make Japan a more inclusive and democratic society.

Note

1 www.moj.go.jp/housei/toukei/toukei_ichiran_index.html (accessed May 2011).

References

Ang, I. 2006. Nation, Migration, and the City: Mediating Urban Citizenship. In *City and Media: Cultural Perspectives on Urban Identities in a Mediatized World*, electronically published proceedings of the ESF-LiU conference, Vadstena, Sweden, 2006. Available at: www.ep. liu.se/ecp/020/ (accessed May 2014).

——2009. Provocation—Beyond Multiculturalism: A Journey to Nowhere? *Humanities Research* XV(2): 17–21.

Appiah, K. A. 2010. *Cosmopolitanism: Ethics in a World of Strangers*. New York: W. W. Norton.

Bhandar, D. 2010. Cultural Politics: Disciplining Citizenship. *Citizenship Studies* 14(3): 331–43.

Delanty, G. 2002. Two Conceptions of Cultural Citizenship: A Review of Recent Literature on Culture and Citizenship. *Global Review of Ethnopolitics* 1: 60–6.

——2007. Citizenship as a Learning Process: Disciplinary Citizenship versus Cultural Citizenship. *Eurozine*. Available at: http://eurozine.com/pdf/2007-06-30-delanty-en.pdf (accessed April 2014).

Donald, J. 1999. *Imagining the Modern City*. London: Athlone Press.

Hage, G. 1998. *White Nation*. Sydney: Pluto Press.

Hall, S. 2000. Conclusion: The Multi-Cultural Question. In *Un/Settled Multiculturalisms: Diasporas, Entanglements, Transruptions*, B. Hesse, ed. London: Zed Books.

Hatano, L. T. 2006. Zainichi Burajirujin wo Torimaku "Tabunka Kyosei" no Shomondai [Issues of Multicultural Co-living for Japanese Brazilians]. *In Kyosei no Naijitsu: Hihanteki Shakaigengogaku Kara no Toikake* [Debunking "Co-living": Appraisal from a View Point of Critical Social Linguistics], K. Ueda and J. Yamashita, eds. Tokyo: Sangensha.

Hermes, J. 2005. *Rereading Popular Culture*. Oxford: Blackwell.

Isin, E. F. and P. K. Wood. 1999. *Citizenship and Identity*. London: Sage.

Iwabuchi, K. 1994. Complicit Exoticism: Japan and its Other. *Continuum: Australian Journal of Media and Popular Culture* 8(2): 49–82.

Kajita, T., K. Tanno, and N. Higuchi. 2005. *Kao no Mienai Teijuka: Nikkei Burajirujin to Kokka, Sijou, Imin Mettowaku* [Invisible Settlement: Japanese Brazilians and the State/Market/ Migrant Networks]. Nagoya: Nagoya University Press.

Kashiwazaki, C. 2011. Internationalism and Transnationalism: Responses to Immigration in Japan. In *Migration and Integration: Japan in Comparative Perspective*, G. Vogt and G. Roberts, eds. Tokyo: Deutsches Institut für Japanstudien.

Kymlicka, W. 1996. *Multicultural Citizenship: A Liberal Theory of Minority Rights*. Oxford: Clarendon Press.

Marshall, T.H. 1992[1950]. *Citizenship and Social Class*. London: Pluto Press.

Matsumiya, A. and K. Yamamoto. 2007. Chiiki Jûmin to Shiteno Gaikokujin wo Megutte [Foreigners as Local Residents]. In Proceedings of 2007 Cultural Typhoon. Association of Cultural Typhoon, Nagoya.

Miller, T. 2007. *Cultural Citizenship: Cosmopolitanism, Consumerism, and Television in a Neoliberal Age*. Philadelphia, PA: Temple University Press.

Morris-Suzuki, T. 2003. Immigration and Citizenship in Contemporary Japan. In *Japan: Change and Continuity*, J. Maswood, J. Graham, and H. Miyajima, eds. London: Routledge Curzon.

Pakulski, J. 1997. Cultural Citizenship. *Citizenship Studies*, 1(1): 73–86.

Pawley, L. 2008. Cultural Citizenship. *Sociology Compass* 2(2): 594–608.

Robins, K. 2000. To London: The City Beyond the Nation. In *British Cultural Studies: Geography, Nationality, and Identity*, D. Morley and K. Robins, eds. Oxford: Oxford University Press.

Rosaldo, R. 1999. Cultural Citizenship, Inequality, and Multiculturalism. In *Race, Identity, and Citizenship: A Reader*, R. D. Torreseds, L. F. Miron, and J. X. Inda, eds. Oxford: Blackwell.

Shipper, A. W. 2008. *Fighting for Foreigners: Immigration and Its Impact on Japanese Democracy*. Ithaca, NY: Cornell University Press.

Stevenson, N. 2003a. *Cultural Citizenship: Cosmopolitan Questions*. Maidenhead: Open University Press.

——2003b. Cultural Citizenship in the "Cultural" Society: A Cosmopolitan Approach. *Citizenship Studies* 7(3): 331–48.

Taylor, C. 1992. The Politics of Recognition. In *Multiculturalism: Examining the Politics of Recognition*, A. Gutmann, ed. Princeton, NJ: Princeton University Press.

United Nations, 2000. Replacement Migration: Is it A Solution to Declining and Ageing Populations? Department of Economic and Social Affairs, Population Division. Available at: www.un.org/en/development/desa/population/publications/ageing/replacement-migration.shtml (accessed April 2014).

van Hensbroek, P.B. 2010. Cultural Citizenship as a Normative Notion for Activist Practices. *Citizenship Studies* 14(3): 317–30.

van Zoonen, L. 2005. *Entertaining the Citizen: When Politics and Popular Culture Converge*. Oxford: Rowman and Littlefield.

Vega, J. and P.B. van Hensbroek. 2010. The Agendas of Cultural Citizenship: A Political-Theoretical Exercise. *Citizenship Studies* 14(3): 245–57.

Young, I. M. 1990. *Justice and the Politics of Difference*. Princeton, NJ: Princeton University Press.

13 National, regional, and global dynamics in East Asia

Historical legacies and contemporary forces

Mark Selden

East Asia, as Sun Ge observes, is a category that has no deep roots, not even a name, in the region that we now call Asia. It emerged as a geopolitical category specifically with "the invasion and interpenetration of the West in modern times" (Ge 2011: 19). This chapter nevertheless intends to assess regional dynamics in the area we now call East Asia during three epochs: first, the eighteenth century at the height of the China-centered tributary-trade order; second, in the years 1840–1975, the era of war, imperialism, revolution, and regional disintegration but also attempts to frame Pan-Asian solutions; and third, the contemporary era of the resurgence of East Asia and the formation of embryonic regional bonds. In each period we examine the changing concerns and possibilities of the region by locating it in national and global contexts (see also Arrighi, Hamashita, and Selden 2003, Saaler and Szpilman 2011).

The dominance of the Western colonial powers and the subjugation of much of Asia, Africa, and Latin America provided the intellectual foundations throughout the nineteenth and much of the twentieth century for essentialist views in both East and West of a permanent state of affairs in which a dynamic and aggressive Western world order would invariably predominate over a weak, inward-looking, and conservative East Asia that collapsed in the face of Western capitalism and military predominance. This Eurocentric world vision, characteristically framed in terms of European predominance from at least the sixteenth century, reified the perspective of the colonial powers and their successors and provided the historical grounding for modernization theory applied not only to Asia but to Africa and Latin America as well (Landes 1969, Rostow 1962).

Such a view misconstrues in particular the East-West relationship between the sixteenth and eighteenth century and presumes the inevitability of European predominance. An alternative paradigm that has emerged in recent years recognizes the salience of China not only as the economic and geopolitical center of an East Asian regional order, but also as a major actor in the global political economy from at least the sixteenth to the eighteenth century and arguably continuing up to the arrival of the Western powers in full force to establish military predominance in the mid-nineteenth century (Arrighi, Hamashita, and Selden 2003, Hamashita 2008). China's economic strides, and, above all, the resurgence of East Asia with China, Japan, and South Korea as an expansive and inter-connected core of the capitalist world economy in the final decades of the long twentieth century and continuing into the new millennium, lend plausibility to an approach that reassesses not only China but reconceptualizes East Asia as a coherent and interdependent region that invites comparison with Europe and also permits assessment of the interaction between East Asia and the broader world.

East Asian regionalism: the eighteenth century

The work of Reid (1988, 1993), Wong (1997), Frank (1998), Pomeranz (2000), Sugihara (2005), and Hamashita (2008), among others, shows that between the sixteenth and eighteenth century, coincident with the dawn of European capitalism, East Asia was the center of a vibrant geopolitical and economic zone. Arrighi, Hamashita, and Selden (2003) have drawn on this literature to frame an understanding of three epochs in the rise, decline, and resurgence of East Asia from a regional and global perspective, a formulation that is extended and modified here. Two elements of the East Asian order in tandem defined its historically distinctive features.

First, among the important linkages that shaped the political economy and geopolitics of the East Asian world was the China-centered tributary-trade order, a regional system pivoting on political and economic transactions negotiated through formal state ties as well as providing a framework for informal trade complementing official tributary missions. The system encompassed principles for governing interstate relations, including investing local rulers with the imprimatur of the Qing, as well as a robust legal and semi-legal trade, much of it linking port cities that were largely beyond the control of the Chinese imperial state and other states. This suggests the need for a new and fluid spatial understanding of the relationship between land and sea, between coastal and inland regions, and between port cities and their hinterlands in the formation of East Asia, one that ebbs and flows over time with the expansion and contraction of China and other states and markets. In other words, while much attention has focused on inter-state tributary relations, regional bonds were created simultaneously through market and intra-city relations, some of which flourished independent of state networks and at times in defiance of them.

Second, East Asian commercial linkages with the world economy from the sixteenth century onward, mediated by silver exchange, transformed East-West trade relations as well as the domestic Chinese and regional economies. This was not, in short, an insular regionalism. East Asia was linked to the world economy in significant ways. Silver flows, to pay for tea, silk, ceramics, spices, and opium among other high value products, were critical in binding Europe and the Americas with East Asia, particularly China, with Manila as the key port of transit. Indeed, the large-scale flow of silver from the Americas to China beginning in the sixteenth century and peaking in the mid-seventeenth century linked the major world regions and transformed both intra-Asian trade and China's domestic economy. Anthony Reid locates Chinese–Southeast Asian trade in a global perspective in the years 1450–1680:

The pattern of exchange in this age of commerce was for Southeast Asia to import cloth from India, silver from the Americas and Japan and copper cash, silk, ceramics and other manufactures from China, in exchange for its exports of pepper, spices, aromatic woods, resins, lacquer, tortoiseshell, pearls, deerskin, and the sugar exported by Vietnam and Cambodia.

(Reid 1993: 33)

Massive silver flows to China from other parts of Asia, Europe, and the Americas paid for silk, tea, porcelain, and miscellaneous manufactures. Specifically, China's sophisticated manufactures were prized in Europe and North America, while the latter had little to offer except silver from the colonies. The significance of this pattern transcends the international sphere. China's domestic economy was simultaneously transformed as silver became the medium for taxation in the Ming dynasty's single whip reform, deeply affecting the agrarian economy as well as urban-rural exchange.

At its height in the eighteenth century, large regions of East Asia experienced protracted peace and prosperity on the foundation of a tributary-trade order at a time when Europe was more or less continuously engulfed by war. If tributary and private trade lubricated the regional order, so too did common elements of statecraft and ritual in the neo-Confucian orders that extended from China to Japan, Korea, the Ryūkyūs, and Vietnam. In contrast to European colonialism in the eighteenth and nineteenth century, this Sinocentric order placed fewer demands for assimilation on neighboring kingdoms incorporated within the Chinese sphere or empire. Moreover, in contrast with European conquerors, it appears to have been less exploitative in economic and political terms, with tributary trade frequently providing lucrative sources of income for local rulers, as well as the legitimating imprimatur of the Chinese court for rulers throughout the region. Tribute, ritual power, diplomacy, and economic bonds structured relatively stable inter-state relations across East Asia at the height of the Qing era.[1]

It was also, to be sure, an order that encompassed its own hierarchies, deep tensions and military conflicts, as illustrated, for example, by the fact that Japan did not send a single tribute mission to China in the nearly three centuries of the Tokugawa era. Yet Japan not only traded with China and the Dutch through Deshima, it also hijacked for its own purposes Okinawa's tribute missions to China. In the eighteenth century the Manchus extended the borders of the Qing empire deep into inner Asia, yet at the same time East Asia enjoyed a protracted peace.

The Chinese empire under Manchu rule may be viewed as the hegemonic power in East Asia and beyond during the long eighteenth century in the triple sense of:

(1) being the region's most powerful state presiding over a protracted regional peace and legitimating selective regimes within a hierarchical order;
(2) being the region's most robust economy, its leading manufacturing exporter, and magnet for the world's silver;
(3) by radiating cultural-political norms as exemplified by the predominance of Neo-Confucian thought and modes of statecraft that shaped norms of order in Japan, Korea, Vietnam, the Ryūkyūs, and beyond.

The demise of the East Asian regional order: disintegration, war and revolution, 1840–1975

The decline of the Qing in the early nineteenth century set the stage for the onslaught of the Western imperialist powers in China and East Asia, shattering the regional order and the protracted peace that had extended across East and Inner Asia to parts of Southeast Asia. With China facing invasion and rebellion and then carved up by the Western powers and Japan, with much of Southeast Asia colonized by the British, Dutch, French, Spanish, Portuguese, and Americans, and with Okinawa, Korea, Taiwan, and the Ryūkyūs incorporated within the Japanese empire by the first decade of the twentieth century, a century of inter-colonial conflict, war and revolution was underway. These fissiparous forces also coincided with rapid if highly unequal economic development and social transformation across a region whose dynamics were predominantly governed by bilateral relations with invading or colonizing powers. In contrast to the East Asian regional order of the eighteenth century, what might be called Pax Sinica, war and bilateral metropolitan-periphery relations became hallmarks of the new disorder. Through it all, Asian port cities continued to extend their reach, albeit they too were absorbed into bilateral colonial networks centered on Europe, Japan, and North America.

In the course of the nineteenth century, as the East Asian order crumbled—the extraordinarily stable rule of Qing China (1644–1911), Tokugawa Japan (1600–1868), and Joseon Korea (1392–1897) all entered their death throes—European imperial power advanced, and a reordering of power relations took place across East Asia and the Asia-Pacific. Particularly notable was Japan's rise and the replacement of China–Korea tributary relations with Japan's colonization of Korea, as well as its colonization of Taiwan and formal incorporation of Hokkaido and Okinawa in the course of the Meiji era. These events were punctuated by China's defeat in the China–Japan War of 1894–5 and, shortly thereafter, the collapse of the Qing dynasty and the descent into civil war, and Japan's ascent as an industrial and colonial power—though one that would be perpetually at war over the half century that began in 1895.

The collapse of the tributary order spurred a race not only to secure colonies throughout East Asia and the Pacific but also to craft diverse Pan-Asian ideologies. Japan would eventually bid to preside over a new East Asian order, articulated as a form of Pan-Asianism. Emerging as the dominant power in Asia in the wake of World War I, Japan continued to expand its power with the creation of Manchukuo in 1931 and the extension of power in North China from the late 1930s and across Southeast Asia from 1942. But both empire and ideology were contested in the form of challenges by the United States and its allies, as well as by a plethora of national independence movements. The result was that Japan's Great East Asia Co-Prosperity Sphere never gained traction. The extension of Japanese power across virtually the entirety of East and Southeast Asia would prove a pyrrhic victory. It was never able to consolidate or enjoy the fruits of empire.

Other critical dynamics played out over the century of colonialism and war that would recast the balance of nation and region. As the Chinese state crumbled internally and was battered by waves of foreign invaders from the mid-nineteenth century onward, tens of millions of Chinese migrants spread across the Asia-Pacific and the world. Stated differently, China's disintegration sowed the seeds for the global expansion of ethnic Chinese who would redefine China's place in the world in the course of the twentieth century and eventually play critical roles in the resurgence of East Asia's intertwined economies and linkages between East Asian economies and the world economy. And not only Chinese. If the largest number of migrants were Chinese (an estimated 40 to 60 million), millions of Japanese, Okinawans, and Koreans, among others, formed diasporas extending across the Asia-Pacific, to Hawaii, the Americas and beyond. Each group created networks and flows of commodities, labor, capital, and culture that linked East Asia and the world. While the colonial powers, led by the British, dominated long-distance trade across Asia and the Pacific in the nineteenth century, they relied on Chinese, Indian, Islamic, and other trade and financial networks to penetrate the societies of the region (Latham and Kawakatsu 2006, Sugiyama and Grove 2001). Thus, even as colonial and semi-colonial nations were subordinated to predominantly bilateral relations by their Euro-American and later Japanese masters, a rich mixture of nationalities and ethnicities defined the new economies taking root across Asia and beyond.

The standard periodization for both global and East Asian purposes emphasizes World War II or the Asia-Pacific War as the critical breakpoint. In many respects it was: both the US and Japanese empires reached the zenith of their reach and power in the course of the war, and while the US used the war to consolidate its power across the Asia-Pacific and globally, Japan's Asian empire was dismantled, touching off great waves of anti-colonial and socialist revolutions that would transform large parts of East and Southeast Asia and set the stage for subsequent conflicts. The war also heralded the emergence of the United States as the hegemonic power in the sense that it enabled the United States to restructure the postwar international order: the Bretton Woods System, including the World Bank, the International Monetary Fund, the world trading order, and the dollar as the international currency, as well as the United Nations. As Shigeru Akita (2010: 91, quoting Patrick O'Brien) observes, "A hegemonic state provides public goods for the international system as a whole. These international public goods include 'peace, safe access to international waterways, international laws for the protection of property rights, an open regime for foreign trade, and an international monetary system'."

The United States would not only dominate all of these institutions, it would also create a formidable empire of Pacific colonies (notably Okinawa and Micronesia, but briefly Japan and South Korea), and military bases pivoting on Okinawa and Micronesia. Above all, it wielded its power to tame Japan, first as an occupied territory and from 1952 as a client state and crucial economic ally, as well as South Korea, while isolating China and challenging the Soviet Union. In the case of Japan, Okinawa, Korea, and Taiwan, the US consolidated its power through the long-term presence of troops and military bases, through the sale of weapons, and mutual defense treaties.

Yet from another perspective, the United States was a flawed hegemon whose weaknesses, notably in the Asia-Pacific, would grow more apparent with the passage of time. The comparison with the protracted peace and stability of eighteenth century East Asia is fruitful. The US drew on the new order to maximize its primacy in world political economy and geopolitics, which is to say that it emerged from World War II with no rival in economic or military strength (all potential challengers having been decimated in the war, including the Soviet Union, its primary adversary), and it successfully bound both Western Europe and Japan to its geopolitical vision. However, it also proved incapable of taming the forces unleashed by war in the years 1945–75. Indeed, like Japan, which was more or less continually at war from early Meiji to its defeat in 1945, the US proved incapable of halting the march of revolutions in China, Korea, and Vietnam. The United States not only went to war in all three cases in the three decades after 1945, but its policies resulted in the division of all three nations and the pursuit of protracted, enormously destructive, and ultimately unwinnable wars in each instance. In short, the United States was continuously tested, and frequently stalemated or bested, in wars in East and Southeast Asia after 1945: the Chinese revolution and civil war (1947–49), the US–Korean War (1950–present), and the US–Indochina Wars (1945–75).

Viewed from the perspective of East Asia and the Asia-Pacific, the years 1945–75 are notable for the continued predominance of war, revolution, instability, and bilateral over multilateral relation—that is, the absence of regional integration, accommodation, or peaceful development despite the relatively rapid economic growth of these years. New nations, or nation fragments (China, Korea, Vietnam), established primary relationships with either the US or the Soviet Union, forging bilateral relationships that were paramount in defining each nation's international relations and shaping its developmental, trade, and geopolitical trajectory while multilateral intra-Asian economic and political linkages were weak. East and Southeast Asia became the primary zone of world conflict in the three decades subsequent to the Asia-Pacific War.

Prasenjit Duara has argued that:

> The Cold War division of the world into two camps controlled militarily by nuclear superpowers seeking to dominate the rest of the developing and decolonizing nations may be seen as a kind of supraregionalism. While in fact the two camps or blocs represented transterritorial spaces including noncontiguous nations, the contiguity of core Eastern and Western Europeans nations within each camp served as a stepping stone for subsequent regionalism to develop within Europe.
>
> (Duara 2010: 973)

This formulation seems to me appropriate for Europe where the Soviet Bloc and Comecon in Eastern Europe stood against NATO and the European Union in Western Europe with the United States playing a pivotal role in the latter. While deep conflicts divided Eastern and Western Europe, the region was largely at peace in the decades after 1945 and in each formation, Comecon and the European Union/NATO, regional processes and institutions gained traction. In Asia, however, because of the nature of anti-colonial movements and wars in the initial postwar decade, in part because the Sino–Soviet split led to fierce rivalry between the two powers by 1960, and because ASEAN was long so weak a reed, it is difficult to discern any effective region formation in economic or security terms. That would change from the 1970s.

The resurgence of East Asia: economic development, integration and geopolitical challenges

Since the 1970s, China's rapid and sustained economic growth and social transformation, coming on the heels of the advance of Japan, South Korea, and the newly industrializing countries of East Asia, has riveted global attention. The rapid development of Japan and the newly industrializing economies of East Asia in the 1950s and 1960s took place within the framework of a bipolar order in which ties centered on either the US or the Soviet Union and deep conflicts were played out in successive wars and national divisions. By contrast, East Asian development since the 1970s is notable for the economic and financial interpenetration of the three dominant national economies within a regional and global setting that is driving a changing intra-Asian and global division of labor. How are we to assess this dynamic, economically driven region-in-formation?

We begin by noting that the emerging regional character coincided with the end of both the golden age of postwar capitalist growth and protracted war in East and Southeast Asia. This did not end the deep suspicions and hostilities immanent in the historical memory and territorial conflicts that have repeatedly pitted China–Japan, Japan–Korea, and also, at times, China–Korea against each another. Thus, not only is the division between China and Taiwan and between North and South Korea unresolved, but even in the aftermath of the collapse of the Soviet Union, no peace treaty has been signed to end the US–Korean War—and, indeed, the conflict embodies the bipolar divisions of the earlier global Cold war conflict. What is the nature of the region-in-formation in light both of the eighteenth century tributary world and contemporary regionalisms, notably the European Union? In what ways does the United States, within broader global dynamics, shape the character of and the prospects for regional outcomes in East Asia?

The precondition for the resurgence of East Asia qua region was a fundamental geopolitical shift. 1970 set the stage for new East Asian regional possibilities and a global reconfiguration of power: in the wake of the China–Soviet rift of the 1960s followed by the end of the radical phase of China's Great Proletarian Cultural Revolution in 1970, the US–China geopolitical entente and burgeoning economic relationship opened the way for ending the bifurcation that had characterized not only postwar Asia but eventually East–West global geopolitics and economics. China's re-entry on the world stage in 1970, its assumption of a UN Security Council seat, its access to US and global markets, and its eventual position as the world's leading trading nation, the center of East-West trade and investment, and a member of the World Trade Organization, opened the way for the re-knitting of economic and political bonds across Asia and strengthening Asian linkages with the global economy.

Within decades, China emerged as the workplace and motor driving the East Asian and world economies, facilitated by the deepening and/or opening of Japan–China and South Korea–China relations and the expansive trade and investment role of overseas Chinese linking China with East and Southeast Asian and the global economy. With the reunification of Vietnam (1975), Germany (1989), and subsequently China with Hong Kong (1997) and Macau (1999), only a divided Korea and the China–Taiwan division remain of the major national ruptures that were the legacy of colonialism, World War II and subsequent conflicts pivoting on the US and Soviet blocs, and in the case of China and Taiwan, substantial economic integration has occurred. These profound changes illustrate the interface of geopolitics and political economy both in global (particularly US–China) and regional (China–Japan–Korea as well as mainland China–Taiwan–Hong Kong and halting steps toward North–South Korea) integration. Together, these developments paved the way for China's surge and for the reknitting of East Asian economic and financial bonds. As in the case of the EU and NATO, the United States has played a major role in facilitating the re-emergence of East Asia as a coherent region of interdependent and intertwined economies, though as we note below, important differences exist between European and East Asian regionalisms.

Particularly notable in East Asian region formation has been the transformation of South Korea from anti-Communist mecca to a regional player of importance. Having fought China and North Korea in the US–Korean War and then provided yeoman mercenary service for the US in the US–Vietnam War, South Korea emerged as one of China's most important trade and investment partners from the 1980s. Within decades, China, Japan, and South Korea would become one another's leading trade and investment partners—but also in some fields competitors—surpassing in significant ways even their economic and financial bonds with the United States. All three were deeply enmeshed in and indeed driving forces of the East Asian and world economies. In 2010 they were the world's second, third, and fifteenth largest economies by IMF reckoning, measured by nominal GDP, and their trade surpluses were among the world's largest.[2]

Another regional development with profound geopolitical consequences has been the trade, investment, and technological partnership that has linked Taiwan and mainland China ever more closely since the 1990s. From virtually no trade or economic relations over the previous half-century, in less than two decades the core of Taiwan's high tech industry would migrate across the Straits. Perhaps as many as one million Taiwanese workers, engineers, managers, and family members presently work and live on the mainland, most of them in Guangdong, Fujian, and especially in the Shanghai-Suzhou corridor.[3] With China-Taiwan trade soaring from $8 billion in 1991 to $102 billion in 2007 and with Taiwan investors pouring an estimated $150 billion into the mainland's export-oriented sectors, the island's economic future has become inseparable from that of the mainland. Taiwan exports to the mainland (including Hong Kong) totaled $114.8 billion in 2010, up 37 percent year-on-year and accounting for a record 42 percent of Taiwan's total exports (Taiwan External Trade Development Council 2011). In 2010 China was Taiwan's number one trade partner, taking 28 percent of Taiwan's exports and providing 13 percent of imports (excluding Hong Kong). Taiwanese capital and technology are central to China's industrialization and export drive. Consider, for example, Taiwan's Foxconn. With approximately 1.4 million employees in Guangdong, Shanghai, Sichuan, and other parts of China in 2014, it dominates production of electronic products for Apple, Samsung, Nokia, HP, and other leading global brands while facilitating China's position as the world's leading manufacturing exporter (Chan, Pun, and Selden 2013, Zhou 2008).

The 2008 electoral victory of the Guomindang's Ma Ying-jeou as president of the Republic of China strengthened cross-Strait ties, as indicated by the initiation of regularly scheduled flights as well as direct shipping and postal links between Taiwan and mainland China, the signing of oil development agreements, and China's offer of a $19 billion loan package to Taiwan enterprises in China— all factors suggestive of further possibilities for economic, social, and political integration. The Taiwan-Hong Kong flight has reportedly become the world's second busiest international route, following New York–London, with many business, pleasure, and family/lineage travelers continuing on to complete a Taiwan–mainland trip and vice versa. The Taiwan–China connection was also a factor in making Hong Kong the world's second busiest cargo hub in 2009.

Again, geopolitics is critical. Immediately after China's entry into the World Trade Organization in 2001, Taiwan gained entry as "Chinese Taipei," one of many signs that China has relaxed or redirected efforts to isolate Taiwan diplomatically. A June 2010 Taiwan–China Economic Cooperation Framework Agreement strengthened the legal structure of the relationship, lowered tariffs, and opened the cross-Strait market to services such as banking. The same year, memoranda of understanding extended the scope of economic and financial interpenetration to the insurance, banking, and securities sectors. Nevertheless, tensions have continued to erupt over such issues as Republic of China's purchase of advanced US military technology, and, in 2014, high-handed government policies violating due process in pressing for stronger Taiwan–China relations (Sui 2014). Whether clashes like the student occupation of the legislature will jeopardize the progress toward economic interdependence and multi-faceted social and cultural exchange remains to be seen.

In short, in economic and financial terms, the reknitting of East Asian economies has gone far toward overcoming two of the three deepest divisions of the bipolar order that emerged from World War II in Asia: bringing together China–Japan–South Korea and China–Taiwan while strengthening China-Hong Kong and China–Singapore ties into deep, dynamic, and multifaceted economic relationships. At the same time, the most antagonistic of East Asian conflicts remains in a state of unresolved warfare: the division of Korea and, in the absence of a peace treaty, the unresolved Korean war, whose dangers are exacerbated by the combination of North Korea's emergence as a nuclear power alongside famine conditions,

US-led trade embargo, and Japan–North Korea conflict. We return below to issues of intra-regional conflicts as entangled with unresolved historical memory issues (see also Dudden in this volume).

China's direct economic reach has, of course, extended far beyond East Asia in recent decades. Yet, as in the eighteenth century, and in contrast with the Euro-American imperialisms of the twentieth century, its economic as well as its geopolitical clout is most striking in the areas of East, Southeast, South, and Inner Asia on its peripheries. Surveying China's expansive relations with the major ASEAN countries, for example, Wade (2010) shows that economic ties with China of most countries in the region now overshadow those with ASEAN countries, and in many instances with ASEAN as a group. The same analysis can be extended to all of the countries on China's borders, including India, Pakistan, Russia, and the former Soviet states.

Consider, for example, the Greater Mekong Subregion (GMS). Comprised of Cambodia, Laos, Myanmar, Vietnam, Thailand, and the two Chinese provinces of Yunnan and Guanxi, it was initiated and led by the Asian Development Bank in 1992. However, regional outcomes are now overwhelmingly shaped by initiatives and financing driven by Chinese planners and technocrats, Chinese-supported infrastructure development projects, and the infusion of Chinese capital, labor, and expertise. Current projects range from roads and railroads, hydropower dams and ports, to resource and industrial development. China's "bridgehead strategy" of building transportation infrastructure linkages is evident on numerous Chinese borderlands in the Northeast (Russia, North Korea, South Korea and, across the sea, Japan), in South Asia (India, Pakistan, Bangladesh), and Central Asia (Kazakhstan and other former Soviet territories) (Wade 2010).

For all its dynamism and resurgent power, measured not only in economic terms but also in military strength and influence, in contrast with the eighteenth century, China has not, certainly not yet, achieved regional predominance, still less hegemony. This is a product not only of the limits of Chinese power and the considerable strength of Japan and South Korea, but also of the continued geopolitical primacy of the United States in East Asia, the Asia-Pacific, and globally. It is also significant that both Japan and South Korea, the other two leading East Asian countries, are firmly allied with the US, have major US bases and permanent stationing of US troops, and are protected by a US nuclear umbrella even as their economic and financial ties and a range of cultural relations with China grow. By contrast, China is without firm allies and external bases. This becomes clear as China is enmeshed in territorial conflicts with Japan and South Korea, both US allies and both housing important US bases.

China's rapidly growing strength has coincided with Japan's relative decline. Indeed, Japan, by many yardsticks the world's second economic power and the motor that drove region-wide economic growth in the 1960s through the 1980s, has virtually disappeared from much analysis of Asian regionalism and global geopolitics. In the 1970s and 1980s, Japan both stimulated the advance of East Asian economies and played a critical role in stoking global overproduction posing a fundamental challenge to the global economy, just as China does in the new millennium.

As early as the 1960s, Japan promoted no less than thirty regional projects in the realms of finance, trade, and summitry, notably in the founding and leadership of the Asian Development Bank (Hamanaka 2010: 6). From the 1980s, it spearheaded direct foreign investment in the region. The fact that Japan is no longer the leader in East Asian regionalism projects is a product of multiple factors. While China's economic and financial as well as military strength surged over the last two decades, Japan's economy never fully recovered momentum after the Japanese bubble burst in 1990 and resulted in the collapse of stock market and real estate values and more than a decade of stagnation followed by slow and sporadic growth. In 2011, Japan's difficulties were multiplied by the 3.11 Fukushima earthquake/tsunami/nuclear disaster, the nation's most serious disaster since the defeat and destruction of the final months of the Asia-Pacific War culminating in the loss of empire and US occupation. The intertwined 3.11 disasters have come at a time when the nation is feeling the effects of an aging population and projected long-term population decline and facing the largest budget deficit compared with GDP of any developed nation. In contrast, as Anthony Kennedy (2010) points out, "[b]etween 2000 and 2008, China's demand for energy grew so quickly that it single-handedly accounted for 51 per cent of world demand growth," and in 2010 it overtook the US as the world's largest energy consumer and became the number two economic power measured by GDP.

Our discussion has noted the interplay between geopolitical and economic dimensions of East Asian regionalism past and present. If analysts have rightly differentiated East Asian regionalism from the institutionalized European formation—there is, for example, no Asian equivalent of NATO, the Euro, parliament, court, or region-wide standards for migration and labor—steps toward intra-regional cooperation have been taken in multiple realms. In recent years East Asia, frequently in conjunction with ASEAN, has stepped up cooperation in such diverse areas as economic and financial security, nuclear nonproliferation, resource management, tariff reduction, fishing rights, counterterrorism, drug smuggling, piracy, human trafficking and organized crime control, disaster relief, environmental degradation, and container security. In symbolic terms, an annual East Asia summit since 2008 provides an occasion for addressing regional issues, though as yet the accomplishments in formal and substantive terms appear slight. The summit is one of several forums, including ASEAN Plus Three, in which China, Japan and South Korea debate the merits of an East Asia versus an Asia-Pacific concept, with China stressing East Asia and Japan seeking a broadening to bring in the United States—an issue that remains a flashpoint in shaping the regional future (Hamanaka 2010: 70–6).[4]

As in other milieux, crises have frequently provided incentives for cooperation. The 1997 Asian financial and currency crisis, for example, provided impetus for regional responses. These culminated in the currency swaps commencing with the Chiang Mai initiative of May 2005 to help shore up countries facing currency and financial crises (efforts to do so in 1997 were blocked by the United States), an initiative reinforced in 2008 (Beeson 2009). Clearly, major obstacles challenge East Asian regionalism, obstacles that are in part a result of the very dynamism that has transformed not only East Asia but the nature of the world system, and in part a result of historical legacies and conflicts that challenge architects of a system that extends from economics and finance to geopolitical arrangements. Equally clearly, we have shown multiple strides toward regional integration, a process that remains hotly contested and in the early phases of development.

Geopolitical and historical memory conflicts: challenges to East Asian regional development

The primary explanation for the discrepancy between a flourishing regional economy and lagging political, geopolitical, or other institutional bonds among the East Asian countries lies in interstate tensions. One important source of latent conflicts lies in unresolved issues from the period of colonialism and war, particularly those associated with the rise of the Japanese empire in the years 1895–1945, often exacerbated by the US–Korean War, the US–Indochina War, and other postwar conflicts. A second basis for division lies in the fact that Japan and South Korea remain bulwarks of US military power in East Asia in an alliance that originated in the post-World War II Soviet-American division and was reinforced by the US–Korean and US–Vietnam wars. A third basis for division is a product of the rise of China and growing geopolitical tensions centered on US–China rivalry and territorial and other conflicts, notably those pitting China against various countries in East and Southeast Asia. With full membership of the United States and Russia in the East Asia Summit from November 2011, geopolitical issues will not be limited to East Asian countries but will be enacted on a global scale.

National conflicts are enacted not only on contemporary battlefields but also in the realm of historical memory. Intra-Asian battles have historically revolved around a Japan which has failed to lay to rest memories associated with the Asia-Pacific War and colonial rule amidst intensified international calls for reparation of "historical injustices and human rights violations" across borders and within countries (Barkan 2000, Dudden in this volume). Despite signs of progress toward framing a common future—for example, a joint China–Japan textbook commission charged with writing a common modern history of the two nations and a common China-Japan-Korea modern history crafted by historians of all three nations— historical memory debates in the region, notably in the form of "textbook controversies," have raged intermittently from the early 1980s to the present.[5]

While Japan takes center stage in these controversies, for the most part textbook treatments in China, Korea, and the United States have been ignored. There is ample reason for closely scrutinizing Japanese textbooks for clues concerning the changing face of Japanese nationalism and the character of Japan's relations with its formerly colonized or invaded neighbors. But this exercise is useful only to the extent that it is sensitive to comparative dimensions of textbook nationalism. As Duus (2011: 101) puts it, "the textbook aims at turning the young into 'good citizens' (or 'national subjects' to use the language of cultural studies) by instilling values or lessons 'learned' from the study of an often idealized past." In other words, across the Asia-Pacific, textbook nationalism is the norm rather than the exception (for Japanese policy see Koide 2014; for counter-trends see Penney 2014, Soysal and Wong in this volume). This requires that we pay attention to its specific forms and intensity and its presence across the region, as well as to historical contexts which fuel shifts in its expression. Historical memory issues profoundly shaped China–Japan and Korea–Japan relations during the administration of Prime Minister Junichiro Koizumi, 2001–06, above all as a result of his annual visits to the Yasukuni shrine, Japan's pre-eminent symbol of war and emperor-centered nationalism, and the waters have been further poisoned by the 2013 visit by Prime Minister Shinzō Abe and revisionist statements by members of his party about Japan's war apologies, which in turn provoked internal opposition in Japan, which included a law suit (*Asahi Shimbun* 2014, *Japan Times* 2014).

The single most intractable challenge to peaceful development of East Asian regionalism centers on the United States and China, whose ties make up perhaps the world's most important bilateral economic relationship even as geopolitical conflicts loom larger. To date, geopolitical and historical conflicts have not slowed economic and cultural regional formation either within East Asia or in the wider Asia-Pacific region (Otmazgin and Ari 2012). But this is surely no guarantee of future trajectories.

In contrast to the lagging institutional arrangements among East Asian states, Shambaugh (2004) has pointed to the preponderance of "US-led security architecture" across Asia (see also Katzenstein 2008, McCormack 2007). This system includes five bilateral alliances in East Asia; non-allied security partnerships in Southeast Asia, South Asia and Oceania; a buildup of US forces in the Pacific; US–India and US–Pakistan military relations; and the US military presence and defense arrangements in Southwest and Central Asia. That formulation needs supplementing with reference to the multiple US military bases across the region and beyond (including Okinawa), meaning the militarization of space where the United States has a virtual monopoly, and the predominance of US sea-launched ballistic missiles and aircraft carriers deployed in the Pacific maritime region, another US monopoly. Equally important is the expansive conception of the US–Japan Security Treaty (Ampo), which has encouraged Japan to extend its naval reach to the Indian Ocean and its military involvement in the service of the US to the Iraq and Afghan wars. With the Abe administration promoting a stronger military to compete with China, Japan has also explored security arrangements with India, Australia, and South Korea, while shifting the center of its defense from Hokkaido in the north (directed toward the Soviet Union) to the south, and joint operations at a number of US bases in Japan and Okinawa that directly target China.

The most salient indicators of the geopolitical challenges that confront the emergence of an East Asian community are the multiple crises that have erupted in the region since 2010, notably the China-Japan dispute over the Senkakus/Diaoyu, North and South Korean clashes involving the sinking of the South Korean warship Cheonan and the Yeonpyeong Island shelling in the contested area around the Northern Limit Line dividing North and South, and the pursuit of Chinese territorial claims in the South China Sea (Beal 2010, McCormack 2011,

Sakai 2010, Thayer 2012). In each case we observe the reincarnation of the divisions previously enacted in the US–Korean and US–Indochina wars: the US rallied to the support of Japan and South Korea, in the case of the intra-Korean conflict, taking the case to the United Nations where China and Russia opposed the US while refraining from exercising their veto. The result was a weak resolution but a strong indication of the continuity of the bipolarity that many believed had ended with the collapse of the Soviet Union. Diplomacy aside, the United States responded to the incidents by making clear its intention to respond to any challenge to its military supremacy in the Western Pacific in the form of military exercises involving Japan and South Korea, supported by the US battleship George Washington. The result was to send powerful warning messages to China and North Korea while revealing the fragility, in geopolitical terms, of East Asian regionalism.[6]

One assessment of this pattern of military challenge and response is that the geopolitical divisions reflect striking continuity from the immediate postwar and, especially, the US–Korean and US–Indochina wars that followed. But something more interesting appears to be going on, suggesting that the balance of forces is in flux. I believe that the emergence of East Asia as a coherent economic region coincides with the long-term decline of American power. This decline is well illustrated by the inability of the US to achieve victory in any of the costly wars it has fought more or less continuously for six decades: from Korea to Indochina to Afghanistan to the Gulf. Equally important is the internal disarray that the United States faces in the wake of the Great Recession that began in 2007–08: this is a product of the failure to frame a program promising economic recovery, systemic high level unemployment and underemployment, and a domestic politics of gridlock. If no single nation is in a position to directly challenge US power, the limits on the uses of that power, above all in the Asia-Pacific, have become clear.

The critical question pertaining to the future of East Asia is this: will the decline of American power open the way for the emergence of a vibrant East Asian regionalism predicated on the strength and interpenetration of the East Asian economies, or does a period lie ahead in which geopolitical and historical memory conflicts involving China, Japan, and the US result in tension, turmoil, and perhaps war? The uncertainties of the present in East Asia presage a situation in which the superpower continues in decline while, despite China's dramatic rise, no alternative power center seems likely to emerge at the heart of a new order in the coming decades.

Notes

1 While relations between China and tributary states have been extensively documented, much more needs to be known about relations among the tributary states—Japan–Korea, Vietnam–Japan, Mongols–Korea, Korea–Vietnam, each of which involved tributary-type relationships. In addition, there were important non-tributary trade relations such as those linking Chinese port cities and their counterparts throughout East Asia and the Asia-Pacific.

2 For GDP measured in purchasing power parity terms (as calculated by the IMF), in 2010 China ranked first, Japan second, South Korea fourth, and Taiwan eighth

among Asian countries, with China's $8.7 trillion GDP more than twice Japan's $4.3 trillion (http://en.wikipedia.org/wiki/List_of_Asian_countries_by_GDP_PPP, accessed April 2014).

World Figures for nominal GDP in 2010 (as calculated by the IMF) show China ranked second and Japan third with South Korea fifteenth, if we exclude the European Union (http://en.wikipedia.org/wiki/List_of_countries_by_GDP_(nominal), accessed April 2014).

For per capita GDP (PPP) figures see http://en.wikipedia.org/wiki/List_of_countries_by_GDP_%28PPP%29_per_capita (accessed April 2014).

3 There are no official figures. One source notes estimates of 750,000 to 1,100,000 (http://taiwanmatters.blogspot.com/2007/12/how-many-taiwanese-live-in-china.html, accessed April 2014).

4 For an early discussion of the ASEAN Plus Three concept, see Stubbs (2002). ASEAN Plus Three, initially a response to the 1997 Asian financial crisis, subsequently broadened its brief as one of several regional organizations. In 2007, an "ASEAN Plus Three Cooperation Work Plan (2007–17)" broadened discussion to peace and security, stability, counter-terrorism, and a range of economic and financial cooperation. However, just as ASEAN itself has functioned primarily as an economic and trade group, the focus of ASEAN Plus Three has centered in these realms.

5 For East Asian textbook controversies and attempts to resolve them, see Hein and Selden (2000), Nozaki and Selden (2009), Richter (2008), and Shin and Sneider (2011).

6 By contrast, Japan-South Korea clashes over Dokdo/Takeshima islets heightened tension between the two countries but produced no US military response (Selden 2011).

References

Akita, S. 2010. World History and the Emergence of Global History in Japan. *Chinese Studies in History* 43(3): 84–96.

Arrighi, G., T. Hamashita, and M. Selden, eds. 2003. *The Resurgence of East Asia: 500, 150 and 50 Year Perspectives.* London: Routledge.

Asahi Shimbun. 2014. Lawsuit Seeks Compensation for Mental Stress Caused by Abe's Yasukuni Visit. April 12. Available at: http://ajw.asahi.com/article/behind_news/social_affairs/AJ201404120051 (accessed April 2014).

Barkan, E. 2000. *The Guilt of Nations: Restitution and Negotiating Historical Injustices.* Baltimore, MD: The Johns Hopkins University Press.

Beal, T. 2010. Korean Brinkmanship, American Provocation, and the Road to War: The Manufacturing of a Crisis. *The Asia-Pacific Journal* 8 (51/1), December 20. Available at: http://japanfocus.org/-Tim-Beal/3459 (accessed April 2014).

Beeson, M. 2009. East Asian Regionalism and the Asia-Pacific: After American Hegemony. *The Asia-Pacific Journal* 2(2/9), January 10. Available at: http://japanfocus.org/-Mark-Beeson/3008 (accessed April 2014).

Chan, J., N. Pun, and M. Selden. 2013. The Politics of Global Production: Apple, Foxconn and China's New Working Class. *The Asia-Pacific Journal* 11(32/2), August 12. Available at: http://japanfocus.org/-Pun-Ngai/3981 (accessed April 2014).

Duara, P. 2010. Asia Redux: Conceptualizing a Region for our Times. *Journal of Asian Studies* 69(4): 963–83.

Duus, P. 2011. War Stories. In *History Textbooks and the Wars in Asia: Divided Memories*, G.-W. Shin and D. C. Sneider, eds. Abingdon: Routledge,

Frank, A. G. 1998. *ReORIENT: Global Economy in the Asian Age.* Berkeley: University of California Press.

Ge, S. 2011. The Predicament of Compiling Textbooks on the History of East Asia. In *Designing History in East Asian Textbooks: Identity Politics and Transnational Aspirations*, G. Müller, ed. Abingdon: Routledge.

Hamanaka, S. 2010. *Asian Regionalism and Japan: The Politics of Membership in Regional Diplomatic, Financial, and Trade Groups*. Abingdon: Routledge.

Hamashita, T. 2008. *China, East Asia and the Global Economy: Regional and Historical Perspectives*, M. Selden and L. Grove, eds. London: Routledge.

Hein, L. and M. Selden, eds. 2000. *Censoring History: Citizenship and Memory in Japan, Germany, and the United States*. Armonk, NY: M. E. Sharpe.

Japan Times. 2014. More Activists Sue Over Abe's Shrine Visit. April 21. Available at: www. japantimes.co.jp/news/2014/04/21/national/crime-legal/more-activists-sue-over-abes-shrine-visit/#.U1hSnl64nlI (accessed April 2014).

Katzenstein, P.J. 2008. Japan in the American Imperium: Rethinking Security. *The Asia-Pacific Journal*, October 14. Available at: www.japanfocus.org/-Peter_J-Katzenstein/2921 (accessed April 2014).

Kennedy, A. 2010. Rethinking Energy Security in China. *East Asia Forum*, June 6. Available at: www.eastasiaforum.org/2010/06/06/rethinking-energy-security-in-china/ (accessed April 2014).

Koide, R. 2014. Critical New Stage in Japan's Textbook Controversy. *The Asia-Pacific Journal* 12(13/1), March 31. Available at: http://japanfocus.org/-Koide-Reiko/4101 (accessed April 2014).

Landes, D. 1969. *The Unbound Prometheus. Technological Change and Industrial Development in Western Europe from 1750 to the Present* (second edition, 2003). Cambridge: Cambridge University Press.

Latham, A. J. H. and H. Kawakatsu, eds. 2006. *Intra-Asian Trade and the World Market*. London: Routledge.

McCormack, G. 2007. *Client State: Japan in the American Embrace*. New York: Verso.

——2011. Small Islands–Big Problem: Senkaku/Diaoyu and the Weight of History and Geography in China-Japan Relations. *The Asia-Pacific Journal* 9(1/1), January 3. http://japanfocus.org/-Gavan-McCormack/3464 (accessed April 2014)

Nozaki, Y. and M. Selden. 2009. Japanese Textbook Controversies, Nationalism, and Historical Memory: Intra- and Inter-national Conflicts. *The Asia-Pacific Journal* 24(5/9), June 15. Available at: www.japanfocus.org/-Yoshiko-Nozaki/3173 (accessed April 2014).

Otmazgin, N. and E. B. Ari, eds. 2012. *Popular Culture and the State in East and Southeast Asia*. Abingdon: Routledge.

Penney, M. 2014. "Why on earth is something as important as this not in the textbooks?" Teaching Supplements, Student Essays, and History Education in Japan. *The Asia-Pacific Journal* 12(1), January 6. Available at: http://japanfocus.org/-Matthew-Penney/4055 (accessed April 2014).

Pomeranz, K. 2000. *The Great Divergence: China, Europe, and the Making of the Modern World Economy*. Princeton, NJ: Princeton University Press.

Reid, A. 1988. *Southeast Asia in the Age of Commerce, 1450–1680: The Lands Below the Winds* (Vol. 1). New Haven, CT: Yale University Press.

——1993. *Southeast Asia in the Age of Commerce, 1450–1680: Expansion and Crisis* (Vol. 2). New Haven, CT: Yale University Press.

Richter, S., ed. 2008. *Contested Views of a Common Past: Revisions of History in Contemporary East Asia*. New York: Campus Verlag.

Rostow, W. W. 1962. *The Stages of Economic Growth. A Non-Communist Manifesto*. Cambridge: Cambridge University Press.

Saaler, S. and C. W. A. Szpilman, eds. 2011. *Pan-Asianism: A Documentary History*, 2 Vols. Lanham, MD: Rowman and Littlefield.

Sakai, T. 2010. Rekindling China-Japan Conflict: The Senkaku/Diaoyutai Islands Clash. *The Asia-Pacific Journal* 8(39/3). Sept 27. Available at: http://japanfocus.org/-Tanaka-Sakai/3418 (accessed April 2014).

Selden, M. 2011. Small Islets, Enduring Conflict: Dokdo, Korea-Japan Colonial Legacy and the United States. *The Asia-Pacific Journal* 9(17/2), April 25. Available at: http://japanfocus.org/-Mark-Selden/3520 (accessed April 2014).

Shambaugh, D. L. 2004. China Engages Asia: Reshaping the Regional Order. *International Security* 29(3): 64–99.

Shin, G-W. and D. C. Sneider, eds. 2011. *History Textbooks and the Wars in Asia: Divided Memories*. Abingdon: Routledge.

Stubbs, R. 2002. ASEAN Plus Three: Emerging East Asian Regionalism? *Asian Survey* 42(3): 440–55.

Sugihara, K., ed. 2005. *Japan, China and the Growth of the Asian International Economy, 1850–1949*. Oxford: Oxford University Press.

Sugiyama, S. and L. Grove, eds. 2001. *Commercial Networks in Modern Asia*. Richmond, Surrey: Curzon.

Sui, C. 2014. What Unprecedented Protest Means for Taiwan. *BBC News*, March 26. Available at: www.bbc.co.uk/news/world-asia-26743794 (accessed April 2014).

Taiwan External Trade Development Council. 2011. Taiwan's Exports to China Rose Sharply in 2010. January 11. Available at: www.taiwantrade.com.tw/MAIN/en_front/searchserv.do?method=listNewsDetail&information_id=31167&locale=2 (accessed April 2014)

Thayer, C. A. 2012. ASEAN'S Code of Conduct in the South China Sea: A Litmus Test for Community-Building? *The Asia-Pacific Journal* 10(34/4), August 20. Available at: http://japanfocus.org/-Carlyle_A-Thayer/3813 (accessed April 2014).

Wade, G. 2010. ASEAN Divides. *New Mandala*, December 23. Available at: http://asiapacific.anu.edu.au/newmandala/2010/12/23/asean-divides/ (accessed April 2014).

Wong, R. Bin. 1997. *China Transformed: Historical Change and the Limits of European Experience*. Ithaca, NY: Cornell University Press.

Zhou, Y. 2008. *The Inside Story of China's High Tech Industry: Making Silicon Valley in Beijing*. Lanham, MD: Rowman and Littlefield.

Index

22865147R00163

Printed in Great Britain
by Amazon